Children, Social Science, and the Law

Children, Social Science, and the Law broadens our conceptualization of the topic of children and law, addressing a wide-ranging set of issues in great need of theoretical, empirical, and legislative attention. The chapters, written by an impressive array of social science and legal experts, confront many difficult questions relating to child abuse, children's eyewitness testimony, divorce and custody, juvenile crime, and children's rights. For example, are the rights that our nation's laws ascribe to children commensurate with their capabilities and needs? How should laws governing the punishment of crime acknowledge developmental differences between adult and juvenile offenders? With its unique integration of psychological research, social policy, and legal analysis, the volume is an important resource for any professional concerned with children and the law.

Bette L. Bottoms is Associate Professor of Psychology at the University of Illinois at Chicago. She is President of the American Psychological Association's Division 37 Section on Child Maltreatment. She has been the recipient of the American Psychology-Law Society Dissertation Award, the Amoco Silver Circle Teaching Award, and the University of Illinois at Chicago Excellence in Teaching Award. She is coeditor of *Child Victims, Child Witnesses* and *Children's Testimony*.

Margaret Bull Kovera is Associate Professor of Psychology at Florida International University. She has been the recipient of the American Psychology-Law Society Dissertation Award and the Saleem Shah Early Career Award for Contributions to Psychology and Law Research.

Bradley D. McAuliff is a postdoctoral research associate in the law and psychology program at the University of Nebraska-Lincoln. In 2000, he received the American Psychology-Law Society Dissertation Award.

D1503076

Children, Social Science, and the Law

Edited by

BETTE L. BOTTOMS
University of Illinois at Chicago

MARGARET BULL KOVERA
Florida International University

BRADLEY D. McAULIFF
University of Nebraska-Lincoln

BOWLING GREEN STATE
UNIVERSITY LIBRARIES

PUBLISHED BY THE PRESS SYNDICATE OF THE UNIVERSITY OF CAMBRIDGE
The Pitt Building, Trumpington Street, Cambridge, United Kingdom

CAMBRIDGE UNIVERSITY PRESS
The Edinburgh Building, Cambridge CB2 2RU, UK
40 West 20th Street, New York, NY 10011-4211, USA
477 Williamstown Road, Port Melbourne, VIC 3207, Australia
Ruiz de Alarcón 13, 28014 Madrid, Spain
Dock House, The Waterfront, Cape Town 8001, South Africa

http://www.cambridge.org

© Bette L. Bottoms, Margaret Bull Kovera, Bradley D. McAuliff 2002

This book is in copyright. Subject to statutory exception
and to the provisions of relevant collective licensing agreements,
no reproduction of any part may take place without
the written permission of Cambridge University Press.

First published 2002

Printed in the United Kingdom at the University Press, Cambridge

Typeface Palatino 10.25/13.5 pt.   *System* LATEX 2$_\varepsilon$ [TB]

A catalog record for this book is available from the British Library.

Library of Congress Cataloging in Publication Data
Children, social science, and the law / edited by Bette L. Bottoms,
Margaret Bull Kovera, Bradley D. McAuliff.
p.   cm.
Includes bibliographical references and index.
ISBN 0-521-66298-2 (hardback) – ISBN 0-521-66406-3 (pbk.)
1. Children – Legal status, laws, etc. – United States.   2. Social case work with
children – United States.   3. Child welfare – United States.   I. Bottoms, Bette L. 1964–
II. Kovera, Margaret Bull, 1966–   III. McAuliff, Bradley D., 1971–
KF3735 .C48   2002
346.7301'35 – dc21   2001043219

ISBN 0 521 66298 2 hardback
ISBN 0 521 66406 3 paperback

For my husband, Gary, and for dedicated front-line professionals like my friends Erin Sorenson and Alison Perona, who spend their lives helping children who become entangled in the legal system. (BLB)

For Hope. It is my hope that she will never have need for the wisdom in this book. (MBK)

For my mom Marnie, my dad Bob, and my brother Curtis, who still to this day do not understand exactly what it is that I do and why. I love you all dearly. (BDM)

Contents

Acknowledgments

The seeds of this book were sown while two of us (BLB and MBK) co-chaired the Children and Law Subcommittee of the American Psychology-Law Society's Women and Law Committee. Through conversations with other members of this subcommittee, it became clear that there was a need for a single resource on children and the law to which researchers, legal scholars, policy makers, and front-line professionals could turn for advice and inspiration. We are grateful to those women who so generously gave of their time and knowledge while we began to form our vision of what such a resource would encompass.

We would also like to extend our appreciation to people who supported us throughout the development of this book. Special thanks go to our celebrated colleagues who have contributed the excellent chapters herein. Each of them spent a significant amount of time preparing a chapter highlighting legal and social science issues relevant to children's special circumstances. Julia Hough, our Cambridge editor, has been a model of patient support. We each have special mentors and colleagues, both past and current, whose advice has guided us as we have sculpted our own academic careers. Some of them are authors of chapters in this book. Finally, our family members, including those who arrived midway during the project (baby Hope Kovera), provided the secure base from which we worked.

Bette L. Bottoms; *Chicago, Illinois*
Margaret Bull Kovera; *Miami, Florida*
Bradley D. McAuliff; *Lincoln, Nebraska*

Contributors

Kristen Weede Alexander, B.A., is a doctoral candidate in human development at the University of California, Davis. She received her bachelor's degree in human development at the University of California, Riverside.

Rosemary J. Avery, Ph.D., is Professor and Associate Chair in the Department of Policy Analysis and Management at Cornell University. She received her doctorate from Ohio State University.

Steven L. Berman, Ph.D., is Assistant Professor of Psychology at the University of Central Florida. He received his Ph.D. in developmental psychology at Florida International University.

Paola Castelli received her Laurea in psychology at the University "La Sapienza" in Rome and completed an internship in psychology and law with an emphasis on children's involvement in the legal system at the University of California, Davis.

Rebecca A. Colman, M.A., is a doctoral candidate in the developmental psychology program at the University of Nebraska-Lincoln.

Howard Davidson, J.D., is Director of the American Bar Association Center on Children and the Law. He received his J.D. from Boston College Law School.

Charlene E. Depner, Ph.D., is Supervisor of Research and Grant Programs at the Center for Families, Children, and the Courts in San Francisco. She received her Ph.D. in social psychology from the University of Michigan.

Howard J. Doueck, M.S.W., Ph.D., is Professor of Social Work, Director of the doctorate program, and Chair of the Children and Youth concentration at the State University of New York at Buffalo.

Robin S. Edelstein, M.A., is a doctoral student in the Department of Psychology at the University of California, Davis. She received her B.A. in psychology from the University of California, Berkeley, and her M.A. from the University of California, Davis.

Carrie S. Fried, M.A., is a doctoral candidate in psychology at the University of Virginia. She received her B.A. from Rice University and her M.A. from the University of Virginia.

Megan Fulcher, M.A., is a doctoral candidate in the developmental psychology program at the University of Virginia.

Simona Ghetti, M.A., is a doctoral candidate in the Department of Psychology at the University of California, Davis. She received her Laurea in psychology at the University of Padua, Italy, and her M.A. in psychology from the University of California, Davis.

Gail S. Goodman, Ph.D., is Professor of Psychology at the University of California, Davis. She received her Ph.D. in developmental psychology from the University of California, Los Angeles, and conducted postdoctoral research at the University of Denver and the Université René Descartes in Paris, France.

Ann M. Haralambie, J.D., is an attorney who resides and practices in Tucson. She received her J.D. from the University of Arizona.

Jeffrey J. Haugaard, Ph.D., is Director of Undergraduate Studies and Associate Professor of Human Development at Cornell University. He received his Ph.D. in clinical psychology from the University of Virginia.

William M. Kurtines, Ph.D., is Professor of Psychology at Florida International University. He received his Ph.D. in psychology from the Johns Hopkins University.

Murray Levine, Ph.D., J.D., is Distinguished Service Professor of Psychology and Adjunct Professor of Law at the State University of New York at Buffalo. He received his Ph.D. from the University of Pennsylvania and his J.D. from the State University of New York at Buffalo.

Susan P. Limber, Ph.D., M.L.S., is Director of the Center for Youth Participation and Human Rights at the Institute on Family and Neighborhood Life and Associate Professor of Psychology at Clemson University. She received her Ph.D. in developmental psychology and her M.L.S. from the University of Nebraska-Lincoln.

Thomas D. Lyon, J.D., Ph.D., is Associate Professor of Law at the University of Southern California Law School. He received his J.D. from Harvard Law School and his Ph.D. in developmental psychology from Stanford University.

Mia McFarlane, J.D., M.S.W., is an attorney at the Children's Legal Center in Buffalo, New York. She received her J.D. and M.S.W. at the State University of New York at Buffalo.

Gary B. Melton, Ph.D., is Director of the Institute on Family and Neighborhood Life and Professor of Psychology at Clemson University. He received his Ph.D. in clinical-community psychology from Boston University.

Kari L. Nysse-Carris, M.A., is a doctoral candidate in social psychology at the University of Illinois at Chicago. She received her B.A. from Hope College and her M.A. from the University of Illinois at Chicago.

Charlotte J. Patterson, Ph.D., is Professor of Psychology at the University of Virginia. She received her Ph.D. from Stanford University.

N. Dickon Reppucci, Ph.D., is Professor of Psychology and Director of Graduate Studies at the University of Virginia. He received his Ph.D. in clinical psychology from Harvard University.

Randall T. Salekin, Ph.D., is Assistant Professor of Psychology and Director of the Child Forensic Psychology Laboratory at the University of Alabama. He received his B.A. from Simon Fraser University and his Ph.D. from the University of North Texas.

Jennifer M. Schaaf, Ph.D., is an investigator at the Frank Porter Graham Child Development Center at the University of North Carolina, Chapel Hill. She received her B.A. from the University of California, Los Angeles, and her Ph.D. from the University of California, Davis.

Melinda G. Schmidt, M.A., is a doctoral candidate in community psychology at the University of Virginia, where she received her B.A.

Wendy K. Silverman, Ph.D., is Professor of Psychology and Director of the Child and Family Psychosocial Research Center at Florida International University, Miami. She received her Ph.D. in clinical psychology from Case Western Reserve University, Cleveland.

Mark A. Small, J.D., Ph.D., is Professor of Psychology at the Institute on Family and Neighborhood Life at Clemson University. He received his Ph.D. in social psychology and his J.D. from the University of Nebraska-Lincoln.

Jennifer Wainright, M.A., is a doctoral candidate in the community and developmental psychology programs at the University of Virginia.

Brian L. Wilcox, Ph.D., is Professor of Psychology and Director of the Center on Children, Families, and the Law at the University of Nebraska-Lincoln. He received his Ph.D. in community psychology from the University of Texas at Austin.

Jennifer L. Woolard, Ph.D., is Assistant Professor of Criminology and Psychology at the University of Florida's Center for Studies in Criminology and Law. She received her Ph.D. in psychology from the University of Virginia.

Jennifer M. Wyatt, M.A., is a doctoral candidate in developmental psychology at the University of Nebraska-Lincoln.

Children, Social Science, and the Law

An Introduction to the Issues

Bette L. Bottoms, Margaret Bull Kovera,
and Bradley D. McAuliff

As noted by Goodman, Emery, and Haugaard (1998), "there are few other areas of law where the courts rely as heavily on social science data as they do for decisions about children's welfare" (p. 775). The primary goal of *Children, Social Science, and the Law* is to facilitate that reliance. We believe researchers in this field have an obligation to understand child-relevant law and policy so that they are prepared to conduct research that is useful to courts, policy makers, and practitioners. Legal professionals and practitioners must then understand and use that research. We designed our book specifically to help both groups of professionals meet these critical responsibilities and, in turn, improve children's quality of life under the laws and policies of the United States.

Children, Social Science, and the Law broadens the field's conceptualization of the topic "children and the law" in ways not attempted previously, raising consciousness about a wide-ranging set of issues in great need of theoretical, empirical, and legislative attention. Some chapters address the newest research in subfields that fortunately have burgeoned over the last decade (e.g., children's eyewitness testimony, child abuse and neglect). Other chapters are in-depth considerations of novel issues that have received far less attention than they deserve (e.g., the impact of welfare policies on children, law and policy related to gay and lesbian parenting). Many difficult questions are confronted: Are the rights that our nation's laws ascribe to children commensurate with their capabilities and needs? Are law and policy effective in promoting the best living arrangements for children whose families have changed through divorce, adoption, and so forth? How should laws governing the punishment of crime acknowledge developmental differences between adult and juvenile offenders? Can social policies and laws protect children from maltreatment? Is the testimony of child witnesses adequately received and accommodated in courts of law? These issues necessarily draw the attention of policy makers and politicians who create and change law; professionals such as judges, lawyers, and police officers who interpret and implement law; and social science researchers who study the assumptions behind and the effects of law and policy.

An impressive array of the most well-regarded experts in the field have written the chapters appearing in this volume. They include social scientists, who provide insights gained from their own and others' research programs, and legal experts, who stress legal analysis and synthesis as well as policy implications. All have reviewed current research and law relevant to their particular topic, and they have made recommendations about future trends and needs. Although the contributions are grounded in high-quality work (empirical or legal), our authors have written for a broad audience of novices and experts from various fields. As such, *Children, Social Science, and the Law* can educate multidisciplinary readers about current research and policy, and it can serve as a stimulant for future collaborative thought, research, and action. With its unique integration of psychological research, social policy, and legal analysis, the volume is an important resource for any professional concerned with children and the law, including researchers, attorneys, judges, policy makers, legislators, and mental health, social service, and police professionals. The book will also be of interest to students and instructors in related disciplines.

A PREVIEW OF THE CONTRIBUTIONS

Children, Social Science, and the Law is divided into five interrelated parts: (a) Children's Rights, Their Capabilities, and Society's Responsibilities to Children; (b) Children and Family Change; (c) Juvenile Aggression and Juvenile Justice; (d) Children as

Victims and Witnesses; and (e) Conclusions and Future Directions. Several fundamental themes weave throughout each part: First, what are the current laws and policies relating to children? How do these laws and policies accommodate – or fail to accommodate – children's special needs and rights? Second, how can social science research be used to test assumptions behind child-relevant laws and policies and, in so doing, inform the creation, interpretation, and implementation of laws and policy that will protect and serve our nation's youth? Third, how can courts and legislators become more receptive to social science recommendations? Finally, what challenges are faced in the 21st century as our society continues its struggle to accommodate children's concerns within our legal system? What should future research and policy goals be? All authors address these themes as they consider their individual topics; therefore, all chapters highlight research that can inform current policies and law and outline future challenges that must be met for the field to continue producing scientifically sound research that will have real impact on children's lives. Next, we preview the contributions within each section of our book.

Children's Rights, Their Capabilities, and Society's Responsibilities to Children

The chapters in Part I consider law, policy, and social science relevant to society's attempts to accommodate children as full persons under the law. The competing interests of children's, parents', and states' rights complicate many circumstances faced by children, from receiving welfare assistance to custody determinations. The authors of these chapters champion the children's advocacy perspective, arguing that children should be guaranteed essentials that adults take for granted such as financial assistance, legal representation, and the right to participate in decisions central to their lifestyle and well-being. The authors are also careful, however, to illustrate advocacy that is appropriate (e.g., advocacy for rights commensurate with children's developmental capacities).

First, Wilcox, Colman, and Wyatt examine one of the most sweeping policy changes in decades: the end of welfare as the nation had known it since the 1930s. The authors examine recent research on the implications of the Personal Responsibility and Work Opportunity Reconciliation Act for the well-being of children in poverty – a startling 19% of all children. Specifically, they address opportunities and risks posed by the new laws in the domains of family–child interactions, child development, child maltreatment, and teen parenting. They preview ongoing evaluations of long-term outcomes, research that will surely inform future law and social policy related to poor children and their families.

Next, Small and Limber trace societal and governmental changes relevant to understanding children's rights in our nation, provide a history of diverging advocacy movements (children's right to self-determination versus rights to basic health and safety), and review the implications of the United Nations Convention on the Rights of the Child (United Nations General Assembly, 1989) and influential reports from the U.S. Advisory Board on Child Abuse and Neglect (1991). Their chapter provides a practical blueprint for future research on children's rights and for social action on behalf of children.

Schmidt and Reppucci focus on matches and mismatches between children's rights and children's developmentally determined cognitive and socioemotional capabilities. The authors provide thorough reviews of child and adolescent self-determination and protection rights in juvenile justice, medical, educational, and family contexts. Then, by applying the findings of developmental psychology research, the authors provide a sophisticated analysis of children's understanding of the law and their rights, and of children's competence to make legally relevant decisions. This analysis reveals that children's actual competencies sometimes differ in important ways from the legal system's assumptions about their competencies. Their chapter illustrates that determining the nature of both actual and perceived competencies is essential in ensuring that children are guaranteed all rights commensurate with their competencies.

Finally, Haralambie and Nysse-Carris consider a specific right that has begun to receive an increasing amount of attention within the legal profession: children's right to legal representation. The authors outline the development of the legal subspecialty of children's legal representation and contrast several models for representing children's voices in legal proceedings. They offer concrete suggestions for social science research that could inform future models of legal representation for children. Researchers addressing their suggestions have the potential to start a unique subfield of legally relevant social science research.

Children and Family Change

Next, our book turns to issues that arise when children are involved in special and changing family situations. Social science findings are already frequently represented in adjudications surrounding divorce, custody, and adoption, because psychological research relevant to these situations is well established. But as our authors attest, the field has much more to offer on a variety of issues that arise in these situations. For example, Haugaard and Avery address the competing interests of parents, children, and the state that are necessarily at stake when parental rights must be terminated to free children for adoption. With a focus on situations in which maltreatment drives termination, the authors provide a detailed description of the legal process of parental rights termination, and they review literature on the consequences to children of being involved in termination situations. They illustrate the precarious balance between the risks and benefits associated with prompt versus protracted termination proceedings and between the states' goals of protecting children from harm versus preserving families.

Family change often involves new custody arrangements for children. Depner reviews social science research that has the potential to guide child custody policy. She considers risks and protective factors that determine outcomes for children involved in various family reorganization alternatives, and she shows how a careful consideration of these factors is necessary for effective child-specific custody plans. Depner's chapter provides judges and other decision makers with practical recommendations based on the best research currently available.

Patterson, Fulcher, and Wainwright focus on a unique family law issue: the mismatch between social science evidence and legal assumptions concerning gay and lesbian parenting. The accessibility of vivid examples of this mismatch underscores the growing importance of the topic. For example, a recent Virginia State Supreme Court ruling that denied a lesbian mother custody of her biological child because of her sexual orientation (*Bottoms v. Bottoms*, 1995) stands in direct contrast to research discrediting assumptions that lesbian and gay parents are unfit (e.g., Patterson, 1992, 1995). Patterson and colleagues' detailed examination of law, policy, and science related to lesbian and gay parenting will educate policy makers and spark much new research in this nascent field.

Juvenile Aggression and Juvenile Justice

At the turn of the 20th century, legal reform based on the assumption that juveniles lacked maturity and judgment led to the establishment of the juvenile court system (Whitebread & Heilman, 1988). Some 60 years later, the U.S. Supreme Court deemed this approach a failure (*Kent v. United States*, 1966) and provided children with due process rights (*In re Gault*, 1967). That ruling ironically turned juvenile courts into closer approximations of the adult criminal justice system. One hundred years later, policies that transfer younger and younger juveniles to adult courts have done even more to preclude the consideration of maturational factors that separate juveniles from adults. Enter the role of social science research: to document the developmental progression of capacities relevant to the legal context. Our next group of chapters considers the constellation of factors surrounding today's juvenile justice system and juvenile offender.

First, Salekin describes the historical and contemporary legal context necessary for understanding issues surrounding the transfer of juveniles to adult criminal courts. His exhaustive review of clinical and developmental psychology findings relevant to understanding aggressive behavior in adolescents leads him to conclude that in most cases, the legal assumption that adults and juveniles are equivalent is misguided, and therefore, that many transfers are unwarranted from a psychological perspective. Fried and Reppucci approach similar issues from a different theoretical perspective. They focus on social and community factors that mediate the development of youth violence, and they use prevention and intervention theories to illustrate how policies could help prevent juvenile delinquency. They also offer practical suggestions to improve predictions about juveniles' future dangerousness and their amenability to treatment.

Woolard's chapter complements the earlier chapter by Schmidt and Reppucci by focusing on children's decision-making capacity in the juvenile justice context. She evaluates the match between what courts demand from juvenile defendants and juveniles' actual capacities (e.g., their ability to make mature judgments, to understand their rights and the law, and to reason about their life situations). She underscores the need for juvenile courts and developmentally sensitive policies, both of which are increasingly threatened in today's society.

Children as Victims and Witnesses

Thankfully, at the turn of the 21st century, concerns about child maltreatment and children's eyewitness testimony have resulted in much research and many useful books (e.g., Bottoms & Goodman, 1996; Briere, Berliner, Bulkley, Jenny, & Reid, 1996; Ceci & Bruck, 1995; Goodman & Bottoms, 1993; Melton & Barry, 1994; Schwartz-Kenney, McCauley, & Epstein, 2001; Westcott, Davies, & Bull, in press). *Children, Social Science, and the Law* is unique in its attention to a much broader, and often overlooked, set of circumstances in which children, law, and policy collide. Even so, no book on children and the law could ignore the topic of child maltreatment and the accommodation of child witnesses in the legal system. Thus, the chapters in Part IV address these issues by considering the newest research and legal thinking in the field.

First, Berman, Silverman, and Kurtines address a new and increasingly important area of child maltreatment research: the impact of exposure to and victimization by community violence. Exposure to crime and violence is a way of life for many children in the United States, especially poor minority children, for whom this is yet one more of many serious burdens. Perhaps because of the disenfranchisement of its victims, this form of child maltreatment has been slow to receive attention. Berman and colleagues move the field forward by reviewing the serious adverse effects of community violence on children's well-being and by delineating strategies for clinical intervention to attenuate negative psychological symptoms. They also outline individual, community, and societal strategies that could promote better prevention and treatment efforts.

Next, McFarlane, Doueck, and Levine review available research on the efficacy of prevention policies in deterring child abuse and neglect. This topic is particularly timely as the field attempts to understand reasons for significant recent declines in child maltreatment reports. According to Jones and Finkelhor (2001), nationwide reports of child sexual abuse have declined 26% since 1991, with case substantiations dropping 31% since 1992. Decreases in other forms of child maltreatment have been more recent and less dramatic. Is this the result of prevention policies such as parenting skills training, school-based education programs, mandated reporting policies, and community sex offender notification laws? (Or, as discussed later, do the decreases reflect societal skepticism about children's reports?) McFarlane et al.'s detailed assessment of prevention strategies illustrates why some efforts have failed, particularly those predicated on intuitive assumptions driven by political motive rather than empirical findings and theoretical reasoning.

The remaining chapters in this part consider the basic science contributions and the applied implications of psychological research testing legal assumptions about children's actual and perceived eyewitness competencies. The chapters consider children's actual eyewitness abilities in forensic interviews and court proceedings, as well as the effects of courtroom accommodations on children's perceived and actual eyewitness competence. The authors illustrate how research using ecologically valid techniques has yielded generalizable results of importance to law and policy. They also point, however, to the limits of using research findings in court. Specifically, in a detailed review of children's eyewitness testimony research, Schaaf, Alexander, Goodman, Ghetti, Edelstein, and Castelli illustrate that a multifaceted understanding of individual, developmental, and social factors is needed to understand child witnesses' weaknesses and strengths, and that application of research to actual legal cases must be made carefully. In particular, they worry that overgeneralization of findings from "false memory research" focuses inordinate societal skepticism on children's reports, particularly on their disclosures of child abuse.

Lyon further develops this theme in his consideration of the courts' use of children's eyewitness suggestibility research. In particular, Lyon performs a sophisticated legal analysis of the admissibility of children's testimony research, concluding that courts can no longer exclude such research. In so doing, he has provided a handbook for evaluating expert testimony on children's suggestibility. He argues that the courts' increasing receptivity to social science findings must be coupled with serious scrutiny of the generalizability of child witness studies to specific cases at hand, scrutiny that he believes will exclude many studies often offered to discredit children's testimony.

Recognizing that certain features of traditional trial proceedings may make children reluctant to testify about their abuse and decrease their accuracy, legislatures and courts have introduced various evidentiary and procedural innovations to help facilitate children's accurate testimony in criminal abuse cases. McAuliff and Kovera review social science evidence on the use and effect of these innovations. They conclude that U.S. courts use most innovations infrequently, and that although innovative procedures have little effect on jurors' perceptions of a defendant, they are associated with more negative evaluations of child witnesses under some circumstances. As with Lyon's chapter, legal professionals will appreciate their practical, research-based recommendations that can guide choices about using special techniques in child witness cases.

Conclusions and Future Directions

In the first of two concluding chapters, Gary Melton emphasizes the need not only for appreciating the fruits of the recent bonding of social science and law, but also for recognizing how the bonding can produce even more benefits in the future. He points out that although courts now often reference social science evidence when it is obviously relevant, "reference" does not often mean "acceptance" or even "understanding." Melton highlights two of the most formidable challenges faced by social scientists who hope to influence the law: (a) courts' intuitions about human behavior are often more persuasive than empirical research and (b) the generalizability of social scientists' research to legal issues is often severely limited by inappropriate methodology. His overarching theme, however, is one of optimism for "a new generation of research" that will advance our understanding of the ways in which law influences children's lives.

The book's final chapter, written by the Director of the American Bar Association's Center on Children and the Law, is a frank examination of barriers to child-friendly laws, policies, and practices. With lapsed patience in the face of years of inaction, Davidson indicts legislators for ignoring social science findings while passing "politically correct" legislation, for failing to finance efforts to help children, and for lacking the courage to embrace children's rights formally by signing the United Nations Convention on the Rights of the Child – as has every other recognized nation in the world. We applaud his courage for pointing to some of the most pressing issues our country faces, pressing issues that we hope our book will advance to the forefront of action.

In conclusion, action on behalf of children must be taken by both social scientists and policy makers. Social scientists must use solid psychological theory and ecologically valid methods to test important legal assumptions, and they must find successful ways to disseminate the results to policy and law makers (Bottoms, Reppucci, Tweed, & Nysse, in press; Melton, 1987). In turn, those who make and change law must heed the results of this research. Only when these goals have been realized will research be successful in changing children's lives. We believe that *Children, Social Science, and the Law* can hardly fail to realize its potential to facilitate these goals: For policy makers, the book will serve as a conduit for the latest findings relevant to law and policy, and for social science researchers and students, it will challenge old beliefs and provide new ideas about the types of socially relevant research needed.

The new century presents unprecedented opportunities for researchers and policy makers to join in a partnership to improve children's lives. We hope both groups of professionals recognize the possibilities and listen to the messages so clearly articulated by the field's most well-respected experts in *Children, Social Science, and the Law*.

References

Bottoms v. Bottoms, No. 941166 (Va. 1995).

Bottoms, B. L., & Goodman, G. S. (Eds.). (1996). *International perspectives on child abuse and children's testimony: Psychological research and law*. Newbury Park, CA: Sage.

Bottoms, B. L., Reppucci, N. D., Tweed, J., & Nysse, K. (in press). Children, psychology, and law: Reflections on past and future contributions to science and policy. In J. Ogloff & R. Roesch (Eds.), *Taking psychology and law into the twenty first century*. New York: Kluwar Academic/Plenum Publishers.

Briere, J., Berliner, L., Bulkley, J. A., Jenny, C., & Reid, T. (Eds.). (1996). *The APSAC handbook on child maltreatment* (pp. 51–71). Thousand Oaks, CA: Sage.

Ceci, S. J., & Bruck, M. (1995). *Jeopardy in the courtroom: A scientific analysis of children's testimony*. Washington, DC: American Psychological Association.

Goodman, G. S., & Bottoms, B. L. (Eds.). (1993). *Child victims, child witnesses: Understanding and improving testimony*. New York: Guilford.

Goodman, G. S., Emery, R. E., & Haugaard, J. (1998). Developmental psychology and law: Divorce, child maltreatment, foster care, and adoption. In I. Siegel & A. Renninger (Eds.), *Child psychology in practice* (pp. 775–876), in W. Damon (Series Ed.), *Handbook of child psychology* (Vol. 4). New York: Wiley.

In re Gault, 387 US 1, 87 S Ct. 1428, 18 L. Ed. 2nd 527 (1967).

Jones, L., & Finkelhor, D. (2001). *The decline in child sexual abuse cases*. Washington, DC: U.S. Department of Justice, Office of Justice Programs, Office of Juvenile Justice and Delinquency Prevention.

Kent v. United States, 383 U.S. 541, 86 S.Ct. 1045, 16 L.Ed.2d 84 (1966).

Melton, G. (Ed.). (1987). *Reforming the law: Impact of child development research*. New York: Guilford.

Melton, G. B., & Barry, F. D. (1994). *Protecting children from abuse and neglect: Foundations for a new national strategy*. New York: Guilford.

Patterson, C. J. (1992). Children of lesbian and gay parents. *Child Development*, 63, 1025–1042.

Patterson, C. J. (1995). Lesbian mothers, gay fathers, and their children. In A. R. D'Augelli & C. J. Patterson (Eds.), *Lesbian, gay, and bisexual identities across the lifespan: Psychological perspectives* (pp. 262–290). New York: Oxford University Press.

Schwartz-Kenney, B. M., McCauley, M., & Epstein, M. A. (Eds.). (2001). *Child abuse: A global view*. Westport, CT: Greenwood.

United Nations General Assembly (1989, November 17). *Adoption of a convention on the rights of the child*. U.N. Doc. A/Res/44/25.

U.S. Advisory Board on Child Abuse and Neglect (1991). *Creating caring communities: Blueprint for an effective federal policy on child abuse and neglect*. Washington, DC: U.S. Government Printing Office.

Westcott, H. L., Davies, G. M., & Bull, R. H. C. (in press). *Children's testimony: A handbook of psychological research and forensic practice*. Chichester, UK: Wiley.

Whitebread, C., & Heilman, J. (1988). An overview of the law of juvenile delinquency. *Behavioral Sciences and the Law, 6*, 285–305.

PART I

CHILDREN'S RIGHTS, THEIR CAPABILITIES, AND SOCIETY'S RESPONSIBILITIES TO CHILDREN

2

The Personal Responsibility and Work Opportunity Reconciliation Act of 1996

What Will It Mean for Children?

Brian L. Wilcox
Rebecca A. Colman
Jennifer M. Wyatt

In 1991, presidential candidate Bill Clinton promised to "end welfare as we know it." With the enthusiastic support of a Republican-controlled Congress, President Clinton signed the Personal Responsibility and Work Opportunity Reconciliation Act (PRWORA) in August 1996, thereby effectively carrying out his promise. This legislation fundamentally transformed the nature of the cash welfare program that had been created in 1935 in response to the economic hardships brought about by the Great Depression, replacing a guaranteed entitlement program with a time-limited benefit.

A policy shift of this magnitude raises many questions, but a central concern of many policy analysts and researchers has been the implications of the new welfare system for children in recipient families and in families who may have received welfare benefits under the old law but are now or soon will be excluded from participation. In this chapter we will briefly describe the nature of this policy transformation and review research that offers a glimpse at the potential consequences of these changes for children in low-income families. Additionally, we will briefly describe the work currently in progress on a number of fronts that may provide scholars and

Correspondence concerning this chapter should be addressed to Brian L. Wilcox, Center on Children, Families, and the Law, University of Nebraska, 121 S. 13th Street, Suite 302, Lincoln, Nebraska 68588-0227. Electronic mail may be sent to bwilcox@unl.edu.

policy makers with the data necessary to discern the impact of welfare reform on the well-being of children in low-income families.

THE ROAD TO WELFARE REFORM

The Aid to Families with Dependent Children program (AFDC; originally called the Aid to Dependent Children program), which was the primary cash welfare program between 1935 and 1996, provided cash welfare payments for children who were needy because their mother or father was absent from the home, was deceased, or was unemployed and thus unable to provide economic support or care. In the minds of most people, AFDC was synonymous with welfare, although there have been and continue to be several other components of the federal-state welfare system. Three principal purposes have guided the AFDC program: "to encourage the care of needy children in their own homes (original 1935 purpose), to strengthen family life (added in 1956), and to promote family self support" (Committee on Ways and Means, 1998, p. 401). The characteristics and eligibility criteria for the program evolved substantially over its 61-year history, making it difficult to characterize the program succinctly. Funding of the AFDC program was shared by the federal and state governments, and states were given flexibility to establish the size of the grants given to families, resulting in substantial variation across the states. For example, in 1994 a family of three with no other resources would have received $200 monthly in Mississippi and $680 in Connecticut. The most important characteristic of the AFDC program, however, was the fact that it was an entitlement program; all families meeting eligibility criteria were entitled to receive the established cash payments.

From its inception in 1935, the AFDC program received mixed reviews even from its supporters. President Franklin D. Roosevelt viewed it as a short-term necessary evil and vowed that his goal was "the abolition of relief altogether" (Leuchtenberg, 1963, p. 124). Two fundamental criticisms have been leveled at the AFDC program: (a) it is said to contain disincentives for family formation and incentives for family disruption, and (b) it is widely believed to contain disincentives for paid employment.

Federal welfare programs have been characterized as containing antifamily elements by Presidents Jimmy Carter, Ronald Reagan,

George Bush, and Bill Clinton. Joseph Califano, Carter's Secretary of Health, Education and Welfare, told the Senate Subcommittee on Public Assistance in 1978 that the AFDC program breaks up families. When pressed for specifics and data supporting this claim, Califano was able to provide none (Moynihan, 1986). By this time, the presumed antifamily effects of welfare had become entrenched in both popular and political lore. Empirical evaluations of the claims that AFDC precipitates nonmarital childbirth and divorce have not provided significant support for these propositions (Blank, 1997; Gottschalk, McLanahan, & Sandefur, 1994; Moffitt, 1992; Wilcox, Robbennolt, O'Keeffe, & Reddy, 1996).

Critics of the AFDC program also argued, with substantial supporting data, that the program contained disincentives for employment. The disincentive mechanism is straightforward: Families with unemployed parents who received no other income received the maximum AFDC benefits, and as a family's earnings increased, benefits fell. After 4 months of working and receiving AFDC, recipients lost $1 in benefits for each $1 earned. The major issues of contention within academic and policy circles have been the size and significance of any work disincentive. A comprehensive review of this research by Moffitt (1992), as well as recent analyses by Blank (1997), suggest that the work disincentive effect may be smaller than is commonly thought. Blank concludes that "AFDC dollars do not reduce work dollars at a rate even close to one-for-one. In fact, the work disincentive effect appears to be relatively small" (1997, p. 147).

Welfare reform has held a near-constant spot on the American political agenda (Blank & Blum, 1997; Chase-Lansdale & Vinovskis, 1995; Handler, 1995). As criticisms of the AFDC program mounted in political circles, public support for the program diminished. The debate leading to the passage of the PRWORA defined the "welfare problem" in terms of the failure of able-bodied adults to seek and gain employment, the propensity of many young women to bear children out of wedlock in order to secure welfare benefits, and the long-term dependence of some welfare recipients. Welfare itself became the problem rather than the solution, according to some policy analysts (Murray, 1984). The goal of welfare reform, then, was to restructure the "incentives" assumed to be inherent in the program so as to encourage the poor (particularly poor women) to enter the paid labor force and to reduce childbearing. Subpopulations of particular concern to politicians were young welfare recipients and long-term welfare recipients.

Passage of the PRWORA in 1996 came on the heels of several years of extensive welfare experimentation at the state level. The Clinton administration (and prior administrations dating back to 1962) held the authority to grant states permission to depart from the standard AFDC program, and many states were granted waivers to experiment with a variety of options. Many of the states created a set of carrot-and-stick incentives and disincentives that served as models for the provisions ultimately enacted in the PRWORA.

THE PERSONAL RESPONSIBILITY AND WORK OPPORTUNITY RECONCILIATION ACT

Having vetoed two prior welfare reform bills on the grounds that they were too harsh on children (Presidential Veto Message, 1996), President Clinton signed the Personal Responsibility and Work Opportunity Reconciliation Act on August 22, 1996, and, in doing so, claimed to have met his promise to "end welfare as we know it." The core provision of the new law did just that. It abolished the AFDC open-ended entitlement program and replaced it with a state block grant program: the Temporary Assistance for Needy Families Block Grant Program (TANF). Under TANF no individual has a guarantee of benefits, as was the case under AFDC. Instead, states receive a fixed block grant that they administer, with considerable latitude, regarding benefits and eligibility criteria. Additionally, TANF cash benefits are limited to 60 cumulative months, after which no federal dollars can be used. States have the option of exempting up to 20% of their caseload from this time limit and may also use state dollars to provide a cash benefit beyond the 60-month limit.

A second fundamental provision of the new law is that it requires TANF recipients to work after receiving benefits for 2 years or face the loss of benefits. States may also terminate Medicaid benefits for adults (but not children) who lose their TANF benefits because they fail to work. As of 2000, single parents are required to work 30 hours per week, and parents in two-parent families must work 35 hours per week. States face sanctions if 50% of their TANF families do not meet these targets by 2002. Even parents of infants and toddlers are required to work, although states may exempt parents of infants under 12 months of age. Unlike the provisions of AFDC, under which child care was guaranteed for employed recipients, working TANF recipients have no guarantee of child care. Parents of children under age 6 who cannot secure child care, however, are not to be penalized for not meeting employment goals. Federal funding for child care under the PRWORA is substantially reduced from prior levels. States may use their own funds to assist TANF recipients in paying for child care but are under no obligation to do so. States are also no longer required to pay at least 75% of the market rate for child care subsidized by the Child Care and Development Fund created under the PRWORA.

Teen and nonmarital childbearing are targeted by several PRWORA provisions. Under previous welfare law, states had the option to require minor parents to live with their parents or in a supervised living arrangement. TANF provisions replace this option with a requirement. Under PRWORA, single mothers under the age of 18 cannot receive benefits unless they live with a parent or are under the supervision of an adult, and they must be enrolled in school or participate in training activities. An "illegitimacy bonus" provides up to five states with cash bonuses for reducing their rate of nonmarital births without increasing abortions. A new program provides $50 million annually to states to support "abstinence until marriage" education programs. In addition, a related provision targeted at both marital and nonmarital childbearing gives states the option of denying additional benefits to families with children born while the family is enrolled in the TANF program. At least 20 states have thus far instituted these "family caps."

The PRWORA continued the trend of past welfare reform efforts to strengthen the child support enforcement system. States are expected to establish paternity for at least 90% of nonmarital childbirths. TANF recipients who do not cooperate in efforts to establish paternity will have their benefit reduced by at least 25%. The system for voluntary paternity establishment was streamlined, as were procedures for the direct withholding of child support from wages. Other provisions were designed to strengthen the interstate enforcement of child support orders, track noncustodial parents who change jobs, and require states to suspend or deny drivers or professional licenses for those owing child support.

A final set of provisions with direct implications for the well-being of children altered the Supplemental Security Insurance (SSI) program. New eligibility guidelines were designed expressly to reduce the number of children receiving SSI benefits. Under prior law, children who did not meet the adult eligibility criteria could request an Individual Functional Assessment (IFA), which considered disability-related factors and conditions unique to children. The new law eliminates the IFA. Additionally, the new law changes the eligibility guidelines by removing references to "maladaptive behavior" as criteria for determining disability and by requiring that mental and physical impairments must result in "marked and severe" functional limitations of at least a year's duration. All children receiving SSI benefits under earlier eligibility guidelines are required to be reevaluated using the new criteria.

POVERTY, WELFARE, AND CHILDREN

Who is being affected by these changes? In 1998, approximately 13.5 million children under the age of 18 lived in families falling below the officially designated poverty threshold. These children account for approximately 40% of the population living in poverty in the United States even though they comprise only 25% of the population. At 18.9% the poverty rate for children is substantially higher than the rates for adults aged 18–64 (10.5%) or 65 and older (10.5%) (U.S. Census Bureau, 2000). The rate of poverty for children has been relatively stable since 1980 but well above the low point of 14.4% in 1973. Younger children are especially vulnerable: In 1997, 21.6% of children under the age of 6 were poor. Children are also, not surprisingly, more likely than adults to be recipients of welfare. Children comprised nearly two-thirds of the AFDC recipient caseload in 1995 (Committee on Ways and Means, 1996).

Not all groups of children are equally likely to be poor or to be welfare recipients. Children in single-parent families, particularly mother-headed single-parent families, have higher rates of poverty

TABLE 2.1. *Poverty Rate (Percent) by Race/Ethnicity and Selected Characteristics, 1997*

	All	White	Black	Hispanic
Children under age 18	19.9	16.1	37.2	36.8
Children under age 6	21.6	18.0	39.7	38.3
Married couples w/children	8.2	7.5	11.0	19.5
Female-headed w/children	43.5	39.7	49.0	56.7

(see Table 2.1) and welfare receipt. Children in Black and Hispanic families were over twice as likely as White children to be poor in 1997, with poverty rates especially high in female-headed families. Similarly, the vast majority of children receiving AFDC support in 1995 were living in single-parent families: 25% due to separation/divorce and 57% due to nonmarital childbirth. Thirty-six percent of parents in AFDC families were White, 37% were Black, and 21% were Hispanic (Committee on Ways and Means, 1998). When longer-term trends in poverty rates and AFDC utilization data are examined, the most striking finding is the shift away from parental death or incapacitation as a significant cause of poverty and AFDC receipt to divorce and nonmarital childbearing (Bane & Ellwood, 1994; Duncan & Caspary, 1997; U.S. General Accounting Office, 1994a).

Any set of poverty and welfare statistics gives an incomplete and somewhat misleading picture of the nature of childhood poverty. It is important, for policy-making reasons, to understand the dynamic nature of poverty and welfare receipt so that resources can be targeted to families who are likely to be long-term recipients. Many welfare recipients cycle on and off the welfare rolls. Indeed, nearly three-quarters of new welfare recipients will have more than one period of AFDC receipt (Duncan & Caspary, 1997). Although studies suggest that 36% to 42% of those who ever receive welfare will do so for less than a total of 2 years, this means that a majority will receive welfare for more than 2 years. Estimates by Bane and Ellwood (1994) and Pavetti (1995) suggest that 35% to 39% of new recipients can be expected to be on the rolls for 5 or more years, with roughly 20% likely to receive welfare for 10 years or more. This group would clearly be affected by the new time limits of the PRWORA.

IMPLICATIONS FOR CHILDREN: RECENT RESEARCH

Welfare policy making has generally focused on adults: how to move them from welfare receipt to stable employment and how to prevent them from entering the welfare program in the first place. As noted previously, however, children comprise the large majority of the welfare caseload and will be affected both directly and indirectly by many provisions in the new welfare law. The next section examines previous research that sheds light on the potential effects of the PRWORA on children. Specifically created to reduce welfare dependency among poor parents and to discourage nonmartial childbearing, the PRWORA provisions promise to alter both the physical and social contexts in which poor children are developing. As families adapt to work requirements, time limits, and changing eligibility rules, many crucial aspects of children's daily lives (e.g., family relationships, household income, and child-care practices) will be simultaneously transformed, raising the possibility that children will be among those most strongly affected by the new legislation.

Unfortunately, given the recency of the new law, research documenting the exact nature and extent of these changes, and their corresponding impact on children's development, has yet to be completed. However, findings from basic research on child development and previous welfare reform programs are available and provide a valuable framework for considering the potential implications of the new legislation for children. Although PRWORA constitutes a major break from previous welfare practices, efforts to involve welfare recipients in the work force and to decrease recipients' childbearing rates are not new. In the past decade, several federal- and state-based initiatives have experimented with the welfare service delivery system in the hope of achieving these goals. Viewed in conjunction with the well-established research literature on the ecological factors that influence children's development, these experiments suggest that there is reason to be both optimistic and wary of the new legislation's effects on children. With this in mind, the following sections identify some of the key developmental issues surrounding welfare reform and explore the opportunities and risks posed to children's well-being by the new policy provisions. The first three sections present the overarching concerns with regard to children about the possible effects of the new eligibility requirements of PRWORA: the impacts of poverty and maternal employment on child well-being and the risk of child maltreatment. Next, specific provisions of the new welfare law are discussed in the context of their expected impact on children and families. These include changes in child-care funding, TANF eligibility for unmarried (adolescent) parents, child-support collection, and eligibility for SSI.

Poverty, Income, and Child Development

From a developmental perspective, monitoring PRWORA's effects on child poverty will be essential to formulating a complete understanding of the law's significance for children. Compared to children from more economically advantaged backgrounds, young children who grow up in poor families are more likely to experience a wide array of undesirable outcomes including infant mortality, low birthweight, poor physical health, inadequate nutrition, learning disabilities, cognitive delays, and behavioral and/or emotional disorders. In addition, although the research on adolescents in poverty is far less extensive, available information suggests that older children from poor families have lower rates of school achievement and occupational attainment and are at greater risk for teen pregnancy. Although it is not entirely clear whether these associations are due to low income, common poverty covariates (e.g., single-parent households, low levels of parental education), or some combination of the two, the persistence, timing, and depth of children's poverty experiences appear to be developmentally salient. Children who spend more time in poverty are more likely to be adversely affected by it, and younger children appear to be more vulnerable than older children to negative outcomes. Moreover, children who experience prolonged bouts of poverty are also more likely to experience extreme forms of poverty (i.e., have family incomes far below the poverty line), presumably placing them at greater risk for later developmental problems (for an excellent review of the literature on children and poverty see Duncan & Brooks-Gunn, 1997; Huston, 1991).

Government efforts to combat child poverty have traditionally focused on means-tested cash assistance and in-kind benefit programs such as AFDC and food stamps. Although many have argued that these types of programs are far from sufficient and fail to meet the needs of the majority of the nation's poor children, there is evidence to suggest that such policies have been at least minimally effective. In 1995, AFDC and other cash benefit programs succeeded in lifting approximately 2.4 million American children out of poverty (Lewit, Terman, & Behrman, 1997).

Thus, the extent to which PRWORA's provisions influence the duration, depth, and timing of children's poverty experiences promises to have a profound impact on children's well-being and may be particularly influential in determining the life chances of minority children who are more likely to live in poverty. If efforts to move welfare-receiving parents into the paid work force are successful, the resulting increases in family income may help to alleviate some of the negative outcomes associated with extreme child poverty. Likewise, if mandatory work requirements and knowledge of time limits result in more frequent and rapid transitions, the number of children living in poverty for a prolonged period of time may be meaningfully decreased.

Unfortunately, there is no guarantee that those families who successfully complete the transition from welfare to work will escape from poverty. Data from previous studies exploring the economic impact of employment on welfare indicate that a large proportion of welfare recipients end up in low-wage jobs and are subsequently unable to use work as a means of lifting their families out of poverty (Burtless, 1997; Cancian, Haveman, Kaplan, Meyer, & Wolfe, 1998; Kisker, Rangarajan, & Boller, 1998). Based on data from past studies of welfare-to-work transitions, experts estimate that the typical welfare recipient can expect to earn somewhere between $6 and $7 an hour. Moreover, if the new welfare policies flood the labor market with large numbers of unskilled workers, competition for the dwindling number of low-skill jobs may depress this hourly wage even further (Burtless, 1997). Thus, even if they are fortunate enough to find stable, full-time jobs in the private sector, many former welfare recipients will remain poor. Consequently, even if PRWORA succeeds in moving parents off the welfare rolls, their children may continue to suffer the negative effects of poverty.

This prospect seems even more likely when one considers the type of welfare recipient most likely to be affected by mandatory work requirements and lifetime limits. Despite common perceptions of long-term welfare use, many families receive welfare for a relatively short period of time. A considerable percentage, however, experience prolonged periods of welfare receipt (5 or more years) and may therefore be particularly vulnerable to the changes included in the new law (Bane & Ellwood, 1994; Duncan, 1991; Duncan & Caspary, 1997). Compared to short-term aid recipients, long-term welfare users have lower levels of education and work experience and are more likely to suffer from mental health problems. These characteristics pose considerable barriers to successful employment and are apt to reduce significantly the job prospects and future earnings of long-term recipients (Cancian et al., 1998; Zaslow, Tout, Smith, & Moore, 1998). As a result, there is good reason to believe that the economic well-being of children from families characterized by long-term welfare use will not be meaningfully improved, and may even be diminished, by efforts to move their parents off welfare and into work. Without a government safety net, families experiencing time limits, sanctions, and/or family caps will have fewer economic resources to devote to their offspring, increasing the likelihood that their children will experience longer and more profound periods of poverty.

Finally, the risks associated with these provisions may be compounded by child age. As noted earlier, younger children appear to be more vulnerable to the adverse effects of poverty. Consequently, monitoring the number and age of children whose families experience a loss and/or reduction in their TANF grants will be crucial to developing a complete understanding of PRWORA's impact on children's well-being.

Parent–Child Relationships

In addition to possible income-related effects, mandatory work participation requirements may indirectly influence child outcomes by altering maternal stress, parenting practices, and/or the overall quality of parent–child interactions. Previous research on maternal employment suggests that how mothers respond to work and their type of employment have more of an impact on their children's well-being than their work status per se. If mothers view employment as stressful or are unable to balance the demands of home and work effectively, their interactions with their children may suffer. They may engage in harsher parenting practices or may simply become less attentive and responsive to their children's needs (Ferber, O'Farrell, & Allen, 1991; Wilson, Ellwood, & Brooks-Gunn, 1995). Likewise, research on employment conditions suggests that parents who are employed in repetitive, low-wage jobs are less nurturing and provide less stimulating home environments than do parents who hold more complex jobs. Moreover, moving mothers from welfare to work is unlikely to improve the quality of children's home surroundings if mothers are placed in low-wage, low-complexity jobs. When followed over a 2-year period, unmarried mothers who transitioned from unemployment to low-wage, low-complexity work experienced a drop in the quality of their home environment comparable to that experienced by persistently unemployed mothers (Parcel & Menaghan, 1997). Conversely, if employment activities enhance mothers' mental health and are socially and mentally stimulating, both parenting practices and child outcomes may be improved (Ferber et al., 1991). Thus, depending on how mothers adapt to the work demands placed on them and the type of employment they assume, children's well-being may either be enhanced, diminished, or unaffected by the new policies.

Although research on maternal employment and child well-being among low-income families is limited, there is reason to believe that maternal work may be beneficial for poor children. A small set of completed studies suggests that maternal employment has mildly positive to neutral effects on the quality of parent–child interactions and development outcomes in low-income samples (Brooks-Gunn, Smith, Berlin, & Lee, 1998; Moore & Driscoll, 1997; Parcel & Menaghan, 1997; Wilson et al., 1995; Zaslow & Emig, 1997).

It is important to note, however, that this conclusion is based on the experiences of women who entered the work force voluntarily and may not accurately represent the experiences of all families and all children. Given that parental reactions to work experiences appear to be a crucial mediator of maternal employment's effects on children, many experts fear that mandatory work requirements will place children at greater risk for unhealthy outcomes by increasing parental distress and disrupting parent–child relationships. Children from families characterized by long-term welfare use may be especially vulnerable. Descriptive data from the Child Outcomes Study of the National Evaluation of Welfare-to-Work Strategies indicate that women with long-term welfare use histories have less work experience and less favorable attitudes toward employment than women with shorter welfare use histories (Zaslow, Tout, et al., 1998). As a result, women who receive welfare for long periods of time may be more likely to be placed in low-wage, low-complexity jobs and may adapt less well to the work environment, placing their children at greater risk for poor developmental outcomes.

Research evaluating these concerns is currently limited to the findings of two welfare demonstration project evaluations. Implemented in 1986 in two sites, the Teen Parent Demonstration (TPD) program examined the effects of mandatory work requirements on the self-sufficiency activities and parenting practices of teen mothers enrolling in AFDC for the first time. On their enrollment into AFDC, teens were randomly assigned to either an experimental or a standard AFDC treatment group. Mothers in the TPD experimental group received enhanced support services and were required to participate in work-related activities in order to receive their maximum welfare grant. Mothers in the control group received traditional AFDC services. When mother–child dyads were subsequently observed at home, no differences emerged between the two groups on measures of parent–child interaction or quality of the home environment, suggesting that mandatory work requirements did not adversely affect the parenting behavior of mothers in the experimental group (Brooks-Gunn et al., 1998; Kisker et al., 1998).

This finding is further supported by results from another welfare experiment, the New Chance Demonstration Project. Designed to improve the life chances of young, low-income mothers who had dropped out of high school and their children, the New Chance program sought to involve program participants in employment, parenting, and educational activities at levels similar to those required in TDP. Although it is important to note that participation in program activities was not mandatory and that participants were not sanctioned for failing to comply with program expectations, the fact that high participation demands did not increase maternal depression and had slightly positive impacts on parenting practices at initial follow-up, suggesting that many high-risk mothers may adapt successfully to more stringent program requirements (Granger & Cytron, 1998; Zaslow & Eldred, 1998).

However, a limited body of research suggests that maternal employment during infancy may increase the likelihood of undesirable developmental outcomes. For example, Baydar and Brooks-Gunn (1991) found that children whose mothers worked during the first year of their life had lower scores on preschool measures of vocabulary and higher rates of behavioral problems than did children whose mothers were unemployed. Their results are particularly disturbing given that many states have chosen not to exempt mothers with children less than 1 year of age from mandatory work participation requirements.

In short, PRWORA's work participation requirements will most likely affect different families and different children in different ways. There is reason to hope that most families will not be adversely affected by mandated employment activities and may even benefit from them; however, the impact of work requirements on the development of young children and children from long-term welfare use families should be closely monitored.

Child Maltreatment

Some provisions of the new law may also diminish the well-being of children by increasing known risk factors for child maltreatment. Children who live in low-income and/or poverty-stricken homes are far more likely than their more economically advantaged peers to experience episodes of both child neglect and physical abuse (e.g., Kruttschnitt, McLeod, & Dornfeld, 1994; Strauss, Gelles, & Steinmetz, 1980; U.S. Department of Health and Human Services, 1996; Wolfner & Gelles, 1993). Although the reason behind this well-documented association is often debated (as was the case in our earlier discussion of child poverty, several factors covary with both low income and child maltreatment, including single-parent family structure and parental substance abuse), several income-related mechanisms have been hypothesized. From an economic perspective, low-income parents may simply lack the necessary financial resources to meet their children's basic needs adequately. Consequently, time limits, sanctions, and family caps may make poor children more vulnerable to child neglect by exacerbating both the length and the depth of their families' poverty (Knitzer & Bernard, 1997).

A considerable body of research also suggests that financial stress may predispose parents toward child abuse by increasing parental distress. Parents experiencing economic hardship score higher on measures of depression and report greater dissatisfaction with their parenting role. In turn, these factors are associated with less nurturing and more punitive parent–child interaction styles in several studies (e.g., Conger et al., 1992; Conger, Ge, Elder, Lorenz, & Simons, 1994; Elder, Conger, Foster, & Ardelt, 1992; McLoyd, 1989; McLoyd, Jayarante, Ceballo, & Borquez, 1994), suggesting that economic disadvantage may place parents at greater risk of harming their children.

Consistent with these hypotheses, two studies have documented an increase in child welfare involvement following the loss of welfare dollars. In 1992, a 5.8% reduction in California's welfare grant was followed by a 20% increase in Los Angeles County's child abuse and neglect reporting rates (Knitzer & Bernard, 1997). Similarly, data from the Illinois Department of Human Services indicate that children from families who experience a welfare grant sanction are significantly more likely to be the subjects of a child protection investigation and are twice as likely to be placed outside of the home (Shook, 1998). It is important to note that neither of these studies provides evidence in support of a causal relationship between welfare income loss and child maltreatment; however, they do suggest that the impact of welfare reform on parents' ability to care for their children in a safe, nurturing manner should be closely monitored.

Child Care

As parents receiving TANF benefits are required to work, increasing numbers of children will be in need of child care, creating new opportunities and risks for healthy development. To comply with the new work requirements, many parents will have to find affordable, accessible child-care arrangements for at least part of the day, especially if their children are too young to be enrolled in school (Scarr, 1998). The hours spent in child care can have a significant impact, positive or negative, on children's development. Social science research on the effects of child care has consistently found that the quality of child-care experience combines with the quality of the home environment to determine the outcomes of children who spend moderate to large amounts of time in day care. Additionally, the age of the child can moderate the effects of the child-care experience. In general, findings from studies of child care in a wide variety of populations tend to follow two patterns of results relevant to the PRWORA: High-quality child care can promote improved child outcomes in many areas of development (e.g., cognitive, social, behavioral, and educational), especially if the child comes from a disadvantaged environment (Caughy, DiPietro, & Strobino, 1994; Hayes, Palmer, & Zaslow, 1990; Zaslow, Oldham, Moore, & Magenheim, 1998); and low- quality child care can be detrimental in many of the same areas of development, especially when children are very young (i.e., less than 1 year old) or have an impoverished home environment (Baydar & Brooks-Gunn, 1991; Belsky & Rovine, 1988; Caughy et al., 1994). These results raise questions about the possible positive and negative effects of placing at-risk children into care while their parents work to meet TANF eligibility requirements.

The PRWORA provisions regarding child care focus on increased state flexibility, a goal that may be achieved at a cost to the children in care. The new Child Care and Development Fund is a block grant given to states for their discretionary use in providing and improving child care, especially for children in families receiving TANF. However, the grant provides substantially less funding than was previously given to states for child-care purposes. Although states will still have the option of increasing the amount of their own funds used for child care (and thereby becoming eligible for more federal funding), the decrease in resources will put states in the precarious position of having to choose between increasing the amount of available child care and improving the quality of existing child care. An additional change is the discontinuation of guaranteed child care for single parents on welfare, meaning that states are not required to help find a suitable child-care placement even if they require a parent to work. (However, states cannot penalize parents of children under age 6 if they cannot find affordable child care.) Some parents may be forced to choose informal child-care arrangements, which could mean leaving children in precarious (and possibly even dangerous) situations. Furthermore, the removal of the provision requiring states to pay up to 75% of the market value of child care for which they are reimbursing, coupled with the decreased amount of money available to states, may also lower the quality of care available to all children of parents on welfare.

As states are forced to choose between spending limited resources on more care or better care, the quality of care received by children of parents in welfare-to-work programs is likely to diminish. Further, as states provide lower reimbursement rates to care providers, parents will have more limited child-care options, possibly again leading to poorer-quality care for their children. Parents in jobs requiring work during odd hours (i.e., shifts other than 9 A.M. to 5 P.M. Monday through Friday) will have additional constraints in securing adequate, affordable care. The age at which a child enters nonparental care is also important to consider: Children who enter care before the end of their first year may be at greatest risk for negative outcomes (Baydar & Brooks-Gunn, 1991). If parents on welfare are forced to return to work too soon after a child is born, that child will have additional disadvantages to overcome beyond those mentioned earlier.

The issues of affordability and availability of adequate child care will be central to the success or failure of the most current wave of welfare reform. Parents will not be able to adhere to the work requirements if acceptable-quality child care is not available. In a study of the California Job Opportunity and Basic Skills program (a voluntary welfare-to-work program that allowed AFDC recipients child-care reimbursement while they were in job training), participants who reported that the child-care arrangements they found were low in quality or inaccessible were more likely to drop out of the program prior to completion or job placement (Meyers, 1993). Hofferth and Collins (1996) similarly found higher rates of employment turnover by parents who were dissatisfied with the quality or accessibility of the child-care arrangements. Parents who cannot find or afford appropriate child care will be unable to complete work requirements and will therefore be unable to remove themselves from poverty. Their children, unfortunately, may pay the greatest price.

Single parents, who comprise a sizable proportion of the welfare population, will face even more challenges to securing child care than will married parents. In two-parent families, work shifts can, in theory, be arranged such that formal care for children is not necessary or the need is more limited (although in reality this is even more difficult than it sounds). A single parent generally does not have another resident adult to care for children while he or she is at work. Therefore, child care for single parents will be an especially significant factor in the effectiveness of welfare reform. Not surprisingly, PRWORA is also less sensitive to the needs of single parents in other ways as well.

Nonmarital Childbearing and Teen Parenting

In addition to reducing welfare dependency, one of the primary goals of the new welfare reform law is to discourage nonmarital childbearing, particularly among teenagers. In keeping with this objective, PRWORA authorizes the allocation of funds for abstinence until marriage education and creates financial incentives for states to reduce their annual illegitimacy and abortion rates (U.S. Department of Health and Human Services, Office of the Assistant Secretary for Evaluation and Planning, 1999). Operating under the assumption that previous AFDC practices encouraged unwed pregnancies by reducing the financial burdens traditionally associated with single parenthood (e.g., Murray, 1984; Wilcox et al., 1996) and evidence suggesting that women who become parents as teens spend more time on welfare (Ellwood, 1986; U.S. General Accounting Office, 1994b), PRWORA also attempts to make nonmarital childbearing less attractive by tightening eligibility requirements and granting states greater flexibility in designing their benefit structures. Whereas the old AFDC law guaranteed cash assistance to all poor mothers regardless of age and gave states the option of imposing housing requirements, under the new law unmarried parents under the age of 18 must live at home or in an adult-supervised setting in order to be eligible for federal cash assistance. Likewise, federal law no longer guarantees that the size of a family's benefit package will increase with the birth of a new child. Under PRWORA, individual states can choose to implement what is known as a *family cap* policy and deny additional cash assistance to families bearing more children while on welfare (Office of the Assistant Secretary for Evaluation and Planning, 1999).

If these policies are successful in reducing early and nonmarital pregnancy and childbearing, the quality of children's lives may be positively affected. Children from single-parent and teen-parent homes are significantly more likely than other children to spend a large proportion of their childhood living in poverty (Maynard, 1997; McLanahan, 1995). Not surprisingly, they are also more likely to experience a wide variety of unfavorable developmental outcomes. Compared to other children, children of single and teen parents are more likely to have low scores on measures of cognitive ability (Moore, Morrison, & Greene, 1997) and physical health (Wolfe & Perozek, 1997). They are also more likely to be the subject of a child abuse investigation and to experience prolonged periods of out-of-home care (Goerge & Lee, 1997). In adolescence and early adulthood, they have lower levels of educational attainment (Haveman, Wolfe, & Peterson, 1997; McLanahan, 1995; Moore et al., 1997) and higher incarceration rates (Grogger, 1997) and are at greater risk for becoming teen parents themselves (Haveman et al., 1997). Although the causal relationships underlying these connections are not entirely clear, efforts to delay teenagers' childbearing and to reduce the number of children growing up in single-parent homes may enhance the life chances of the children eventually born to these women.

If the policy changes described earlier are not successful, however, children's well-being may be undermined. Nearly half of the nation's states have chosen to adopt a family cap, even though the ability of such policies to reduce illegitimacy rates is questionable and may place children at risk. Although some states experimenting with family cap policies have found them to be effective in decreasing the childbearing rates of program recipients (e.g., New Jersey's Family Development Program) (New Jersey Department of Human Services, 1998), similar reductions have not emerged in other locations (e.g., Delaware) (Zaslow, Tout, et al., 1998). In either case, those families who are undeterred by family cap policies will be forced to stretch already limited financial resources to cover the needs of their growing family. As a result, the children of these families may grow up in more severely impoverished environments, increasing the likelihood of poor outcomes. Moreover, findings from the New Jersey Family Development Program suggest that family cap policies may have unintended consequences. In addition to decreasing recipients' childbearing rates, implementation of the family cap policy was associated with higher abortion rates (New Jersey Department of Human Services, 1998).

Provisions requiring unmarried teen parents to live in an adult-supervised setting raise additional concerns. Research on children from divorced families indicates that high-conflict environments are detrimental to children's well-being (Amato, 1994). As a result, if the new policies encourage the formation of unhealthy marital relationships or force single teens to live with hostile, unsupportive parents, children may be harmed (see Depner, this volume, for a discussion of the effects of marital stress and divorce on children).

Finally, federal funding for abstinence until marriage programs has generated considerable controversy stemming from the unproven nature of the interventions falling under this rubric as well as disagreement concerning the appropriateness of the program's goals (Wilcox, 1999). Approximately $500 million in state and federal funds will be spent on these programs through this grant program alone. One concern is that abstinence education programs will supplant more effective comprehensive sexuality education and teen pregnancy prevention efforts and potentially place youth at greater risk for unintended pregnancies and sexually transmitted diseases. Partly in response to the criticism that these new programs are largely unproven, Congress allotted $6 million for a national evaluation of the abstinence until marriage education initiative.

Child Support

Many families receiving AFDC in the past were single-parent (specifically single-mother) families who were not receiving child support from the absent spouse. In a further attempt to raise these families out of poverty (and thereby off the welfare rolls), provisions were placed in PRWORA to ensure that these families were receiving child support. The goal was for noncustodial parents, rather than the government, to help pay for raising those children. Developmental and social researchers suggest that there are reasons to question not only the effectiveness of this approach but also its effects. It is generally unquestioned that the additional money received by low-income single parents from a noncustodial parent will improve child outcomes – if for no other reason than via the increase in income, which is associated with better child outcomes. However, the increased collection may also increase the amount of contact the noncustodial parent has with the children and the former spouse (Furstenberg, Morgan, & Allison, 1987); this contact may take various forms and may be beneficial or detrimental for the children. The research on the effects on children of contact with noncustodial parents comes mainly from the field of divorce research and has been relatively consistent: Positive, supportive contact is consistently associated with more positive outcomes, and negative contact (characterized by strained relationships and interactions and/or increased conflict with the custodial parent) is consistently associated with more negative outcomes (Amato, 1993, 2001; Emery, 1982; Hess & Camara, 1979; Hetherington, 1993). As payment of child support for many noncustodial parents will be involuntary, there is an additional question: What will be the effect of mandatory child support payments on the parent–child relationship and on the parent–parent relationship? Some researchers fear that mandatory payments will result in more conflict between parents, especially in the case of never-married parents, which does not predict healthy outcomes for children (McLanahan, Seltzer, Hanson, & Thompson, 1994).

Four provisions of PRWORA were specifically aimed at increasing the amount of child support received by custodial parents. First, the law requires states to strengthen and streamline the process of voluntary in-hospital paternity establishment, which would help in securing child support orders later. Second, states are required to increase their levels of child support collection through the use of "new hire" registries to catch delinquent parents who change jobs and through improved communication across state lines about child support orders. If a noncustodial parent refuses to pay, states now have the right and the responsibility to garnish wages, revoke professional licenses, and seize assets. States refusing to uphold child support orders in this manner may face additional monetary penalties. Third, states can apply for grants to develop programs that increase noncustodial parents' access to and visits with their children. Fourth, efforts to eliminate noncustodial parents' barriers to employment include a state option to use welfare-to-work funds for education and training of noncustodial parents of children receiving TANF. Although these overarching statutes are large-scale efforts focused on the parents, the specific goals of the changes in child support enforcement are intended for the children of non-paying noncustodial parents. States will be required to find more noncustodial parents, secure court orders for those parents to pay child support, and collect the money from them.

There are, unfortunately, reasons to question whether the intended outcomes will actually be achieved in the area of child support enforcement, and whether unintended effects will prove more harmful than the conditions the statutes were designed to improve (Garfinkel, McLanahan, & Robins, 1994). A U.S. General Accounting Office report (U.S. GAO, 1998) found that states have been relatively ineffective collectors of child support. If states are able to improve their identification, adjudication, and collection efforts, the provisions may work in the expected manner. A few states, in addressing this issue, have investigated the possibility of outsourcing to private collection agencies. Additionally, states have the option to raise the $50 "pass-through" and give more of the collected support to the families. Previously, only the first $50 of child support collected was given to a custodial parent receiving welfare; any additional money collected was used to reimburse the state. States may now raise the amount that is given to the custodial parent once collection has begun. Also, money collected retroactively can now be given to families first, then to state and federal pockets. The objectives of the provisions may have unintentional and unpredictable side effects as well. The issues of mandatory child support payment and possibly increased negative contact between noncustodial parents, custodial parents, and children have not been successfully resolved by researchers. Although it is clear that conflictual contact between noncustodial and custodial parents can be detrimental to children's well-being, we cannot be certain that mandatory child support payments will always lead to an increase in parent–parent conflict. The results from the increased efforts by states to collect child support, and answers to questions about long-term effects of mandatory child support and possibly increased negative contact, remain to be answered by future research.

Supplemental Security Income

The stress involved in parenting in poverty may be further exacerbated if one or more children in a family has special needs (i.e., severe mental, emotional, or behavioral impairments) or has a disability. The combined effects of living in poverty and having a disability put children and families at greater risk than if they have only one of those disadvantages. Researchers have found reliable associations between disabilities and poverty: Children with disabilities are more likely to live in poverty, and children in poverty are more likely to have disabilities (Huston, McLoyd, & Garcia-Coll, 1994; Sameroff, 1993). In the past, low-income families with a child with special needs could apply for SSI to help offset the extra costs incurred in caring for and raising that child. However, in an attempt to reduce the amount of money being given to low-income families with children whose disabilities are not severe, the PRWORA provisions substantially tightened the criteria and the qualification process for families to receive SSI; families will now have greater difficulty meeting eligibility requirements (Bazelon Center for Mental Health Law, 1996; Doolittle, 1998). As many as 15% of the children who previously qualified for SSI benefits will no longer do so under the new criteria. Additionally, as the process of applying for Medicaid has been "delinked" from the TANF application process (meaning that families must now navigate through two separate processes to apply for TANF and Medicaid), many of these children will also lose Medicaid benefits (Bazelon Center for Mental Health Law, 1996). The new welfare law discarded criteria that had taken proponents years to cement (Ohlson, 1998). Under the old provisions, children who did not immediately qualify for SSI based on stated criteria (which were mostly based on definitions of adult dysfunction) could request an IFA, by which many children were deemed eligible. This assessment has been removed as an eligibility option. Moreover, other criteria were removed from the eligibility requirements; for example, references to "maladaptive behavior" and emotional and behavioral disturbances are no longer included. The changes in this set of provisions appear to have been a reaction to a series of expansions to the definition of who should qualify for SSI that began with the 1990 *Zebley v. Sullivan* Supreme Court decision (Doolittle, 1998; *Sullivan, Secretary of Health and Human Services v. Zebley* et al., 1990). The new standards were intended to make it more difficult for individuals to qualify for SSI, a goal that appears to have been achieved (Ohlson, 1998).

Families with ineligible children, who already live in poverty, will no longer be able to receive the subsidy, causing their income to fall further below the poverty line. One fear is that families already experiencing stress due to poverty-related concerns and caring for a child with a disability will be under greater stress, possibly leading to less nurturant parenting or even, at the extreme, to incidents of harmful parenting. Additionally, these children, already at risk, are placed at higher risk for a variety of other detrimental outcomes in the domains of physical, psychosocial, educational, and emotional development (Ohlson, 1998).

Summary

Most, if not all, of the families who receive welfare will be affected by the changes in the PRWORA. The provisions regarding work requirements, time limits, and child care (as well as provisions specifically targeting single-parent families and children with disabilities) are likely to have marked effects on children's home environment, parent–child relationships, and overall well-being. The exact nature and extent of these effects, however, cannot be conclusively determined by appeals to previous social science research, as this work was conducted under previous welfare statutes and/or on voluntary welfare-to-work programs. Fortunately, the government and independent organizations have already begun to study the effects of the new welfare law. In the following section, some of the major efforts thus far are outlined.

NEW RESEARCH ON THE IMPACT OF THE PRWORA

The research reviewed in the previous section provides valuable cues to the potential impact of welfare reform on children. However, the best answers to the questions raised by the passage of PRWORA will eventually come from the numerous welfare reform studies currently underway at both the federal and local levels. Although the majority of these studies focus on implementation issues and adult outcomes, growing recognition of and concern for the well-being of children from welfare-receiving families have prompted both government and private sector agencies and foundations to include child outcomes in their monitoring and evaluation activities. Some of the studies focus directly on the children themselves; others concentrate on changes in the financial, social, and educational contexts in which children develop. Some of the studies are surveys; others are based on direct observation and measurement of child and family outcomes. Taken together, these differing methodologies promise to provide both researchers and policy makers with a more comprehensive understanding of children's poverty experiences over time and under different program conditions. In short, how we think and talk about welfare reform and its impacts on child development will most likely be reshaped and redefined by this new generation of welfare research. With this in mind, this section offers a brief description of the major projects currently being conducted and highlights their potential contributions to our understanding of the effects of welfare reform on children. Information on these projects can also be found in the 1998 *Greenbook* (Committee on Ways and Means, 1998) and in a recent policy review by Zaslow, Tout, et al. (1998). A list of relevant websites appears in Table 2.2.

Survey of Program Dynamics

As part of the welfare reform provisions, PRWORA authorizes the annual allocation of $10 million, between fiscal years 1996 and 2002, to the U.S. Census Bureau for the purposes of collecting longitudinal data on a nationally representative sample of families. Known as the Survey of Program Dynamics (SPD), the survey includes measures of household characteristics, family income, family processes,

TABLE 2.2. *Ongoing Welfare Reform Research Projects*

Project	Sponsoring Organization	Related Internet Address
Survey of Program Dynamics	U.S. Census Bureau	http://www.sipp.census.gov/spd/spdmain.htm
Welfare Reform and Children: a Three City Study	Principal Investigators: Ronald Angel, University of Texas Linda Burton, Pennsylvania State University P. Lindsay Chase-Lansdale, Northwestern University Andrew Cherlin, Johns Hopkins University Robert Moffitt, Johns Hopkins University William Julius Wilson, Harvard University	http://www.jhu.edu/~welfare/
National Survey of America's Families	Urban Institute Child Trends	http://newfederalism.urban.org/nsaf/
National Study of Low Income Child Care; Child Welfare Longitudinal Study; Project on State Level Outcomes	U.S. Department of Health and Human Services, Administration on Children and Families	http://www.acf.dhhs.gov/programs/pcmr/rd&e.htm
Child Care Under Welfare Reform	General Accounting Office	http://www.gao.gov/
Early Head Start Research and Evaluation Project	Mathematica Policy Research and Center for Young Children and Families at Columbia University	http://www.tc.columbia.edu/academic/cycf/earlyhead.htm

and child well-being. Participating households are interviewed annually from 1997 to 2002 using a set of survey instruments specifically designed to monitor the causes and consequences of families' participation in welfare-related programs. Thus SPD data should prove useful in examining the impact of welfare policy changes on low-income families over time.

National Survey of America's Families

Valuable population-based information on children's well-being is also being collected by private agencies. Conducted by the Urban Institute in Washington, DC, as part of its Assessing the New Federalism project, the National Survey of America's Families (NSAF) is designed to provide both national- and state-level data on children and families. Approximately half of the survey's 50,000 households have incomes 200% below the poverty line. In 1997 and 1999, respondents were asked to answer questions about family structure, income, child support, child care, maternal employment, maternal psychological well-being, and parental involvement in children's schooling. Other measures specific to children include health status, behavior problems, and involvement in positive activities. The data should allow researchers to monitor the number of children moving into and out of poverty and may help to illuminate how factors like maternal employment and mental health moderate the impact of welfare reform on children's well-being.

Welfare Reform and Children: A Three-City Study

On a more local level, a team of researchers from Chicago, Harvard, Johns Hopkins, and Pennsylvania State are exploring the impact of welfare reform on children and youth growing up in three urban areas (Boston, Chicago, and San Antonio). Survey questions include information on children's physical health, disabilities, cognitive and emotional development, school achievement, and childbearing. In-person interviews, diaries, and observation are also being used to assess neighborhood resources and service delivery. Participating families will be followed over time and include both TANF and working-poor households. Goals of the study include exploring the developmental outcomes associated with growing up in a welfare-receiving household, assessing the impact of income in general on child well-being, and exploring the extent to which local welfare service delivery practices influence child outcomes.

National Study of Low Income Child Care

Funded by the Department of Health and Human Services and carried out by Abt Associates of Cambridge, Massachusetts, and the National Center for Children in Poverty at Columbia University, the National Study of Low Income Child Care is a 5-year project designed to study how welfare policy changes affect the child-care market for families receiving welfare in 25 communities. Issues of interest include the impact of subsidies on the type, amount, and quality of available child care, state policies, practices and regulations, and family decision making. In a subsample of five communities, parent interviews, surveys, and child-care observations will also be used to explore children's care experiences. Given that the success of the latest welfare reform movement is largely dependent on the ability of families to find appropriate child care for their children and the fact that children's well-being will undoubtedly be influenced by the quality of care that they receive, studies like this one should prove invaluable to our understanding of the viability of welfare reform and its effects on children.

Child Care Under Welfare Reform

The General Accounting Office (GAO) will also be producing a report on states' child-care practices following welfare reform. Drawing on data gathered from site visits, administrative records, and telephone interviews, states' efforts to increase the supply of child-care options and resource allocation practices will be monitored. The information gathered should augment our understanding of how states are responding to the new demands placed on them by changes in the welfare law.

Child Welfare Longitudinal Study

PRWORA also requires the Department of Health and Human Services to gather information relevant to concerns regarding the impact of welfare reform policies on the family's involvement with the child welfare system. Conducted by the Research Triangle Institute in North Carolina, the Child Welfare Longitudinal Study should permit researchers to explore the relationships between TANF changes and family experiences with child protective services. Scheduled to begin data collection in the spring of 1999, the 6-year study will select and follow a nationally representative sample of 6,000 children on entry into the child welfare system. Issues to be addressed by the study include family, child, and service-based characteristics that contribute to case outcomes.

Project on State-Level Child Outcomes

As a supplement to adult-focused welfare reform demonstration evaluations currently being conducted in five states (Connecticut, Iowa, Minnesota, Indiana, and Florida), the federal Department of Health and Human Services has agreed to fund child outcome studies in each of these states. The projects focus on children between the ages of 5 and 12 years and include measures of child health, school achievement, behavioral problems, child-care arrangements, and quality of the home environment. The data gathered should provide both researchers and policy makers with a more in-depth understanding of how different welfare program practices influence child outcomes.

Early Head Start Research and Evaluation Project

In order to learn how early intervention programs mediate the effects of welfare reform on children and families, researchers at Mathematica Policy Research and the Center for Young Children and Families at Columbia University are conducting a longitudinal study of approximately 3,000 low-income families who are participating in the Early Head Start Program. Families are recruited into the Early Head Start Program before the birth of the child, and services continue throughout the first 3 years of the child's life; thus, researchers hope to uncover the role that early intervention services may play in buffering children and families from the effects of living in poverty.

CONCLUSION

Over the next several years, a number of the studies just described will begin to provide a clearer picture of the meaning of welfare reform for children growing up in poor families. PRWORA did indeed change the U.S welfare system more fundamentally than any previous reform effort, and in doing so made it exceedingly difficult to predict its impact on those who received welfare benefits in the past. Earlier research on a variety of welfare-to-work demonstration projects took place in a vastly different policy context, as did more general research on maternal employment. Most of this research relied on data from women who chose to work or who voluntarily participated in programs intended to prepare them for employment and support them once employed. The post-PRWORA studies will include women – and the children of women – who may not have entered employment voluntarily, or who may have failed to secure or maintain employment and thus lost access to benefits.

Welfare reform will inevitably return to the top of the policy agenda in the near future. Both critics and supporters of the 1996 reform recognize that it represents an experiment that must be evaluated. The studies we have described here, along with others like them, promise to provide policy makers with a sounder empirical basis on which to make future policy decisions. However, this is not meant to imply that policies are likely to be based solely – or even primarily – on social science findings. Political ideology, public values, and vested interests will always play a significant role in decision making in any arena as significant and contentious as welfare policy (Aaron, Mann, & Taylor, 1994; Steiner, 1981). Nevertheless, psycholegal scholarship can play an important role in shaping policy debates and the actions of policy actors. Studies of the effects of variations in specific elements of welfare policies (e.g., child-care subsidies, family caps), as well as research on the consequences of growing up in poor or near-poor families, can alter the tone of the public's discourse on welfare. Bringing this research to the attention of policy makers and the public, however, will require psycholegal scholars to engage in a more active dissemination strategy than is typical, as these audiences are notoriously poor journal readers. Successful dissemination requires direct interaction with both the press and the policy-making community – and few of us have received either training or encouragement to undertake these types of activities. The studies we have described that are currently underway are likely to provide us with a better understanding of the impact of existing welfare policy and practice on child well-being. If these findings are aggressively brought to the attention of both policy makers and the public, our effectiveness in shaping welfare policy is likely to be greater when we revisit these issues than was the case prior to the 1996 reforms.

References

Aaron, H. J., Mann, T. E., & Taylor, T. (Eds.). (1994). *Values and public policy.* Washington, DC: Brookings Institution.

Amato, P. R. (1993). Children's adjustment to divorce: Theories, hypotheses, and empirical support. *Journal of Marriage and the Family, 55,* 23–38.

Amato, P. R. (1994). Life-span adjustment of children to their parent's divorce. *The Future of Children, 4*(1), 143–157.

Amato, P. R. (2001). The consequences of divorce for adults and children. In R. M. Milardo (Ed.), *Understanding families into the new millennium: A decade in review* (pp. 488–506). Minneapolis: National Council on Family Relations.

Bane, M. J., & Ellwood, D. T. (1994). *Welfare realities: From reform to rhetoric.* Cambridge, MA: Harvard University Press.

Baydar, N., & Brooks-Gunn, J. (1991). Effects of maternal employment and child-care arrangements on preschoolers' cognitive and behavioral outcomes: Evidence from the children of the National Longitudinal Survey of Youth. *Developmental Psychology, 27,* 932–945.

Bazelon Center for Mental Health Law. (1996, December). *A dubious bargain: What states' implementation of the new welfare law will mean for children with mental or emotional disorders and their families.* Issue Paper Series. Washington, DC: Author.

Belsky, J., & Rovine, M. J. (1988). Nonmaternal care in the first year of life and the security of infant–parent attachment. *Child Development, 59,* 157–167.

Blank, R. M. (1997). *It takes a nation: A new agenda for fighting poverty.* Princeton, NJ: Princeton University Press.

Blank, S. W., & Blum, B. (1997). A brief history of work expectations for welfare mothers. *Future of Children, 7*(1), 28–39.

Brooks-Gunn, J., Smith, J., Berlin, L., & Lee, K. (1998, May). *Implementations of welfare changes for parents of young children.* Paper presented at the Family Process and Child Development in Low Income Families Conference, Evanston, Illinois.

Burtless, G. T. (1997). Welfare recipients' job skills and employment prospects. *The Future of Children, 7*(1), 39–51.

Cancian, M., Haveman, R., Kaplan, T., Meyer, D., & Wolfe, B. (1998, November). *Work, earnings, and well-being after welfare: What do we know?* Paper presented at the Welfare Reform and the Macro-Economy Conference, Washington, DC.

Caughy, M. O., DiPietro, J. A., & Strobino, D. M. (1994). Day-care participation as a protective factor in the cognitive development of low-income children. *Child Development, 65,* 457–471.

Chase-Lansdale, P. L., & Vinovskis, M. A. (1995). Who's responsibility? An historical analysis of the changing roles of mothers, fathers, and society. In P. L. Chase-Lansdale & J. Brooks-Gunn (Eds.), *Escape from poverty: What makes a difference for children?* (pp. 11–37). Cambridge: Cambridge University Press.

Committee on Ways and Means, U.S. House of Representatives. (1996, November 4). *1996 green book: Background material and data on programs within the jurisdiction of the Committee on Ways and Means (WMCP 104–14).* Washington, DC: U.S. Government Printing Office.

Committee on Ways and Means, U.S. House of Representatives. (1998, May 19). *1998 green book: Background material and data on programs within the jurisdiction of the Committee on Ways and Means (WMCP 105–17).* Washington, DC: U.S. Government Printing Office.

Conger, R. D., Conger, K. J., Elder, G. H., Lorenz, F. O., Simons, R. L., & Whitbeck, L. B. (1992). A family process model of economic hardship and adjustment of early adolescent boys. *Child Development, 63,* 526–541.

Conger, R. D., Ge, X., Elder, G. H., Lorenz, F. O., & Simons, R. L. (1994). Economic stress, coercive family process and developmental problems of adolescents. *Child Development, 65,* 541–561.

Doolittle, D. K. (1998). Welfare reform: Loss of Supplemental Security Income (SSI) for children with disabilities. *Journal of the Society of Pediatric Nurses, 3,* 33–44.

Duncan, G. J. (1991). The economic environment of childhood. In A. C. Huston (Ed.), *Children in poverty* (pp. 23–50). New York: Cambridge University Press.

Duncan, G. J., & Brooks-Gunn, J. (1997). *Consequences of growing up poor.* New York: Russell Sage Foundation.

Duncan, G. J., & Caspary, G. (1997). Welfare dynamics and the 1996 welfare reform. *Notre Dame Journal of Law, Ethics and Public Policy, 11,* 605–632.

Elder, G. H., Conger, R. D., Foster, E. M., & Ardelt, M. (1992). Families under economic pressure. *Journal of Family Issues, 13*(1), 5–37.

Ellwood, D. (1986). *Targeting strategies for welfare recipients.* Princeton, NJ: Mathmatica Policy Research Inc.

Emery, R. E. (1982). Interparental conflict and the children of discord and divorce. *Psychological Bulletin, 92,* 310–330.

Ferber, M. A., O'Farrell, B., & Allen, L. R. (1991). *Work and family: Policies for a changing workforce.* Washington, DC: National Academy Press.

Furstenberg, F. F., Morgan, S. P., & Allison, P. D. (1987). Paternal participation and children's well-being. *American Sociological Review, 52,* 695–701.

Garfinkel, I., McLanahan, S. S., & Robins, P. K. (1994). Child support and child well-being: What have we learned? In I. Garfinkel, S. S. McLanahan, & P. K. Robins (Eds.), *Child support and child well-being* (pp. 239–256). Washington, DC: Urban Institute.

Goerge, R. M., & Lee, B. J. (1997). Abuse and neglect of the children. In R.A. Maynard (Ed.), *Kids having kids: Economic costs and social consequences of teen pregnancy* (pp. 205–230). Washington, DC: Urban Institute Press.

Gottschalk, P., McLanahan, S., & Sandefur, G. D. (1994). The dynamics and intergenerational transfer of poverty and welfare participation. In S. H. Danziger, G. D. Sandefur, & D. H. Weinberg (Eds.), *Confronting poverty: Prescriptions for change* (pp. 85–108). Cambridge, MA: Harvard University Press.

Granger, R. C., & Cytron, R. (1998). *A synthesis of the long-term effects of the New Chance Demonstration, Ohio's Learning, Earning and Parenting (LEAP) Program, and the Teenage Parent Demonstration (TPD).* New York: Manpower Demonstration Research Corporation.

Grogger, J. (1997). Incarceration-related costs of early childbearing. In R. A. Maynard (Ed.), *Kids having kids: Economic costs and social consequences of teen pregnancy* (pp. 231–256). Washington, DC: Urban Institute Press.

Handler, J. F. (1995). *The poverty of welfare reform.* New Haven, CT: Yale University Press.

Haveman, R. H., Wolfe, B., & Peterson, E. (1997). Children of early child-bearers as young adults. In R. A. Maynard (Ed.), *Kids having kids: Economic costs and social consequences of teen pregnancy* (pp. 257–284). Washington, DC: Urban Institute Press.

Hayes, C. D., Palmer, J. L, & Zaslow, M. J. (Eds.). (1990). *Who cares for America's children? Child care policy for the 1990s.* Washington, DC: National Academy Press.

Hess, R. D., & Camara, K. A. (1979). Post-divorce family relationships as mediating factors in the consequences of divorce for children. *Journal of Social Issues, 35,* 79–97.

Hetherington, E. M. (1993). An overview of the Virginia Longitudinal Study of Divorce and Remarriage with a focus on early adolescence. *Journal of Family Psychology, 7,* 39–56.

Hofferth, S., & Collins, N. (1996, May). *Child care and employment turnover*. Paper presented at the Annual Meeting of the Population Association of America, New Orleans.

Huston, A. C. (1991). *Children in poverty*. New York: Cambridge University Press.

Kisker, E. E., Rangarajan, A., & Boller, K. (1998). *Moving into adulthood: Were the impacts of mandatory programs for welfare-dependent teenage parents sustained after the program ended?* Washington, DC: U.S. Department of Health and Human Services, Office of Assistant Secretary for Planning and Evaluation.

Knitzer, J., & Bernard, S. (1997). The new welfare law and vulnerable families: Implications for child welfare and child protection systems. *Children and Welfare Reform Issue Brief 3*. New York: National Center for Children in Poverty.

Kruttschnitt, C., McLeod, J. D., & Dornfeld, M. (1994). The economic environment of child abuse. *Social Problems, 41*(2), 299–315.

Leuchtenberg, W. E. (1963). *Franklin D. Roosevelt and the New Deal*. New York: Harper & Row.

Lewit, E. M., Terman, D. L., & Behrman, R. E. (1997). Children and poverty: Analysis and recommendations. *The Future of Children, 7*(2), 4–21.

Maynard, R. A. (Ed.). (1997). *Kids having kids: Economic costs and social consequences of teen pregnancy*. Washington, DC: Urban Institute Press.

McLanahan, S. S. (1995). The consequences of nonmarital childbearing for women, children and society. In *Report to Congress on out-of-wedlock childbearing* (DHHS Pub. No. PHS 95-1257) (pp. 229–239). Washington, DC: Government Printing Office.

McLanahan, S. S., Seltzer, J. A., Hanson, T. L., & Thomson, E. (1994). Child support enforcement and child well-being: Greater security or greater conflict? In I. Garfinkel, S. S. McLanahan, & P. K. Robins (Eds.), *Child support and child well-being* (pp. 239–256). Washington, DC: Urban Institute.

McLoyd, V. (1989). Socialization and development in a changing economy: The effects of paternal job loss and income loss on children. *American Psychologist, 44*(2), 293–302.

McLoyd, V., Jayaratne, T. E., Ceballo, R., & Borquez, J. (1994). Unemployment and work interruption among African American single mothers: Effects on parenting and adolescent socioemotional functioning. *Child Development, 65*, 562–589.

Meyers, M. (1993). Child care in JOBS employment and training program: What difference does quality make? *Journal of Marriage and the Family, 55*, 767–783.

Moffitt, R. (1992) Incentive effects in the U.S. welfare system: A review. *Journal of Economic Literature, 30*, 1–61.

Moore, K. A., & Driscoll, A. K. (1997). Low-wage maternal employment and outcomes for children: A study. *The Future of Children, 7*(1), 122–127.

Moore, K. A., Morrison, D. R., & Greene, A. D. (1997). Effects on children born to adolescent mothers. In R. A. Maynard (Ed.), *Kids having kids: Economic costs and social consequences of teen pregnancy* (pp. 145–180). Washington, DC: Urban Institute Press.

Moynihan, D. P. (1986). *Family and nation.* New York: Harcourt, Brace, Jovanovich.

Murray, C. (1984). *Losing ground: American social policy 1950–1980.* New York: Basic Books.

New Jersey Department of Human Services. (1998). *A final report on the impact of New Jersey's Family Development Program: Results from a pre-post analysis of AFDC case loads from 1990–1996.* [On-line] available at: http://www.state.nj.us/humanservices/rutfdp.html

Ohlson, C. (1998). Welfare reform: Implications for young children with disabilities, their families, and service providers. *Journal of Early Intervention, 21,* 191–206.

Parcel, T. L., & Menaghan, E. G. (1997). Effects of low-wage employment on family well-being. *The Future of Children, 7*(1), 116–121.

Pavetti, L. A. (1995). How long do families stay on AFDC? Who spends longer periods of time receiving welfare? Why do people who leave welfare for jobs return to the rolls? In R. K. Weaver & W. T. Dickens (Eds.), *Looking before we leap: Social science and welfare reform* (pp. 127–162). Washington, DC: Brookings Institution.

Presidential veto message. (1996, January 13). *Congressional Quarterly, 54,* 103.

Sameroff, A. (1993). Stability of intelligence from preschool to adolescence: The influence of social and familial risk factors. *Child Development, 64,* 80–97.

Scarr, S. (1998). American child care today. *American Psychologist, 53,* 95–108.

Shook, K. (1998). *Assessing the consequences of welfare reform for child welfare.* [On-line]. Available at: http://www.jcpr.org/winter98/article2.html

Steiner, G. Y. (1981). *The futility of family policy.* Washington, DC: Brookings Institution.

Strauss, M. A., Gelles, R. A., & Steinmetz, S. (1980). *Behind closed doors: Violence in the American family.* New York: Doubleday.

Sullivan, Secretary of Health and Human Services v. Zebley et al. (1990, Feb. 20). 110 S. CT. 885.

U.S. Census Bureau (2000). *Poverty 1998.* [Online]. Available at: http://www.census.gov/hhes/poverty/poverty98/pv98est1.html

U.S. Department of Health and Human Services, National Center on Child Abuse and Neglect. (1996). *Third national incidence study of child abuse and neglect: Final report (NIS-3).* Washington, DC: Government Printing Office.

U.S. Department of Health and Human Services, Office of the Assistant Secretary for Planning and Evaluation (1999). *Comparison of the prior law and the Work Reconciliation Act of 1996 (P.L. 104–193).* [Online]. Available at: http//aspe.os.dlhs.gov/hsp/isp/reform.htm

U.S. General Accounting Office. (1994a, May). *Families on welfare: Sharp rise in never-married women reflects societal trend* (GAO/HEHS-94-92). Washington, DC: Author.

U.S. General Accounting Office. (1994b, May). *Families on welfare: Teenage mothers least likely to become self-sufficient* (GAO/HEHS-94-115). Washington, DC: Author.

U.S. General Accounting Office. (1998, August). *Child support: An uncertain income supplement for families receiving welfare* (GAO/HEHS 98–168). Washington, DC: Author.

Wilcox, B. L. (1999). Sexual obsessions: Public policy and adolescent girls. In N. G. Johnson, M. C. Roberts, & J. Worell (Eds.), *Beyond appearance: A new look at adolescent girls* (pp. 333–354). Washington, DC: American Psychological Association.

Wilcox, B. L., Robbennolt, J. K., O'Keeffe, J. E., & Reddy, M. E. (1996). Teen nonmarital childbearing and welfare: The gap between research and political discourse. *Journal of Social Issues, 52*(3), 71–90.

Wilson, J. B., Ellwood, D. T., & Brooks-Gunn, J. (1995). Welfare to work through the eyes of children. In P. L. Chase-Lansdale & J. Brooks-Gunn (Eds.), *Escape from poverty: What makes a difference for children* (pp. 63–86). New York: Cambridge University Press.

Wolfe, B., & Perozek, M. (1997). Teen children's health and health care use. In R. A. Maynard (Ed.), *Kids having kids: Economic costs and social consequences of teen pregnancy* (pp. 181–204). Washington, DC: Urban Institute Press.

Wolfner, G. D., & Gelles, R. J. (1993). A profile of violence toward children: A national study. *Child Abuse and Neglect, 17*, 197–212.

Zaslow, M. J., & Eldred, C. A. (1998). *Parenting behavior in a sample of young mothers in poverty: Results of the New Chance observational study*. New York: Manpower Demonstration Research Corporation.

Zaslow, M. J., & Emig, C. A. (1997). When low-income mothers go to work: Implications for children. *The Future of Children, 7*(1), 110–115.

Zaslow, M. J., Oldham, E., Moore, K. A., & Magenheim, E. (1998). Welfare families' use of early childhood care and education programs, and implications for their children's development. *Early Childhood Research Quarterly, 13*, 535–563.

Zaslow, M., Tout, K., Smith, S., & Moore, K. A. (1998). Implications of the 1996 welfare legislation for children: A research perspective. *Social Policy Report of the Society for Research in Child Development, 12*(3), 1–35.

3

Advocacy for Children's Rights

Mark A. Small
Susan P. Limber

Advocacy on behalf of children is more than simply the provision of needed services to children. Advocacy efforts represent an attempt to increase the responsiveness and accountability of all institutions affecting children. As Melton (1983) notes, "whether the intent is to increase children's self-determination or to enhance the social, education, and medical resources to which children are entitled, child advocates have as their mission social action on behalf of children" (p. 1).

Although social scientists often conduct and report research related to child well-being, these efforts frequently fail to take into account larger social trends affecting children and families. Moreover, they often fall short of informing advocacy efforts – either in helping to set an agenda for advocacy or in evaluating advocacy efforts. The intent of this chapter is to provide an overview of child advocacy issues for social scientists in order to facilitate a greater connection between social scientists and child advocates. We begin by noting some significant social trends influencing the nature of child advocacy. These include the changing nature of the American family, the changing nature of social institutions, and the shift in responsibility for children's welfare from the federal government to state and community organizations. Next, a brief history of advocacy is presented, noting philosophical differences between those

Institute on Family and Neighborhood Life, Clemson University who push for increasing self-determination of children and those who primarily advocate for improved health and safety conditions for children. Finally, we describe two overarching frameworks that could guide the work of advocates and social scientists – the United Nations Convention on the Rights of the Child (United Nations General Assembly, 1989) and a landmark report from the United States Advisory Board on Child Abuse and Neglect (1991). Both provide comprehensive blueprints for research and advocacy. Within these contexts, social scientists may create useful knowledge, disseminate such knowledge to relevant decision makers, and individually advocate within their professional capacity.

TRENDS

The Changing Nature of the American Family

Over the past 20 years, no social trend has had greater influence on the welfare of children than the changing nature of the American family. According to U.S. Census data, from 1970 to 1990, the percentage of married-couple households with children declined from 40% to 26% of all households but since then has held steady at 25% in 1997 (Bryson & Casper, 1998). In 1970, 89% of families with children had both parents living in the household, 10% of children lived only with their mothers, and 1% lived only with their fathers. In 1997, the percentage of mother-only and father-only families had risen to 23% and 5%, respectively (Bryson & Casper, 1998).

The absence of an additional parent in the household is largely the result of the decision not to marry. As noted, the largest percentage of single-parent families consists of mother-only families. In 1997, 58% of Black female householders who had children under 18 and no spouse present had never been married compared to 42% of Hispanics and 25% of Whites (Bryson & Casper, 1998). The numbers are even higher for single mothers with children under the age of 6 who had never married: Blacks 85%, Hispanics 73%, and Whites, 56% (Bryson & Casper, 1998).

The trend away from marriage before childbearing is perhaps best reflected in the premarital birth statistics. Between 1930 and 1934, only one in six (16.6%) first children born to women

15 to 29 years old was conceived or born premaritally; the number increased to one in every two (50%) between 1990 and 1994 (Bachu, 1999). For women 15 to 19 years old, 85% of first-born children during the early 1990s were either conceived or born premaritally (Bachu, 1999). Because marriage is rarely exercised as an option by pregnant teenagers, children born to teenagers are at special risk; not only are they likely to have fewer advocates available, but also teenage parents are less likely than older parents to be educated about possible advocacy choices to meet their child's needs.

Not only are families experiencing shrinking adult human resources, but the material support for families also has not improved in recent years. The changing demographics of the American family and the consequences for children have prompted a number of public and private organizations to keep a tally of indicators of child well-being. At the most basic sustenance level, the plight of the poorest, most vulnerable population has not improved. Despite the economic boom of the 1990s, the percentage of children who remain in poverty has remained relatively constant, hovering around 20% (Children's Defense Fund, 1997; Dalaker, 1999). The current Census Bureau data indicate the number of poor children to be 13.5 *million* (Dalaker, 1999). The number of children uninsured for health care coverage is estimated at 11.1 million, or 15.4% of all children (Campbell, 1999).

The most significant private organization to document child well-being is the Annie E. Casey Foundation, which annually publishes the *KIDS COUNT Data Book*, a state-by-state report of 10 indicators of child well-being. The indicators include rates of low-birth-rate babies; infant mortality; child death; teen death by accident, homicide, and suicide; teen births; juvenile violent crime arrests; high school dropouts; teens not attending school and not working; children living in poverty; and single-parent families. As the most recent *KIDS COUNT Data Book* (Annie E. Casey Foundation, 2000) notes, although the 1990s were a decade of unparalleled prosperity in the United States, approximately 9.2 million children could be viewed as "particularly vulnerable" because their families had significant risk factors, such as a lack of education and work experience, single parenthood, and welfare dependency. Viewing indicators across states and across domains localizes the challenges facing children and the corresponding need for advocacy for children. Although there is genuine need for attention to the needs of children from all economic brackets, some classes of children are especially vulnerable – minorities, immigrants, and children with physical disabilities, mental illness, or mental retardation.

The Changing Nature of Social Institutions

A second major trend affecting the nature of child advocacy is the changing nature of social institutions responsible for children. Juvenile courts, schools, and welfare agencies are all undergoing substantial changes. State by state, the juvenile justice system is slowly changing from a court system premised on rehabilitation to one focused on accountability and punishment (see, e.g., Juvenile Accountability Incentive Block Grant Act of 1999). (For discussions of the Juvenile Accountability Incentive Block Grant Act, see the chapters in this volume by Salekin, by Fried & Reppucci, and by Woolard.). Transformation is also taking place in educational settings as schools are pressured to provide more secure environments for children, meet the counseling and mental health needs of troubled children, and reduce truancy – all without significant increases in resources or reduction in the emphasis on the traditional educational mission. Finally, although the effects of the Personal Responsibility and Work Opportunity Reconciliation Act of 1996 (PRWORA) are still being studied, one early conclusion emphasizes an increased need for child care, as newly working parents struggle to find alternative custodial arrangements (U.S. General Accounting Office, 1998). (See Wilcox, Colman, & Wyatt, this volume, for additional discussion of the PRWORA.)

The changing nature of social institutions requires new advocacy approaches. As traditional missions of social institutions are reconsidered old advocacy strategies may no longer be applicable. Whereas previously attorneys representing juveniles accused of committing crimes might advocate for appropriate mental health services and intense supervision in lieu of imprisonment, new statutes automatically transfer some juveniles to adult court, often removing the possibility of any diversionary treatment. In schools, zero tolerance policies result in compulsory suspension and expulsion, negating any efforts to negotiate on a case-by-case basis. Examples of how advocacy strategies need to change also relate to accessing children or their parents. One unintended consequence of welfare reform legislation for parents who are removed from welfare rolls is that they lose contact with the state, and as a result are unaware that their children may still be eligible for Medicaid benefits. As these examples illustrate, to best influence the direction of changes taking place in social institutions, advocacy strategies should be targeted at legislative and policy levels.

Devolution

A third social trend influencing the nature of advocacy is devolution. Broadly construed, *devolution* refers to the shifting of responsibility for governance from the federal government to state and local governments. Practically, this means turning over to states the responsibility for legislating and administering a variety of social programs, including those aimed at providing a social safety net for the most vulnerable citizens. The most dramatic example of devolution applied to child and family policy is the elimination of the Aid to Families with Dependent Children program and its replacement with the Temporary Assistance to Needy Families bloc grant established in PRWOA. With the intent to "end welfare as we know it," the PRWOA gave states a great deal of latitude to modify welfare programs.

Child advocates became alarmed that with such wide discretion there would be a "race to the bottom" among states as each state attempted to establish programs with lower benefits than neighboring states. This administrative tactic was thought to discourage nonresidents from moving into a particular state for the express purpose of collecting greater benefits, and to encourage residents to move to other states offering greater benefits. Interestingly, the federal legislation makes available federal funding that would allow states to externalize welfare funding, but thus far there is little discussion in the literature regarding a "race to the top" (Brinig & Buckley, 1997).

Because of the recency of the legislation, it is still unclear how these changes ultimately will affect families and children, but there are clear implications for the nature of advocacy efforts undertaken on behalf of children and families. Devolution shifts the venue of advocacy from the federal government to all 50 state governments. Whereas previous legislative efforts on behalf of children could be concentrated at the federal level, with benefits accruing to all children regardless of their residential location, new legislative efforts must take place in each state legislature, with benefits dependent upon state residence. Regardless of one's stance on the proper balance of federal and state sovereignty, the efficiency of child advocacy is reduced by the necessity of advocating for change in 50 locations rather than 1. An additional consequence of devolution is the increased importance of geographic space for a child's well-being. Because devolution allows potentially meaningful disparities in state policies regarding child welfare, where a child is born and where her or she resides take on greater importance.

HISTORY OF CHILD ADVOCACY

Although these trends represent current forces affecting child advocacy, it is useful to view these developments within the longer history of childhood and advocacy efforts on behalf of children in the United States. Phillip Ariès, in his comprehensive work *Centuries of Childhood* (1962), notes that in previous epochs, children were alternately seen as miniature adults, souls to be saved, private property of fathers, or natural resources to be exploited. Although parental concern with child raising has always existed, societal concern with the experience of childhood and, consequently, advocacy efforts on behalf of children are relatively new phenomena that originated in the child-saving era of the late 19th and early 20th centuries (1880–1914) (Takanishi, 1978). Only recently, and largely in modern western culture, have children been viewed as a distinct class worthy of special consideration.

Images of children still greatly influence advocacy efforts. Children are often viewed either as vulnerable individuals in need of protection or as young adults who ought to be given autonomy to make decisions. These two contrasting views of children influence the nature and direction of much advocacy. Sometimes characterized as *kiddie libbers* and *child savers* (Mnookin, 1978), these two groups differ fundamentally in their conceptualization of child-hood and how they would balance child, family, and state inter-ests. Additionally, at least three different perspectives regarding the proper balance between state and family interests exist within the child savers' group alone (Melton, 1987). The common thread among the child-saver perspectives is the desire for legislation to protect children, though there are different ideas about when inter-vention should occur (Small & Schwartz, 1990).

In contrast to the child savers, who focus on establishing the proper relationship between state and family interests, the kiddie libbers focus on fostering children's autonomy and self-determination. This group conceptualizes children as "more like than unalike adults and favors public policies designed to protect the autonomy and privacy of children and youth" (Melton, 1987, p. 347). Although there has been some legal and judicial success in recognizing the autonomy of children and adolescents, both legislation and judicial decisions are rife with conflicting views of the nature of childhood and the ideal relationships of children, families, and the state (see, e.g., *Fare v. Michael C.*, 1979; *Parham v. J. R.*, 1979). (See Schmidt & Reppucci, this volume, for a discussion of *Parham v. J.R.*).

The lack of consensus on the proper political and legal status of children and youth in the United States is reflected in positions taken by various child advocacy groups. Child advocacy groups may actually be opposed to one another on particular issues (e.g., notification and consent laws regarding abortion). For example, premised on the notion that adolescents are legally competent de-cision makers, child advocates favoring children's autonomy have argued that the best interests of juveniles are served by allowing them to obtain abortions without parental notification or consent. In contrast, other advocates believe that the juvenile ultimately will benefit from parental involvement in whatever decision is made.

Legislative Advocacy

Images of children as vulnerable persons in need of protection dominated legislation on behalf of children in the first half of the 20th century. Child advocates focused largely on raising the consciousness of the American public regarding the dismal plight of many children and the need for protective legislation. Creating secure, healthy environments for children became a priority. As concern for the proper development of children grew, advocates began to argue that what previously had been seen as children's needs should become entitlements and rights of children. Extending adults' rights to children and securing special rights based on unique needs of children became a priority. Moreover, transmuting needs into rights shifted the responsibility from the individual caretaker to the larger society and provided an opportunistic target for advocacy – in many cases, the legislative branch of government.

Thus, legislative advocacy efforts were undertaken to reduce child mortality, improve or eliminate working conditions for children, and mandate compulsory education. Although not meant to be exhaustive, Table 3.1 lists a number of significant advocacy milestones in the history of child protection legislation, as well as important events and influential publications.

The legislative success of child and family advocates is reflected in the broad range of federal legislation that provides services to children and their families. For example, according to a recent report from the U.S. General Accounting Office (GAO) (1996), there are at least 131 federal programs administered by 16 different federal agencies that serve at-risk or delinquent youth. The majority are administered by the federal Health and Human Services Department (58) and the Justice Department (22). Total appropriations for youth in fiscal year 1995 exceeded $4 billion.

The services and target groups identified in the GAO report reveal a wide range of at-risk subpopulations of youth and a wide variety of services. They also illustrate a variety of images of young people and the prevailing view of how they may be helped. Specifically targeted subpopulations include youth who are economically disadvantaged; abused or neglected; drug or alcohol abusers; missing, exploited, or abducted; runaways or homeless; school dropouts; victims of crime; minorities; juvenile offenders; delinquents; or children considered at risk or high risk. The services focused on in the report include self-sufficiency skills, crime/violence intervention, gang intervention, mentoring, tutoring, conflict resolution, counseling, substance abuse intervention, job training

TABLE 3.1. *Selected Milestones Affecting Child Advocacy Efforts in U.S. History*

1899	First Juvenile Court Established, Chicago, Illinois
1904	Founding of the National Child Labor Committee
1909	First White House Conference on the Care of Dependent Children
1912	Establishment of the Children's Bureau
1919	White House Conference on Child Welfare Standards
1920	Founding of the Child Welfare League of America
1924	Founding of the American Orthopsychiatric Association
1930	White House Conference on Child Health and Protection
1934	Founding of the Society for Research in Child Development
1938	Fair Labor Standards Act (first enforceable laws protecting children from work)
1940	White House Conference on Children in a Democracy
1950	Midcentury White House Conference on Children and Youth
1960	Golden Anniversary White House Conference on Children and Youth
1961	President's Panel on Mental Retardation
1963	Establishment of the National Institute on Child Health and Human Development
1965	Initiation of Project Head Start
1970	White House Conference on Children and Youth
1970	Report issued by Joint Commission on Mental Health of Children
1974	Passage of the Child Abuse Prevention and Treatment Act
1980	Passage of the Adoption Assistance and Child Welfare Act
1984	Passage of the Missing Children's Assistance Act
1986	Passage of the Children's Justice Act
1988	Establishment of the U.S. Advisory Board on Child Abuse and Neglect
1990	First report issued by the U.S. Advisory Board on Child Abuse and Neglect
1990	First *KIDS COUNT Data Book* published by the Center for the Study of Social Policy
1990	Passage of the Victims of Child Abuse Act
1992	Passage of the Family and Medical Leave Act
1993	Passage of the National Child Protection Act
1995	Signing of the United Nations Convention on the Rights of the Child by UN Ambassador Madeline Albright
1996	Passage of the Child Pornography Prevention Act
1996	Temporary Assistance to Needy Families block grant established in the Personal Responsibility and Work Opportunity Act
1997	Passage of the Adoption and Safe Families Act
1998	Development of the Safe Schools/Healthy Students initiative (collaboration between the U.S. Departments of Justice, Health and Human Services, and Education)
2000	Surgeon General's Conference on Children's Mental Health (leading to a Call to Action on Children's Mental Health)
2001	Surgeon General's report on youth violence issued

Source: Modified from Takanishi (1978).

assistance, support services, focused activities, parental/family intervention, planning and program development, training and technical assistance, research/evaluation, capital improvements, and clearinghouses (U.S. GAO, 1996).

Advocacy in the Courts

Although they obtained some initial legislative success, child advocates additionally began to focus in the second half of the 20th century on increasing the self-determination rights of children in the courts. Historically, only adults were ascribed rights protected in courts of law. Children, for the most part, were seen as in need of protection and incapable of conceiving of their own present and future interests. Consequently, the welfare of children was placed in the hands of their parents and others in authority who were assumed both to know and to act on children's interests. The merits of this paternalistic approach toward children recently have been challenged in a number of contexts, most often by demonstrating the rational decision-making abilities of youth and noting conflicts of interest in parental decisions regarding children's welfare (see Schmidt & Reppucci, this volume, for a more detailed discussion).

FUTURE FRONTIERS FOR ADVOCACY

As the history of child advocacy in the legislative and judicial spheres illustrates, the United States has long lacked a coherent, unified policy on children's rights (Walker, Brooks, & Wrightsman, 1999). However, in recent years, several blueprints have been developed that provide a comprehensive, coherent vision of policy for children's rights and unprecedented guidance for child advocacy efforts – the United Nations Convention on the Rights of the Child (United Nations General Assembly, 1989) and a landmark report of the United States Advisory Board on Child Abuse and Neglect (1991). In this final section, we will explore these documents as future frontiers for advocacy efforts and the corresponding roles social scientists may play in their realization.

The United Nations Convention on the Rights of the Child:
An International Consensus on Children's Rights

Although the international community had formally voiced its concern for children's rights as early as 1924, with the adoption of the Geneva Declaration on the Rights of the Child by the League of Nations (see Table 3.2), it was not until 1989, with the passage of the United Nations Convention on the Rights of the Child, that minimum standards were established for the civil, political, economic, social, and cultural rights of children in the form of a legally binding treaty (Limber & Flekkøy, 1995). As Melton (1991a) argued, "the Convention is the first official bill of rights with a coherent, comprehensive vision of children's policy" (p. 70). Indeed, as will be described, the Convention provides a guidepost for advocacy on behalf of children in virtually all domains of their lives (Melton, 1991a, 1998).

In what ways is the Convention exceptional? The Convention on the Rights of the Child is remarkable in at least three respects. First, it has enjoyed wide and rapid acceptance by members of the international community. With the exception of Somalia and the United States, the Convention has been ratified by all of the world's nations (Walker et al., 1999). Moreover, although the drafting process was lengthy, once adopted by the General Assembly, the Convention was accepted more rapidly than any other human rights treaty in history (Limber & Flekkøy, 1995; Melton, 1998). The Convention was opened for signature in January 1990. Within 6 months it had been ratified by 20 countries, enough to put it into force on September 1, 1990. By 1991, the Convention had been ratified by nearly 100 countries. Thus, the Convention embodies a resounding worldwide consensus that children are persons, that they deserve respect and protection, and that nations should use the force of law to ensure that children's rights are upheld (Melton, 1991b).

Second, the Convention articulates a far wider variety of rights for children than had been set forth in any previous human rights document (Walker et al., 1999). Previous international documents had considered civil and political rights, traditionally championed by western countries, to be separate from economic, cultural, and social rights, favored by the nations of the former

TABLE 3.2. *Significant Events in the Development and Ratification of the United Nations Convention on the Rights of the Child*

1923	Save the Children International Union (SCIU) drafted and approved the Declaration of the Rights of the Child (later referred to as the Geneva Declaration). The document asserted that children should be the first to receive relief in emergencies (Walker et al., 1999).
1924	The Geneva Declaration was adopted by the Assembly of the League of Nations. A resolution was passed inviting its members to follow its principles (Cantwell, 1992).
1948	The UN General Assembly passed A Universal Declaration of Human Rights. Although the document did not specifically refer to children's rights, it arguably accorded rights to children by conferring rights on "all members of the human family" (Walker et al., 1999).
1959	The United Nations adopted the Declaration of the Rights of the Child, an aspirational document that significantly expanded upon the protections outlined in the Geneva Declaration (Limber & Flekkøy, 1995; Walker et al., 1999).
1979	In honor of the International Year of the Child, Poland drafted the precursor to the Convention on the Rights of the Child, a 10-article document that reiterated the rights set forth in the 1959 Declaration of the Rights of the Child and included implementing provisions. The UN Commission on Human Rights referred the draft to an open-ended Working Group to redraft the convention (Limber & Flekkøy, 1995).
1989	The Convention on the Rights of the Child was adopted by acclamation by the UN General Assembly.
1990	The Convention on the Rights of the Child was put into force after being ratified by 20 countries.

Eastern bloc. The Convention has 54 articles that cover virtually all aspect of children's lives. Among the substantive rights that the Convention recognizes are the rights to survival, protection, development, and participation.[1] Examples of protection rights include protection from physical, sexual, and psychological abuse and neglect (article 19); economic exploitation (article 32); and abduction, sale, and trafficking (articles 11 and 35). Conditions that the Convention recognizes as necessary to a child's adequate development include the right to an education (articles 28–30), the right to a family environment (Preamble), and the opportunity to engage in play, leisure activities, and cultural events (article 31). Such rights are

[1] These categories are not used in the Convention but are used here for explanatory purposes.

commonly referred to as *nurturance rights*, as they all contribute to or nurture a child's healthy development. Rights to participation (also referred to as *self-determination rights*) include the child's right to express opinions and have his or her opinions taken into account in any matter or procedure affecting the child (articles 12 and 13); the right of access to information (article 13); the rights to freedom of association and assembly (article 15); the right to freedom of thought, conscience, and religion subject to appropriate parental guidance and national law (article 14); and the right to protection against interference with a child's privacy, family, home, and correspondence (article 16).

Third, despite being a lengthy, wide-ranging document that reflects a diversity of international views of children (Melton, 1996; Murphy-Berman, Levesque, & Berman, 1996), the Convention is an extraordinarily coherent instrument in its focus on children's sense of *dignity* (Melton, 1991a,b, 1996). References to children's dignity appear seven times throughout the Convention in diverse contexts, emphasizing the drafters' concerns that adults acknowledge the "personhood" of children and take seriously those aspects of life that are of most importance to children (Limber & Flekkøy, 1995). Thus, rather than limiting their statement to prescribing either nurturance or self-determination rights for children (as has been the strategy of advocates with child saver or kiddie libber agendas, respectively), the drafters recognized that respect for children's dignity requires promotion of their liberty, privacy, *and* nurturance rights (Melton, 1991a,b, 1996).

Finally, not only does the Convention spell out the full panoply of rights to be accorded children, but it also provides a mechanism for evaluating the progress that nations have made in realizing their obligations (article 43). State Parties to the Convention must submit periodic reports to an international committee of experts, which reviews each report, solicits feedback from nongovernmental organizations (if deemed appropriate), and provides feedback to the State Party. The purpose of the Convention's reporting requirement is not to provide a means for condemning those nations with poor human rights records, but rather to create a cooperative, nonconfrontational atmosphere that will promote constructive dialogue among the committee, the nation's official representatives, and other nonofficial country representatives (including child advocates) (Limber & Flekkøy, 1995). For example, in response to the expert committee's criticism of Jamaica's juvenile confinement practices, several of Jamaica's governmental ministries met with nongovernmental organizations to discuss ways of improving the nation's juvenile justice system (Limber & Flekkøy, 1995).

Implications for U.S. Law, Policy, and Practice. Although the United States signed the Convention in 1995, it has not ratified the treaty, which requires approval by the Senate Foreign Relations Committee and a subsequent two-thirds majority vote of the Senate. Such approval appears unlikely in the near future, particularly given the current membership of the Senate Foreign Relations Committee, chaired by the staunch conservative Jesse Helms. This inaction within the Senate likely stems both from a general historical reluctance to ratify international human rights treaties and from a particular concern with the content of the Convention. The Senate's hesitancy to ratify international human rights treaties is not a recent phenomenon (Kaufman, 1990). The Convention on the Prevention and Punishment of the Crime of Genocide was not ratified by the United States until 1986, some 40 years after it was approved by the United Nations at the end of World War II (Centre for Human Rights, 1987). Added to this historical reluctance is a concern on the part of conservative organizations (e.g., the Eagle Forum, the National Center for Home Education), advocates, and politicians that the Convention's provisions undermine the rights of parents (Limber & Flekkøy, 1995; Limber & Wilcox, 1996). As noted subsequently, however, these criticisms are unfounded, because the Convention explicitly protects families and stresses parental responsibility.

Although the Senate has not taken action on the Convention, arguably its provisions are legally binding in the United States. Because the Convention has been adopted nearly universally by the international community, it may be considered customary international law (which may be preempted in U.S. law only by the Constitution or an international treaty) (Melton, 1998; Melton & Kaufman, 1997; see also Kaufman, 1990, for a discussion of this point with regard to human rights treaties).

Regardless of its legal status, however, the Convention on the Rights of the Child should be used, first and foremost, as a guide for advocacy and professional practice (Cohen & Naimark, 1991; Limber & Flekkøy, 1995; Melton, 1991a). The Convention provides at least six broad principles to guide the efforts of advocates and practitioners.

1. *Policies and practices should promote a child's sense of dignity.*
   As noted previously, policies and practice should be guided, above all, "by respect for the dignity of children as members of the human community" (Melton, 1991a, p. 344). Special care should be taken to preserve the dignity of children who may be particularly vulnerable, notably those with mental or physical disabilities (article 23); those who have been arrested, detained, or imprisoned (articles 37, 39); and those exposed to abuse, neglect, or exploitation (article 39) (Limber & Flekkøy, 1995).

2. *The provision of services for children should assume highest priority* (Melton, 1991a,b). Echoing the principle of "children first," which was first enunciated in the Geneva Declaration, the Convention asserts that children have a right to "special care and assistance" (Preamble). Children, for the most part, exist within a state of de jure or de facto dependency (in most cases, either being unable or not permitted to provide for themselves). A sense of fairness dictates that children should not be penalized for their dependent status, but rather that states make provision of services to children their highest priority. Unfortunately, this principle is not embraced in United States, where children receive an insufficient proportion of the available human service dollars (Melton, 1991b).

3. *Children should be viewed as important actors in all matters affecting them* (Melton, 1991a,b, 1998). Provision of services to children is inadequate, however, regardless of their quality or intensity, if the child is treated merely as a passive recipient of those services. The Convention guarantees any "child who is capable of forming his or her own views . . . the right to express those views freely in all matters affecting the child"

(article 12, section 1). Encouraging children to express their opinions and feelings about their own lives and events in their world and to participate actively in the world around them signals a respect for children as human beings (Weithorn, 1998). Communicating this respect to children will help them to develop a positive sense of self and self-respect.

4. *Policies and services for children should respect parents and support the family's integrity* (Melton, 1991a,b, 1998). The Convention acknowledges that parents are primarily responsible "for the upbringing and development of the child" (article 18, section 1) and requires that the state respect parents' "responsibilities, rights, and duties . . . to provide, in a manner consistent with the evolving capacities of the child, appropriate direction" in exercising children's rights under the Convention (article 5). This principle need not conflict with principle 3. As Melton notes, "the Convention appears to presume a model of *shared* decision making by parents and children . . . who are all taken seriously as persons by authorities (1991b, p. 69, citation omitted).

5. *Children have a right to a family environment.* The Convention recognizes that children have a right to a "family environment" (Preamble), a phrase that emphasizes the quality and climate of care provided to children, not the identity of providers (Kaufman, 1994). The drafters of the Convention deemed that a family environment was so important that they decreed that all placements outside of the child's biological family be subject to judicial review (Melton, 1991b). Moreover, the Convention asserts that state authorities should have a wide range of noninstitutional services available to them (articles 23, 40). When the state does undertake the custody and care of children, it should be in a family-like setting with "due regard" for preserving the "continuity in a child's upbringing" (article 20).

6. *Prevention of harm should be the foundation of policy and practice on behalf of children.* Respect for the personhood of children requires that efforts be made to prevent assaults on children's physical, mental, and social integrity (see, e.g., articles 19, 14, and 27; Melton, 1991a).

In sum, although proponents of the Convention face stiff political opposition to ratification of the treaty in the United States (Limber & Wilcox, 1996), the Convention offers a guide for enormous advances in advocacy efforts on behalf of children. As Carol Bellamy (UNICEF's (Executive Director of the United Nations International Children's Education Fund) recently noted, "a century that began with children having virtually no rights is ending with children having the most powerful legal instrument that not only recognizes but protects their human rights" (1997, cited in Walker et al., 1999, p. 28). It is too early to evaluate the success of this legal instrument in helping to bring about real change in children's realization of their rights (e.g., in totalitarian regimes that have ratified the Convention with no apparent intention of altering practices such as using children as soldiers or confining or torturing children in prisons). Nevertheless, policy makers, child advocates, and practitioners should embrace this opportunity and use its principles to guide policy and practice at individual, local, state, federal, and international levels (Limber & Flekkøy, 1995).

The U.S. Advisory Board on Child Abuse and Neglect's Blueprint for an Effective Child Protection Policy

The Convention on the Rights of the Child requires States Parties to craft specific national policies based on the Convention's articles and principles. As noted earlier, the United States has long lacked a comprehensive, coherent policy for enhancing the welfare of children (Walker et al., 1999).

To date, the most ambitious attempt at formulating such a policy has been the work of the U.S. Advisory Board on Child Abuse and Neglect (U.S. Advisory Board, 1991). The U.S. Advisory Board, a blue-ribbon panel appointed by the secretary of health and human services, was given a broad statutory charge to evaluate progress in fulfilling the goals of the Child Abuse Prevention and Treatment Act of 1974 (CAPTA). Through a series of reports, the U.S. Advisory Board had documented the woeful status of the current scheme of child protection and provides a blueprint for how a national policy might be structured (U.S. Advisory Board, 1990, 1991, 1992, 1993, 1995). Although federal leadership is still lacking, specific principles and recommendations are being implemented and considered in many jurisdictions (Melton, Thompson, & Small, in press).

The U.S. Advisory Board's national policy rests on the following principles (which echo those underlying the United Nations Convention on the Rights of the Child). First, children deserve the respect and dignity that emanate from being members of the human family. Moreover, as the family (broadly construed) is the natural place for children to grow up safe and healthy, children should have the right to live safely in a family environment. Finally, communities should be encouraged to develop an atmosphere in which neighbors help neighbors and all look out for the protection of children. In short, the U.S. Advisory Board's plan advocates a comprehensive, child-centered, family-focused, and neighborhood-based approach.

In arguing for a comprehensive policy, the Advisory Board acknowledged the multiplicity of academic and disciplinary approaches to understanding child maltreatment, as well as the widespread fragmentation of service agencies that currently address the needs of child abuse and neglect victims. The diffusion of programs for children and the corresponding gaps in services for children and families create hardships for advocates – both in obtaining treatment for children and in targeting policy and legislative reform. Understanding all of the possibilities for services for a particular child in a specific state requires a vast knowledge of a bewildering set of government agencies and their regulations, a task well beyond most parents and difficult even for seasoned advocates.

The policy envisioned by the Advisory Board is also child-centered, thus restoring children to their rightful place as the centerpiece of state efforts to address child maltreatment. Current state child protection schemes focus not on the child but on the investigation of potential abusers. To change the status quo, the U.S. Advisory Board proposes a new role for children, one in which they are taken seriously and their needs are addressed by including them in decisions regarding their lives, providing them necessary therapeutic and legal services, and ensuring that they are placed in safe, healthy environments. In every possible scenario, consideration of the best possible outcome for the child replaces investigation as the pivotal point around which all other decisions would be made.

In addition, the U.S. Advisory Board recommended family-focused policies that directly and indirectly strengthen families.

Families are viewed as a critical ingredient for child well-being, and their potential as a resource for children should be supported. Because of the harmful consequences for many children who are removed from the home, whenever possible, services should be organized to help families remain functional as well as reduce the risk of child maltreatment. Special efforts should be made to provide family preservation services to reduce the number of children removed unnecessarily from homes. The U.S. Advisory Board also called for a federal role in improving the quality of deteriorating family environments through legislative efforts ranging from improved housing and transportation assistance to the development of community centers and mobile van services that would connect rural communities.

Finally, the U.S. Advisory Board championed the use of neighborhood-based strategies to support families. Such strategies include fostering an ethic of mutual assistance, as well as placing support services within easy reach of community residents (e.g., school-based family resource centers). These support services should include not only the formal services typically provided by state agencies but also informal services (volunteer, community) that originate from local grass-roots efforts. The recently created White House Office on Faith-Based and Community Initiatives is one example of how the federal government might build and enhance the capacity of neighborhood-based organizations to strengthen families through increased services.

In sum, there is a clear need for child-centered, family-focused, neighborhood-based approaches to child protection. Although the U.S. Advisory Board's recommendations were based on a state-of-the-art review of empirical literature available at the time, there is still much to be learned about improving the overall welfare of children and families. The conceptual vision and concrete recommendations within the plan of the U.S. Advisory Board provide a solid foundation for consideration of future empirical efforts.

SETTING A RESEARCH AGENDA TO FURTHER CHILD ADVOCACY

Not only do the Convention and the U.S. Advisory Board report establish an agenda for child advocacy, they also suggest research agendas for social scientists that may, in turn, further inform advocacy efforts to promote children's rights. Several directions for such research will now be discussed.

Children's Views of Their Rights

Social scientists should continue to pursue research to assess children's perceptions of their rights at different ages and under varied circumstances (e.g., Cherny & Perry, 1996; Helwig, 1995; Melton, 1982; Melton & Limber, 1992; Schmidt & Reppucci, this volume). Such research will help to refine an agenda for child advocacy[2] (Melton & Limber, 1992) and assist in efforts to teach children about their rights and how to express them (Limber & Flekkøy, 1995). These efforts may, for example, help policy makers determine how children of different ages can best express their participation rights (e.g., expression of views, freedom of assembly, access to information, participation in cultural life).

Children's Subjective Understanding of Key Constructs

Research also is needed to illuminate children's subjective understanding of various constructs that are basic to children's rights (Melton, 1998; Melton & Kaufman, 1997). For example, many of the principles underlying the Convention (and the U.S. Advisory Board report) are based on children's *perceptions*. Social scientists may assist advocates and policy makers in understanding those elements that are, in the eyes of a child, critical to a *family environment*. Similarly, researchers may provide insight into the conditions that promote a child's sense of *dignity*, *privacy* or *honor*. In this regard, particular attention should be paid to perceptions of the most vulnerable children (e.g., racial and ethnic minorities, abused or exploited children, economically disadvantaged children).

Children's Evolving Capacitites

Experts in child development also can help to illuminate ways in which children's rights can best be fulfilled consistent with

---

[2] Adults frequently are not adept at identifying those issues that are most important to children (Melton & Limber, 1992).

children's *evolving capacities* (article 5), a theme that is pervasive in the Convention (Limber & Flekkøy, 1995). Policy makers, advocates, and practitioners frequently are poorly attuned to children's needs at different ages (or under various conditions) and to their ability to exercise their own rights. As noted previously, research may be particularly useful in advising adults about ways to empower children to fulfill their own rights in significantly broader ways, consonant with their evolving capacities.

Social Indicator Data

As noted earlier, in the last generation, we have witnessed extraordinary changes in the American family and in social institutions that affect and serve families. Within this ever-changing landscape, continued collection of survey and archival data is needed to assess children's rights in such domains as health care, child care, protection from maltreatment, and education (to name only a few). For each identified area, the data collection should provide a snapshot of the level of need at the national, state, and local levels.

Evaluation of Interventions

Researchers also can provide advice about child advocacy efforts by examining the response to children's needs at the national, state, and local levels. To what extent are efforts for ensuring children's rights both available and effective (Melton & Kaufman, 1997)? For example, in examining the degree to which a community's policies and practices support children's right to participate, researchers should evaluate the existence of community institutions, practices, and policies to facilitate meaningful participate by children and youth and explore means to develop, maintain, and enhance them. Evaluating children's perceptions of these policies, institutions, and practices also should be part of any such efforts.

CONCLUSIONS

In the 100 years since the first child advocacy efforts were launched in the United States, numerous legislative, administrative, and judicial reforms have been conceived and implemented to promote children's rights to nurturance and self-determination. However, these efforts, as a whole, have been incomplete and have lacked a coherent philosophy (as evidenced by the conflicts between the kiddie libber and child-saving movements). In recent years, models have been developed that provide advocates, policy makers, and practitioners alike with unprecedented guidance in the formation of coherent, unified policies for children that are rooted in respect for children's dignity. The United Nations Convention on the Rights of the Child offers the most comprehensive conceptual and practical framework to date for wide-ranging child advocacy efforts in the United States and throughout the world. The 1993 report of the U.S. Advisory Board on Child Abuse and Neglect similarly provides a blueprint for advocacy efforts to prevent and ameliorate the effects of child maltreatment. Such models are more critical than ever amid the dramatic changes in the family and social institutions and the shifting of responsibility for governance from federal to local levels of government. Social scientists have the opportunity to play key roles in both informing the advocacy agenda and evaluating advocacy efforts. In both regards, particular attention should be paid to ensuring that children's own views are heard, understood, and promoted. To do so will signal respect for the dignity of children.

References

Annie E. Casey Foundation (2000). *2000 KIDS COUNT Data Book*. Baltimore: Author.

Ariès, P. (1962). *Centuries of childhood: A social history of family life*. New York: Vintage Books.

Bachu, A. (1999). *Trends in premarital childbearing: 1930 to 1994* (P23-197). Washington, DC: U.S. Census Bureau.

Brinig, M. F., & Buckley, F. H. (1997). Welfare magnets: The race for the top. *Supreme Court Economic Review, 5*, 141–178.

Bryson, K., & Casper, L. M.. (1998). *Household and family characteristics: March 1997* (P20-509). Washington, DC: U.S. Census Bureau.

Campbell, J. A. (1999). *Health insurance coverage* (P60-208). Washington, DC: U.S. Census Bureau.

Centre for Human Rights. (1987). *Status of human rights instruments*. New York: United Nations.

Cherny, I., & Perry, N. W. (1996). Children's attitudes toward their rights: An international perspective. In E. Verhellen (Ed.), *Monitoring children's rights* (pp. 241–250). New York: Kluwer Law International.

Children's Defense Fund (1997). *Poverty matters: The cost of child poverty in America*. Washington, DC: Author.

Cohen, C. P., & Naimark, H. (1991). United Nations Convention on the Rights of the Child: Individual rights concepts and their significance for social scientists. *American Psychologist, 46*, 60–65.

Dalaker, J. (1999). *Poverty in the United States*. Washington, DC: U.S. Census Bureau.

Fare v. Michael C., 442U.S. 707 (1979).

Helwig, C. C. (1995). Adolescents' and young adults' conceptions of civil liberties: Freedom of speech and religion. *Child Development, 66*, 152–166.

Kaufman, N. H. (1990). *Human rights treaties and the Senate: A history of opposition*. Chapel Hill, NC: University of North Carolina Press.

Kaufman, N. H. (1994, May). *The concept of family in international law*. Paper presented at the International Colloquium on the U.N. Convention on the Rights of the Child. Charleston, S.C.

Limber, S. P., & Flekkøy, M. G. (1995). The U.N. Convention on the Rights of the Child: Its relevance for social scientists. *Social Policy Report, 9*(2), 1–15.

Limber, S. P., & Wilcox, B. L. (1996). Application of the U.N. Convention on the Rights of the Child to the United States. *American Psychologist, 51*, 1246–1250.

Melton, G. B. (1982). Children's rights: Where are the children? *American Journal of Orthopsychiatry, 52*, 530–538.

Melton, G. B. (1983). *Child advocacy: Psychological issues and interventions*. New York: Plenum.

Melton, G. B. (1987). The clashing of symbols: Prelude to child and family policy. *American Psychologist, 42*, 345–354.

Melton, G. B. (1991a). Preserving the dignity of children around the world: The U.N. Convention on the rights of the Child. *Child Abuse and Neglect, 15*, 343–350.

Melton, G. B. (1991b). Socialization in the global community: Respect for the dignity of children. *American Psychologist, 46*, 66–71.

Melton, G. B. (1996). The child's right to a family environment: Why children's rights and family values are compatible. *American Psychologist, 51*, 1234–1238.

Melton, G. B. (1998). Children's rights in the health care system: The evolving framework in international human rights law. *Childrenz Issues, 2*(2), 37–41.

Melton, G. B., & Kaufman, N. H. (1997). Monitoring of children's rights. In A. Ben-Arieh & H. Wintersberger (Eds.), *Monitoring and measuring the state of children: Beyond survival* (Eurosocial Report No. 62, pp. 81–88). Vienna: European Centre for Social Welfare and Policy Research.

Melton, G. B., & Limber, S. P. (1992). What children's rights mean to children: Children's own views. In M. Freeman & P. Veerman (Eds.), *The ideologies of children's rights* (pp. 167–187). Dordrecht, the Netherlands: Kluwer.

Melton, G. B., Thompson, R. A., & Small, M. A. (in press). *Toward a child-centered, neighborhood-based child protection system.* Westport, CT: Praeger.

Mnookin, R. H. (1978). Children's rights: Beyond kiddie libbers and child savers. *Journal of Clinical Child Psychology, 7,* 163–167.

Murphy-Berman, V., Levésque, H. L., & Berman, John J. (1996). U.N. Convention on the Rights of the Child: A cross cultural view. *American Psychologist, 51,* 1257–1261.

Parham v. J.R., 442 U.S. 584 (1979).

Personal Responsibility and Work Opportunity Reconciliation Act of 1996, Pub. L. No. 104–193, 110 Stat. 2105.

Small, M. A., & Schwartz, I. M. (1990). Policy implications for children's law in the aftermath of *Maryland v. Craig. Seton Hall Constitutional Law Journal, 1,* 109–130.

Takanishi, R. (1978). Childhood as a social issue: Historical roots of contemporary child advocacy movements. *Journal of Social Issues, 34,* 8–28.

United Nations General Assembly. (1989, November 17). *Adoption of a Convention on the Rights of the Child.* U.N. Doc. A/Res/44/25.

U.S. Advisory Board on Child Abuse and Neglect. (1990). *Critical first steps in response to a national emergency.* Washington, DC: U.S. Government Printing Office.

U.S. Advisory Board on Child Abuse and Neglect. (1991). *Creating caring communities: Blueprint for an effective federal policy on child abuse and neglect.* Washington, DC: U.S. Government Printing Office.

U.S. Advisory Board on Child Abuse and Neglect. (1992). *The continuing child protection emergency: A challenge to the nation.* Washington, DC: U.S. Government Printing Office.

U.S. Advisory Board on Child Abuse and Neglect. (1993). *Neighbors helping neighbors: A new national strategy for the protection of children.* Washington, DC: U.S. Government Printing Office.

U.S. Advisory Board on Child Abuse and Neglect. (1995). *A nation's shame: Fatal child abuse and neglect in the United States.* Washington, DC: U.S. Government Printing Office.

U.S. General Accounting Office. (1996). *At-risk and delinquent youth: Multiple federal programs raise efficiency questions* (GAO/HEHS-96-34). Washington, DC: U.S. Governent Printing Office.

U.S. General Accounting Office. (1998). *Welfare reform: States' efforts to expand child care programs* (GAO/HEHS-98-27). Washington, DC: U.S. Government Printing Office.

Walker, N. E., Brooks, C. M., & Wrightsman, L. S. (1999). *Children's rights in the United States: In search of a national policy*. Thousand Oaks, CA: Sage

Weithorn, L. A. (1998). Youth participation in family and community decision making. *Family Futures, 2*(1), 6–9.

4

Children's Rights and Capacities

Melinda G. Schmidt
N. Dickon Reppucci

The notion that children possess rights is relatively recent in U.S. history. In the last 150 years, children's nurturance rights have been established, and some rights to self-determination for minors have also begun to emerge. The extension of certain rights to minors has raised a number of questions regarding their understanding of and capacity to exercise these rights in legally relevant contexts. In the last several decades, psychology has made important strides toward answering these questions. In this chapter, we first offer a historical context for the emergence of children's rights; then we outline five areas of the law that have witnessed significant change in recent years. Finally, we discuss social science research on children's understanding of the law and their rights, as well as children's competence to make legally relevant decisions.

A BRIEF HISTORICAL CONTEXT

For hundreds of years, children in the United States were valued mainly as economic assets in a largely agrarian society. It was not until the mid-1800s that children began to be valued sentimentally and recognized as requiring nurturance and protection (Hart, 1991; Walker, Brooks, & Wrightsman, 1999). To meet these needs, the family was given the responsibility as well as the autonomy to provide for the best interests of children (Chisholm, 1981; Reppucci & Crosby, 1993). Thus, children's nurturance rights were enveloped in the rights of the family, which were accorded respect and privacy guided by two postulates: "(1) children, by virtue of their age and experience, lack the ability and/or the capacity to be completely autonomous directors of their own lives; and (2) the private and autonomous family is the institution most suited to provide for the best interests of society's children" (Reppucci & Crosby, 1993, p. 2). According to Melton (1982), "the underlying premise is that children's and parents' interests are coextensive because of the child's need for protection which the family is assumed to provide. The child's liberty interest becomes expressed as the *parents' right* to choose how they rear their children" (p. 531). Indeed, two Supreme Court cases, *Meyer v. Nebraska* (1923) and *Pierce v. Society of Sisters* (1925), cemented the right of parents to direct the upbringing of their children.

The state has intervened and restricted parental rights when parents have been found unwilling or unable to act in their children's best interest (see, e.g., *Prince v. Massachusetts*, 1944). Although the state began to intervene as *parens patriae* to protect children's interests in the late 1800s and early 1900s, it paid little regard to the child's perspective. At about this same time, in 1899, the first juvenile court was established to rehabilitate rather than punish children, and the need for due process rights for juveniles was dismissed (Hart, 1991).

Nurturance and Self-Determination Rights and Children's Emergence as Persons

During the 19th and 20th centuries, increases in children's rights were largely protection-oriented, though recent years have seen an increase in children's self-determination rights (Hart, 1993). Whereas nurturance rights emphasize children's entitlements to nutrition, medical care, and other benefits, self-determination rights allow children to make autonomous decisions and exercise control over their environments. Mnookin (1978) has referred to advocates of nurturance rights who call for state interventions to protect children as *child savers* and champions of self-determination rights as *kiddie libbers*. (See Small & Limber, this volume, for an extended discussion of the history, current status, and future of child advocacy efforts.)

Only in the second half of the 20th century did children's status as persons begin to emerge, and with that status came a recognition of some rights to self-determination (Hart, 1993). Although many people favor the extension of nurturance rights, a great deal of ambivalence surrounds whether (and which) self-determination rights should be accorded to children (see, e.g., Grisso, 1981; Rogers & Wrightsman, 1978). In fact, the lack of national consensus and unified policy surrounding children's rights is one reason that the United States has not yet ratified the popular 1989 United Nations Convention on the Rights of the Child (UNCRC). (See Small & Limber, this volume, and Walker et al., 1999, for further discussion of the UNCRC).

Following the civil rights movement of the 1960s, and grounded in some of its ideologies, the children's rights movement targeted paternalistic legal policies (Davis, Scott, Wadlington, & Whitebread, 1997). In the cases of *In re Gault* (1967) and *Tinker v. DesMoines Independent Community School District* (1969), as well as in Justice William O. Douglas's dissent in *Wisconsin v. Yoder* (1972), the Supreme Court first recognized children as persons with constitutionally protected rights separate from those of their parents.

In re Gault. *In re Gault* (1967) was a landmark case that fundamentally changed the juvenile justice system. Gerald Gault was 15 years old when he allegedly made a lewd telephone call to a neighbor. Gault was subsequently adjudicated delinquent and given an exorbitant disposition of 6 years in a detention home. Gault claimed that his commitment to a state institution was a denial of liberty without due process of law required by the Constitution. In a decision that "constitutionalized the juvenile justice process" (Davis et al., 1997, p. 746), the U.S. Supreme Court held that "neither the Fourteenth Amendment nor the Bill of Rights is for adults alone" (*In re Gault*, p. 13). *In re Gault* established that children are entitled to some (though not all) due process rights accorded to adults in the adjudicatory phase, including the rights to notice of charges, legal counsel, confrontation and cross-examination, and silence. Although due process rights for children may be considered protection rights, the *Gault* case signaled a fundamental shift in treating children not only as persons but to some degree as adults (Manfredi, 1998).

Tinker v. DesMoines. Two years later, in *Tinker v. DesMoines* (1969), the Supreme Court upheld the fundamental right to freedom of expression for children. *Tinker* involved the expulsion of children from school for wearing black armbands to protest the Vietnam War. Justice Abe Fortas stated in the majority opinion that "students in school as well as out of school are 'persons' under our Constitution" (p. 511). Although *Tinker* is seen by many as the first true children's (self-determination) rights case, Melton (1989) argues that when examined closely, *Tinker* may be a case of parents' rights disguised as children's rights. In fact, the parents of the children involved were antiwar protesters, and the children were as young as 8 years old. Melton notes that an 8-year-old's capacity to understand and protest against a war is disputable. He suggests that a stronger case for children's rights would have been made had the children's views been unbiased by those of their parents.

Wisconsin v. Yoder. In *Wisconsin v. Yoder* (1972), the Supreme Court decided in favor of the right of Amish parents to terminate their children's formal educational training at the eighth grade. Although the majority opinion favored parents' rights, Justice Douglas's famous dissent officially recognized that the interests of parents and children may conflict, and suggested that there may be some situations in which the rights of children to make decisions about their own future outweigh the rights of their parents (Davis et al., 1997; Reppucci & Crosby, 1993). In short, Douglas portrayed the child as a person with individual rights, separate from those of parents. Although the current state of the law continues to weigh more heavily the rights of parents than those of children, many legal and mental health professionals have emerged in recent years in favor of increased recognition and protection of children's – and especially adolescents' – rights over and above the right of family privacy (Portwood, Reppucci, & Mitchell, 1998). Moreover, the courts have begun to see that the constitutional rights of children may reign in the exercise of parental and/or state authority (Reppucci & Crosby, 1993; see, e.g., *Planned Parenthood of Missouri v. Danforth*, 1976).

Children's emergence as persons and the accompanying change in emphasis from the right of protection to the right of self-determination has resulted in a somewhat confusing coexistence of "independence" and "dependence" rights for children (Grossberg, 1993). Melton (1983) acknowledged this confusion, stating, "Since [*Gault* and *Tinker*], the Court has wavered numerous times in its perception of whether minors are fully persons entitled to basic legal rights" (p. 99). Children's rights have come about through a number of narrowly applied court decisions, which fail to lay a definitive groundwork for policy on children's rights (Davis & Schwartz, 1987). According to Scott, Reppucci, and Aber (1988), "the law increasingly gives minors the liberty to make decisions which directly or indirectly restrict the authority of their parents and the state. Paradoxically, expanded legal rights of adolescents are supported and constrained by paternalistic as well as libertarian goals" (pp. 1064–1065). In the next section, we highlight areas of case law that have seen drastic changes in children's rights in recent years. Following this overview, we discuss in greater detail the Court's inconsistencies in its extension of rights to children.

CASE LAW ON CHILDREN'S RIGHTS

Though Mnookin (1978) first made note of it more than 20 years ago, it remains true that, in general, children have both less liberty and less accountability than adults. However, five areas of the law have witnessed significant change with regard to children's rights in recent years: due process rights in juvenile justice proceedings, medical and abortion rights, rights surrounding mental health treatment, rights in school, and participation and protection rights (e.g., the rights to participation in custody proceedings and protection from child abuse).

Due Process Rights in Juvenile Justice

One year before the monumental Supreme Court decision in *Gault*, Justice Fortas's opinion in *Kent v. United States* (1966) set the stage for a series of cases that would delineate certain due process rights for children. *Kent* gave juveniles their first legal protection in the juvenile justice system – the right to a hearing and to counsel before being transferred to adult criminal court. With regard to the juvenile court, Justice Fortas wrote, "There is evidence . . . that the

child receives the worst of both worlds: that he gets neither the protections accorded to adults nor the solicitous care and regenerative
treatment postulated for children" (p. 555).

Following *Kent*, *In re Gault* (1967) extended due process rights
to children and further recognized juveniles as persons with constitutionally protected liberty interests (Walker et al., 1999). This
trend continued with the Court's decisions in *In re Winship* (1970)
and *Breed v. Jones* (1975). The *Winship* decision required that the
standard of proof "beyond a reasonable doubt" rather than "a
preponderance of the evidence" be applied in juvenile court proceedings, whereas *Breed* gave children the right to protection from
double jeopardy. In addition, though not a juvenile case, *Miranda v.
Arizona* (1966) required that defendants be informed of their Fifth
Amendment right against self-incrimination as well as their Sixth
Amendment right to counsel at the time of their arrest. (Whether
juveniles have the capacity to understand and invoke those rights
is the subject of much debate and social science research and is cov-
ered later in this chapter.) Finally, some state courts jumped on the
due process rights bandwagon as well. For example, the Wisconsin
Supreme Court concluded in *Winburn v. State* (1966) that children
are entitled to the insanity defense, as did the Louisiana Supreme
Court in the 1978 case of *State in Interest of Causey*.

However, other Supreme Court decisions indicated that *Gault*'s
impact would not transform the juvenile court completely into an
adult court (Crosby & Reppucci, 1993). In *McKiever v. Pennsylvania*
(1971) the Court denied children the right to a trial by jury in juvenile court proceedings. A year later, *Kirby v. Illinois* (1972) held
that minors, like adults, do not have an absolute right to counsel
at a preindictment lineup. More recently, in *Schall v. Martin* (1984),
the Court upheld a New York statute that authorized broad discretion in detaining juveniles before trial. In its decision, the Court
invoked the *parens patriae* doctrine and relied on the assumption
that juveniles have a lesser interest in liberty and freedom than
adults because, as minors, they are under the control of their parents (Worrell, 1985). Worrell points out, however, that the equation
of state and parental constraints of children's liberty is false, and
that even parents cannot encroach on their children's fundamental
rights. Moreover, Worrell argues that because adults and minors

are similarly situated in their right to freedom from institutional restraint, the broad discretion in detaining juveniles before trial authorized by the *parens patriae* doctrine constitutes a denial of equal protection of the laws.

Two additional criticisms surrounding the extension of due process rights in the juvenile justice system are worth noting. First, although the promise of rehabilitation is one of the tenets of the juvenile court, the Supreme Court has not addressed an explicit right to treatment for children in the juvenile justice system (Crosby & Reppucci, 1993). Second, although the *Gault* decision gave juveniles the right to counsel in a delinquency hearing in 1967, Caeti, Hemmens, and Burton (1996) found that state juvenile courts vary greatly in the extent to which they have adopted the standards for provision of counsel to juveniles laid down in *Gault*. Thus, despite the great strides that have been made in extending due process rights to juveniles in recent years, for better or for worse, children continue to be granted fewer due process protections than adults in the legal system.

Medical and Abortion Rights

Minors are presumed to be immature and incompetent under U.S. law. As a result, they are generally deemed incapable of giving informed and voluntary (competent) consent to medical treatment (Davis et al., 1997; Walker et al., 1999). In most cases, parents are given the right to make medical decisions affecting their children. Recent years have seen the expansion of exceptions to this rule, however, with the notion that a mature minor should be given some rights to bodily self-determination regarding medical treatment (Davis & Schwartz, 1987; Walker et al., 1999). Increasingly, states are drafting statutes allowing minors to give consent to specific medical treatments, such as treatments for pregnancy, pregnancy prevention (i.e. birth control), venereal disease, or substance abuse (Davis et al., 1997). Moreover, the "mature minor" doctrine has been invoked by courts in recent years to allow minors who exhibit adultlike maturity to obtain a range of treatments without the consent of their parents (Penkower, 1996). Though *mature minor* is never clearly defined, Wadlington (1973) explains that the doctrine is generally applied in cases in which "(a) treatment was undertaken for the benefit of the minor, not a third person, (b) the minor was near majority age (at least 15) and was considered to have sufficient mental capacity to understand the nature and importance of the medical procedure, [and] (c) the medical procedure was not serious in nature" (p. 119).

Probably the most controversial issue with regard to adolescents' medical rights in the past several decades has been a minor's right to obtain an abortion without parental consent. Only a few years after *Roe v. Wade* (1973) legalized abortion in the United States, *Planned Parenthood of Central Missouri v. Danforth* (1976) applied this right to minors. In a turning-point decision for children's rights, the Supreme Court found unconstitutional a Missouri statute that required parental consent for a minor to obtain an abortion during the first 12 weeks of her pregnancy. In its 5–4 decision, the Court declared that neither the state nor the parent may have complete veto power over a minor's decision to terminate her pregnancy. The Court did raise the issue of maturity, however, recognizing that not all minors can give effective, informed consent and allowing for the possibility of additional regulation of adolescent abortion.

Three years later, in *Bellotti v. Baird* (1979), the Court struck down a Massachusetts statute that required parental consent for minors' abortions but allowed a minor who had been denied parental consent the chance to have a higher court overrule her parents. Justice Lewis Powell, Jr., concluded, in writing for the majority, that a minor must have access to the court without first seeking parental consent. Thus, states requiring parental consent for abortion were forced to provide an alternative means (called *judicial bypass*) by which an adolescent may demonstrate either that she is mature enough to make the abortion decision (a *mature minor*) or that it is in her best interests to obtain an abortion. The irony, of course, is that if a minor is not mature enough to make an abortion decision, how can she be mature enough to raise a child? Not surprisingly, in practice, judges rarely deny adolescents abortions through judicial bypass (see, e.g., Mnookin, 1985; Pliner & Yates, 1992).

H.L. v. Matheson (1981) was the first case to test parental notification requirements. The Court upheld a Utah statute that required physicians to notify the parents of immature and dependent minor girls "if possible" prior to performing an abortion. In finding parental notification provisions constitutional for dependent minors, the Court declared that the state's interest in protecting children from harm and maintaining family integrity outweighed the minor girl's liberty interest in making her own abortion decision. However, Scott (1984) highlights Justice Warren Burger's untested psychological assumption that the abortion decision is more serious than medical decisions surrounding childbirth. Scott emphasizes the need for empirical research to test such assumptions.

In more recent years, the Supreme Court has continued to strike down parental consent statutes that do not allow for judicial bypass (see, e.g., *City of Akron v. Akron Center for Reproductive Health*, 1983) but has upheld notification statutes and even waiting periods so long as they contain necessary bypass procedures (see, e.g., *Hodgson v. Minnesota*, 1990; *Ohio v. Akron Center for Reproductive Health*, 1990). No consensus exists in the Supreme Court on the issue of adolescent abortion (Scott, 1984). It is likely that increasingly restrictive state statutes regulating adolescent abortion will continue to be tested in the courts (Crosby & Reppucci, 1993).

Rights Surrounding Mental Health Treatment

Opposing its trend toward self-determination rights in adolescent abortion, the Court clearly classified minors as children in the 1979 case of *Parham v. J.R.* (Melton, 1989). In *Parham*, the Court upheld a Georgia statute that allowed the parents or guardians of a minor child to admit him or her to a state mental hospital without a hearing on the matter, despite claims that this violated the child's liberty interest under the due process clause of the Fourteenth Amendment. In the decision, the Court relied on the presumption that parents act in the best interests of their children when admitting them to psychiatric hospitals (Appelbaum, 1989); thus, due process rights may be waived. Justice Burger wrote, "[P]arents possess what children lack in maturity, experience, and capacity for judgment required for making life's difficult decisions. . . . Most children, even in adolescence, simply are not able to make sound judgments concerning many decisions, including their need for medical care" (pp. 602–603).

In addition to this questionable psychological assumption, the Court relied on the assumption that state psychiatric hospitals would have no interest in furthering unnecessary admissions (Appelbaum, 1989). As Weithorn (1988) has pointed out, however, the shift from public to privately run psychiatric facilities appears to have undercut this assumption. (See Melton, Lyons, & Spaulding, 1998, for a thorough analysis of the legal framework surrounding the civil commitment of minors.)

In addition to protection from civil commitment, minors have sought the right to obtain mental health treatment without parental consent. Although the issue of a right to mental health treatment has not come before the Supreme Court, many state legislatures have created statutes allowing minors to consent to outpatient as well as inpatient services without parental consent (Crosby & Reppucci, 1993).

Rights in School

A number of cases have tested constitutional protections as they apply to students in school. Discussed earlier in this chapter, *Tinker v. DesMoines* (1969) was the first case to find that children have some constitutionally protected rights in school. Six years later, the Court continued on this course by upholding students' rights to procedural due process (i.e., notice and a hearing) on suspension from school (*Goss v. Lopez*, 1975).

The trend did not last long, however. Two years later, the Court found in *Ingraham v. Wright* (1977) that corporal punishment in schools did not violate the Eighth Amendment's ban of cruel and unusual punishment on the basis that constitutional protection is not necessary because public schools are open institutions that children are free to leave (Melton, 1989). Nor did the Court find that notice and a hearing prior to the enforcement of corporal punishment were required under the due process clause (Melton, 1989).

More recently, *New Jersey v. T.L.O.* (1985) addressed the question of minor students' independent privacy right to protection from unreasonable searches and seizures in schools. The Court found that school personnel may conduct a search of students' belongings so long as they have "reasonable suspicion" to believe that the student is violating a school rule (Davis et al., 1997). Finally, in *Hazelwood School District v. Kuhlmeier* (1988), the Court abandoned the test of First Amendment protections it had devised in *Tinker*. Although in *Tinker* the Court established that schools may not prohibit children's freedom of expression merely to avoid being associated with an unpopular viewpoint, in *Hazelwood* the Court stated that school officials retain the right to control what is published in a school-sponsored newspaper. The Court found that the principal's deletion of two pages of the student newspaper did not constitute an infringement of students' First Amendment rights.

Participation and Protection Rights

The increasing focus on self-determination and personhood has brought about greater participation rights for children in custody decisions during divorce proceedings. However, recent years have also seen fewer protections accorded to children. With regard to participation in custody decisions, the passage of the Uniform Marriage and Divorce Act in 1970 helped clarify the best interests of the child standard by providing a list of factors to be considered by judges in deciding custody. This list of factors included, among others, "the wishes of the child as to his custodian" (Section 402, 1970, as amended 1971, 1973). Today, all 50 states explicitly include the consideration of a child's wishes in laws concerning children in contested custody cases (Crosby-Currie, 1996). In fact, in at least one state, Georgia, the preference of a child 14 years of age or older solely determines the child's custody (*Harbin v. Harbin*, 1976).

On the other hand, constitutional protections reserved for minors have begun to be chipped away. Crosby and Reppucci (1993) cite the example of the death penalty. In the 1988 decision in *Thompson v. Oklahoma*, the Court found that societal consensus opposed the execution of juveniles 15 years of age and younger as cruel and unusual punishment under the Eighth Amendment. One year later, in *Stanford v. Kentucky* (1989), however, Justice Antonin Scalia's opinion for the majority stated that "neither a historical nor a modern societal consensus forbid the imposition of capital punishment on any person who murders at 16 or 17 years of age" (p. 4978). Furthermore, Justice Scalia denounced the relevance of social science evidence to the question of whether to execute juveniles (Crosby & Reppucci, 1993).

The Court has also been somewhat hesitant in protecting children from abuse. Although the state does act against child abusers through police, social science, and prosecutorial systems, in cases of child abuse the state has found for itself interests in rather than duties to protect the liberties of children (Crosby-Currie & Reppucci, 1999). In a monumental case that came down against children's rights, the Court in *DeShaney v. Winnebago County* (1984) refused to declare an affirmative duty to protect children from the violence of their parents even when the abuse has been acknowledged by the state. (See Crosby-Currie & Reppucci, 1999, for a thorough legal analysis of the *DeShaney* case.)

Inconsistency in the Extension of Rights to Children

In general, case law has marked forward but inconsistent progress in children's rights over the last several decades. For example, in the extension of due process rights within the juvenile justice system, children have been accorded a right to counsel but not to a trial by jury. Moreover, in the realm of medical and mental health rights, the court has expanded children's rights to bodily self-determination in regard to adolescent abortion (e.g., *Bellotti v. Baird*, 1979; *Planned Parenthood of Central Missouri v. Danforth*, 1976) while at the same time refusing to grant children the right to a hearing prior to being placed by their parents in a state mental hospital (*Parham v. J. R.*, 1979).

Inconsistency in the extension of rights to children may be accounted for in part by the shift from a more liberal to a more conservative Supreme Court in the last 20 years. Walker et al. (1999) noted that conservative justices have tended to favor nurturance rights but not rights to self-determination. In addition, in spite of the improvements in and the increasing relevance of social science evidence, the contributions of social science researchers have continued to be eyed warily rather than wholeheartedly accepted. Finally, justices' conservative or liberal leanings have influenced their beliefs about and application of information regarding the development of children's capacities.

Regardless of its conservative or liberal makeup, the Court extends rights to minors based on its perception of minors' competence (Melton, 1983). Children are generally viewed as developmentally immature and without the capacity to make independent choices that reflect their own best interests (Melton, 1983, 1989; Reppucci & Crosby, 1993). Melton suggests that as a result, the Court may presume that children lack autonomy and liberty interests, justifying the limitation of minors' rights in ways that would be unconstitutional for adults.

In an effort aimed at reconciling some of the issues inherent in extending rights to children, the legal system has recently begun to distinguish adolescents as a special category, separate from children or adults. In doing so, the courts have continuously faced the question of whether adolescents' cognitive developmental capacities require that they be given the autonomy of an adult or the protection owed a child in making decisions (Crosby & Reppucci, 1993). Moreover, depending on whether the issue is protection of minors from harm or punishment of minors for wrongdoing, the courts have come down inconsistently on the rights and capacities of minors (Davis et al., 1997; Reppucci, 1999). Melton (1989) highlights the paradox of proportionality when he asks, "does recognition of due process rights for juveniles accused of delinquency imply that juveniles should be viewed as fully responsible for their behavior and subject to adult criminal sanctions?" (p. 284). Both Melton (1989) and Zimring (1982, 1998) argue that the age at which autonomous rights are first given to minors might rightfully be lower than the age at which they are first held fully responsible for their conduct. This argument is supported by research on children's decision-making competence in legal contexts, discussed later in this chapter. We next summarize social science research findings about children's understanding of the law and their rights. (For a broad overview of social science research used to test legal assumptions, see Bottoms, Reppucci, Tweed, & Nysse, in press.)

CHILDREN'S UNDERSTANDING OF THE LAW AND THEIR RIGHTS

Although recent years have seen the extension of certain rights to minors, children's cognitive and emotional developmental maturity may impact their ability to understand the legal system and assert their rights. According to Melton (1982), "if children are to participate more fully in self-determination as individuals, then increased awareness of children's comprehension of their rights (both 'natural' and 'legal') is necessary in order to facilitate legal education and to establish reasonable limits on the exercise of these rights" (p. 535). Research on children's understanding of the law and their rights has focused on two areas: children's conceptualizations of rights and the legal system and children's ability to invoke or protect their rights.

Children's Conceptualizations of Rights and the Legal System

June Tapp (1976; Tapp & Levine, 1974) initiated the study of children's understanding of the law within a cognitive developmental framework with her studies of the development of legal socialization in children in the 1970s. Relying on the developmental theories of Piaget and utilizing Kohlberg's terminology, Tapp and Levine (1974) introduced a cognitive developmental model of legal reasoning, which conceptualized children's problem-solving strategies and mental framework toward the law. Tapp and Levine combined moral development and legal reasoning theories into a three-stage model of development described by Tapp (1976) as involving a shift from "preconventional law-obeying, to a conventional law-and-order maintaining, to a postconventional law-making orientation" (p. 374). Their research showed that most adults in the United States maintain a conventional level of legal reasoning and suggested that children shift from preconventional to conventional legal reasoning in adolescence. (See Tapp, 1976, for a detailed review of this research.)

Melton (1980) furthered this research by testing the hypothesis that children develop a conception of their rights along a continuum similar to Tapp and Levine's three-stage model. In Melton's model, children progress in a stagelike manner beginning at Level I, in which they view rights egocentrically as anything they have or can do, but in which they also believe that rights may be revoked by an adult at any time. As children progress to Level II, they view rights as privileges granted for obeying rules. Progression to Level III involves a conceptualization of rights as principles required by dignity and freedom (Melton, 1980; Melton & Limber, 1992). Melton hypothesized that progress along this continuum would be a function of both developmental maturity and social class, with older and higher socioeconomic status (SES) children being more likely to view rights positively and assert rights for themselves. Melton's participants were 80 first, third, fifth, and seventh graders drawn evenly from a poor and an affluent suburb of Boston. Melton found strong support for his hypothesis that maturational factors in cognitive ability influence children's perceptions and assertions of both due process and self-determination rights. He also found that the higher SES children moved toward more mature views of rights about 2 years earlier than the lower SES children. Specifically, Melton found that regardless of social class, children in the first grade used Level I reasoning. By third grade, the majority of higher SES children had shifted to Level II reasoning; however, the lower SES children did not reach this level until fifth grade. In seventh grade, all of the children remained at Level II regardless of social class.

Subsequent research has supported the cognitive stage theories of legal development. Saywitz (1989) studied 48 children aged 4–14, half of whom had experience with the legal system as victim witnesses of child abuse. Concurring with Melton's (1980) finding that children have a concept of rights by third grade (age 8), Saywitz found that 8- to 9-year-olds had accurate conceptions of the court and its players. It was not until early adolescence (12–14 years old) that children demonstrated Tapp and Levine's (1974) conventional or Melton's Level II reasoning. Moreover, experience with the court system was not found to increase children's understanding and conceptualization of the court process (see also Grisso, 1981). Warren-Leubecker, Tate, Hinton, and Ozbek (1989) also found support for the developmental model but noted that children may experience a stage of misperceptions between lack of knowledge and understanding, in which they believe they understand a term but are actually confusing it with another (e.g., confusing *jury* with *jewelry*). Recently, Perry et al. (1995) have also found that the developmentally inappropriate language used by attorneys when questioning children (termed *lawyerese*) significantly impairs children's ability to comprehend and answer questions accurately.

In general, studies of children's concepts of their rights have shown that by the end of grade school, children have considerable knowledge of the legal process and an understanding of key legal vocabulary. However, understanding may develop at slightly different ages based on the difficulty of the legal concept, and knowledge of the process precedes understanding of vocabulary (Melton & Limber, 1992; see also Flin, Stevenson, & Davies, 1989; Peterson-Badali & Abramovitch, 1992; Peterson-Badali, Abramovitch, & Duda, 1997; Ruck, Keating, Abramovitch, & Koegl, 1998; Saywitz, Jaenicke, & Camparo, 1991). Unfortunately, the majority of these studies involve only White, middle-class participants, and none of them examine children's understanding of the law in legal settings. However, Melton and Limber suggest that children from disadvantaged backgrounds may be especially vulnerable to the legal system, because they may not be convinced that they really have rights and thus will not assert them. Moreover, the circumstances of arrest may impede children's ability to understand and assert their rights. In these cases, the extension of rights to children becomes meaningless (Peterson-Badali, Ambramovitch, Koegl, & Ruck, 1999).

Children's Ability to Invoke or Protect Their Rights

The Court first addressed children's ability to waive their rights prior to interrogation in the 1979 case of *Fare v. Michael C.* Michael was a 16-year-old boy with an extensive police record who had been brought in for questioning regarding a murder. He was read his *Miranda* warnings but was denied his request to have his probation officer present during the questioning. Michael subsequently made incriminating statements and drew pictures suggesting that he had been involved in the murder. The Court ruled that Michael's request for his probation officer did not constitute an invocation of his right to counsel, and that examination of the "totality of the circumstances" found that he had waived his rights knowingly, intelligently, and voluntarily. The Court cited Michael's previous experience with the police as evidence that he had sufficient understanding of the law to have knowingly and voluntarily waived his *Miranda* rights to counsel and to protection from self-incrimination.

The Court's decision in *Fare v. Michael C.* was the impetus for research on children's capacities to understand and invoke or waive their due process rights. The groundbreaking work in this area was Grisso's (1980, 1981) studies of juveniles' capacities to waive their *Miranda* rights. (See Woolard, this volume, for a detailed description of Grisso's work.) Grisso compared juveniles' capacities to waive their rights to silence and to a lawyer against an adult standard of understanding. He studied an ecologically valid sample consisting of juveniles recently admitted to a detention center, residents of a boys' town and a correctional boys' school, adult ex-offenders living in halfway houses, and adult nonoffenders from custodial and maintenance crews. In addition, he used multiple measures to assess comprehension of the words and phrases employed in the *Miranda* warning, as well as understanding of how *Miranda* rights function protectively during interrogation. Grisso found that, as a class, children under the age of 15 had significantly poorer understanding of both the content and the function of their rights of silence and counsel than adults of comparable intelligence. In contrast to Melton's (1980) findings, Grisso found that juveniles' understanding of *Miranda* rights was not significantly related to SES. Moreover, experience with the court system did not improve their comprehension of the words and phrases comprising the *Miranda* warning, but it was related to greater understanding of the protective function of rights during interrogation. Finally, Grisso found that although a majority of juveniles were able to apply rights to themselves in hypothetical legal situations, very few successfully invoked their rights during actual interrogations.

Grisso's findings reinforced earlier research (Grisso & Pomiciter, 1977), which also found that children rarely invoked their right against self-incrimination. In an examination of a random sample of juvenile felony referrals over a 3-year period (1974–1976), the researchers found that juveniles were questioned by police in 65–75% of the referrals and chose to talk in about 90% of these cases. Of the 10% of juveniles who refused to talk, almost all were older (15–16 years of age). Moreover, an increase in due process protections instituted in 1975 had no effect on the frequency with which children waived their right to silence.

More recently, Peterson-Badali et al. (1999) again established that children infrequently invoke their due process rights. In semistructured interviews with young offenders in Canada, these investigators found that whereas 63% of participants reported having been informed of their a right to silence, 59% of participants questioned by police waived their right to silence and to consult with a parent. Similarly, although 61% stated that they had been told of their right to counsel, 75% reported that they did not obtain a lawyer prior to questioning. The researchers noted practical limitations (e.g., not knowing *how* to call a lawyer) or misconceptions of rights as barriers to children's invocation of their rights.

Belter and Grisso (1984) further examined children's practical understanding of their rights in a study of minors' ability to recognize and protect themselves from rights violations in a hypothetical client–counselor relationship in a mental health setting. The researchers found that providing rights information to 15- and 21-year-olds significantly improved their ability to recognize rights violations and to recommend protective actions. However, 9-year-olds who received rights information prior to witnessing violations were no better at recognizing violations or protecting rights than same-age peers who had not received this information. In essence, although 9-year-olds could understand and accurately paraphrase their rights, they could not apply them in practice.

Abramovitch, Peterson-Badali, and Rohan (1995) found similar age effects in understanding and assertion of due process rights using hypothetical vignettes with a sample of 192 Canadian students in grades 6, 8, 10, and 13, as well as a group of 72 university students. Abramovitch and her colleagues found a significant difference in understanding of rights between grades 8 and 10, with only a third of the younger students displaying understanding. Moreover, about three-quarters of the sixth grade students indicated that they would waive their right to silence compared to about half of the students in grades 8, 10, and 13 and 40% of the university students.

What can be done to improve children's understanding and assertion of their rights? Researchers have generally concluded that experience with the juvenile justice system does not improve children's understanding of their rights (Grisso, 1980; Lawrence, 1983; Peterson-Badali and Koegl, 1998). Moreover, parents may not be of assistance; studies have shown that parents' understanding of the consequences of rights waiver is no better than that of their children (see, e.g., Grisso, 1981; Lawrence, 1983). Finally, Lawrence's research indicates that attorneys and juveniles alike may overestimate the juvenile client's understanding of the law.

Several suggestions have been made that might improve the situation for children. Peterson-Badali et al. (1999) underscore the need to educate children about their rights and the legal system before they encounter the courts. Once in the system, children should be offered a neutral, noncoercive atmosphere during questioning and should be provided with practical information such as how to contact a lawyer. In addition, lawyers and court personnel should take responsibility for ensuring children's understanding (Lawrence, 1983). Finally, Peterson-Badali et al. (1999) suggest that lawyers' effectiveness in assisting their juvenile clients may be enhanced by providing them with instruction based on relevant developmental research on children's legal knowledge, as well as developmentally appropriate communication techniques.

CHILDREN'S COMPETENCE TO MAKE LEGALLY RELEVANT DECISIONS

In establishing children as persons possessing rights, *In re Gault* (1967) brought to light the question of children's competence to exercise their rights (Melton, 1983). Whereas adults are presumed to be competent and must be demonstrated to be incompetent, the reverse is true for children. Moreover, a determination of competence in one setting does not deem a juvenile competent to make decisions in other contexts (Britner, LaFleur, & Whitehead, 1998; Koocher & DeMaso, 1990). Although competence may be seen as a prerequisite for the extension of self-determination rights, a more persuasive explanation for the concern over children's competence is rooted in the state's desire to protect children from harms incurred by their own poor decisions (Melton, 1984). According to Melton, "the overriding contemporary issue in the law affecting children is the limits of their competence, a question which on its face invites the attention of developmental psychologists" (p. 448).

In response to the Court's reliance on assumptions about children's competence, psychology has made tremendous contributions to the study of children's capacities in legal and medical contexts in the last 25 years. The study of competence was advanced with the publication of a book by Melton, Koocher, and Saks (1983) outlining knowledge and directions for social science research on children's competence. Since then, the study of competence has become a major subfield of study in psychology. In the remainder of this chapter, we highlight the issues of informed consent and competence and review research on children's competence to make legally relevant decisions with regard to medical treatment. (See Woolard, this volume, for an extended discussion of the research on the competencies relevant in a juvenile justice context, such as competence to assist counsel, to stand trial, and to waive *Miranda* rights.)

Informed Consent and Competence

The doctrine of informed consent is at the crux of the issue of children's competence to make their own medical decisions. Minors wishing to obtain medical treatment without parental consent must be able to render informed consent (Crosby & Reppucci, 1993). Three elements must be satisfied for legally valid informed consent (Grisso & Vierling, 1978; McCabe, 1996; Scherer & Reppucci, 1988; Weithorn & Campbell, 1982). First, the consent must be informed. *Informed* consent calls on a child's knowledge and understanding of the information given, as well as his or her cognitive capacities to consider reflectively the relevant alternatives, examine potential long- and short-term consequences, and weigh risks and benefits. Second, consent must be voluntary (i.e., free from coercion) and not simply based on deference to authority. Third, informed consent must be given competently. Although the Court has never outlined criteria for assessing adolescents' competence to consent to medical treatment (Crosby & Reppucci, 1993), competent consent has generally been defined as that in which the child demonstrates expression of a choice, a reasonable outcome of the decision, rational reasoning processes, and an understanding of the risks, benefits, and alternatives surrounding the decision (Meisl, Roth, & Lidz, 1977; Melton & Ehrenreich, 1992; Weithorn &

Campbell, 1982). Weithorn (1984) notes, however, that in practice, assessments of juveniles' competence are often based largely on factual understanding rather than appreciation and reasoning processes.

Social Science Research on Children's Competence

Informed Consent. In an initial examination of informed consent, Grisso and Vierling (1978) reviewed developmental theory and research and concluded that "[t]here appear to be no psychological grounds for maintaining the general legal assumption that minors at age 15 and above cannot provide competent consent" (p. 424). Moreover, Grisso and Vierling suggested that ages 11–14 constitute a transition period in which some adolescents may be able to provide competent informed consent and should be allowed to on a case-by-case basis.

Medical Treatment. Weithorn and Campbell (1982) were among the first to address empirically the issue of children's competence to make medical decisions. In a groundbreaking study comparing the decision-making capacities of children and adults, they presented a set of four hypothetical treatment vignettes followed by a structured interview to 9-, 14-, 18-, and 21-year-olds. Participants were instructed to pretend they were the story character, and treatment decisions were scored using the criteria of competence outlined previously. The researchers found that 14-year-olds demonstrated adult-level competence and that even 9-year-olds provided evidence of a choice and a reasonable outcome of that choice.

Several years later, Scherer and Reppucci (1988) explored the element of voluntariness in children's competence to provide informed consent. Using five hypothetical treatment dilemmas within which parental influence was either nonexistent, noncoercive, or coercive, the authors examined the treatment decisions of 40 14- and 15-year-olds. They found that, in general, adolescents deferred to parents' influence. This was especially true when the medical treatment in question had less serious consequences and when adolescents believed that the family stress caused by opposing the treatment was not worth enduring. However, adolescents were less likely to defer to parents' opinions when the treatment was of greater consequence (a kidney donation), especially when the parental influence was coercive. In a follow-up study, Scherer (1991) found that 9- to 10-year-old children were more likely to defer to parents than either 14- and 15-year-olds or young adults (21- to 25-year-olds) in the kidney donation scenario.

Abortion. The Supreme Court in *Bellotti v. Baird* (1979) outlined several assumptions about adolescents' vulnerability, inability to make reasoned decisions, and the criticality of the role of parents in child rearing. As the courts have continued to increase restrictions on adolescent abortion through the enforcement of parental consent and notification laws, social scientists have struggled to examine empirically the assumptions underlying these restrictions (Melton, 1987; Melton & Pliner, 1986).

Lewis (1980) was the first to examine adolescent girls' capacity to make an abortion decision in the ecologically valid context of a pregnancy clinic. She found that minors did not differ from adults in their ability to envision the potential consequences of the pregnancy decision, though they were more likely than adults to perceive their abortion decision as determined by external influences (e.g., lack of a job with which to support a child). In a later review of the research, Lewis (1987) drew four conclusions about minors' competence to consent to abortion. First, younger minors were more likely than older minors to consult their parents about the abortion decision. Second, minors making abortion decisions were *not* highly influenced by their peers. Third, developmental tasks of adolescence such as identity formation and increased autonomy were not found to impede adolescents' ability to forecast the potential consequences of their acts. Fourth, Lewis concluded that minors may demonstrate adult-level competence in reasoning ability but perform differently than adults in actual decision situations. Thus, Lewis' conclusions are generally positive regarding minors' ability to make independent decisions about abortion, although minors' differences in comparison to adults the actual decision situation suggest that they may be engaging in a distinct decision-making process and call for greater attention to this issue.

The debate surrounding adolescents' competence to consent to abortion was ignited among psychologists in 1987, when the American Psychological Association' Interdivisional Committee on Adolescent Abortion submitted an *amicus curiae* brief to the Supreme Court in the case of *Hartigan v. Zbaraz*. The brief's authors cited research by Weithorn and Campbell (1982) and Lewis (1980) in arguing the unconstitutional nature of a parental consent law for young women 14 years of age and older. In response to the brief, Gardner, Scherer, and Tester (1989) argued that it overstated the findings of psychological research on adolescents' decision-making skills. They outlined the limitations of the research used in the brief and underscored the difficulty in confirming a hypothesis that two groups do not differ appreciably, thus opening the door for more vigorous research on adolescents' competence in abortion decision making.

Ambuel and Rappaport (1992) took this research to a new level in their study of 75 young women, aged 13–21, in the midst of seeking a pregnancy test at a medical clinic. Participants took part in audiotaped interviews that were scored later on criteria of legal competence including voluntariness, reasoning ability, and depth of understanding of decision consequences. Comparing two groups of adolescents (youths who were 15 years old and younger and youths who were 16 to 17 years old) to a group of legal adults (aged 18–21), Ambuel and Rappaport found that only adolescents 15 years of age and younger who were *not* considering abortion did not appear as legally competent as adults.

Conclusions, Limitations, and Future Directions for Research

Over the course of the 20th century, children's nurturance rights have been fairly clearly delineated, though much discourse still surrounds the extension to minors of rights to self-determination. The last several decades have witnessed the initiation of empirical research designed to test empirically assumptions about children's understanding of and capacity to exercise their rights, not only within the arena of juvenile justice but also in medical, mental health, school, and family settings. With few exceptions (e.g., Ambuel & Rappaport, 1992), most studies of children's competence have been limited by majority White, middle-to upper-class, small samples and the use of hypothetical vignettes (McCabe, 1996; Scherer, 1991; Scherer & Reppucci, 1988; Weithorn & Campbell, 1982). Despite these limitations, researchers have generally concluded that minors 14 years of age and older are similar to adults with regard to cognitive capacities surrounding decision making (Britner et al., 1998).

Future research should address sample limitations and continue to compare children's capacities to an adult standard of competence in ecologically valid contexts (Britner et al., 1998; McCabe, 1996). Although adultlike cognitive capacities may exist, an adolescent's performance may be compromised by the demands of the decision at hand or the surrounding context (Britner et al., 1998; Melton & Stanley, 1996; Woolard, Reppucci, & Redding, 1996). According to Melton (1984), "that children have the *capacity* to perform competently and responsibly does not mean that they will exercise such maturity of judgment, particularly when the decision is made under circumstances of great stress, or when social norms elicit undesirable behavior" (pp. 465–466).

Scott, Reppucci, and Woolard (1995) and Steinberg and Cauffman (1996) have proposed an expanded framework through which to examine children's decision-making competence. Previous research has defined and examined competence solely in terms of cognitive capacities, neglecting developmental factors related to judgment in decision making. Scott et al. argue for the inclusion of judgment factors in assessing decision making competence on two accounts. First, if adolescents as a class demonstrate poorer judgment in decision making than adults, society's interest in preventing harm to adolescents (resulting from damaging decision outcomes) may rightfully outweigh the benefit of according adolescents freedom and accountability. Second, although adults are given the autonomy to make *poor* decisions on the basis of their established values and preferences, an adolescent's *poor* decision may actually reflect developmental factors that will change over time. As a result, Scott et al. proposed the examination of three developmental judgment factors in addition to cognitive capacities. These factors are attitude toward risk, including the focus on potential gains versus losses; temporal perspective, involving the weighing of short- and long-term consequences and risks versus benefits; and peer and parental influences. Steinberg and Cauffman (1996) have added to this list three "psychosocial" factors relating to maturity of judgment: responsibility, temperance (impulsivity), and perspective. (See Woolard, this volume, for a thorough discussion of children's decision-making competence in legal contexts.)

In the future, the Court will likely continue to extend to and withhold rights from children based on perceptions of their competence, raising additional questions about the balance of children's self-determination rights and their accountability for actions. As Zimring (1982) aptly states, however, "one cannot legislate maturity" (p. 241). According to Zimring, we must give juveniles the opportunity to learn to make independent decisions while at the same time minimizing harm to both the juvenile and the community. Psychologists can build on their past contributions to the law by continuing to examine empirically the Court's assumptions about children's understanding of their rights, as well as their competence to make legally relevant decisions across varying decision-making contexts.

References

Abramovitch, R., Peterson-Badali, M., & Rohan, M. (1995). Young people's understanding and assertion of their rights to silence and legal counsel. *Canadian Journal of Criminology, 37*, 1–18.

Ambuel, B., & Rappaport, J. (1992). Developmental trends in adolescents' psychological and legal competence to consent to abortion. *Law and Human Behavior, 16*, 129–154.

Appelbaum, P. S. (1989). Admitting children to psychiatric hospitals: A controversy revived. *Law & Psychiatry, 40*, 334–335.

Bellotti v. Baird, 443 U.S. 622 (1979).

Belter, R. W., & Grisso, T. (1984). Children's recognition of rights violations in counseling. *Professional Psychology: Research and Practice, 15*, 899–910.

Bottoms, B. L., Reppucci, N. D., Tweed, J. A., & Nysse, K. L. (in press). Children, psychology, and law Reflections on past and future contributions to science and policy. In J. Ogloff & Ron Roesch (Eds.), *Taking psychology and law into the 21st century.* New York: Kluwar Academic/Plenum Publishers.

Breed v. Jones, 421 U.S. 519 (1975).

Britner, P. A., LaFleur, S. J., & Whitehead, A. J. (1998). Evaluating juveniles' competence to make abortion decisions: How social science can inform the law. *The University of Chicago Roundtable, 5,* 35–62.

Caeti, T. J., Hemmens, C., & Burton, V. S., Jr. (1996). Juvenile right to counsel: A national comparison of state legal codes. *American Journal of Criminal Law, 23,* 611–632.

Chisholm, B. A. (1981). Children's rights. *Early Child Development and Care, 7,* 45–56.

City of Akron v. Akron Center for Reproductive Health, 462 U.S. 416 (1983).

Crosby, C. A., & Reppucci, N. D. (1993). The legal system and adolescents. In P. H. Tolan & B. J. Cohler (Eds.), *Handbook of clinical research and practice with adolescents* (pp. 281–304). New York: Wiley.

Crosby-Currie, C. (1996). Children's involvement in contested custody cases: Practices and experiences of legal and mental health professionals. *Law and Human Behavior, 20,* 289–311.

Crosby-Currie, C., & Reppucci, N. D. (1999). The missing child in child protection: The constitutional context of child maltreatment from *Meyer* to *Deshaney. Law & Society, 21,* 129–160.

Davis, S. M., & Schwartz, M. D. (1987). *Children's rights and the law.* Lexington, MA: D.C. Heath.

Davis, S. M., Scott, E. S., Wadlington, W., & Whitebread, C. H. (1997). *Children in the legal system* (2nd ed.). New York: Foundation Press.

DeShaney v. Winnebago County Department of Social Services, 489 U.S. 189 (1984).

Fare v. Michael C., 442 U.S. 707 (1979).

Flin, R. H., Stevenson, Y., & Davies, G. M. (1989). Children's knowledge of court proceedings. *British Journal of Psychology, 80,* 285–297.

Gardner, W., Scherer, D., & Tester, M. (1989). Asserting scientific authority: Cognitive development and adolescent legal rights. *American Psychologist, 44,* 895–902.

Goss v. Lopez, 419 U.S. 565 (1975).

Grisso, T. (1980). Juveniles' capacities to waive Miranda rights: An empirical analysis. *California Law Review, 68,* 1134–1166.

Grisso, T. (1981). *Juveniles' waiver of rights: Legal and psychological competence.* New York: Plenum.

Grisso, T., & Pomiciter, C. (1977). Interrogation of juveniles: An empirical study of procedures, safeguards, and rights waiver. *Law and Human Behavior, 1,* 321–342.

Grisso, T., & Vierling, L. (1978). Minors' consent to treatment: A developmental perspective. *Professional Psychology, 9,* 412–427.

Grossberg, M. (1993). Children's legal rights? A historical look at a legal paradox. In R. Wollons (Ed.), *Children at risk in America: History, concepts, and public policy* (pp. 111–140). Albany: State University of New York Press.

H.L. v. Matheson, 450 U.S. 398 (1981).

Harbin v. Harbin, 238 Ga. 109 (1976).

Hart, S. N. (1991). From property to person status: Historical perspective on children's rights. *American Psychologist, 46*, 53–59.

Hart, S. N. (1993). Children's rights in a civilized society. In M. A. Jensen & S. G. Goffin (Eds.), *Visions of entitlement* (pp. 85–131). Albany: State University of New York Press.

Hartigan v. Zbaraz, 484 U.S. 171 (1987).

Hazelwood School District v. Kuhlmeier, 484 U.S. 260 (1988).

Hodgson v. Minnesota, 497 U.S. 417 (1990).

In re Gault, 387 U.S. 1 (1967).

In re Winship, 397 U.S. 358 (1970).

Ingraham v. Wright, 430 U.S. 651 (1977).

Kent v. United States, 383 U.S. 541 (1966).

Kirby v. Illinois, 405 U.S. 951 (1972).

Koocher, G. P., & DeMaso, D. R. (1990). Children's competence to consent to medical procedures. *Pediatrician, 17*, 68–73.

Lawrence, R. A. (1983). The role of legal counsel in juveniles' understanding of their rights. *Juvenile & Family Court Journal, 34*, 49–58.

Lewis, C. C. (1980). A comparison of minors' and adults' pregnancy decisions. *American Journal of Orthopsychiatry, 50*, 446–453.

Lewis, C. C. (1987). Minors' competence to consent to abortion. *American Psychologist, 42*, 79–83.

Manfredi, C. P. (1998). *The Supreme Court and juvenile justice*. Lawrence: University Press of Kansas.

McCabe, M. A. (1996). Involving children and adolescents in medical decision making: Developmental and clinical considerations. *Law and Human Behavior, 21*, 505–516.

McKeiver v. Pennsylvania, 403 U.S. 528 (1971).

Meisl, A., Roth, L. H., & Lidz, C. W. (1977). Toward a model of the legal doctrine of informed consent. *American Journal of Psychiatry, 134*, 285–289.

Melton, G. B. (1980). Children's concepts of their rights. *Journal of Clinical Child Psychology, 9*, 186–190.

Melton, G. B. (1982). Children's rights: Where are the children? *American Journal of Orthopsychiatry, 52*, 530–538.

Melton, G. B. (1983). Toward "personhood" for adolescents: Autonomy and privacy as values in public policy. *American Psychologist, 38*, 99–103.

Melton, G. B. (1984). Developmental psychology and the law: The state of the art. *Journal of Family Law, 22*, 445–482.

Melton, G. B. (1987). Legal regulation of adolescent abortion: Unintended effects. *American Psychologist, 42*, 79–83.

Melton, G. B. (1989). Are adolescents people? Problems of liberty, entitlement, and responsibilty. In J. Worrell & F. Danner (Eds.), *The adolescent as decision-maker: Applications to development and education.* Educational psychology (pp. 281–306). San Diego, CA: Academic Press.

Melton, G. B., & Ehrenreich, N. S. (1992). Ethical and legal issues in mental health services for children. In C. E. Walker & M. C. Roberts (Eds.), *Handbook of clinical child psychology,* (2nd ed., pp. 1035–1055). New York: Wiley.

Melton, G. B., Koocher, G. P., & Saks, M. J. (1983). *Children's competence to consent.* New York: Plenum.

Melton, G. B., & Limber, S. P. (1992). What children's rights mean to children: Children's own views. In M. Freeman & P. Veerman (Eds.), *The ideologies of children's rights* (pp. 167–187). Dordrecht, the Netherlands: Martinus Nijhoff.

Melton, G. B., Lyons, P. M., Jr., & Spaulding, W. J. (1998). *No place to go: The civil commitment of minors.* Lincoln: University of Nebraska Press.

Melton, G. B., & Pliner, A. J. (1986). Adolescent abortion: A psychological analysis. In G. B. Melton (Ed.), *Adolescent abortion: Psychological and legal issues* (pp. 1–39). Lincoln: University of Nebraska Press.

Melton, G. B., & Stanley, B. H. (1996). Research involving special populations. In B. H. Stanley & Joan E. Sieber (Eds.), *Research ethics: A psychological approach* (pp. 177–202). Lincoln: University of Nebraska Press.

Meyer v. Nebraska, 262 U.S. 390 (1923).

Miranda v. Arizona, 384 U.S. 436 (1966).

Mnookin, R. H. (1978). Children's rights: Beyond kiddie libbers and child savers. *Journal of Clinical Child Psychology, 7,*163–167.

Mnookin, R. H. (1985). *Bellotti v. Baird*: A hard case. In R. H. Mnookin (Ed.), *In the interest of children: Advocacy, law reform, and public policy* (pp. 149–264). New York: W. H. Freeman.

New Jersey v. T.L.O., 469 U.S. 325 (1985).

Ohio v. Akron Center for Reproductive Health, 497 U.S. 502 (1990).

Parham v. J.R., 442 U.S. 584 (1979).

Penkower, J.A. (1996). The potential right of chronically ill adolescents to refuse life-saving medical treatment – Fatal misuse of the mature minor doctrine. *Depaul Law Review, 45,* 1165–1216.

Perry, N. W., McAuliff, B. D., Tam, P., Claycomb, L., Dostal, C., & Flanagan, C. (1995). When lawyers question children: Is justice served? *Law and Human Behavior, 19,* 609–629.

Peterson-Badali, M., & Abramovitch, R. (1992). Children's knowledge of the legal system: Are they competent to instruct legal counsel? *Canadian Journal of Criminology, 34,* 139–160.

Peterson-Badali, M., Abramovitch, R., & Duda, J. (1997). Young children's legal knowledge and reasoning ability. *Canadian Journal of Criminology, 39,* 145–170.

Peterson-Badali, M., Abramovitch, R., Koegl, C. J., & Ruck, M. D. (1999). Young people's experience of the Canadian youth justice system:

Interacting with police and legal counsel. *Behavioral Sciences and the Law,* *17,* 455–465.

Peterson-Badali, M., & Koegl, C. J. (1998). Young people's knowledge of the Young Offenders Act and the youth justice system. *Canadian Journal of Criminology, 40,* 127–152.

Pierce v. Society of Sisters, 268 U.S. 510 (1925).

Planned Parenthood of Central Missouri v. Danforth, 428 U.S. 52 (1976).

Pliner, A. J., & Yates, S. M. (1992). Psychological and legal issues in minors' rights to abortion. *Journal of Social Issues, 48,* 203–216.

Portwood, S. G., Reppucci, N. D., & Mitchell, M. S. (1998). Balancing rights and responsibilities: Legal perspectives on child maltreatment. In J. R. Lutzker (Ed.), *Handbook of child abuse research and treatment* (pp. 31–52). New York: Plenum.

Prince v. Massachusetts, 321 U.S. 158 (1944).

Reppucci, N. D. (1999). Adolescent development and juvenile justice. *American Journal of Community Psychology, 27,* 307–326.

Reppucci, N. D., & Crosby, C. A. (1993). Law, psychology, and children: Overarching issues. *Law and Human Behavior, 17,* 1–10.

Roe v. Wade, 410 U.S. 113 (1973).

Rogers, C. M., & Wrightsman, L. S. (1978). Attitudes toward children's rights: Nurturance or self-determination? *Journal of Social Issues, 34,* 59–68.

Ruck, M. D., Keating, D. P., Abramovitch, R., & Koegl, C. J. (1998). Adolescents' and children's knowledge about rights: Some evidence for how young people view rights in their own lives. *Journal of Adolescence, 21,* 275–289.

Saywitz, K. J. (1989). Children's conceptions of the legal system: "Court is a place to play basketball." In S. J. Ceci, D. F. Ross, & M. P. Toglia (Eds.), *Perspectives on children's testimony* (pp. 131–157). New York: Springer-Verlag.

Saywitz, K. J., Jaenicke, C., & Camparo, L. (1991). Children's knowledge of legal terminology. *Law & Human Behavior, 14,* 523–535.

Schall v. Martin, 467 U.S. 253 (1984).

Scherer, D. G. (1991). The capacities of minors to exercise voluntariness in medical treatment decisions. *Law & Human Behavior, 15,* 431–449.

Scherer, D. G., & Reppucci, N. D. (1988). Adolescents' capacities to provide voluntary informed consent: The effects of parental influence and medical dilemmas. *Law and Human Behavior, 12,* 123–141.

Scott, E. S. (1984). Adolescents' reproductive rights: Abortion, contraception, and sterilization. In N. D. Reppucci, L. A. Weithorn, E. P. Mulvey, & J. Monahan (Eds.), *Children, mental health, and the law* (pp. 125–150). Beverly Hills, CA: Sage.

Scott, E. S., Reppucci, N. D., & Aber, M. (1988). Children's preference in adjudicated custody decisions. *Georgia Law Review, 22,* 1035–1078.

Scott, E. S., Reppucci, N. D., & Woolard, J. L. (1995). Evaluating adolescent decision making in legal contexts. *Law and Human Behavior, 19,* 221–244.

Stanford v. Kentucky, 492 U.S. 361 (1989).

State In Interest of Causey, 363 So. 2d 472 (1978).

Steinberg, L., & Cauffman, E. (1996). Maturity of judgment in adolescence: Psychosocial factors in adolescent decision making. *Law and Human Behavior, 20,* 249–272.

Tapp, J. L. (1976). Psychology and the law: An overture. *Annual Review of Psychology, 27,* 359–404.

Tapp, J. L., & Levine, F. J. (1974). Legal socialization: Strategies for an ethical legality. *Stanford Law Review, 27,* 1–72.

Thompson v. Oklahoma, 487 U.S. 815 (1988).

Tinker v. DesMoines Independent Community School District, 393 U.S. 503 (1969).

Uniform Marriage and Divorce Act 402, 9 Uniform Laws Annotated 35 (1970, as amended 1971, 1973).

Wadlington, W. (1973). Minors and health care: The age of consent. *Osgood Hall Law Journal, 11,* 115–125.

Walker, N. E., Brooks, C. M., & Wrightsman, L. S. (1999). *Children's rights in the United States: In search of a national policy.* Thousand Oaks, CA: Sage.

Warren-Leubecker, A., Tate, C. S., Hinton, I. D., & Ozbek, N. (1989). What do children know about the legal system and when do they know it? First steps down a less traveled path in child witness research. In S. J. Ceci, D. F. Ross, & M. P. Toglia (Eds.), *Perspectives on children's testimony* (pp. 158–183). New York: Springer-Verlag.

Weithorn, L. A. (1984). Children's capacities in legal contexts. In N. D. Reppucci, L. A. Weithorn, E. P. Mulvey, & J. Monahan (Eds.), *Children, mental health, and the law* (pp. 125–150). Beverly Hills, CA: Sage.

Weithorn, L. A. (1988). Mental hospitalization of troublesome youth: An analysis of skyrocketing admission rates. *Stanford Law Review, 40,* 773–838.

Weithorn, L. A., & Campbell, S. B. (1982). The competency of children and adolescents to make informed treatment decisions. *Child Development, 53,* 1589–1598.

Winburn v. State, 32 Wis. 2d 152 (1966).

Wisconsin v. Yoder, 406 U.S. 205 (1972).

Woolard, J. L., Reppucci, N. D., & Redding, R. E. (1996). Theoretical and methodological issues in studying children's capacities in legal contexts. *Law and Human Behavior, 20,* 219–228.

Worrell, C. (1985). Pretrial detention of juveniles: Denial of equal protection masked by the parens patriae doctrine. *Yale Law Journal, 95,* 174–193.

Zimring, F. E. (1982). *The changing legal world of adolescence.* New York: Free Press.

Zimring, F. E. (1998). *American youth violence.* New York: Oxford University Press.

5

Children's Legal Representation in Civil Litigation

Ann M. Haralambie
Kari L. Nysse-Carris

Children's legal representation has developed in a largely ad hoc manner among the states, with little concern for traditional ethical principles of zealous advocacy, children's constitutional rights, or attorneys' malpractice liability (Haralambie, 1993). It has not even been clear whether children have any right to be represented in civil litigation by counsel, either appointed or privately retained. Although the U.S. Supreme Court articulated a constitutional right to independent representation for children in certain delinquency cases (*Arizona v. Gault*, 1967), no similar constitutional right has been declared for children involved in the child welfare system or family courts. (For a discussion of the history, current status, and future of the children's legal rights advocacy movement, see Small & Limber, this volume.)

Children most often have independent representation in child welfare proceedings filed by child protective services agencies to free children temporarily or permanently from their parents' care because of abuse, neglect, or abandonment. Much less frequently, children have independent representation in custody cases between the child's parents or between a parent and a private third party such as a grandparent. Children are more likely to have independent representation in custody cases when issues of abuse

Correspondence concerning this chapter should be addressed to Ann M. Haralambie, 3499 N. Campbell Avenue, Suite 901, Tucson, Arizona 85719-2376. Electronic mail may be sent via the Internet to ann.haralambie@azbar.org.

or neglect are raised by one of the private parties.[1] The rationale for appointing independent representation for children is (a) to provide an independent person to advocate for their best interests and (b) to give children a voice for their expressed position in cases that so directly impact their lives. These dual purposes sometimes put a child's attorney in conflicting roles. For example, if an attorney thinks that returning a child to the birth parents is not in the child's best interests, but the child expressly desires reunification with the parents, the attorney may be forced to choose between advocating for the child's best interests and advocating for the child's expressed wishes. Therefore, there has been a move toward clearly separating the roles, even having two representatives appointed for the child, one to advocate best interests and one to advocate expressed wishes.

The legal system, particularly the child welfare and domestic relations areas of law, has struggled to balance the competing interests of (a) children's beneficence and autonomy, (b) parental rights to family autonomy and privacy and states' rights to safeguard the well-being of children, and (c) whether other parties to litigation or the court can adequately represent children's legal interests. On the

---

[1] Appointment of counsel for children in custody cases is not nearly as widespread as in child welfare cases. Although most states permit such appointments, very few provide government funding for them, and even fewer require appointment (Haralambie, 1993). In most cases, counsel fees are paid by the parents, whose finances are often already depleted due to their own legal expenses. Courts have been reluctant to add to the parents' financial stress by requiring a third attorney for the child (American Academy of Matrimonial Lawyers [AAML], 1995). It has been argued that when courts have access to full time court-connected professionals who provide custody evaluations, there is no need for children to have independent legal representation. Some judges believe that the evaluator is in the best position to inform the court of the child's best interests and wishes. Some psychologists disagree, however, arguing that experts should not provide testimony as to the child's best interests (e.g., Goodman, Emery, & Haugaard, 1998). The idea of empowering children in their parent's divorce and postdivorce litigation is controversial. On the one hand, conventional wisdom says not to "put the children in the middle." On the other hand, children are already in the middle when their custody and visitation are being litigated. Children may become frustrated with their lack of voice in proceedings that directly affect them. Nevertheless, judges and matrimonial attorneys have tended to discourage appointment of attorneys for children in custody and visitation cases (AAML, 1996; National Council of Juvenile and Family Court Judges [NCJFCJ], 1998). For further discussion of issues relevant to children, divorce, and custody, see Depner, this volume.

one hand, the end of the 20th century saw increased professionaliza-
tion of legal child advocacy and a more sophisticated understanding
of what legal representation can and should be. The legal representation of children has become a recognized subspecialty, with its
own professional organizations, literature, and jurisprudence. On
the other hand, however, financial pressures reduced services of
all types for children and families. Legislatures are often reluctant
to provide funding for attorneys and are increasingly considering
models of representation that rely heavily on volunteers.

In this chapter we explore (a) the development of children's legal
representation, (b) various models of children's legal representation, and (c) the role of social science in legal representation. We
conclude by offering suggestions to improve children's representation. Although some attention is given to nonattorney models
for representing children in legal proceedings, we deal primarily with the various roles attorneys may play when representing
children. Because attorneys in quasi-criminal juvenile delinquency
cases function for the most part as they would for adult clients, we
do not discuss children's legal representation in delinquency cases.
For a discussion of children's legal representation in delinquency
cases, see Woolard, this volume.

HISTORICAL DEVELOPMENT OF LEGAL REPRESENTATION FOR CHILDREN

Historically, children were not perceived as having a legal right to
any kind of legal representation (Ventrell, 1995). When a child's
legal interests were at stake, it was assumed that either the parents, the child welfare agency, or the court could adequately protect
those interests (National Center on Child Abuse and Neglect, 1980).
Courts usually assumed that parents were the natural guardians of
their children's interests, and that until parents were proven to be
unfit, they were to act as their children's legal representatives in
court. This position has been advocated by some social scientists as
well (Goldstein, Solnit, Goldstein, & Freud, 1996). When the government brought an action against parents, the fact that the state agency
served more than one constituency (the public interest in protecting the child as *parens patriae* – the state acting to protect children,

the goal of family reunification, and stewardship over its budget) raised obvious conflicts of interest. Nevertheless, many courts and legislatures continued to assume that agency attorneys could serve children's interests in all but exceptional cases (Haralambie, 1997).

When independent counsel did represent children, the attorney's role was unclear. In some cases it was assumed that the attorney would act as a guardian *ad litem*, or an "arm of the court," to investigate and report the child's best interests or to advocate the position of the child's best interests. In other cases, the attorney was expected to act as a traditional attorney, advocating for the child's expressed position. Many times attorneys were expected to blend the roles, or attorneys assumed that they had the inherent authority to define their role as they saw fit. In most cases, neither statutes under which the attorneys were appointed, case law, ethical opinions, nor court order clarified the attorney's role (CSR, Inc., 1994; Haralambie, 1993).

When Congress enacted the Child Abuse Prevention and Treatment Act (CAPTA) in 1973, federal money was made available to states for guardians *ad litem* for children in child welfare cases. (The statute did not require that the guardians *ad litem* be attorneys.) When children in maltreatment cases were provided with attorneys during the 1970s, the representation tended to be paternalistic, based on the model of the guardian *ad litem* who advocated the "child's best interests" as determined by the attorney. States received federal credit for their CAPTA compliance, and attorneys could feel good about what they were doing for abused and neglected children. Attorneys operating under such undefined roles often failed to fulfill even the most basic duties ordinarily required of attorneys, such as meeting with the client, attending all hearings, and contacting the caseworker assigned to the case (CSR, Inc., 1994; Green & Dohrn, 1996). Even when attorneys acted zealously, their zeal often exceeded their knowledge, and their good intentions were not adequately informed by the social and behavioral sciences or by what was important from the child's perspective. The attorney's personal biases, prejudices, life experiences, and philosophies dictated the content of the representation in a very subjective manner. It may not be possible to eliminate the subjective from the determination of what is in the child's best interests (Mnookin, 1985), but today's trend is clearly to advocate a more objective process (American Bar Association [ABA], 1996; National Association of Counsel for Children [NACC], 2001; Proceedings, 1996).

Some early children's attorneys were well trained and thoughtful and ensured optimal legal outcomes for their clients. The legal system in general, however, did little to ensure consistency of representation. Judges often appointed newly admitted attorneys because they had time, needed the experience, and would work for little or no pay. Usually there were no experienced children's attorneys to mentor them, and there were no law books devoted to the field in which to find direction or assistance. Attorneys were left to their own devices both to define their own role and to educate themselves on how to perform it.

In the 1980s, pediatric law began to form as a distinct subspecialty within the law. The multidisciplinary National Association of Counsel for Children (NACC), founded in 1977, established early collaborations among pediatricians, psychologists, social workers, and attorneys and provided a rich resource for attorneys struggling to represent child clients competently. The NACC provided a structure (however informal and loosely organized) within which the profession and its jurisprudence could incubate. The fellowship of child advocates, often disrespected by other attorneys, derisively labeled as practicing "kiddie law," and largely underpaid, provided emotional support and encouragement that allowed many early child attorneys to remain involved in the field. Attorneys charged with representing abused and neglected children realized that they needed to be well versed in the social sciences, psychology, and medicine. The new subspecialty of attorneys became partners in a multidisciplinary model, at least with respect to ongoing training and consultation. This multidisciplinary focus continues to be an important characteristic of modern child advocacy (ABA, 1996; American Academy of Matrimonial Lawyers [AAML], 1995; NACC, 2001; National Council of Juvenile and Family Court Judges [NCJFCJ], 1998; Proceedings, 1996).

By the first half of the 1990s there still was no uniformity with respect to what it meant for an attorney to represent a child. The central question debated among attorneys and commentators was whether the attorney was expected to advocate the child's expressed wishes (the traditional attorney or client-centered model) or the attorney's perception of the child's best interests (the typical role of a guardian *ad litem*). Statutory language regarding appointment of representation for children tended to be vague and unhelpful. The statutes usually did not address the possible conflict between the child's expressed wishes and the attorney-determined best interests (e.g., a child wants to be reunited with an abusive parent, but the attorney deems separation to be in the child's best interests). Sometimes the statutory language was confusing or inconsistent, requiring the child's attorney to perform the two potentially conflicting duties of representing the child's best interests and advocating for the child's articulated wishes. Statutes used many words and phrases to refer to the child's representative, but they often did not define those terms. An appointment as *attorney* might or might not mean the same thing as appointment as *guardian ad litem, attorney ad litem,* or *law guardian.* An appointed guardian *ad litem* might actually be expected to function as a traditional attorney, representing the child's expressed wishes instead of the guardian *ad litem*'s traditional role of advocating what is believed to be the child's best interests (Haralambie, 1993; Ichikawa, 1997). The fact that these terms had no meaning beyond the particular state legislature's word to refer to the child's representative created much confusion.

Existing ethical rules still fail to provide adequate guidance to children's attorneys. Most states have adopted one of the two existing American Bar Association (ABA) model ethical codes. States have sometimes adopted one of the model codes, sometimes adapted them, and sometimes adopted their own independent ethical rules. The ethical rules of each state are binding on the attorneys practicing in that state. In this chapter, we use the ABA codes because most state ethical rules are based at least in part on one of these models. Whereas the Model Code of Professional Responsibility did not provide any direct guidance for attorneys representing children (ABA, 1969), the newer ABA Model Rules of Professional Conduct (1983) at least mentions the issue of the child's attorney. Specifically, Ethical Rule (ER) 1.14 of the Model Rules concerns clients under a disability, including the "disability of minority." ER 1.14(a) adopts the general principle that attorneys for children must, "as far as reasonably possible," maintain the traditional attorney's role toward child clients. Neither the rule nor its commentary, however, provides direction on how the child's attorney is supposed to modify the traditional representation to take account of the "disability." To address this lack of guidance, various professional organizations have introduced standards of practice (discussed in greater detail subsequently; e.g., AAML Standards [1995], which the first author criticized for theoretical and practical reasons [Haralambie & Glaser, 1995]), and several published law books on child advocacy (Duquette, 1990; Haralambie, 1993; Jacobs, 1995; Peters, 1997b) provide practical guidance and scholarly and theoretical underpinnings for the legal subspecialty of child advocacy. Further, professional journals, conferences, and multidisciplinary organizations also exist to assist attorneys who practice pediatric law.

The second half of the 1990s saw a remarkable consensus among scholars and commentators regarding the proper role of the child's attorney. The consensus tipped the autonomy-beneficence scale toward autonomy, adopting a traditional attorney–client model (with some modification) and an objective determination of the child's best interests for attorneys charged with determining the child's position. This consensus, however, is not universally shared by judges or practitioners, many of whom continue to prefer a blended role (e.g., NACC, 2001). Thus, the history of children's legal representation was initially marked by a lack of representation followed by often confusing and ill-defined roles. More recent developments have resulted in widespread agreement among professionals that children's attorneys should structure that relationship in light of the traditional attorney–client model. In the section that follows, we describe various models of representation available to children's attorneys. Where appropriate, we draw attention to professional standards that offer guidance on the attorney's role.

MODELS OF REPRESENTATION AND PROFESSIONAL STANDARDS
FOR REPRESENTING CHILDREN IN LEGAL SETTINGS

Attorneys provide legal representation for children pursuant to a number of models and roles. In some communities, representation

is provided through government agencies such as public de-
fender offices staffed with salaried attorneys, support staff, and
(occasionally) multidisciplinary staff resources. Some private child
advocacy centers and clinics provide representation through con-
tracts with the government and/or nonprofit donations and grants.
These private centers and clinics may be staffed by full-time attorneys, or the center's staff may train, coordinate, and supervise
volunteer attorneys from the community. Next, we discuss the
various attorney models, the barriers to effective use of attorney models, and nonattorney model alternatives. Various professional organizations such as the ABA, the American Academy
of Matrimonial Lawyers, legal scholars and practitioners who at-
tended the Fordham Conference on Ethical Issues in the Legal Representation of Children, and the National Council of Juvenile and
Family Court Judges have endorsed various components of these
representational models. Throughout the discussion we highlight
these professional organizations' stance on the various models.

Attorney Models

Traditional Attorney. The trend among scholars and commentators is to return child advocacy to the client-directed, traditional
attorney model, with some modifications to account for children's
developing capabilities (e.g., NACC, 2001). Under the traditional
attorney model, the attorney represents the child's expressed
wishes, regardless of what the attorney believes is the child's best
interests. For example, if a child expressed a desire to reside with
a maternal grandmother, the attorney operating under the traditional attorney model would zealously advocate for the child's wish
even if the attorney personally believed that the child would be
best served by residing with the paternal grandmother. The ABA
(1996) clearly stated that a child's attorney should be a lawyer who
provides the child with the same legal services and "undivided
loyalty, confidentiality, and competent representation" granted to
adult clients (p. 1).

   Suggested modifications of the client-directed, traditional attorney model acknowledge that children's cognitive and social development may limit their ability to assist their attorney. For example,

infants and young children with a limited vocabulary are unable to provide meaningful direction to their attorneys. In these cases, the attorney may need to make a principled, objective determination of the child's position (Proceedings, 1996). When a child is unable to assist the attorney, some legal scholars and practitioners suggest that lawyers consult multidisciplinary resources (e.g., social workers, psychologists, doctors) to make an objective determination of the child's best interests (ABA, 1996; Proceedings, 1996). Other professional organizations, however, recommend that lawyers do not take a position and that the court appoint a multidisciplinary expert as the child's guardian *ad litem* (AAML, 1995).

The ABA, American Academy of Matrimonial Lawyers, and legal scholars at the Fordham Conference (Proceedings, 1996) endorse the client-directed, traditional attorney model as the model of choice for children's representation. The traditional model allows attorneys to play a very familiar role – advocating for their client's wishes. Following a traditional model eliminates concerns about paternalism when making difficult decisions about the child's best interests because the lawyer is not called on to make "best interests" decisions. Traditional attorney models maximize the child's perspective and direct voice and minimize the attorney's ability to filter or undermine the child's position. Under this model, the child's attorney can propose creative solutions, focus attention on the child's perspective, and highlight how court decisions will impact important aspects of the child's life. The model also allows the child's attorney to pursue the child's objectives vigorously while pressuring the system and service providers to respond in a timely fashion to child desires.

The client-directed, traditional representation model is not without its critics, who argue that the model sacrifices children's beneficence for autonomy. The National Council of Juvenile and Family Court Judges (NCJFCJ, 1998) contends that the role of a child's court-appointed representative should vary as a function of case needs. For example, the National Council of Juvenile Family Court Judges argues that in some cases the child's representative should provide a fact-finding service for the court rather than zealously present the child's wishes. Such an investigative mission would be hampered by a traditional attorney model that emphasizes client loyalty.

Attorney as Guardian Ad Litem. Sometimes the court may appoint an attorney to act as the child's guardian *ad litem,* an officer of the court who is charged with protecting the child's best interests and whose determinations are not bound by the child's expressed wishes. Whether or not attorneys should act as guardians *ad litem* has become increasingly controversial. Most professional organizations such as the ABA (1996) and the scholars at the Fordham Conference (Proceedings, 1996) state a clear preference for attorneys to be appointed as the child's attorney and not as a guardian *ad litem* because the guardian *ad litem's* duties clearly conflict with advocating for the child's expressed wishes. Professional organizations recognize, however, that courts may appoint attorneys as guardians *ad litem.* Under the AAML Standards (1995), when an attorney is explicitly appointed as guardian *ad litem,* the attorney is prohibited from making recommendations about the outcome or contested issues of the litigation. The role of the attorney guardian *ad litem* is not to determine or advocate for the child's best interests but rather to focus on what is the best *process* by which the case should be decided. The ABA (1996) states that although an attorney may accept a dual appointment as attorney and guardian *ad litem,* the lawyer's primary duty should be to protect the child's legal rights and to perform all the functions of a client-directed, traditional attorney.

In contrast to the client-directed, traditional model, the guardian *ad litem* model maximizes the child's beneficence at the expense of the child's autonomy. Current guardian *ad litem* models require the child's representative to inform the court of the child's wishes, but the guardian *ad litem* is free to advocate against the child's own position. Most professional organizations recommend that lawyers not be appointed as guardians *ad litem* because lawyers are not trained to substitute their judgment for that of their clients in this way.

Attorney as Attorney and Guardian Ad Litem. Before the 1990s, the most common role adopted by or assigned to attorneys for children in child welfare cases was a dual attorney/guardian *ad litem* role. This position is fraught with ethical difficulties for attorneys because the functions of the client-directed, traditional attorney and those of the guardian *ad litem* may be diametrically opposed. As a result, most of the current scholarship and commentary discourage attorneys from assuming this dual role (AAML, 1995; ABA, 1996; Proceedings, 1996). When there is a direct conflict between the roles of traditional attorney and guardian *ad litem*, ABA Standard B-2 (1996) requires the attorney to continue to serve as attorney and to withdraw as guardian *ad litem*, requesting appointment of a separate guardian *ad litem* without revealing the basis for the request.

The benefit of the model of the attorney as attorney and guardian *ad litem* is that it provides maximum flexibility for the child's representative to define the role according to the shifting needs of the child's circumstances. The model is best suited to representation of a very young child or a child who is otherwise unable to direct the representation. Once the child is able to provide direction, however, attorney–client confidentiality may create an irreconcilable conflict between the dual roles. An attorney's duty of confidentiality ordinarily precludes divulging client confidences without the client's permission. If the attorney must also act as a guardian *ad litem*, making a recommendation regardless of the child's wishes, that recommendation may be based on information that was received by the attorney confidentially, and the guardian *ad litem* may even be required by his or her role to divulge the confidence itself to the court. Thus, although this model provides maximum flexibility, it can also present attorneys with ethical dilemmas.

Attorney Plus Separate Guardian Ad Litem. The ABA (1996) and Fordham Conference attendees (Proceedings, 1996) both addressed situations in which children may have both an attorney and a separate guardian *ad litem*. For example, in some cases, the attorney may have serious concerns about the safety of the position the child wishes to advocate. Although the two representatives may be arguing at cross-purposes, this model maximizes the child's voice and autonomy while also providing the court with objective information concerning the child's best interests. This model poses few if any ethical conflicts because the attorney (a) advocates the child's perspective of his or her own best interests and (b) is in a position to challenge any bias or inadequacy of the guardian *ad litem*'s position. The primary criticism of this model is the expense of having two separate representatives, which may make this approach impractical for many jurisdictions.

Attorney for Guardian Ad Litem. Some courts appoint a lay guardian *ad litem* for the child and an attorney to represent that guardian *ad litem*. In this model, the lawyer assumes a traditional role, being bound by the ethical and lawful directions of the client, who is the adult guardian *ad litem*. The court obtains the child's best interests position through the lawyer's advocacy of what the guardian *ad litem* has determined by independent investigation and analysis. This model is consistent with all of the existing national standards of practice. It avoids the ethical problems of the lawyer acting directly as guardian *ad litem*. However, this model does not provide the child with a direct voice in the proceeding and requires the appointment of two separate adults. Therefore it continues to disenfranchise the child who wishes to express a position and may be impractical because of the expense.

Attorney/Expert Team. The growing recognition that lawyers lack the training to make an independent determination of a child's best interests has caused a majority of legal scholars and commentators to reject the idea that lawyers should accept representation that requires them to make a best interests determination. It has been suggested, however, that lawyers can function in this traditional guardian *ad litem* role by joining with psychologists or social workers to form a representational team (Duquette, 1992; Jones & Snow, 1997; Weinberg, Weinberg, & Shea, 1997). Under this model, the expert determines the child's best interests, and the lawyer advocates for that position.

On the one hand, this model may not provide the child with a direct voice in the proceeding. Further, the role of the expert is not always well defined. If the expert is a consultant to the attorney, helping to formulate the position to be advocated, then the combined team becomes, in effect, a guardian *ad litem*. On the other hand, the expert may serve as a resource to assist the attorney to communicate effectively with the child client and to analyze and present evidence in furtherance of the child's position. It should be noted that experts disagree about the usefulness of this model.

For example, Goodman, Emery, and Haugaard (1998) suggest that experts such as psychologists and social workers should not offer expert testimony or advice as to the best interests of a particular child because of the difficulty associated with (a) making an objective determination and (b) making idiographic predictions from a nomothetic science.

Law Student Clinic Model. Another model of representation is for children to be represented by law students under the supervision of law school faculty through law school clinics (Hill, 1998). Some programs may have ancillary resources from affiliated schools of social work, medicine, and psychology. Law students are often extremely motivated to spend time investigating and preparing their cases. In prolonged child welfare proceedings, however, several different student lawyers are likely to represent the child before the case is concluded, which hampers continuity of representation and rapport between the child and legal representative.

Peters Model. A state-of-the-art model for children's legal representation formulated by Peters (1997b) attempts to provide lawyers with principled and objective guidance about the child's best interests. Fordham Conference attendees (Proceedings, 1996), in essence, adopted the Peters model concerning how children's attorneys should determine the child's best interests. Peters advocates for a "deeply contextual representation" of the child and rejects the best interests versus child's wishes dichotomy. Her model provides attorneys with a process that is guided by three defaults, three principles, and self-assessment questions. The three defaults require attorneys to (a) become acquainted with the child, (b) explore fully the child's competence to contribute to his or her case, and (c) either advocate for the child's desires (even if the attorney disagrees) or, when the attorney is explicitly required, represent the child's best interests and express the child's wishes within the context of representing the child's best interests. Peters recommends that attorneys' actions be guided by three principles as a case unfolds. Specifically, attorneys are to (a) act in ways that reflect their developing understanding of the child-in-context and the theory of the case, (b) respect one's client, whether present or absent, and (c) cultivate right relationships with people in the child's life, keeping in mind the ways in which the child values each of these relationships. These principles require attorneys to familiarize themselves with the rich texture of the child's life, to appreciate the child's perspective, and to recognize the limitations of the ephemeral involvement of the attorney and the legal system in the child's long-term life. Finally, Peters urges attorneys to assess continually their actions on the child's behalf. For example, attorneys should continually ask themselves if they are viewing the case through the eyes of the child, if they are altering their actions in ways that they would not for an adult client, if they are explaining as much about the case as the child can understand, and if they are making decisions based on their own desires rather than the child's desires.

The Peters model provides a continuum and a context that allow the attorney to act as an attorney and to recognize when the child cannot assist the attorney. The model reminds attorneys that they are transient and relatively unimportant players in their child clients' lives, and that they must respect the relationships and systems that will remain with the child long after the attorneys are gone. The model does not allow for subjective substitute decision making. Rather, it requires a time-intensive and objective process of determining the child's position. When the child does not provide direction, this model permits the attorney to present multiple alternatives if analysis does not lead to one clearly superior position or to decline to take a position if there is no objective basis for doing so. The model strikes an appropriate balance between autonomy and beneficence, allows for the flexibility necessary for dealing with an ever-developing child client, and avoids many ethical conflicts. The primary criticism leveled against the model is that it may be unrealistic to expect attorneys to commit the time and resources necessary to implement it.

Barriers to Effective Use of Attorney Models. Obviously, lawyers may be asked to represent children's legal interests under the guidance of various models. Standards of practice authored by professional organizations such as the ABA (1996) and the AAML (1995) strongly recommend that attorneys represent children under the direction of the client-directed, traditional attorney model. As discussed next, there are barriers to effective use and implementation of these attorney models.

Attorneys have at their disposal a wide array of investigative and advocacy tools to represent children effectively in court cases. Lawyers are trained to analyze the facts and issues of the case and to advocate vigorously for their child clients. Lack of time and resources often limit their ability to provide competent and ethical services. Even the most diligent attorney may not be able to provide excellent advocacy in the face of a heavy caseload and a lack of resources. In most jurisdictions, multidisciplinary support services are not available to court-appointed attorneys. Similarly, courts often do not fund independent expert consultants or witnesses or reimburse out-of-pocket expenses.

In custody and visitation. cases, most states require that the attorney be paid, if at all, by the parents, who usually have enough difficulty paying their own attorneys. Even in child welfare cases, in which government payment is more likely, appointed attorneys are generally poorly paid. If attorneys are paid an hourly rate, it is usually very low compared to what those same attorneys charge paying clients, and in many cases the payment may not even cover the attorney's basic overhead expenses. If attorneys are paid on a per case or other flat fee basis, there is a financial disincentive to spend adequate time on a case. Conscientious and diligent attorneys may gross less than the minimum wage on some cases. Worse yet, some courts rely largely or entirely on *pro bono* representation. Although all attorneys have an ethical obligation to provide *pro bono* services, it is not possible for most attorneys to specialize in an area when they are never paid for their services. Because there is now a clear recognition that representing children requires specialized and ongoing training, it is disheartening to see increased pressure to rely on volunteer attorneys to represent children.

Society does not expect pediatricians and child psychologists to provide all or most of their services to children at no cost, but many courts, legislatures, and even local bar associations expect attorneys who specialize in child advocacy to do so. Nor does society entrust our children's medical care to moonlighting gerontologists and proctologists, but it encourages corporate attorneys and personal injury attorneys to take child welfare cases on a *pro bono* basis. Such expectations devalue the need for specialized training and render it difficult for attorneys to develop and maintain their expertise as child advocates unless they do so as a sideline to another area of practice.

A careful reading of all of the new standards for child representation, particularly the Peters model, reveals how short attorneys fall in meeting the legitimate legal needs of child clients. It is humbling to realize how much damage attorneys can do to a young life by cavalier and perfunctory representation. In the reality of a legal practice, attorneys cannot represent children as they are instructed. But they must. The poetic admonition to let our reach exceed our grasp comes readily to mind. Peters' model defines our reach, and child advocates from all disciplines, in turn, will need to renew the effort to fight for the systemic changes (such as appropriate caseloads, adequate compensation, and the availability of multidisciplinary resources) that will allow attorneys to come closer to what ethics, risk management, and beneficence call them to do.

Nonattorney Models

Courts are not limited to attorney-based means of child representation. Sometimes, courts turn to nonattorneys or laypersons to provide children with much needed representation. Nonattorneys do not provide *legal* representation for children; instead, they perform a fact-finding role or advocate for a specific position. We briefly discuss these models in this chapter because in some jurisdictions a nonattorney or layperson is the only person considered by the court as representing solely the interests of the child. We will specifically highlight the guardian *ad litem* and court-appointed special advocate models.

Guardian Ad Litem. In some states, guardians *ad litem* are considered to be independent parties to the proceeding, but in many they are not, serving only as investigators who function as an arm of the court. They are sometimes described as "the eyes and ears of the court." Guardians *ad litem* are expected to determine and inform the court of the child's best interests.

Representation provided by nonattorney guardians *ad litem* may involve lay guardians *ad litem* or experts serving in that role. Often guardians *ad litem* are volunteers, making their use fiscally attractive to courts. Experts such as psychologists, social workers, physicians, or educators who serve as guardians *ad litem* may provide special assistance to the court by helping to assess the child's particular needs and to provide objective analysis of the opinions of other experts. When the court determines that a guardian *ad litem* should be appointed for a child, some scholars suggest that a layperson should fulfill that role because (a) attorneys may not have any special qualifications that allow them to determine a child's best interests and (b) there may be ethical dilemmas with attorneys doing so (ABA, 1996; NCJFCJ, 1998; Proceedings, 1996). As mentioned earlier, however, some scholars do not recommend that psychologists, social workers, or physicians be called on to make an objective determination of the child's best interests (e.g., Emery & Rogers, 1990; Goodman et al., 1998).

Court-Appointed Special Advocate. Perhaps the most popular form of lay volunteer advocacy for children is the court-appointed special advocate (CASA). Organized CASA programs exist in all 50 states; however, there are various CASA models. The National Court Appointed Special Advocate Association provides various services to state and local CASA programs as well as to individual CASAs. CASAs may serve as the child's sole representative, but some juvenile courts appoint both a CASA and an attorney for the child, a model encouraged by one comprehensive national study of legal representation for children (CSR, Inc., 1994).

The CASA investigates the case and provides the court with information, and perhaps recommendations, concerning the child's best interests. Under this model, the attorney and CASA may or may not act as a team. When the CASA and the attorney take similar positions, they can often be of great assistance to one another. For example, the CASA may have more time to investigate facts and collect information. The attorney may be able to subpoena records, take depositions, and otherwise obtain information through formal legal discovery procedures. In other cases, the CASA and the child's attorney take inconsistent positions, especially when the attorney is functioning in the traditional role of advocating for the client's expressed position.

Some CASA programs provide a staff or contract attorney who is available to represent the CASA in court. However, not all CASA programs operate on a guardian *ad litem* model. In such circumstances, the CASA may not be considered a separate party entitled to independent legal representation.

ROLE OF SOCIAL SCIENCE IN ADVANCING KNOWLEDGE RELEVANT TO CHILDREN'S LEGAL REPRESENTATION

Social scientists with interests in children and law use the scientific method to test legal assumptions relevant to children. Their findings can inform the law and bring about policy change. For example, in an influential decision about testimonial accommodations for children such as closed circuit television (*Maryland v. Craig*, 1990), the U.S. Supreme Court relied heavily on social science evidence about children's abilities. The information reached the court in the form of an *amicus curiae* brief prepared largely by psychologists (e.g., Goodman, Levine, Melton, & Ogden, 1991). Likewise, social scientists are equipped to address legal issues surrounding children's legal representation, and we suggest that they should. In this chapter, we have discussed various models of representation available to attorneys and nonattorneys who represent children. Social scientists ought to be able to contribute to society's understanding of children's legal representation by using social scientific research methods to test legal assumptions. For example, researchers could evaluate the effectiveness of the various representation models in terms of child, parent, and attorney satisfaction or in terms of other measures such as the stability of the child's placement in custody cases. A large body of social psychological research and theory suggests that, in other domains, adults and children express greater satisfaction with and acceptance of outcomes when they believe they have had a voice in the process leading to those outcomes (e.g., Folger, 1977; Lind, Kulik, Ambrose, & De Vera Park, 1993; Lind & Tyler, 1988). Social scientists could investigate whether children express greater satisfaction with custody decisions when they express their desires and feel those desires are seriously represented, as opposed to when they are not given an opportunity to voice their concerns.

Another topic open to scientific inquiry is the effect of child age and maturation on children's ability to assist their legal representative and the appropriateness of the various representation models. When are children mature enough to express desires based on reasonable considerations? Should the child's age dictate the use of one representation model over another? Further, an important component of guardian *ad litem* models is the ability of experts to determine a child's best interests. Currently, social scientists disagree about whether this is ethical or even possible. Even so, through evaluation studies of custody placements, social scientists should be able to move closer to the identification of criteria that should be considered when making such a determination. Finally, psychologists could explore educational partnerships in which they could educate lawyers about child development issues that affect the ability to communicate effectively with children.

CONCLUSION

Despite a growing consensus that attorneys should represent children under the direction of the client-directed, traditional attorney model, states and individual judges still sometimes hold other expectations for children's attorneys. Existing standards and various legal commentators and organizations agree that children's attorneys require multidisciplinary training in a variety of areas. As the ABA (1996) and the Fordham Conference attendees (Proceedings, 1996) urge, judges who hear child maltreatment cases must insist on appropriate multidisciplinary training for all attorneys who represent children and must use their influence to ensure realistic caseloads, reasonable compensation, and adequate access to multidisciplinary resources for court-appointed attorneys for children.

To achieve multidisciplinary training, the mental health, medical, and social service communities must be willing to educate and mentor children's attorneys. Few would dispute that the standard of practice in the child welfare arena is a multidisciplinary one (Sorenson, Bottoms, & Perona, 1997), and the child's attorney is an important part of the process. Even though other child advocates may be frustrated by an attorney who advocates what the child wants irrespective of what the attorney deems to be in the child's best interests, they must respect the legitimacy of the attorney's role. There is nothing inappropriate about trying to persuade the child's attorney concerning the child's best interests; the attorney can then use that information in advising the child client. In the end, however, the attorney may be bound by what the child wishes.

At this time it appears that children will be given a greater role in their own representation. It should be remembered, however, that the child's articulated position is only one position to be considered by the judge. It is not the final decision in the case. The child's attorney gives the child a personal voice in the proceedings. Other parties and witnesses contribute to the judge's overall view of the case. The judge must evaluate the facts and the law and render a decision, not merely defer to recommendations made by a particular expert or the child's attorney.

As experienced child advocates recognize the paucity of good outcome data, the shortage of substantial better alternatives for children, and the long-term damage that can be done to children and their families from shortsighted interventions, many choose to give children a real voice in legal proceedings rather than merely the illusion of a voice. Whether or not the position prevails, respect for the child – the subject of our best interests analysis – demands that the child's position, as advanced from the child's unique perspective, be represented in court. Experienced and principled attorneys for children do not all reach the same conclusions in balancing the goals of maximizing the child's autonomy and voice with extending protective beneficence to children who have already been victimized (Federle, 1996; Guggenheim, 1996; Haralambie & Glaser, 1995; Marguilies, 1996; NACC, 1997; Peters, 1997a). The challenge is to provide a context in which the child's legal representative can assess the child's position and provide informed and meaningful guidance to the child. Partnerships between the courts and social scientists may bring us closer to meeting this challenge.

References

American Academy of Matrimonial Lawyers. (1995). *Representing children: standards for attorneys and guardians ad litem in custody or visitation proceedings*. Chicago: Author.

American Bar Association. (1969). *Model code of professional responsibility*. Chicago: Author.

American Bar Association. (1983). *Model rules of professional conduct*. Chicago: Author.

American Bar Association. (1996). *Standards of practice for lawyers who represent children in abuse and neglect cases*. Chicago: Author.

Arizona v. Gault, 387 U.S. 1 (1967).

Child Abuse Prevention and Treatment Act (CAPTA), P.L. 93–247.

CSR, Inc. (1994). *Final report on the validation and effectiveness study of legal representation through guardians ad litem*. Washington, DC: U.S. Department of Health and Human Services.

Duquette, D. (1990). *Advocating for the child in protection proceedings: A handbook for lawyers and court appointed special advocates*. Lexington, MA: Lexington Books.

Duquette, D. (1992). Child protection legal process: Comparing the United States and Great Britain. *Pittsburgh Law Review, 54*, 239–294.

Emery, R. E., & Rogers, K. C. (1990). The role of behavior therapists in child custody cases. In M. Hersen & R. M. Eisler (Eds.), *Progress in behavior modification* (pp. 60–89). Beverly Hills, CA: Sage.

Federle, K. H. (1996). The ethics of empowerment: Rethinking the role of lawyers in interviewing and counseling the child client. *Fordham Law Review, 64*, 1655–1697.

Folger, R. (1977). Distributive and procedural justice: Combined impact of "voice" and improvement on experienced inequity. *Journal of Personality and Social Psychology, 35*, 108–119.

Goldstein, J., Solnit, A. J., Goldstein, S., & Freud, A. (1996). *The best interests of the child: The least detrimental alternative*. New York: Free Press.

Goodman, G. S., Emery, R. E., & Haugaard, J. J. (1998). Developmental psychology and law: Divorce, child maltreatment, foster care, and adoption. In I. Siegel & A. Renninger (Eds.), *Child psychology in practice* (pp. 775–876), in W. Damon (Series Ed.), *Handbook of child psychology* (Vol. 4). New York: Wiley.

Goodman, G. S., Levine, M., Melton, G. B., & Ogden, D. (1991). *Craig vs. Maryland.* Amicus brief to the U.S. Supreme Court on behalf of the American Psychological Association. *Law and Human Behavior, 15*, 13–30.

Green, A., & Dohrn, B. (1996). Forward: Children and the ethical practice of law. *Fordham Law Review, 64*, 1281–1298.

Guggenheim, M. (1996). A paradigm for determining the role of counsel for children. *Fordham Law Review, 64*, 1399–1433.

Haralambie, A. M. (1993). *The child's attorney: A guide to representing children in custody, adoption, and protection cases.* Chicago: American Bar Association.

Haralambie, A. M. (1997). Current trends in legal representation. *Child Maltreatment, 2,* 193–201.

Haralambie, A. M., & Glaser, D. L. (1995). Practical and theoretical problems with the AAML Standards for representing "impaired" children. *Journal of the American Academy of Matrimonial Lawyers, 13,* 57–94.

Hill, F. G. (1998). Clinical education and the "best interest" representation of children in custody disputes: Challenges and opportunities in lawyering and pedagogy. *Indiana Law Journal, 73,* 605–633.

Ichikawa, D. P. (1997). An argument on behalf of children. *Child Maltreatment, 2,* 202–212.

Jacobs, T. A. (1995). *Children and the law: Rights and obligations.* St. Paul, MN: West Group.

Jones, L. R., & Snow, J. E. (1997). *Two voices, one vision: The ethical imperative for mental health professional-attorney representation of children.* Unpublished manuscript.

Lind, E. A., Kulik, C. T., Ambrose, M., & De Vera Park, M. V. (1993). Individual and corporate dispute resolution: Using procedural fairness as a decision heuristic. *Administrative Science Quarterly, 38,* 224–251.

Lind, E. A., & Tyler, T. R. (1988). *The social psychology of procedural justice.* New York: Plenum.

Marguilies, P. (1996). The lawyer as caregiver: Child client's competence in context. *Fordham Law Review, 64,* 1473–1504.

Maryland v. Craig, 497 U.S. 836 (1990).

Mnookin, R. (1985). *In the interest of children: Advocacy, law reform, and public policy.* New York: W. H. Freeman.

National Association of Counsel for Children. (2001). Recommendations on the representation of children in abuse and neglect cases. *Advocacy for children and families: Moving from sympathy to empathy* (pp. 95–112). Denver, CO: Author.

National Center on Child Abuse and Neglect. (1980). *Representation for the abused and neglected child: The guardian ad litem and legal counsel.* Washington, DC: U.S. Department of Health and Human Services.

National Council of Juvenile and Family Court Judges. (1998). *Principles for appointment of representatives for children in custody and visitation proceedings.*

Peters, J. K. (1997a). The lawyer in the interdisciplinary meeting. *Child Maltreatment, 2,* 226–244.

Peters, J. K. (1997b). *Representing children in child protective proceedings: Context, ethics and practice.* Charlottesville, VA: Michie Company.

Proceedings of the conference on ethical issues in the legal representation of children: Recommendations of the conference. (1996). *Fordham Law Review, 64,* 1301–1323.

Sorenson, E., Bottoms, B. L., & Perona, A. (1997). *Intake and forensic interviewing in the children's advocacy center setting: A handbook.* Washington, DC: National Network of Children's Advocacy Centers.

Ventrell, M. R. (1995). Rights and duties: An overview of the attorney–child client relationship. *Loyola University of Chicago Law Review, 26,* 259–285.

Weinberg, L. A., Weinberg, C., & Shea, N. M. (1997). Advocacy's role in identifying dysfunctions in agencies serving abused and neglected children. *Child Maltreatment, 2,* 212–225.

PART II

CHILDREN AND FAMILY CHANGE

6

Termination of Parental Rights to Free Children for Adoption

Conflicts between Parents, Children, and the State

Jeffrey J. Haugaard
Rosemary J. Avery

Before a child can be adopted into a new family, the rights of the child's birth parents must be totally and irrevocably terminated. As a result, thousands of children every year are affected by the legal process of terminating parental rights. In many cases of infant adoption, a birth mother and birth father voluntarily relinquish their rights over a child – a process that they may agree to months before their child is born. In other cases of infant adoption, and often when an older child is adopted, parental rights are terminated involuntarily as a result of a judicial determination that the birth parents are unable to provide adequate parenting. Consequently, every adoption is preceded by a termination, and public policy on adoption is always entangled in legal proceedings regarding the termination of parental rights.

In this chapter we focus on the process and consequences of the termination of parental rights, and in particular on cases in which termination of parental rights is being pursued because children have been chronically or severely maltreated by their parents or other caregivers. We start with a discussion of the need to balance the rights of parents and children in termination cases and efforts of current and past policy to do so. We then describe current laws regarding the legal process involved in the termination of parental rights and the ways in which the needs, rights, and obligations of parents, children, and the state are balanced in such proceedings. We then explore some of the consequences of current policy by focusing on social science research that examines the consequences to children of protracted versus rapid termination of their parents' rights in cases where the children have been abused or neglected. We focus almost exclusively on the consequences to children because of the lack of research on the consequences to parents of having their parental rights terminated. Finally, we discuss the ways in which changes to public policy might benefit children, their birth families, and potential adoptive families.

BALANCING THE RIGHTS OF PARENTS, FAMILIES, AND CHILDREN

The involuntary termination of parental rights is a striking example of the ways in which the needs, rights, and obligations of parents, families, children, and the state can come into conflict. Many of these cases are the result of situations in which parents have chronically or severely maltreated their children. When parental maltreatment threatens the well-being of a child, the state's interest in preserving and strengthening families can conflict with its interest in protecting children and providing them with the opportunity to develop in a healthy way. Parents' rights to raise their children as they see fit can conflict with laws placing limits on parents' actions and with laws mandating removal of children from their homes when it appears that their right to a reasonably safe existence is being threatened. Children's need to remain connected to their parents and siblings may conflict with their need to be raised by parents who can provide an adequate environment for their development.

When a child is identified as neglected or maltreated, agents of the state (typically a department of social services and/or a family court) must initially decide whether it is safe to leave the child in the home and work to rehabilitate the family by providing services or whether it is in the child's best interest to place the child in temporary foster care until such a time as it is safe to return the child to the home. They must later decide whether children who have been temporarily placed in foster care should be returned home, remain in temporary care, or be placed in a permanent adoptive home. There are some situations in which timely rehabilitation of a birth family is likely, such as when a young mother neglects the needs of her child because of a lack of knowledge of child development.

There are other situations, however, in which successful reunification with birth parents appears very unlikely, such as when a parent murders one of several siblings (Hardin & Lancour, 1996). Difficulties arise when it is not clear whether the parents can be helped to provide adequate parenting to their children within a reasonable period of time. Although reasonable efforts to support and preserve birth families are both desirable and required by law, undertaking extensive and long-term but futile efforts to preserve a birth family absorbs scarce resources and requires that a child remain in one or more long-term foster placements, substantially damaging the child's prospect for permanency in adoptive placement.

Policy shifts over the past few decades have reflected changing beliefs about the balance between the importance of maintaining children in their birth homes and removing children permanently from their birth homes so that they are available for adoption by another family. Prior to 1980, the prolonged placement of children in foster care was a long-standing concern of child welfare professionals, as evidenced by the accumulation of a substantial body of research following Maas and Engler's (1959) landmark study of foster care drift – a situation in which children spend a prolonged amount of time in foster care, possibly in several placements, without ever being placed in a permanent home. In response to this looming public policy problem, the federal Adoption Assistance and Child Welfare Act (AACWA) became law in 1980, with the goals of preventing unnecessary foster care placements, reunifying families when possible, and limiting time spent in foster care by encouraging adoption when return to a birth parent is not possible. Child welfare agencies were compelled to pursue family rehabilitation efforts vigorously because of the law's requirement of extensive and diligent efforts to rehabilitate the parents and preserve the family (Hardin & Lancour, 1996). Critics of the AACWA argued that many states interpreted these efforts to mean every possible effort and that these vigorous efforts often delayed the inevitable permanent separation of children from their birth parents. In fact, evidence suggests that the law was largely unsuccessful in achieving the goals of keeping birth families together or of having children adopted swiftly when adoption was necessary (White, Albers, & Bitonti, 1996).

In response to the continuing escalation of the foster care problem during the 1990s, the U.S. Congress passed the Adoption and Safe Families Act (ASFA) in 1997. One of the primary purposes of ASFA was to correct many of the deficiencies of its predecessor regarding the termination of parental rights. The AACWA's requirement that states use extensive and diligent efforts to rehabilitate the parents and preserve the family was criticized as going too far to ensure family preservation. ASFA clarified the reasonable-efforts requirement and stated that child safety was paramount in all foster-care decisions. In effect, ASFA tightened two important time lines for children in foster care: those regarding the state's development of a plan for the permanent placement of the child and those regarding the termination of parental rights. The ASFA requires that a permanency hearing (a court hearing presided over by a family court judge that reviews a child's temporary status and permanency goals) be held within 12 months of the child's entering foster care. It also requires that the state file or join a petition to terminate the parent's rights over any child if the child has been in foster care for 15 of the 22 most recent months, unless a relative is caring for the child or a compelling reason exists why termination would not be in the best interests of the child. Although the ASFA remedied some of the more glaring deficiencies in the AACWA, it has drawn sharp criticism. Of particular concern is the provision that requires states to seek the termination of parental rights, with few exceptions, in the case of any child who has been in foster care for 15 of the most recent 22 months. Opponents of the ASFA hold that it may terminate the rights of parents who could eventually provide a stable home, and that it fails to take account of the fact that adoptive families might not be available for children whose parents' rights have been terminated – thus putting children in the position of having no legally recognized parents (O'Laughlin, 1998).

In summary, many competing rights and interests must be considered in most cases involving the termination of parental rights. Over the years, our society has struggled to find the correct balance between these competing rights, and this process continues today. In the next section, we describe the process of the termination of parental rights and the ways in which the process attempts to balance the rights of those involved.

THE LEGAL PROCESS OF TERMINATING PARENTAL RIGHTS

The termination of parental rights is one of the most momentous procedures in the U.S. legal system. In part this is because of the fundamental right, in our society, of families to be free from state interference and the right of parents to raise their children as they see fit (e.g., *Meyer v. Nebraska*, 1923; *Santosky v. Kramer*, 1982; for reviews, see Faupel, 1994; Korn, 1994; Warzynski, 1994). Consequently, terminating a parent's rights strikes at one of the core legal and social values of our society. Termination is also important because it is irreversible, barring a finding that fraud occurred during the termination (*Santosky v. Kramer*, 1982). Termination of parental rights effectively severs a birth parent's rights over his or her child and places the child under the legal guardianship of the state. Whereas custody determinations can be reviewed periodically, by law a parent whose rights have been terminated can never apply to a court to have those rights restored.

Termination of parental rights is a relatively rare occurrence for children in foster care. The overwhelming majority of children who are removed from their homes for reasons of abuse or neglect are eventually reunited with their birth families. Data from the 1996–1997 Adoption and Foster Care Reporting System (AFCARS) indicate that approximately two-thirds of all children who exited the child welfare system during that year were reunited with a birth parent, approximately 15% experienced earlier termination of parental rights and were adopted in that year, and the remaining 18% of children who may or may not have experienced termination of parental rights exited the system to live with relatives, became emancipated, or experienced another nonfamily placement.

Voluntary Termination of Parental Rights

Parents can have their rights voluntarily terminated in a legal proceeding. This typically happens when parents have decided voluntarily to relinquish their child for adoption. Voluntary terminations are most common in the adoption of infants. However, in some cases involving the abuse or neglect of children by their parents, the parents may agree voluntarily to relinquish their rights as part of a bargain with a district attorney or a department of social services

(Haralambie, 1993). Some voluntary terminations include provisions allowing birth parents some ongoing contact with the child, and others result in the birth parents having no further contact with their child (Grotevant, McRoy, Elde, & Fravel, 1994).

All voluntary terminations must be made freely by a parent, and most state laws prohibit the child's mother or father from being coerced or tricked into terminating their rights (Carrieri, 1991). Further, parents must fully understand what it is that they are relinquishing for the decision to be made freely. The majority of states do not allow a mother to relinquish rights to her infant until after the birth of the child, and the other states allow for revocation of consent given before the child's birth for a time shortly after the birth. These laws are based on the belief that the mother will not fully understand what it means to relinquish the rights to her child until after she has given birth (Selman, 1994). Despite the legal expectations, some evidence suggests that some birth mothers do experience feelings of coercion and indecision regarding the relinquishment of their child. De Simone (1995, 1996) reports higher levels of grief among birth mothers who perceived that they had been coerced into relinquishment, and Baran and Pannor (1993) report that birth parents who assume more responsibility for the decision to relinquish are better able to cope with feelings of loss, mourning, and grief.

Birth fathers, including unwed fathers, have rights similar to those of birth mothers in termination proceedings (*Caban v. Mohammed*, 1979; *In re Raquel Marie X.*, 1990; Shanley, 1995). Efforts must be made to locate a father who is not aware of the birth of his child so that he can choose whether to terminate his rights. In addition, efforts must be made to identify the father if the mother is unwilling or unable to identify him (e.g., *In re Doe*, 1994). However, a father who knows of the existence of his child and who has made no effort to participate in the child's life may be considered to have abandoned or neglected the child, thus permitting termination of his rights (Haralambie, 1993; *Lehr v. Robertson*, 1983).

Two cases in the mid-1990s highlighted the rights of birth fathers (*In re Adoption of B.G.S.*, 1992; *In re Doe*, 1994). In both cases, fathers learned of the existence of their child soon after the mother's rights to the child had been terminated and the child had been placed with an adoptive family. Both fathers immediately applied to the court to have the child returned to them, based on the argument that their rights had been fraudulently terminated. The terminations were reversed, and both fathers were awarded custody of their child. Even though appeals by the adoptive families resulted in delays of 2 years in returning the child to the birth father, appellate courts continued to hold that the child would have to be returned to the birth father because his rights had never been terminated. Although the courts acknowledged that there would likely be negative consequences to the children and the adoptive parents when they were separated, the rights of the birth fathers, and the interest of the state in maintaining the rights of birth parents, were seen as more important (for discussion see Appell & Boyer, 1995).

When all parties agree to a voluntary termination of parental rights, few conflicts between parents, children, and the state arise. Parents who cannot or who prefer not to raise a child are relieved of that responsibility; the child, it is hoped, will be placed in a loving home; and the state's interest in promoting child development and family life is maintained. One area in which conflict has emerged involves situations in which adoptive parents have changed previous agreements with birth parents or other birth relatives regarding visitation once an adoption has been finalized. The courts have followed two general paths in resolving these cases. Some states have been guided by the principle of the best interest of the child. Courts have permitted the enforcement of visitation agreements based on this principle in some cases (e.g., *People ex rel. Sibley v. Sheppard*, 1981), and visitation has been prohibited in other cases in which the court believed that it was not in the child's best interest (e.g., *In re Department of Public Welfare*, 1981). Other states have been guided by the principle that once an adoption is finalized, the adoptive parents have control over visitation and the birth parents have no standing to pursue contact (e.g., *Colorado Ex rel M.M.*, 1986; *Hill v. Moorman*, 1988).

Involuntary Terminations

Involuntary terminations involve the state, usually through a department of social services, petitioning a court to have a parent's

rights terminated against the parent's wishes. Most of these cases involve children who have been removed from their parents because
of chronic or severe abuse or neglect. Termination of parental rights
is undertaken because the department believes that the parents will
not be able to provide adequate care for their child.

Initial and permanent removal of a child from his or her parents
must follow specific legal guidelines. Initial removal of children to
a foster home or other temporary placement can be done at the recommendation of the department of social services. However, the
removal must be reviewed by a judge, with the child's birth parents having the right of legal representation during the review (for
additional discussion see Cahn & Johnson, 1993). The department
of social services must then develop a case plan that includes reasonable efforts to rehabilitate the family so that the child can return
home. If a parent develops the ability to parent adequately, then
the child is returned home by the department. If conditions that
led to the removal of the child do not improve, the department
can pursue termination of the parents' rights. Prior to 1998, social
work practice regarding reasonable efforts was not clearly guided
by the law, and reasonable efforts were fairly universally accepted
to mean all possible efforts by caseworkers to reunify families. The
AFSA provided more clarity on the guiding principle of the law by
limiting the amount of time a birth family has to demonstrate adequate rehabilitation efforts. However, exactly what *reasonable efforts*
must include has never been defined clearly – partly because these
efforts may need to vary from family to family. Consequently, differences in expectations regarding reasonable efforts appear among
the states and among locales within states.

Termination proceedings are adversarial and result in a judge's
weighing the efforts that the agency has made to provide services to
the parent, the parent's improvement in areas that had been identified as problematic, and the parent's general capacity to provide adequate parenting (Cahn & Johnson, 1993). Although not obligated
by federal law (*Lassiter v. Dept. of Social Services*, 1981), 46 states
require that birth parents be supplied with a lawyer if they cannot afford one during termination procedures, and 46 states require
that a guardian *ad litem* (usually a lawyer) be appointed to represent
the best interests of the child (Cressler, 1993–1994). A judge must

rule that the birth parents are unfit as parents before their rights can be terminated (*Quilloin v. Walcott*, 1978) and that the statutory grounds for termination have been met by clear and convincing evidence (*Santosky v. Kramer*, 1982). Whether it would be in a child's best interest to remain with his or her birth parents or to live in another home is not an issue at this stage of the legal proceedings; the sole issue is whether the state can show that the parents are unfit. "If best interests of the child were a sufficient qualification to determine child custody, anyone with superior income, intelligence, education, etc., might challenge and deprive the parents of their right to their own children" (*In re Doe*, 1994, pp. 182–183).

Because of the irreversible nature of the termination of parental rights, many judges are reluctant to grant terminations (Sommer, 1994). As a result, lawyers for departments of social services may hesitate to initiate termination procedures except in the most obvious cases of parental unfitness (Cahn & Johnson, 1993). In addition, judges may continue cases rather than terminating parental rights or sending a child home to his or her birth parents, hoping that the birth parents will make the necessary improvements in their ability to parent. The result can be many children in foster care who are unable to return home because of their parents' continuing problems and unable to be adopted because the problems are not sufficiently severe to provide the level of certainty needed for termination to occur. This lack of permanence for children can negatively influence a child's long-term probability of adoption and can result in both psychological damage and serious long-term life impacts (Ford, 1996; Lyman & Bird, 1996).

Can Children Seek to Terminate Their Parents' Rights? In 1992, 12-year-old Gregory Kingsley petitioned to terminate his birth parents' rights after the state department of social services decided, against Gregory's wishes, to remove him from a foster home and return him to his birth parents. The initial legal issue was whether Gregory, as a minor, had standing to bring a termination petition to court. The trial judge ruled that Gregory did have standing, and the rights of Gregory's birth parents were terminated at trial. However, an appellate court overruled the trial court, stating that Gregory did not have standing to initiate court proceedings, citing Florida Civil

Procedure statutes stating that "unemancipated minors do not have the legal capacity to initiate legal proceedings in their own names" (*Kingsley v. Kingsley*, 1993, p. 782). However, the appellate court let stand the ruling terminating Gregory's parents' rights.

Currently, most children can gain access to the courts only through a guardian *ad litem*, although children do have direct access to the courts in a few states (Haralambie, 1993). Although the roles of guardians *ad litem* continue to evolve, their basic function is to represent what the guardian perceives to be the child's best interest (see Haralambie and Nysse-Carris, this volume, for a discussion of children's access to legal representation generally). The legal assumption is that children do not have the capacity to consider both the short- and long-term implications of possible legal courses of action and thus need the intermediary of a guardian. Legal arguments against this practice state that children should be afforded the same rights as adults to use the courts directly, through a lawyer who vigorously represents the child's point of view (e.g., Russ, 1993; Sommer, 1994).

Summary

Cases involving the termination of parental rights are often difficult to decide because of the legal conflicts they involve. Termination cases challenge the fundamental right of parents to be free of state interference in raising their children and the fundamental right of family and individual privacy. Balanced against these rights is the right of children to be raised in a family atmosphere that will allow them to develop in a healthy way. When the state initiates termination proceedings against a parent, the state is taking the stand that the child's right to a healthy upbringing is impossible to attain in the child's current family and that the child's right to a healthy upbringing supersedes the parent's rights to family and individual privacy. Conversely, if the state decides not to terminate birth parents' rights in cases of abuse or neglect, the state reaffirms the importance of parents' right to raise their children and/or implies that it would be in the child's best interest to remain with his or her birth parents, even if time in a foster family is required to provide the birth parents with the chance to improve their parenting abilities.

THE RELATION OF THE PROCESS AND TIMING OF TERMINATIONS
TO CHILD OUTCOMES

Although it is clear that parents' rights cannot be terminated involuntarily without a finding of parental unfitness, with passage of
the ASFA, predictions are that time lines for termination of parental
rights will be shorter and that the courts will become increasingly
sensitive to considering the needs of children in potential termination cases rather than focusing almost exclusively on the rights of
parents. This increases the importance of understanding whether
the timing of termination procedures might have an influence on
the health and development of children whose parents' rights might
be terminated. After all, the state's interest in healthy children can
be met only if termination of parental rights and other interventions
result in healthier children. At issue, then, is whether termination of
parental rights has the desired outcome of helping children develop
in a healthier way and whether the process or timing of terminations
has an influence on child outcomes.

It is generally assumed that in most cases it is beneficial for a
child whose birth parents' rights have been terminated to be placed
in an adoptive home (Barth & Berry, 1987). There is some evidence
that children raised away from abusive or neglectful parents do
experience a healthier life. For example, research has shown that
children raised in adoptive homes have better outcomes than those
who are returned to problematic birth homes (Bohman, 1971). In addition, the reabuse rate for children removed to foster care because
of abuse or neglect has been shown to be lower than the rate for
children who are not removed and who remain with their families
(Runyan & Gould, 1985). It is worth noting, however, that the rate
of abuse in foster care is greater than the rate of abuse in nonfoster
homes generally (Goodman, Emery, & Haugaard, 1998).

Because adoption is a desired outcome for children whose parents' rights have been terminated, it is important to understand
whether the process or timing of the termination process influences
whether children can be successfully adopted into new homes.
The research suggests that the timing of termination can influence
the success of adoptive placement in two ways: (a) by influencing the likelihood that a child will be adopted and (b) by influencing

the likelihood that the adoption will be successful. We explore these issues in this section.

Characteristics of Protracted Termination Decisions

As already noted, many termination cases proceed slowly and cautiously because many possible risks are involved if parental rights are terminated in error. Most important, a child might lose the chance to return home and have ongoing contact with a birth family and extended kin to whom the child may be very attached. In addition, permanently losing contact with a child may be tremendously stressful to a parent. Ratterman (1991) reported that in some cases it took 5 years for a child, who could clearly not be returned to a birth parent, to be freed for adoption. Interestingly, she found that most significant problems contributing to delays in termination proceedings were not predominantly driven by legal delays but were more likely to result from staff shortages, bad communication between caseworkers and lawyers, bad staff training, and lack of written procedures.

Several studies have reported systematic differences in the amount of time for termination proceedings to be completed. Using an event history analysis that controls for time and duration dependence in the system, Avery (1998) found that the age at which a child enters the system is related to a child's permanency-planning horizon. She found that, controlling for all other factors in the model, children entering the system between age 2 and 5 years were particularly vulnerable to delays in termination of parental rights, whereas children entering the system as infants were freed significantly more quickly. She suggested that delays in freeing children aged 2 to 5 might be related to factors such as stronger attachment to birth parents and prolonged attempts by social workers to reunify the child and birth family. Other studies have found similar results. McMurty (1992) found that children entering care at older ages and those with disabilities were freed significantly more slowly, and Ratterman (1991) found that cases involving physically or emotionally abused children took longer to reach termination. Jacobs (1996) found that both race and age at entry were associated with delays in termination proceedings. White children were freed more quickly on average than minority race children in his sample, and children entering care before age 2 or after age 8 were freed significantly more quickly than children entering care between the ages of 3 and 7.

Parental characteristics have also been found to be related to delays in termination of parental rights. Ratterman (1991) reported that termination of parental rights in cases involving birth parents who were substance abusers, mentally ill, developmentally disabled, incarcerated, or missing took longer than average to complete and become legal. On the other hand, Jacobs (1996) found that voluntary relinquishment of a child by his or her birth parent was associated with a shorter time to termination. Goodman et al. (1998) found that children for whom it is more difficult to find an adoptive home (older, ethnic minority, and/or disabled children) experience termination proceedings that are more protracted. As discussed in the next section, the importance of protracted termination proceedings lies in the fact that it impacts a child's chance of being adopted, thus decreasing even further the chance for a successful adoptive placement (Avery, 1998).

Consequences of Protracted Termination Proceedings

Protracted termination proceedings may be beneficial to children and their birth families if the children are eventually returned home. Parents who may not respond to several months of intervention to increase their parenting abilities may respond to longer interventions that involve steadily increasing contact with their children. This may allow the children to be reunited with their birth families – resulting in stability for the child and a higher probability of appropriate parenting in the long run.

Delays in termination decisions can have negative consequences for children who are not returned to their birth homes because the delays may reduce the children's likelihood of being adopted, resulting in their languishing in foster care (Avery, 1998). More than a half million children are in the foster care system in the United States, nearly double the number a decade ago. O'Laughlin (1998) reported that children placed in foster care spend an average of 3 years in the system, and 1 in 10 spend more than 7 years in foster care. Children who eventually leave the foster care system through adoption typically wait between 3½ and 5½ years for adoptive placement, with the majority of children having several placements during their time in care. Many children "age out" of the system (turn 18) without ever being placed in a permanent adoptive home.

Delays in terminating parents' rights increase the already existing barriers to adoption experienced by those who have been abused, neglected, or abandoned. Delays are inevitably linked to the child's being older when available for adoption and, as children grow older, it becomes harder to find adoptive families for them and harder to ensure a successful adoptive placement (Barth & Berry, 1988; Barth, Courtney, & Berry, 1994; Finch, Franshel, & Grundy, 1986; McMurty & Lie, 1992).

Avery (1998) found that increased time spent in the child welfare system makes children less likely to be adopted, a phenomenon she refers to as *duration dependence*. Her study found that even relatively short delays in termination of parental rights, such as a year, reduced the probability of adoption by approximately 40% each year thereafter. Moreover, Avery found that the caseloads of social workers significantly influenced their ability to serve children in their care. Higher child protective service and foster care caseloads in local areas were significantly associated with a decreased probability of adoption for children in that area.

Another potential negative consequence of protracted termination proceedings is that they may result in negative outcomes once an adoption placement has been made. Of particular concern is the increased risk of adoption disruption. Adoption disruption occurs when the adoptive parents request that the child be returned to the agency that placed the child prior to adoption finalization (Barth & Berry, 1988). Several studies have found that outcomes related to delays (e.g., older age of a child, higher number of previous foster care placements) are associated with an increased risk of disruption. For example, studies have found that adoptions of older children are more likely to be disrupted even when only school-age children are considered (e.g., Festinger, 1986; Partridge, Hornby, & McDonald, 1986). Longer waits for adoption have been associated directly with disruption in some studies (Boneh, 1979; Partridge et al., 1986) but not in others (Festinger, 1986; Zwimpfer, 1983).

Evaluating the Stability of Reunification and Adoption

As just noted, there are potential advantages and disadvantages to delaying the process of termination of parental rights. But what of the consequences of an incorrect decision regarding prompt termination? One must also consider the potential liabilities of incorrect prompt decisions regarding termination of return to birth parents when determining general directions for policy.

Risks Associated with Reunification. Most children in foster care have experienced severe or long-standing abuse or neglect, and the risk that a child will be reabused after being returned to his or her birth family is a concern in reunification efforts. Studies of child maltreatment have found reabuse rates after return to birth homes of 17–25% (Jones, 1983; Runyan & Gould, 1985).

Another concern after reunification is recidivism, or return to foster care. Several studies have found recidivism rates of 24–32% (Block, 1981; Block & Libowitz, 1983; Fein, Maluccio, Hamilton, & Ward, 1983; Mech, 1983; Rzepnicki, 1987; Wulczyn, 1991). Recidivism rates have been found to vary by child and birth family characteristics. Block (1981) found higher recidivism rates for children 13–15 years old at the time of reunification (43%), lower rates for children 16–18 years old (32%), lower rates still for children 10–12 years old (22%), and the lowest rates among children 0–9 years old at the time of reunification (14%). Furthermore, Block (1981) found lower recidivism rates for those with siblings (12–36%) than for those without siblings (40%) and higher rates for children discharged to two-parent families (42%) compared to those discharged to one-parent families (27%). Courtney (1994) reported foster care recidivism rates of approximately 25% for children returning to a birth family within the first year of placement and lower recidivism rates for those returning after the first year in foster care. English, Marshall, and Orme (1999) found that the probability of recidivism increased with the number of prior referrals to foster care, a birth family with a history of a domestic violence, a history of a parent experiencing abuse/neglect as a child, and substance abuse by the parent. From their extensive review of the reunification literature, Barth and Berry (1987) concluded that there is much evidence to suggest that children who have been abused or neglected are very often not safe at home after reunification and that of all placement options, reunification with birth parents fails most often to be free from abuse and fails to result in developmental well-being for the child.

Risks Associated with Adoption. The risk associated with adoption that has been the focus of most research is adoption disruption. Using data from five states, Urban Systems Research and Engineering (1985) reported national disruption rates for special needs children (children with disabilities, older children, sibling groups, and children of color) to be 6–20%. About 12% of placements made by the Oklahoma Department of Social Services from 1982 to 1985 resulted in disruption (Rosenthal, 1986), and a 1986 New England study of predominantly special needs placements yielded a disruption rate of 27% (Partridge et al., 1986). Festinger's (1986) study of 879 adoptive placements in New York found an 8% disruption rate, Kadushin and Martin (1988) found an 11% disruption rate across 11 special needs placement studies, and 15% of 1,981 placements of children 3 years of age and older in 13 California counties ended in disruption (Barth & Berry 1988).

Rosenthal (1993) noted that the sociodemographic factor most powerfully associated with the risk of adoption disruption is the child's age at the time of placement, with the risk increasing with age. Coyne and Brown (1985) found a disruption rate of 3% for children adopted at age 7 or younger compared to a rate of 18% for those 8 years of age or older. Physical disabilities and serious medical conditions are not risk factors for disruption, but emotional and behavioral problems are strong predictors of disruption. In addition, adoption by foster parents consistently predicts a reduced risk (Rosenthal, 1993).

Summary

Currently, many children must wait several years after being removed to foster care before termination of their birth parents' rights occurs and they are freed for adoption by another family. The benefits of a protracted wait in foster care – primarily eventual reunification with birth parents who are able to provide adequate parenting – must be weighed against the problems associated with a protracted wait if the child cannot be reunited with his or her birth family – primarily a reduced chance of being adopted and an increased chance of a disrupted or troubled adoption. Research indicates that, compared to recidivism and reabuse rates, adoption may be a more stable and permanent outcome for children. This suggests that earlier termination of parental rights, even if this involves error in some cases, may be a better policy when all children in foster care are considered.

IMPLICATIONS FOR CHILD WELFARE POLICY AND PRACTICE

The federal ASFA reinforces the philosophy that reunification of a child with his or her birth family remains the primary goal of child welfare services while simultaneously limiting the time a birth family has to demonstrate adequate rehabilitation efforts. The emphasis on reunification in this act and parallel planning for alternative child outcomes reflects society's respect for children's and parents' rights. There is no philosophical contradiction between taking prompt action to free children for adoption in some cases and working diligently to preserve families in others. The state should try to support and preserve families, but only when such efforts are realistic. But what is a realistic time frame to expect in resolutions involving termination of parental rights? Both Courtney (1994) and Goerge (1990) suggest that efforts to reunify a child with his or her parents will most often either succeed or fail in far less than 2 years – a significantly shorter time than the average time to termination reported by Ratterman (1991), Jacobs (1996), or Avery (1998) in their empirical studies.

The research suggests that to maximize the likelihood of positive outcomes for children whose parental rights have been terminated because of abuse or neglect, terminations need to occur in a way that minimizes the time a child waits in foster care. As noted previously, however, judges are often loath to terminate parental rights except in the most extreme cases and in cases in which the parents have been given an opportunity (often over many years) to rehabilitate themselves. There is clearly a need for state child welfare agencies to concentrate on making assessments of which cases should be allowed to go to early termination of parental rights and in which circumstances family preservation and rehabilitation will be in the best interest of the child (Harden & Lancour, 1996). Delays in assessment can often render early termination a moot issue, and efforts to secure successful outcomes for children can increase dramatically when parental rights are terminated in a timely manner.

A possible reason for the low rate of permanency success in the case of reunifications could be inadequate services rendered to the families. To reduce the incidence of recidivism among children discharged from foster care, the families to which they are discharged must be strengthened to the point where they can accept the return of the child and cope with the difficulties in reestablishing a functional family unit. Intensive family services must be provided as soon as possible after the child is placed in foster care and should continue for an appropriate length of time after discharge. Studies have found, however, that services to reunified families often end prematurely and are inadequate to secure permanency, despite evidence that greater and longer provision of services does help to prevent abuse and recidivism (Berry, 1988; Broeck & Barth, 1986). Barth and Berry (1987) note that current permanency planning time limits work against rather than for reunification efforts and make reunification a more common but risky outcome for children by returning children to their homes with brief or minimal supervision and services.

CONCLUSIONS

As described throughout this chapter, legal proceedings to terminate parents' rights over their children often pit the rights and responsibilities of parents, children, and the state against each other. In our society, parents have the fundamental right to raise their children as they see fit, with no governmental interference, children have the right to a healthy upbringing, and the state has interests in maintaining family privacy and ensuring that its children are raised in a healthy way. Laws to balance these rights have changed over the past years. Laws making it relatively easy for the state to remove a child from his or her birth parents were superseded by laws making permanent removal much more difficult, and those laws, in turn, have been superseded by recent laws making termination easier to accomplish in a shorter period of time. The difficulty of balancing the rights of parents, children, and the state is clearly shown in these changing laws – as is society's changing beliefs about the relative importance of parents' and children's rights when these come into conflict. Ongoing changes in these laws and the way they are used by the courts and social work agencies are likely to continue as our society continues to struggle to arrive at a good balance between the rights and responsibilities of parents, children, and the state.

References

Appell, A. R., & Boyer, B. (1995). Parental rights vs. best interests of the child. *Duke Journal of Gender Law & Policy, 2*, 63–96.
Avery, R. J. (1998). *Foster Case histories of children freed for adoption in New York State: 1988–1993*. Public Agency Adoption in New York State, Phase I Report. Grant number 5 R01 HD27529-05, Washington, DC: National Institute for Health and Human Development, Department of Health and Human Services.
Baran, A., & Pannor, R. (1993). Perspectives on open adoption. *Future of Children, 3*(1), 119–124.
Barth, R. P., & Berry, M. (1987). Outcomes of child welfare services under permanency planning. *Social Service Review, 61*, 71–90.
Barth, R. P., & Berry, M. (1988). Child abuse and child welfare services. In M. Wald & M. Kirst (Eds.), *Conditions of children in California* (pp. 78–95). Berkeley: Policy Analysis for California Education.
Barth, R. P., Courtney, M., & Berry, M. (1994). Timing is everything: An analysis of the time to adoption and legalization. *Social Work Research, 18*, 139–148.
Block, N. M. (1981). Toward reducing recidivism in foster care. *Child Welfare, 60*, 597–610.
Block, N. M., & Libowitz, A. S. (1983). *Recidivism in foster care*. New York: Child Welfare League of America.
Bohman, M. (1971). A comparative study of adopted children, foster children, and children in their biological environment born after undesired pregnancies. *Acta Paediatrica Scandinavia, 221* (Suppl.), 5–38.
Boneh, C. (1979). *Disruptions in adoptive placements*. Boston: Department of Public Welfare.
Caban v. Mohammed, 441 U.S. 380 (1979).

Cahn, K., & Johnson, P. (1993). Critical issues in permanency planning. In K. Cahn & P. Johnson (Eds.), *Children can't wait* (pp. 3–18). Washington, DC: Child Welfare League.

Carrieri, J. R. (1991). *Child custody, foster care, and adoptions.* New York: Lexington Books.

Colorado Ex rel M.M., 726 P. 2d 1108 (1986).

Courtney, M. (1994). Factors associated with the reunification of foster children with their families. *Social Service Review, 68*, 81–108.

Coyne, A., & Brown, M. E. (1985). Developmentally disabled children can be adopted. *Child Welfare, 64*, 607–615.

Cressler, D. E. (1993–1994). Requiring proof beyond a reasonable doubt in parental rights termination cases. *Journal of Family Law, 32*, 785–815.

De Simone, M. (1995). Unresolved grief in women who have relinquished an infant for adoption. *Dissertation Abstracts International Section A Humanities and Social Sciences, 55*(9-A), 2987.

De Simone, M. (1996). Birth mother loss: Contributing factors to unresolved grief. *Clinical Social Work Journal, 24*(1), 65–76.

English, D. J., Marshall, D. B., & Orme, M. (1999). Characteristics of repeated referrals to child protective services in Washington State. *Child Maltreatment, 4*(4), 297–307.

Faupel, M. L. (1994). The "Baby Jessica case: And the claimed conflict between children's rights and parents' rights. *Wayne Law Review, 40*, 285–331.

Fein, E., Maluccio, A. N., Hamilton, J. V., & Ward, D. E. (1983). After foster care: Outcomes of permanent planning for children. *Child Welfare, 62*, 485–562.

Festinger, T. (1986). *Necessary risk: A study of adoption and disrupted adoption placements.* Washington, DC: Child Welfare League of America.

Finch, S., Franshel, D., & Grundy, J. (1986). Factors associated with the discharge of children from foster care. *Social Work Research and Abstracts, 29*, 10–18.

Ford, H. A. (1996). Exploring stability and change processes in foster care: An application of organizational ecology to human populations. *Dissertation Abstracts International Section A Humanities and Social Sciences, 57*(4-A), 1846.

Goerge, R. M. (1990). The reunification process in substitute care. *Social Service Review, 64*, 422–457.

Goodman, G., Emery, R., & Haugaard, J. J. (1998). Developmental psychology and the law: Divorce, child maltreatment, foster care, and adoption. In I. Sigel & A. Renninger (Eds.), *Handbook of child psychology (5th ed.), Vol. 4. Child psychology in practice* (pp. 775–876). New York: Wiley.

Grotevant, H. D., McRoy, R. G., Elde, C. L., & Fravel, D. L. (1994). Adoptive family system dynamics: Variations by level of openness in the adoption. *Family Process, 33*, 125–146.

Haralambie, A. M. (1993). *Handling child custody, abuse and adoption cases.* Colorado Springs, CO: Shepard's/McGraw-Hill.

Hardin, M., & Lancour, R. (1996). *Early termination of parental rights: Developing appropriate statutory grounds.* Washington, DC: ABA Center on Children and the Law.

Hill v. Moorman, 525 So. 2d 681 (1988).

In re Adoption of B.G.S., 614 A. 2d 1161 (1992).

In re Department of Public Welfare, 419 N. E. 2d 285 (1981).

In re Doe, 638 N. E. 2d 181 (1994).

In re Raquel Marie X., 559 N. E. 2d 418 (1990).

Jacobs, B. A. (1996). *An analysis of characteristics affecting the length of time until termination of parental rights in New York State adoption cases.* Unpublished honors thesis, Cornell University, Department of Policy Analysis and Management.

Jones, M. A. (1983). *A second chance for families – five years later: Follow-up of a program to prevent foster care.* New York: Child Welfare League of America.

Kadushin, A., & Martin, J. (1988). *Child welfare services* (4th ed.). New York: Macmillan.

Kingsley v. Kingsley, 623 So. 2d 780 (1993).

Korn, K. (1994). The struggle for the child: Preserving the family in adoption disputes between biological parents and third parties. *North Carolina Law Review, 72*, 1279–1331

Lassiter v. Dept. of Social Services, 452 U.S. 18 (1981).

Lehr v. Robertson, 463 U.S. 248 (1983).

Lyman, S. B., & Bird, G. W. (1996). A closer look at self-image in male foster care adolescents. *Social Work, 41*(1), 85–96.

Maas, H., & Engler, R. E. (1959). *Children in need of parents.* New York: Columbia University Press.

McMurtry, S. L. (1992). Evaluating efforts to free foster children for adoption. *Journal of Social Service Research, 16*, 89–116.

McMurty, S. L., & Lie, G. W. (1992). Differential exit rates of minority children in foster care. *Social Work Research and Abstracts, 28*, 42–48.

Mech, E. V. (1983). Out of home placement rates. *Social Service Review, 57*, 659–667.

Meyer v. Nebraska, 262 U.S. 390 (1923).

O'Laughlin, M. (1998). A theory of relativity: Kinship foster care may be the key to stopping the pendulum of terminations vs. reunification. *Vanderbilt Law Review, 51*(5), 1427–1457.

Partridge, S., Hornby, H., & McDonald, T. (1986). *Legacy of loss: Visions of gain, an inside look at adoption disruption.* Portland: University of Southern Maine, Human Services Department Institute.

People ex rel. Sibley v. Sheppard, 445 N. Y. S. 2d 420 (1981).

Quilloin v. Walcott, 434 U.S. 246 (1978).

Ratterman, D. (1991). *Termination barriers: Speeding adoption in New York State through reducing delays in termination of parental rights cases.* Washington, DC: ABA Center on Children and the Law.

Rosenthal, J. A. (1986). *Final report on factors associated with Oklahoma special needs adoptive disruptions.* Unpublished manuscript. University of Oklahoma, Norman.

Rosenthal, J. A. (1993). Outcomes of adoption of children with special needs. *The Future of Children, 3,* 77–88.

Runyan, D. K., & Gould, C. (1985). Foster care for child maltreatment: Impact on delinquent behavior. *Pediatrics, 75,* 562–568.

Russ, G. H. (1993). Through the eyes of a child, "Gregory K.": A child's right to be heard. *Family Law Quarterly, 27,* 365–933.

Rzepnicki, T. (1987). Recidivism of foster children returned to their own homes: A review and new directions for research. *Social Service Review, 61*(1) 56–70.

Santosky v. Kramer, 455 U.S. 745 (1982).

Selman, M. E. (1994). For the sake of the child: Moving toward uniformity in adoption law. *Washington Law Review, 69,* 841–867.

Shanley, M. L. (1995). Unwed fathers' rights, adoption, and sex equality: Gender-neutrality and the perpetuation of patriarchy. *Columbia Law Review, 95,* 60–97.

Sommer, C. D. (1994). Empowering children: Granting foster children the right to initiate parental rights termination proceedings. *Cornell Law Review, 79,* 1200–1262.

Urban Systems Research and Engineering. (1985). *Evaluation of state activities with regard to adoption disruption.* Washington, DC: Urban Systems Research and Engineering.

Warzynski, V. L. (1994). Termination of parental rights: The "psychological parent" standard. *Villanova Law Review, 39,* 737–771.

White, M., Albers, E., & Bitonti, C. (1996). Factors in length of foster care: Worker activities and parent–child visitation. *Journal of Sociology and Social Welfare, 23,* 755–784.

Wulczyn, F. (1991). Caseload dynamics and foster care reentry. *Social Service Review, 65,* 133–156.

Zwimpfer, D. M. (1983). Indicators of adoption breakdown. *Social Casework, 64,* 169–177.

7

Child Custody Research at the Crossroads

Issues for a New Century

Charlene E. Depner

Domestic relations cases, including divorce, child custody, child support, paternity, domestic violence, and adoption filings, compose the fastest-growing sector of cases that come before our states' courts. The National Center for State Courts reports a 65% increase in domestic relations filings between 1985 and 1997 (Ostrom & Kauder, 1997).

The widesweeping impact of child custody policy and practice is evident when we consider that more than half of all children born today will live apart from one parent at some time during their childhood (Furstenberg & Cherlin, 1991). All of these children are potentially subject to child custody orders. Although a great deal of research has focused on custody following divorce, this literature is not sufficient to advise child custody policy makers. Divorce accounts for little more than half of the children who live in single-parent households. The others are born to parents who do not marry (U.S. Bureau of the Census, 1992). Child custody cases may enter the courts because a divorce is in progress, a paternity case is being heard, child support orders are being established, or as part of domestic violence restraining orders. Because divorce is only one family law proceeding that involves child custody orders, the term *family reorganization* is used in this chapter to refer the wider spectrum of family circumstances that lead to child custody decisions.

Due to the profound formative effects that custody and visitation laws may have on future generations, social science has played a highly influential role in the policy and practice of family law. This chapter reviews some of the key research guiding current child custody policy. It begins by summarizing outcome variables linked to family reorganization. It then provides a brief overview of research on risks and protective factors that influence these outcomes. Following this is a discussion of the application of social science data to legal custody decision making. The chapter concludes with recommendations for future research.

FAMILY REORGANIZATION AND CHILD OUTCOMES

Research conceptualizes family reorganization as raising particular transitional demands for the child (Hetherington, Bridges, & Insabella, 1998). The child's physical and social world becomes, at least for a time, less stable and predictable. Disruptions and nonnormative transitions (e.g., changes in schedules, residence, schools; new partners of parents; birth of new children) are added to or interact with the particular developmental milestones a child may be negotiating.

The disruptions and transitions that the child experiences may take different forms, depending on the type of proceeding that prompted child custody decisions. For the breakup of marital or for cohabiting relationships, there may be a great deal of financial uncertainty and change in the resources available to the child. Parents may reduce time at home in order to work to make ends meet (McLanahan & Sandefur, 1994). With reduced resources in finances and parental time, some children may also suffer reduced access to professional assessment and intervention. For other children, the establishment of child custody orders may introduce a parent who had not been actively involved in their lives. Custody orders associated with domestic violence proceedings can curtail contact with a parent or relegate access to a supervised visitation context. Most of the research knowledge is based on either analyses of divorced families (a category that may include never-divorced parents who are now in a new relationship) or single-parent families (a category that may include never-married parents).

An analysis of the various risks and protective factors associated with the reorganization of a child's family can lead to a clearer understanding of potential consequences for the child. The consequences most frequently evaluated in social science research are emotional well-being, behavior problems, academic achievement, social development, and the transition to adulthood. Research and policy point to other child outcomes that merit further research. These include the financial well-being of the child, the child's recovery from trauma experienced in troubled families, the child's physical health, growth status, and neurological functioning, and social competencies (e.g., interpersonal skills, ability to establish satisfying interpersonal relationships; ability of the child to become a good parent).

Prominent reviews (Amato & Keith, 1991; Emery, 1999) document deficits among children of divorce on a wide spectrum of indicators of emotional well-being, including self-esteem, "externalizing" problems (defiance, aggression, poor self-control, excessive risk-taking), and "internalizing" problems (anxiety, depression, dependence). Laumann-Billings and Emery (2000) caution that this literature often cannot adequately differentiate between long-standing symptoms and short-term reactions to family reorganization, because most studies employ a cross-sectional design and include young children.

Children from divorced or single-parent households score lower in academic achievement tests and school grades, although these differences are not large in magnitude. These children also have a somewhat higher dropout rate and are less likely to complete college (Kelly, 2000).

Nonnormative timing of the developmental milestones of late adolescence and early adulthood is also more common among children who are not reared in two-parent households. Children whose parents divorce more commonly exhibit antisocial behavior, delinquency, substance abuse, lower educational attainment, unemployment, precocious sexual activity, adolescent childbearing, and lower socioeconomic attainment (Amato & Keith, 1991; Simmons, 1996).

Other research suggests that the divorce of one's parents may have implications for an individual's ability to form and sustain intimate relationships. Several studies observed a somewhat elevated rate of marital instability among those whose parents divorced

(Amato & Keith, 1991; Bumpass, Martin, & Sweet, 1991; McLanahan & Bumpass, 1988).

The adverse consequences linked to family reorganization typically are not large in magnitude. Effect sizes are small, with only modest differences in the relative proportions of children from intact and divorced households who fall below clinical cutoff levels (Amato & Keith, 1991; Cherlin & Furstenberg, 1994; Furstenberg & Cherlin, 1991, Kelly, 2000; Seltzer, 1994). Further, the outcomes reported in this literature frequently co-occur. Failure to recognize this nonindependence can lead to exaggerated estimates of the prevalence of poor outcomes in the full population (Hetherington et al., 1998).

There is also great diversity in how children are affected by family reorganization. Most people who were subject to custody orders as children function as normal, healthy adults, but some do not. For some children, the effects are particularly profound (Hetherington et al., 1998; McLanahan & Sandefur, 1994). Adults who experienced family reorganization as children often recount painful childhood experiences. It is likely that children could benefit from support to cope with the many often unpredictable changes that accompany family reorganization.

Why do some children suffer poor outcomes? Can research suggest points of intervention that will optimize results for them? The next section of this chapter examines the variables that differentiate children with good outcomes from those with poor ones.

Individual Differences in Outcomes

Research on the differential impact of family reorganization has focused primarily on the characteristics of the child, such as age, gender, and temperament. Research on the effects of age is inconclusive (Hetherington et al., 1998). Certainly the age of the child affects both the types of experiences associated with the transition (e.g., change in school, friendship networks) and the child's cognitive capacity to make sense of the changes taking place in the family environment (Bray, 1991). Researchers and practitioners have focused attention on the potential vulnerability of young children (Amato & Keith, 1991; Kelly, 2000), speculating that such children may be at greater risk because they have the greatest need for a predictable, responsive environment and the least capacity to articulate and mobilize resource needs. Family courts have devoted considerable attention to the types of visitation arrangements that meet the developmental needs of very young children while providing opportunities for both parents to stay involved. California data show that most (73%) custody disputes result in young children residing exclusively with their mothers. This picture changes over time, however. Five years after the custody order, a substantial proportion of these children have moved to shared arrangements or reside with their fathers. The proportion of children residing exclusively with their mothers decreases to 55% (Sciortino, 2000).

Gender differences have captured the attention of the research and policy communities alike. Do boys and girls have different responses to divorce? Should the gender of the child inform custody arrangements (Warshak, 1992)? Most investigators find remarkable similarities for boys and girls (Amato & Keith, 1991; Hetherington et al., 1998). Girls do, however, appear to be at somewhat greater risk for early childbearing and school dropout (Cherlin & Furstenberg, 1994; McLanahan & Sandefeur, 1994). They also show greater evidence of resilience and coping with the stresses of family dissolution (Hetherington et al., 1998; Werner, 1993).

Among individual difference variables in children, temperament appears to be the variable most strongly linked to outcomes. Adaptable children with easy temperaments are better able to manage the stresses of family reorganization (Hetherington et al., 1998). Researchers speculate that this may reflect the child's temperamental capacity to adapt to change and to draw in resources as well as the contribution of the child's temperament to the emotional climate of a stressed family. Those with appealing characteristics and engaging personalities may be more successful in drawing in the support resources that they need (Werner, 1993). Children who react unpleasantly to transitions are also more likely to elicit negative reactions from parents, who are themselves experiencing stress (Rutter, 1987).

Because the research design of most individual differences studies involves group comparisons at a particular point in time, the data do not provide a good test of the mechanisms that might account for differential outcomes. One area that deserves further research attention is the cognitive capacity that a child brings to the challenges of family breakup. Children with developmental delays or disabilities need greater support to comprehend and adapt to the changes associated with family transition. Given the importance of early intervention, it is also crucial to make certain that changes in financial resources or residence do not delay assessment or interrupt services. Children who have experienced trauma prior to the breakup are also often in need of services. Because of the high proportion of custody cases involving family violence, assessment and treatment should be a priority in cases involving these children (Rossman, 1998).

Risk Factors

Family reorganization poses particular challenges for each family member. In many contested child custody cases, it also plays out against a backdrop of adverse family circumstances. In California, for example, 41% of contested child custody cases involve parents below the poverty line, 25% include allegations of parental substance abuse, and 45% have domestic violence restraining orders (Depner, 2001). Poverty, parental substance abuse, and violence can each have direct deleterious effects on a child. So, an analysis of the impact of family reorganization would consider the separate and cumulative impact of risk factors in a child's environment, as well as the cluster of risk factors that confront a child at any particular time (Masten & Coatsworth, 1998).

Financial Risks. Socioeconomic disadvantages resulting from family reorganization adversely affect the quality of children's housing, communities, and schools. Family breakup also reduces access to opportunities for education and employment (McLanahan & Sandefur, 1994). Despite vigorous state and federal efforts to increase the financial resources of children through child support enforcement, research shows that custodial mothers and their children still suffer disproportionate financial loss, relative to fathers, in their standard of living following divorce (Bianchi, Subaiya, &

Kahn, 1997). This poses substantial risk to children. In California, 5-year follow-up data on contested custody cases show that 8% of the children in these cases had been homeless (Depner, 2001). Added risks associated with financial disadvantage are pernicious housing conditions (e.g., lead poisoning, rodent infestation, inadequate plumbing or heating), exposure to community violence (see Berman, Silverman, & Kurtines, this volume), firearms, crime, and drugs (McLoyd, 1998).

Loss of Parental Time and Support. Parents may be less available to the child due to reduced custodial access, transition tasks associated with setting up new arrangements for housing and child care, or the financial and legal burdens of the legal process of dissolution (Hetherington et al., 1998; Simons, 1996).

In addition, the stress of the breakup and transition can reduce the quality of parenting available to the child. New demands to change residence, adapt work schedules, and/or respond to legal and financial pressures all may adversely affect family functioning. It has also been hypothesized that parental availability can facilitate child adjustment by affording opportunities for the child to talk openly about the transition and to formulate a storyline that explains events in terms that are developmentally appropriate (Gorell-Barnes, 1999; Rutter, 1987). Cognitive and academic deficits have been linked to the limited availability of adults to provide stimulating interaction, help with homework, ensure that the child is not truant, and promote strong academic functioning (Clark-Stewart, Vandell, McCartney, Owen, & Booth, 2000; Nord, Brimhall, & West, 1997).

Antisocial Peers . Children who lack access to supportive adults may rely more heavily on peers. The work of Patterson and his colleagues suggests that when paired with poor parenting, associating with antisocial peers can map a disturbing trajectory of antisocial behavior and juvenile offenses. Their research shows a sequence of precursor variables, including early externalizing behavior, disrupted family functioning, ineffective discipline, and formation of relationships with antisocial peers (Patterson, Forgatch, Yoerger, & Stoolmiller, 1998; Vuchinich, Bank, & Patterson, 1992).

Exposure to Family Conflict. One of the most replicated findings in the literature is the adverse effect of family conflict on children (Amato & Keith, 1991; Cummings & Davies, 1994; Emery, 1999; Johnston & Roseby, 1997). Often conflict precedes the family breakup by many years. Early exposure to conflict may have physiological effects on the child, reducing the long-term capacity for self-regulation (Jouriles & Norwood, 1996). High-conflict families offer poorer conflict resolution skills, providing instead greater exposure to impulsive, aggressive behavior. Although family breakup may diminish the child's exposure to conflict, many children continue to suffer the consequences of protracted parental battles long after the breakup (Johnston & Roseby, 1997). Parental conflict creates an emotional environment for the child that is often hostile and critical. Siblings may act as buffers to the conflict, but they too can be drawn into the family warfare (Caya & Liem, 1998). Buchanan, Maccoby, and Dornbusch (1996) reported that potential advantages of frequent and continued contact with both parents were not realized when children felt caught in the middle between warring parents.

The effects of domestic violence on children appear to be even more pernicious than those of nonviolent conflict (Depner, Leino, & Chum, 1992; Leiberman & Van Horn, 1998; McNeal & Amato, 1998). These effects are often compounded by coexisting factors such as sibling violence, child abuse, and psychiatric illness (Appel & Holden, 1998). Further adverse consequences for children are associated with the coercive, erratic parenting that is common in violent households (Margolin, 1998).

Pathogenic Family Functioning. Prospective research on divorce has demonstrated that many of the problems originally considered poor outcomes of divorce could be traced to pathogenic family functioning prior to the family breakup (Amato & Keith, 1991; Cherlin et al., 1991). Higher rates of parental substance abuse, depression, and psychological disorders are noted in some studies (Amato, 1993; Capaldi & Patterson, 1991; Forgatch, Patterson, & Ray, 1995). California's statistics show that in over half (55%) of contested child custody cases, parents raised concerns about child abuse, either physical or sexual, child neglect or abduction, substance abuse, or domestic violence. In 30% of all cases more than one such matter arose, usually in the form of counterallegations between parents (Depner, 2001).

Noting that some poor outcomes attributed to divorce, such as problems of internalizing, externalizing, and self-regulation, are heritable qualities, some analysts (Jockin, McGue, & Lykken, 1996; McGue & Lykken, 1992) caution that inheritance of these problematic characteristics is an alternative plausible explanation for the emotional status of children after divorce. They argue that emotional and behavioral problems may have been inherited rather than specifically linked to family breakup. Present during this stressful period, they could, in fact, exacerbate the difficulties of family disruption.

Protective Factors

Caregiving. Early childhood research emphasizes the critical role of caregiving in the development and adaptation of the child. Not only nutrition and physical care are consequential for a child to reach his or her full potential. A burgeoning literature on early development points to the significance of a nurturing, reciprocal connection between the child and caretaker(s) for the optimal development of the child (Arredondo & Edwards, 2000). For a baby, this may mean feeding the baby when it is hungry or comforting it when it is distressed. For older children, it may be logical consequences for violation of rules. In each case, the child's overture is met with a contingent response from a caregiver.

Parent–Child Relationships. Findings that support the crucial role of caregiving raise concerns when paired with the long-documented effects of divorce on parenting capacity. Some research finds that the stresses of the breakup leave parents particularly vulnerable to diminished mental and physical health, reducing parent availability, adversely affecting the efficiency of day-to-day family functioning, and heightening the number of negative interactions between parent and child (Clarke-Stewart & Hayward, 1996; Emery, 1999; Simons, 1996). As a result, supportive family relationships may be less available to the child at a time when they are most needed.

Poor parenting practices, including problems with communication, supervision, emotional availability, and consistent rules and routines, have been linked to the emotional stress of the family reorganization, conflict, and reduced financial resources (Capaldi & Patterson, 1991; Forgatch et al., 1995). The functioning of the primary caretaker, most often the mother, is an important correlate of child adjustment (Furstenberg & Cherlin, 1991).

Family reorganization may affect the relationship of the child with significant caregivers and influence other key parenting inputs such as cognitive stimulation, verbal interaction, and coaching. The structure and predictability of the home environment have long been considered significant not only to the healthy development of the child but also to adaptation to stressful transitions such as family breakup (Buchanan et al., 1996).

Recently, a separate body of research has looked at the particular contributions fathers can make to children's adjustment to family reorganization (Braver, 1998). This literature also points to adverse effects of severed father–child bonds (Lamb, 1999). Some theorists believe that the impact of sustained father involvement may be particularly beneficial for boys (Amato & Keith, 1991; Clarke-Stewart & Hayward, 1996). In most families, fathers remain only minimally or sporadically involved (Seltzer, 1994). Although many policy makers assume that close and continued contact with both parents is beneficial to the child, research offers little evidence that the quantity of contact alone ensures good outcomes for children. Instead, the variables most strongly associated with good outcomes reflect the quality of the parent–child relationship and the payment of child support (Amato, 1993; Amato & Keith, 1991; Furstenberg & Cherlin, 1991; McLanahan & Sandefur, 1994).

Other Interpersonal Resources. Family reorganization absorbs time that parents might otherwise have available for interaction with and supervision of children. Without the assistance of other adults in the environment, children must rely exclusively on the single parent for modeling, assistance, supervision, and other resources. Kinship and friendship networks offer supplemental resources for the child whose parents live apart. Following family reorganization, one out of five children will live at some time with a grandparent (Seltzer, 1994). Grandparents have visitation rights in every state (Stanton, 1998). In a 5-year follow-up of 672 California families who brought custody disputes to court in 1991, 90% of all parents reported that at least one other adult had a strong quasi-parental role in the life of their child (e.g., helping with homework, attending games and school functions, spending time playing or talking together). Many children had more than one such person. Half of the parents (53%) said that grandparents played this role; nearly half (47%) named a stepparent (Depner, 2001).

Cohabitation and remarriage following family reorganization often also introduce added complexities to the social network of the child, with the addition of new partners (and their family members), stepsiblings, and half-siblings. These new relationships can offer additional resources for the child as well as present a set of new challenges (Bray & Kelly, 1998; Cherlin & Furstenberg, 1994). Supportive stepfamilies have the potential to avert adverse effects of dissolution (Bray & Kelly, 1998). Research on stepparenting shows some direct benefits, particularly for boys. The tenor of the relationship appears to be a crucial factor. Supportive stepfathers enhanced boys' achievement and reduced their antisocial behavior (Amato & Keith, 1991). Adverse effects are more common for girls with step-parents (Hetherington et al., 1998).

Teachers. Little research attention has been devoted to the role of other figures in the social world of the child. Teachers, community figures, and spiritual leaders each can play pivotal roles in the life of a child during family transition. Hetherington, Cox, and Cox (1982) found that teachers could support children during the family transition by working with parents to monitor and bolster their child's day-to-day functioning. Considering the pervasiveness of family breakup, it is likely that adults in academic settings interact with many children going through the experience. Yet their contributions to good outcomes for the child remain unevaluated.

Professional Care and Intervention. The high rates of violence and other pathogenic processes among families contesting child custody raise concerns that children receive appropriate professional care and treatment. For various reasons children may, in fact, be less

likely to receive good pediatric care, early assessment, and intervention. Family dissolution taxes the time and financial resources
of parents. Professionals recognizing the stresses and instabilities of
the postdissolution family may inappropriately advise a "wait and
see" attitude. Training of medical and legal professionals may assist
them in making appropriate referral decisions. Sound planning for
postdissolution families will factor in the appropriate use of good
professional support for children (Ricci, 1997).

Appropriate Custody and Visitation Arrangements. One useful
policy application of social science research would be to determine
whether children fare better when custody is assigned primarily
to the mother, the father, or jointly to both parents. Demonstrable
salutary benefits of any particular form of custody would give policy makers a clear basis for child custody presumptions. This line of
research has proven more difficult than was originally anticipated
and has generated inconclusive results. There are several reasons.
First, given variation in local cultures and legal definitions, custody
labels alone cannot precisely define a unique set of residence and
visitation arrangements. A second reason is that child custody research does not employ standard terminology. The term *custody* is
used generically to refer to circumstances that the law painstakingly
differentiates. In family law, *legal custody* refers to decision-making
responsibilities for the health, education, and welfare of the child;
physical custody refers to where the child resides. *Visitation* or *access*
is the legal label for the amount of time that each parent can spend
with the child. *De facto custody* refers to actual decision making,
residence, and access arrangements that a family follows. De facto
custody may deviate substantially from the specifications of legal
custody orders. The lack of specificity in research terminology con-
founds different effects that custody may have, including decision
making, contact, and residence.

Even when terminology is precise, researchers find that many
families make formal or informal modifications to child custody
and visitation over time (Buchanan et al., 1996; Depner, 1993). As a
result, children categorized under the same custody label may have
very different interactions and relationships with their parents over
the course of their minority. In a California sample of 1,032 children

for whom custody orders were established in 1991, 73% reported that they had made informal changes in visitation and residential arrangements within the first 2 years after going to court. At the 5-year mark, 65% had changed the residence of the child at least once, and 40% of all of the children had changed their residence four times or more (Depner, 2001; Sciortino, 2000).

The heterogeneity of circumstances within general categories of custody makes it difficult to isolate one form of child custody that is advisable in most cases. Instead, research needs to address a more sophisticated question: How can custody plans be structured to mitigate particular risks and vulnerabilities associated with family reorganization?

INCORPORATING RISK AND PROTECTIVE FACTORS
INTO CUSTODY DECISIONS

The goal of the researcher and the child custody decision maker is essentially the same. Each is identifying vulnerabilities of the child, seeking resources to address them, and building on strengths that support good outcomes. Custody determination may employ an analysis of risks and protective factors at several critical junctures. Parents can apply these notions in designing parenting plans. Child custody evaluation ideally involves an assessment of risks and a strategy for mobilizing protective factors. Standards governing judicial decision making also demand an analysis of the factors most likely to promote the child's healthy adjustment.

To avoid intruding on competent parental decision making, some states rely extensively on private ordering. Private ordering allows parents substantial discretion to set up their own custody arrangements, based on the reasoning that parents, not the courts, are best equipped to determine the custody and access arrangements that will be in their children's best interest. With private ordering, courts intervene in custody determination only when parents cannot agree on custody arrangements or when there is a risk to the welfare of the child (Maccoby & Mnookin, 1992). The growing availability of parent education programs provides parents with unprecedented access to information to support decision making about custody decisions (Geisler & Blaisure, 1999).

Best interest standards govern judicial decision making in many states. Derived from juvenile court guidelines, this standard may bring a wide array of considerations to bear on custody determination, weighed according to judicial discretion in the individual case (Kelly, 1997). The Uniform Marriage and Divorce Act [9(a) U.L.A.91 (1976)], adopted by 44 states, outlines several key principles, including parental preferences, child preferences, the child's relationship with each child and with other key members of the family network, the child's adjustment, and the mental health of the parties (Goodman, Emery, & Haugaard, 1998).

Mounting evidence of the high rate of violence between parties with custody disputes has turned policy attention to principles that should govern custody determination in domestic violence cases (Jaffe & Geffner, 1998). Some states have reformulated their best interest standards, assigning priority to the health, safety, and welfare of the child. Others have taken the additional step of restricting custodial rights and access of batterers to their children.

More generally, documentation of dysfunctional and dangerous parents in family law cases is introducing appropriate cautions in the assignment of caregiving responsibilities. It is becoming more common for judicial decision makers to examine critically whether and how a proposed custody arrangement will, in fact, contribute to the healthy development of the child. As a result, judicial officers are ordering more investigations of parental adequacy (Kelly & Lamb, 2000).

With changes in child custody standards that require the court to consider the health, welfare, and safety of the child, it is likely that mental health professionals will be called into court to offer clinical information that has a bearing on child custody decisions. For mental health professionals, this is a clarion call to examine critically the assessment tools and strategies that are most appropriate to that goal (Gould & Stahl, 2000), as well as to ensure that mental health professionals in the court have sufficient training about their appropriate role in the court's deliberations and about the custody implications of the circumstances that may afflict the parties in question (e.g., violence, substance abuse). Mental health practitioners in several disciplines have established ethical and practice guidelines for their work in the courts.

NEW DIRECTIONS FOR FUTURE RESEARCH

Researchers in the field of child custody are painfully aware of the shortcomings of their work (Depner, 1994). The policy utility of the field is compromised by small, descriptive studies with insufficiently rigorous sampling, measurement, or statistical analysis. Custody research credibility is undermined by the prevalence of thinly veiled advocacy scholarship (Felner & Terre, 1987). There is an emerging consensus about the kind of research that would ideally guide custody policy, along with growing recognition of the barriers to meeting that gold standard. Ideally, family law and social science would build on an interdisciplinary research agenda that targets the development of knowledge in key areas. Multiple coordinated studies would address these issues, conforming to rigorous methodological standards. Longitudinal research would trace family functioning over time.

Even with greater methodological sophistication, the nature of the phenomenon under investigation poses serious challenges to child custody research. Pioneering custody researchers have called for recognition of vast differences in family histories, circumstances, and resources (Kelly, 2000) and of variations in the adaptive responses of parents and children (Hetherington et al., 1998). This population is large and diverse, including never-married and divorcing parents, those who remarry and those who maintain long-term single-parent households, those who build strong intergenerational and community supports and those who are isolated, those whose major task is negotiating family transition and those who struggle with problems of violence, drugs, or poverty.

Because many of the most potent predictors and outcomes are highly correlated, it is difficult to isolate variables for intervention. Certain family characteristics (e.g., poverty) predispose a family to reorganization as well as poor outcomes. Without longitudinal data, particularly those from measures of the predivorce household, causal inferences are speculative; but longitudinal work is challenged by the multiple concurrent timetables relevant to the family: the developmental progress of the child, the progress of legal proceedings, and the time frames of family breakup and reorganization.

Despite these challenges, the conceptual and empirical under-pinnings of child custody research have become increasingly so-phisticated. To illustrate some of the paradigmatic shifts that have taken place in the field, we contrast the "old thinking" that dictated early research with some of the new conceptual and theoretical ap-proaches that will guide research in the 21st century.

Old thinking severely underestimated the number of children who were exposed to pathogenic family functioning. The preva-lence of violence, substance abuse, and poverty was not recognized, nor did research address these issues directly as problems attendant to the breakup of many families. New research seeks a clearer un-derstanding of factors that may compromise the health, welfare, and safety of the child.

Although specific developmental vulnerabilities of children have long been known, old thinking regarded children as capable of easily rebounding from severe trauma. Today there is mounting evidence that although the young child has a strong capacity to recover from trauma, early experiences can have a decisive impact on the architecture of the brain and on the nature and extent of adult capacities.

Early custody research placed a great deal of emphasis on the relative impact of mothers and fathers. Today there is recognition of the importance of both parents, as well as the wider range of interpersonal relationships in the child's social world, including siblings, caretakers, stepparents, grandparents, peers, teachers, and the community.

Early custody theories pitted alternative caretakers against one another, concerned about the effects of disrupted attachments on development and learning. New research recognizes that, more important than either bonding or attachment, is the reciprocal con-nection between a child and at least one caregiver. The capacity of the child to form this connection with each parent is recog-nized.

Early research searched for the strongest or critical determi-nants of outcomes for children subject to custody orders. More recently, it has become clear that because many of the lead-ing determinants (e.g., individual attributes, family structure, stresses, parental distress, and family processes) are interrelated, attempts to name the leading determinant have little practical significance.

At one time, social science and law sought universal principles to guide custody determination. Today there is a growing recognition that development is highly variable and contextualized. Children relate to themselves and others in qualitatively different ways at different points in their lives. Early stages are the building blocks for later advances. In addition to these paradigmatic shifts, a critical new direction for research is to represent more clearly the broad spectrum of families and issues that enter family court. There are several promising new directions.

Research on understudied populations is a critical imperative in child custody research. Based almost exclusively on parents of European descent, the child custody literature provides scant information that is generalizable to a wider spectrum of families seeking custody orders. There is a critical need for understanding the circumstances, issues, and preferred solutions of all families facing child custody decisions. Such an approach should not rely on simplistic or essentialist characterizations of ethnic groups (Kline, 1993).

Future research will also be directed to the high proportion of children with custody orders whose life experience does not match the *divorce-event* model. For example, increasing numbers of child custody orders (30% in California) involve children of unmarried parents. Regardless of the marital history of parents, there is a major research gap on the topic of reestablishing relations with a long-absent parent. For parents who have never lived in the same household with the child or who have been estranged for a substantial portion of the child's life, research on issues, alternatives, and outcomes would be extremely beneficial.

Many children who are subject to custody orders live in poverty, yet most custody research is done on middle-class samples. Elite issues dominate inquiry into the relationship of financial and custodial decisions in a literature that looks at the division of assets, not debts, and rarely includes child support issues for low-income or indigent parents. Yet, in 1,996 California contested custody cases, 38% of all mothers and 21% of all fathers were unemployed or earning wages below the poverty level (Depner, 2001). Given substantial evidence of the direct effects of poverty on child development (McLoyd, 1998), future research must integrate the poverty and custody perspectives.

A high proportion of children are exposed to experiences, such as drug use violence, and poverty, that can put them at risk for poor developmental outcomes. These risk factors deserve substantially greater attention in child custody research. Although court reforms to prevent domestic violence make provisions for the inclusion of custody in restraining orders, custody research has given little attention to how these orders are formed and whether they adequately protect the best interest of the child. Custody research currently proceeds with the naive assumption that these cases constitute a minor segment of custody actions. In California, statewide statistics show that nearly half of all contested cases have domestic violence restraining orders.

Another new direction for child custody research is to make more sophisticated distinctions between conflict and violence. Old thinking often did not discriminate between the two dynamics and often portrayed domestic violence as a primarily crisis-engendered response to the breakup. A new direction for research is to trace more carefully the history and etiology of violence, its impact, and its implications for children.

Sibling relationships and the differential impact of custody arrangements on each child in a family also deserve greater attention in future custody research. Although developmentally based models have been invoked in considering the optimal parenting plan for a particular child, these models need to be extended to consider both separate and combined developmental issues of all children in the family.

The prevailing assumption underlying research is that custody cases occur at the time of divorce, and initial custody agreements are adhered to during the minority of the child. Future research should incorporate the wider spectrum of case trajectories – noncompliance with orders, modifications, geographical moves, and blended families.

Although there are no solid statistics, family law professionals are pointing to a rise in the number of crossover cases between the family and juvenile systems. Throughout the minority of a child, the family may have matters in family court, juvenile dependency court, delinquency matters, or child protective services. This overlap should be considered in future custody research. Future custody research should also factor in major social changes, such as child support enforcement and welfare reform, which substantially affect social demands for parental involvement.

CONCLUSION

At the beginning of the 21st century, child custody research is at the crossroads. Social science research has made major strides in identifying risks and resources for children who are subject to child custody orders. There are also important new directions for the future, including broadening the research to include the diverse spectrum of parents who make child custody decisions, forging interdisciplinary relationships, and building a collaborative research agenda to provide solid research that supports family law policy and practice. The family law system will touch the lives of a majority of the current generation of children. This fact alone compels the finest efforts that can be mustered by family law and social science.

References

Amato, P. R. (1993). Children's adjustment to divorce: Theories, hypotheses, and empirical support. *Journal of Marriage and the Family, 55*(1), 23–38.

Amato, P. R., & Keith, B. (1991). Parental divorce and the well-being of children: A meta-analysis. *Psychological Bulletin, 110*, 26–46.

Appel, A., & Holden, G. (1998). The co-occurrence of spouse and physical child abuse: A review of and appraisal. *Journal of Family Psychology, 12*(4), 578–599.

Arredondo, D. E., & Edwards, L. P. (2000). Attachment, bonding, and reciprocal connectedness: Limitations of attachment theory in the juvenile and family court. *Journal of the Center for Families, Children and the Courts, 2*, 109–129.

Bianchi, S. M., Subaiya, L., & Kahn, J. (1997, March). *Economic well-being of husbands and wives after marital disruption.* Paper presented at the annual meeting of the Population Association of America, Washington, DC.

Braver, S. (1998). *Divorced dads: Shattering the myths.* New York: Tarcher/ Putnam.

Bray, J. H. (1991). Psychosocial factors affecting custodial and visitation arrangements. *Behavioral Science and the Law, 9,* 419–437.

Bray, J. H., & Kelly, J. (1998). *Stepfamilies*: Love, marriage, and parenting in the first ten years – based on a landmark study. New York: Broadway Books.

Buchanan, C., Maccoby, E., & Dornbusch, S. (1996). *Adolescents after divorce.* Cambridge, MA: Harvard University Press.

Bumpass, L. L., Martin, T. C., & Sweet, J. A. (1991). The impact of family background and early marital factors on marital disruption. *Journal of Family Issues, 12,* 22–42.

Capaldi, D, M., & Patterson, G. R. (1991). Relation of parental transitions to boy's adjustment problems: I. A linear hypothesis: II. Mothers at risk for transitions and unskilled parenting. *Developmental Psychology, 27,* 489–504.

Caya, M. L., & Liem, J. H. (1998). The role of sibling support in high-conflict families. *American Journal of Orthopsychiatry, 68,* 327–333.

Cherlin, A. J., & Furstenberg, F. F. (1994). Stepfamilies in the United States: A reconsideration. In J. Blake & J. Hagen (Eds.), *Annual review of sociology* (pp. 359–381). Palo Alto, CA: Annual Reviews.

Cherlin, A. J., Furstenberg, F. F., Chase-Lansdale, P. L., Kiernan, K. F., Robins, P. K., Morrison, D. R., & Teitler, J. O. (1991). Longitudinal studies of effects of divorce in children in Great Britain and the United States. *Science, 252,* 1386–1389.

Clarke-Stewart, K. A., & Hayward, C. (1996). Advantages of father custody and contact for the psychological well-being of school-age children. *Journal of Applied Developmental Psychology, 17,* 239–270.

Clarke-Stewart, K. A., Vandell, D. L., McCartney, K., Owen, M. T., & Booth, C. (2000). Effects of parental separation and divorce on very young children. *Journal of Family Psychology, 14*(2), 304–326.

Cummings, E. M., & Davies, P. (1994). *Children and marital conflict.* New York: Guilford Press.

Depner, C. E. (1993). Parental role reversal: Mothers as nonresidential parents. In C. E. Depner & J. H. Bray (Eds.), *Nonresidential parenting: New vistas in family living* (pp. 37–60). Newbury Park, CA: Sage.

Depner, C. E. (1994). Revolution and reassessment: Child custody in context. In A. E. Gottfried and A. W. Gottfried (Eds.), *Redefining families: Implications for child development* (pp. 99–130). New York: Plenum.

Depner, C. E. (2001, March). *Risk and resilience in contested child custody cases.* Paper presented at the California Family Law Institute, Costa Mesa.

Depner, C. E., Leino, V., & Chun, A. (1992). Interparental conflict and child adjustment: A decade review and meta-analysis. *Family and Conciliation Courts Review, 30*(3), 323–341.

Emery, R. E. (1999). *Renegotiating family relationships: Divorce, child custody, and mediation.* New York: Guilford Press.

Felner, R. D., & Terre, L. (1987). Child custody dispositions and children's adaptation following divorce. In L. Weithorn (Ed.), *Psychology and child custody determinants: Knowledge, roles and expertise* (pp. 106–149). Lincoln: University of Nebraska Press.

Forgatch, M. S., Patterson, G. R., & Ray, J. A. (1995). Divorce and boys' adjustment problems: Two paths with a single model . In E. M. Hetherington & E. A. Blechman (Eds.), *Stress, coping and resiliency in children and families* (pp. 67–105). Mahwah, NJ: Erlbaum.

Furstenberg, F. F., Jr., & Cherlin, A. J. (1991). *Divided families: What happens to children when parents part.* Cambridge, MA.: Harvard University Press.

Geisler, M. J., & Blaisure, K. R. (1999). 1998 nationwide survey of court-connected divorce education programs. *Family and Conciliation Courts Review, 37*(1), 36–63.

Goodman, G. S., Emery, R. E., & Haugaard, J. J. (1998). Developmental psychology and law: Divorce, child maltreatment, foster care and adoption. In W. Damon, I. E. Sigel, & K. A. Renniger (Eds.), *Handbook of child psychology: Child psychology in practice* (Vol. 4, pp. 775–876). New York: Wiley.

Gorell-Barnes, G. (1999). Divorce transitions: Identifying risks and promoting resilience for children and their parental relationships. *Journal of Marriage and the Family, 25*(4), 425–441.

Gould, J. W., & Stahl, P. M. (2000). The art and science of child custody evaluations: Integrating clinical and forensic mental health models. *Family and Conciliation Courts Review, 38*(3), 392–414.

Hetherington, E. M., Bridges, M., & Insabella, G. M. (1998). Five perspectives on the association between marital transitions and child adjustment. *American Psychologist, 53*(2), 167–184.

Hetherington, E. M., Cox, M., & Cox, R. (1982). Effects of divorce on parents and children. In M. E. Lamb (Ed.), *Nontraditional families: parenting and child development* (pp. 233–288). Hillsdale, NJ: Erlbaum.

Jaffe, P. G., & Geffner, R. (1998). Child custody disputes and domestic violence: Critical issues for mental health, social service, and legal professionals. In G. W. Holden, R. Geffner, & E. N. Jouriles (Eds.), *Children exposed to marital violence: Theory, research, and applied issues* (pp. 371–408). Washington, DC: American Psychological Association.

Johnston, J., & Roseby, V. (1997). *In the name of the child: A developmental approach to understanding and helping children of conflict and violent divorce.* New York: Free Press.

Jockin, V., McGue, M., & Lykken, D. T. (1996). Personality and divorce: A genetic analysis. *Journal of Personality and Social Psychology, 71*, 288–299.

Jouriles, E., & Norwood, W. (1996). Physical violence and other forms of marital aggression: Links with children's behavior problems. *Journal of Family Psychology, 10*, 223–234.

Kelly, J. (1997). The best interests of the child: A concept in search of meaning. *Family and Conciliation Courts Review, 35*(4), 377–387.

Kelly, J. (2000). Children's adjustment in conflicted marriage and divorce: A decade review of research. *Journal of the Academy of Child Adolescent Psychiatry, 39*(8), 963–973.

Kelly, J., & Lamb, M. E. (2000). Using child development research to make appropriate custody and access decisions for young children. *Family and Conciliation Courts Review, 38*(3), 297–311.

Kline, M. (1993). Race, racism, and feminist legal theory. In D. K. Weisberg (Ed.), *Feminist legal theory: Foundations* (pp. 371–382). Philadelphia: Temple University Press.

Lamb, M. E. (1999). Non-custodial fathers and their impact on the children of divorce. In R. A. Thompson & P. Amato (Eds.), *The post-divorce family: Research and policy issues* (pp. 105–125). Thousand Oaks, CA: Sage.

Laumann-Billings, L., & Emery, R. E. (2000). Distress among young adults from divorced families. *Journal of Family Psychology, 14*(4), 671–687.

Lieberman, A., & Van Horn, P. (1998). Attachment, trauma, and domestic violence: Implications for child custody. *Child and Adolescent Psychiatric Clinics of North America, 7*(2), 423–443.

Maccoby, E., & Mnookin, R. (1992). *Dividing the child*. Cambridge, MA: Harvard University Press.

Margolin, G. (1998). Effects of domestic violence on children. In P. K. Trickett & C. J. Shellenbach (Eds.), *Violence against children in the family and the community* (pp. 57–102). Washington, DC: American Psychological Association.

Masten, A. S., & Coatsworth, J. D. (1998). The developmental competence in favorable and unfavorable environments: Lessons from research on successful children. *American Psychologist, 53*(2), 205–220.

McGue, M., & Lykken, D. T. (1992). Genetic influence on risk of divorce. *Psychological Science, 6*, 368–373.

McLanahan, S., & Bumpass, L. (1988). Intergenerational consequences of family disruption. *American Journal of Sociology, 94*, 130–152.

McLanahan, S., & Sandefur, G. (1994). *Growing up with a single parent: What hurts, what helps*. Cambridge, MA: Harvard University Press.

McLoyd, V. C. (1998). Socioeconomic disadvantage and child development. *American Psychologist, 53*(2), 185–204.

McNeal, C., & Amato, P. (1998). Parents' marital violence: Long-term consequences for children. *Journal of Family Issues, 19*(2), 123–139.

Nord, C. W., Brimhall, D., & West, J. (1997). *Fathers' involvement in their children's schools*. Washington, DC: National Center for Educational Statistics, U.S. Department of Education.

Ostrom, B. J., & Kauder, N. B. (1997). *Examining the work of state courts*. A joint project of the Conference of State Court Administrators, the State Justice Institute, the Bureau of Justice Statistics, and the National Center for State Courts' Court Statistics Project. Williamsburg, VA: National Center for State Courts.

Patterson, G. R., Forgatch, M. S., Yoerger, K. L., & Stoolmiller, M. (1998). Variables that initiate and maintain an early-onset trajectory for juvenile offending. *Develoment and Psychopathology, 10,* 531–547.

Ricci, I. (1997). *Mom's house, dad's house: Making two homes for your child.* New York: Simon & Schuster.

Rossman, B. B. R. (1998). Decarte's error and post-traumatic stress disorder: Cognition and emotion in children who are exposed to parental violence. In G. W. Holden, R. Geffner, & E. N. Jouriles (Eds.), *Children exposed to marital violence: Theory, research, and applied issues* (pp. 223–256). Washington, DC: American Psychological Association.

Rutter, M. (1987). Psychosocial resilience and protective mechanisms. *American Journal of Orthopsychiatry, 57,* 316–331.

Sciortino, S. (2000). *Children's residence five years after mediation* (Research Update 6). San Francisco: California Center for Families, Children, and the Courts.

Seltzer, J. A. (1994). Consequences of marital dissolution for children. *Annual Review of Sociology, 20,* 235–266.

Simons, R. L. (1996). The effect of divorce on adult and child adjustment. In R. L. Simons & Associates (Eds.), *Understanding differences between divorced and intact families: Stress, interaction, and child outcomes* (pp. 65–77). Thousand Oaks, CA: Sage.

Stanton, A. M. (1998). Grandparents' visitation rights and custody. *Child and Adolescent Psychiatric Clinics of North America, 7*(2), 423–443.

U.S. Bureau of the Census. (1992, March). *Marital status and living arrangements* (No. 468, Current Population Reports, Series P-20). Washington, DC: U.S. Government Printing Office.

Vuchinich, S., Bank, L., & Patterson, G. R. (1992). Parenting, peers, and the stability of antisocial behavior in preadolescent boys. *Developmental Psychology, 28*(3), 510–521.

Warshak, R. (1992). *The custody revolution: The father factor and the motherhood mystique.* New York: Poseidon Press.

Werner, E. E. (1993). Risk, resilience, and recovery: Perspectives from the Kauai Longitudinal Study. *Development and Psychopathology, 54,* 503–515.

8

Children of Lesbian and Gay Parents

Research, Law, and Policy

Charlotte J. Patterson
Megan Fulcher
Jennifer Wainright

On December 20, 1999, in a groundbreaking decision, the Vermont Supreme Court ruled that the state must guarantee exactly the same protections for same-sex couples that it does for heterosexual couples (Goldberg, 1999). The court left it to the state legislature to decide whether to accomplish this by legalizing same-sex marriages in Vermont, by adopting a domestic partnership law that would provide all the protections afforded by marriage, or by some other means. To extend equal rights to gay and lesbian couples "who seek nothing more, nor less, than legal protection and security for their avowed commitment to an intimate and lasting relationship is simply, when all is said and done," the opinion stated, "a recognition of our common humanity" (*Baker et al. v. State of Vermont et al.*, 1999, p. 45).

Thus began a new chapter in the history of legal and policy issues affecting children of lesbian and gay parents. The Vermont legislature responded to the court's ruling by creating the possibility for *civil unions* among same-sex partners. A civil union is a "comprehensive legal status parallel to civil marriage for all purposes under Vermont state law" (ACLU, 2001) but does not affect the partners' status under federal law. The new statute, which took effect on July 1, 2000, allows same-sex couples who undertake civil unions to

Address correspondence to Charlotte J. Patterson, Department of Psychology, Gilmer Hall, P.O. Box 400400, University of Virginia, Charlottesville VA 22904 or via the Internet at cjp@virginia.edu move from the status of *legal strangers* with regard to one another to the status of *legal next of kin*, at least for purposes of Vermont law. The creation of civil unions for same-sex couples created new protections for children of lesbian and gay couples who undertake civil unions, including improved access to family health insurance coverage and protection of family relationships by the courts in case of parental separations or dissolution of civil unions. Civil unions for same-sex couples in Vermont, then, are likely to result in benefits to children of lesbian and gay parents in that state.

Although Vermont has thus recently taken a major step toward equal rights for lesbian and gay Americans, events of the past few years in other states have moved in a different direction. For instance, policies forbidding openly lesbian or gay adults to adopt minor children, which by 1998 had been discarded by every state except Florida, have had a resurgence in the last few years, with Arkansas, Utah, and Mississippi all adopting antigay adoption statutes. The issues surrounding lesbian and gay parents and their children are currently the subject of spirited debate across the United States, and the legal and policy landscape relevant to children of lesbian and gay parents remains in flux.

In view of the rapidly changing legal and policy environments, our aims in this chapter are three: to summarize the current status of legal and policy issues relevant to children of lesbian and gay parents in the United States today, to provide an overview of the research evidence about development among these children, and – in light of the current knowledge base – to outline some changes in law and policy that would benefit children growing up with lesbian and gay parents. In short, we hope to provide a snapshot of the current legal terrain, to give an overview of the relevant social science literature, and to offer some suggestions for future legal and policy initiatives.

A preliminary question can be raised about the number of children involved in such discussions. How many children of lesbian and gay parents are there in the United States today? Many estimates have been offered, but reliable estimates of the number of lesbian and gay parents and their children are difficult to find (Badgett, 1998; Michaels, 1996; Patterson & Friel, 2000). Early attempts to create such estimates were based on nonrepresentative samples and were subject to a number of biases. More recent efforts (Badgett, 1998; Patterson & Friel, 2000) have drawn on population-based representative (or near-representative) samples. Even so, difficult assessment dilemmas must be resolved regarding the ways in which participants are identified as lesbian or gay, on the one hand, and as parents, on the other. The impact of these decisions on the size of estimates can be dramatic. If, for example, women are asked, "Are you a parent?", many more lesbian women apparently respond in the affirmative than if they are asked, "Have you had a biological child?" (Badgett, 1998; Patterson & Friel, 2000). The result is that although there is common agreement that there are many lesbian and gay parents in the United States today, and although most commentators suggest that parenthood is becoming more common in lesbian and gay communities, there is little agreement as to the precise number of lesbian and gay parents and their children. The clearest conclusion is that there are very substantial numbers – almost certainly millions – of children with lesbian and gay parents in the United States today (Patterson & Friel, 2000), and hence that legal and policy issues relevant to them affect sizable numbers of Americans.

When considering lesbian and gay parents and their children, it is helpful to recognize the diversity of family constellations. One important distinction is between families in which children were born or adopted in the context of heterosexual marriages that later dissolved when one or both parents came out as lesbian or gay, on the one hand, and those in which children were born or adopted after parents had affirmed lesbian or gay identities, on the other. Families of the first type have undergone the tensions, separations, and reorganizations characteristic of parental divorce and separation, whereas families of the second type have not experienced these transitions. Thus, children's experiences are likely to be different in the two kinds of families.

Within each of these two general types of families, there are, of course, many additional kinds of diversity. Apart from the ethnic, religious, economic, and other forms of diversity that characterize other families, there are also a number of forms of diversity that are more specific to lesbian and gay family formation (Martin, 1993; Patterson, 1995b). For instance, a lesbian couple and a gay couple may agree to conceive children together and raise them jointly. Variants on this arrangement might involve a gay couple and a single lesbian or a lesbian couple and a single man. The adults might or might not live in the same home or in close proximity to one another. Children may be conceived by lesbian mothers using sperm from a known or an unknown donor, or by gay men with the help of a surrogate mother, or children may be adopted either in domestic arrangements or from abroad. For a number of reasons (e.g., international adoptions), many families also include members of more than one ethnic group.

Different kinds of lesbian- and gay-parented families have given rise to different types of legal and policy issues. For instance, child custody cases involving lesbian and gay parents may arrive in court when previously married heterosexual parents are divorcing, after one has come out as lesbian or gay, and the parents cannot agree on custody and visitation arrangements. In some jurisdictions, these cases raise the question of whether a parent's sexual orientation should be considered in making custody and visitation arrangements for minor children; in others, they do not. If a lesbian couple has adopted a child together and subsequently separates, questions about custody and visitation may also find their way into court. Here, however, the issues raised are likely to be different ones. Because only one member of the couple is likely to be recognized as a parent by the law, questions may revolve around the standing of the other member to bring a custody matter at all. Other kinds of lesbian- and gay-parented families may raise a variety of other legal and policy issues, including those involving the use of reproductive technology, surrogacy, adoption, and foster care arrangements.

In the next section, we provide an overview of the legal and policy terrain for children of lesbian and gay parents in the United States today, with an eye to the diversity of issues and families involved. This is followed by a discussion of the research literature on children of lesbian and gay parents, and by recommendations for changes in law and policy that would benefit children in lesbian- and gay-parented families.

LEGAL STATUS OF LESBIAN AND GAY PARENTS AND THEIR CHILDREN

Although the right to marry and the right to raise children as one sees fit are regarded by American law as fundamental, these rights have not been extended to lesbian or gay Americans. The rights to marry (*Loving v. Virginia*, 1967), to procreate (*Skinner v. Oklahoma*, 1942), and to raise children (*Meyer V. Nebraska*, 1923) have long been held by the U.S. Supreme Court to be fundamental and, as such, have been seen as guaranteed by the Constitution. But however taken for granted these rights may be by the majority of Americans, they have often been denied to lesbian and gay Americans. At the time of this writing, legal recognition of same-sex marriage has not yet occurred in any jurisdiction within the United States (Chambers, 1996; Eskridge, 1993; Rubinstein, 1996). Lesbian and gay parents have endured many challenges to their custody of and visitation with children from previous heterosexual marriages, as well as limitations on their opportunities to become foster or adoptive parents after acknowledging their lesbian or gay identities (Rubinstein, 1991, 1996).

Sodomy Laws

Important underpinnings of discrimination against lesbian women and gay men in many states are provided by the so-called sodomy laws (Rivera, 1991; Rubinstein, 1996). In 1950, every state in the Union had such laws on the books, making private oral or anal sexual conduct between consenting adults a criminal act – often a felony. Over the years, sodomy laws have gradually undergone repeal in many states (ACLU, 2000). Many sodomy statutes have been voided by legislatures or by courts, but sodomy restrictions are still on the books in 15 states. In Arkansas, Kansas, and Oklahoma, the laws apply to same-sex but not to opposite-sex couples; in Arkansas, the law is currently under challenge (ACLU, 2001). Twelve states still have sodomy laws that apply to both same-sex and different-sex couples (ACLU, 2000).

Despite the undisputed fact that behavior prohibited by these laws is widespread among heterosexual as well as nonheterosexual adults in the United States today (Laumann, Gagnon, Michael, & Michaels, 1994), courts have often used the illegality of lesbian and gay parents' presumed sexual conduct to justify the denial of child custody or the curtailment of visitation (e.g., *Bottoms v. Bottoms*, 1995; *Roe v. Roe*, 1985; *Thigpen v. Carpenter*, 1987). Despite the private nature of sexual behavior between consenting adults, sodomy laws have often been invoked against lesbian and gay parents seeking custody of their children, and sodomy laws represent an important barrier to equal treatment of lesbian women and gay men. This point was recognized by the Georgia Supreme Court in *Powell v. State* (1998) when it struck down laws forbidding oral and anal sex between consenting adults, saying that "we cannot think of any other activity that reasonable persons would rank as more private and more deserving of protection from governmental interference than consensual, private, adult sexual activity" (ACLU, 2000). State sodomy laws were, however, upheld as constitutional by the U.S. Supreme Court in *Bowers v. Hardwick* (1986) on the grounds that sodomy laws do not violate the right to privacy guaranteed by federal law. In the wake of the *Bowers v. Hardwick* decision, efforts to overturn sodomy laws must proceed on a state-by-state basis.

Child Custody and Visitation by Lesbians and Gay Men

The extent to which a parent's sexual identity is considered relevant in deciding a child's best interest, for purposes of child custody and visitation, varies from state to state (Brantner, 1992; Lambda Legal Defense and Education Fund, 1996; see Depner, this volume, for a general discussion of divorce and custody issues). In many states, parental sexual orientation is considered relevant to custody and visitation disputes only if it can be shown to have an adverse impact on the child. Before parental sexual orientation can be considered as a factor relevant to the child's best interests, in these states, a connection, or *nexus*, must be demonstrated between a person's sexual orientation, on the one hand, and a negative outcome for the child, on the other. For instance, in *S.N.E. v. R.L.B.* (1985), an Alaska court awarded custody to a lesbian mother, noting that there was "no suggestion that [her sexual orientation] has or is likely to affect the child adversely." Similar rulings have emerged recently in a number of states. For instance, in a recent Maryland visitation case (*Boswell v. Boswell*, 1998), the court refused to limit children's visitation with their gay father in the presence of his same-sex partner because there was no evidence of harm to the children from such visitation.

At the other end of the spectrum, some states have in place presumptions against lesbian or gay parents. Even though these may no longer rise to the level a of per se rule against parental fitness among lesbian and gay adults, they may nevertheless remain influential. In the *Bottoms v. Bottoms* (1995) case, for example, the Virginia Supreme Court reiterated its earlier holding that a lesbian mother is not per se unfit, but it included the mother's sexual orientation among factors considered to make her an undesirable parent. It viewed the fact that "conduct inherent in lesbianism is punishable as a . . . felony" (i.e., the mother's violation of the state's sodomy laws) as an "important consideration in determining custody" (*Bottoms v. Bottoms*, 1995, p. 108).

The legal standards for custody in a number of states fall somewhere between these two extremes. In one recent case (*Burgess v. Burgess*, 1999), the Indiana Supreme Court denied a gay father's request for review of a lower court's decision that denied him custody of his son. Indiana law does not allow parental sexual orientation to be considered as a determinative factor in placement of a child, but the court noted in its decision that the father's sexual orientation "raises the specter of an aberrant lifestyle" (*Burgess v. Burgess*, 1999). In another recent North Carolina case, a gay father was denied custody of his two sons because of the court's concern about his long-term relationship with a male partner, who was helping to care for the boys (*Pulliam v. Smith*, 1998). Despite legal progress in many states, child custody and visitation for lesbian and gay parents after the breakup of heterosexual marriages continue, in some jurisdictions, to be adjudicated in an atmosphere of antigay prejudice.

Adoption and Foster Care

Legal adoptions of minor children by lesbian and gay adults can be seen as falling into one of two categories (Patterson, 1995c). When biological parents are unable or unwilling to care for a child and an adoptive parent who is not related to the biological parents offers to provide that child with a home, the result is called a *stranger adoption*. In such cases, the courts dissolve existing legal bonds and create a new legal relationship between the child and the adoptive parent. *Second-parent adoptions* are pursued by lesbian and gay couples who raise a child together, although only one member of the couple – the biological parent or legal adoptive parent – is viewed as a parent in law. These couples seek legal recognition of the relationship between the other parent and the child. In recent years, both types of adoption have been completed by openly lesbian and gay individuals in the United States (Polikoff, 1990).

Like laws on custody and visitation, those governing adoption vary considerably across the states (Patterson, 1995c; for a discussion of adoption and foster care in the context of heterosexual relationships, see Haugaard and Avery, this volume). At the time of this writing, adoption of minor children by lesbian or gay adults is specifically barred by statute in Arkansas, Florida, Mississippi, and Utah. New Hampshire had a statute barring lesbian and gay individuals from becoming adoptive parents until recently, but the legislature repealed it in 1999 (Love, 1999). In other states, such as New York and Massachusetts, the law allows adoptions by openly lesbian and gay prospective adoptive parents. For example, in a landmark New York second-parent adoption case, *In re Adoption of Evan* (1992), the court noted that "[t]he fact that the petitioners here maintain an open lesbian relationship is not a reason to deny adoption. . . . A parent's sexual orientation or sexual practices are presumptively irrelevant" (*In re Adoption of Evan*, 1992, pp. 1001–1002).

Even though state adoption laws vary, both stranger adoptions and second-parent adoptions by openly lesbian and gay adults have occurred in numerous jurisdictions. Openly lesbian or gay adults have completed stranger adoptions in many states, including California, Ohio, and the District of Columbia. Many more stranger adoptions have no doubt been accomplished by lesbian or gay adults in other states without their sexual orientation becoming a topic of public discussion. Second-parent adoptions have been granted in 17 states and in the District of Columbia. State supreme courts in Massachusetts, Vermont, and Wisconsin have ruled on the legality of second-parent adoptions, and two of the three – Massachusetts (*Adoption of Tammy*, 1993) and Vermont (*Adoptions of B.L.V.B. & E.L.V.B.*, 1993) – have affirmed them.

Summary

Across the United States today, the legal and policy landscape for lesbian and gay parents and their children is remarkably varied. At one end of the spectrum, in a state such as Massachusetts – in which sodomy laws have been repealed, in which parental sexual orientation is considered irrelevant to child custody and visitation proceedings, and in which the State Supreme Court has affirmed the legality of second-parent adoptions – the legal climate for lesbian and gay parents and their children is generally positive. At the other end of the spectrum, in a state such as Virginia – in which sodomy laws make private oral and anal sexual conduct between consenting adults illegal, in which lesbian and gay parents are disadvantaged in custody and visitation proceedings by negative presumptions about their parental fitness, and in which second-parent adoptions have not yet been reported – the legal atmosphere for lesbian and gay parents and their children is less desirable. Although the pace of change may vary from state to state, the direction of movement over time during the last 50 years is clearly toward provision of greater legal recognition of the many different family types formed by lesbian and gay adults.

SOCIAL SCIENCE RESEARCH ON LESBIAN AND GAY PARENTS
AND THEIR CHILDREN

How do the results of social science research address legal and policy issues raised by child custody, visitation, and adoption by lesbian and gay parents? In this section, we provide an overview of studies focused on children of lesbian and gay parents. When they have denied or curtailed custody or visitation, courts have voiced three main concerns about development among children of lesbian and gay parents. Research in each of the three main areas of judicial concern – namely, children's sexual identity, other aspects of children's personal development, and children's social relationships – will now be summarized. For other recent reviews of this material, see Green and Bozett (1991), Parks (1998), Patterson (1992, 1995b, 1995d, 1997, 1998), Perrin (1998), and Tasker and Golombok (1991, 1997).

Children of Divorced Lesbian and Gay Parents

Reflecting the issues relevant to the largest number of custody disputes, most of the research compares development among children with divorced custodial lesbian mothers to that of children with divorced custodial heterosexual mothers. For children living in families headed by lesbian mothers who are divorced from the children's fathers, it has been widely believed that children living in families headed by divorced but heterosexual mothers provide the best comparison group. Thus, most studies have compared children in divorced lesbian mother–headed families with children in divorced heterosexual mother–headed families, and we review these here.

One major concern is that development of sexual identity might be compromised for children with lesbian or gay parents. For example, it has been suggested that children reared by lesbian or gay parents may show disturbances in gender identity (i.e., a person's self-identification as male or female), gender role behavior (i.e., the degree to which a person's activities are regarded by the culture as conforming to masculine or feminine norms), and/or sexual orientation (i.e., a person's choice of sexual partners, whether heterosexual, homosexual, or bisexual). To examine the possibility that children in the custody of lesbian or gay parents experience disruptions of development in this area, research has addressed each of these three major facets of sexual identity.

In general, research has failed to reveal important differences in the development of children's gender identity or gender role behavior as a function of parents' sexual orientation (Golombok, Spencer, & Rutter, 1983; Green, 1978; Green, Mandel, Hotvedt, Gray, & Smith, 1986; Kirkpatrick, Roy, & Smith, 1981). For example, in interviews with children of lesbian and heterosexual mothers, Green and his colleagues (1986) found no differences among children as a function of their mothers' sexual orientation with respect to favorite television programs, television characters, games, or toys. These investigators did report that daughters of lesbian mothers were more likely to be described as engaging in rough-and-tumble play, or play with toys such as trucks or guns that are usually thought of as masculine, but they found no comparable tendency for sons' play to be feminized, nor have other investigators replicated the difference for daughters. Taking all the available information together, the similarities in development of gender identity and gender role behavior between children of lesbian mothers and children of heterosexual mothers are very striking.

A number of investigators have also studied sexual orientation, the third component of sexual identity. For example, Huggins (1989) interviewed a group of teenagers, half of whom were the offspring of heterosexual mothers and half of lesbian mothers. No child of a lesbian mother self-identified as lesbian or gay, but one child of a heterosexual mother did. Similar results have been reported by others (e.g., Golombok & Tasker, 1996; Gottman, 1990). Studies of the offspring of gay fathers have yielded similar results (Bozett, 1987).

Further studies, conducted from a behavior genetic perspective, have added to this literature. Pattatucci and Hamer (1995) studied a large sample of women, some of whom self-identified as lesbian or bisexual. Using loose criteria for identification (i.e., average Kinsey scores of 2 or higher), there were 19 such women in their sample with daughters old enough that their sexual orientation could be reported. Of these, six daughters were identified as lesbian or bisexual. However, when more restrictive criteria were used to identify lesbian and bisexual women (i.e., average Kinsey scores of 5 or above), only one of seven adult daughters who were interviewed by the researchers identified herself as lesbian. No significant results emerged for sons of lesbian mothers in this sample. In another, similar study, Bailey and his colleagues (1995) interviewed gay fathers and inquired about the sexual orientation of their adult sons. They reported that 7 of 75 (9%) of the sons in their sample were identified as gay or bisexual. No information about the daughters of gay fathers was collected in this study. Appropriate interpretation of these numbers depends on the population base rates for nonheterosexual identities, and for many reasons, these remain a matter of dispute. Thus, the clearest conclusion from these and the earlier studies would seem to be that although the extent of possible genetic contributions to sexual orientation remains unknown, the great majority of children with lesbian or gay parents grow up to identify themselves as heterosexual (Bailey & Dawood, 1998).

A broad array of other aspects of personal development has been assessed by researchers (Patterson, 1995b; Tasker & Golombok, 1991). Among these have been psychiatric evaluations and assessments of behavior problems, personality, self-esteem, self-concept, locus of control, moral judgment, and intelligence. Concerns about possible difficulties in personal development among children of lesbian and gay parents have not been sustained by the results of this research (Patterson, 1992, 1995b, 1997). As was the case for sexual identity, studies of other aspects of personal development have revealed no important differences between children of lesbian/gay and heterosexual parents. Fears that the children of lesbian or gay parents suffer deficits in personal development appear to be without empirical foundation.

Studies assessing potential differences between children of gay and lesbian versus heterosexual parents have sometimes included assessments of children's social relationships. Because of concerns voiced by the courts that children of lesbian and gay parents might encounter difficulties among their peers, the most common focus of attention has been on peer relations (Patterson & Redding, 1996). Studies in this area have consistently found that children of lesbian mothers report normal peer relations and that adult observers agree with this judgment (Patterson, 1992). Anecdotal and first-person accounts describe children's worries about being stigmatized as a result of their parents' sexual orientation (e.g., Pollack & Vaughn, 1987). The research literature in this area remains sparse, but findings to date provide little if any evidence for the proposition that children of lesbian mothers have difficulty in peer relations (Tasker & Golombok, 1997).

Research has also been directed to the description of children's relationships with adults, especially fathers. For instance, Golombok and her colleagues in the United Kingdom (1983) found that children of divorced lesbian mothers were more likely than children of divorced heterosexual mothers to have contact with their fathers. Most children of lesbian mothers who participated in this study had some contact with their fathers during the year preceding the study, but most children of heterosexual mothers had not. Kirkpatrick and her colleagues (1981) also reported that the lesbian mothers in their sample were more concerned than the heterosexual mothers that their children have opportunities for good relationships with adult men, including their fathers. Overall, the results of research to date suggest that children of lesbian mothers have satisfactory relationships with adults of both genders.

Concerns that children of lesbian or gay parents are more likely than children of heterosexual parents to be sexually abused have also been voiced by judges in the context of child custody disputes (Patterson & Redding, 1996). Results of research in this area show that the great majority of adults who perpetrate sexual abuse are male; sexual abuse of children by adult women is extremely rare. Existing research findings suggest that gay men are no more likely than heterosexual men to perpetrate child sexual abuse (Jenny, Roesler, & Poyer, 1994). Fears that children in the custody of gay or lesbian parents might be at heightened risk of sexual abuse are thus without empirical foundation (Patterson, 1995b, 1997, 1998).

Research on Children Born to or Adopted by Lesbian Mothers

Many writers have recently noted an increase in childbearing among lesbians, but research on these families is relatively new (Kirkpatrick, 1996; Martin, 1993; Patterson, 1992, 1994b; Perrin, 1998). In this section, we summarize the research to date on children born to or adopted by lesbian mothers. Although some gay men are also undertaking parenthood after coming out, no research has yet been reported on their children.

In one of the earliest studies of children born to lesbians, Steckel (1987) compared the progress of social and personality development among preschool children conceived via donor insemination to lesbian couples with that of same-age children conceived in the conventional way by heterosexual couples. Using parent interviews, parent and teacher Q sorts, and structured doll play techniques, Steckel compared independence, ego functions, and object relations among children in the two types of families. Her main results documented impressive similarity in psychological development among children in the two groups. Similar findings, based on extensive interviews with five lesbian mother families, were also reported by McCandlish (1987).

The first study to examine psychosocial development among preschool and school-age children born to or adopted by lesbian mothers was conducted by Patterson (1994a, 1995a; Patterson, Hurt, & Mason, 1998). Thirty-seven 4- to 9-year-old children were studied using a variety of standardized measures. The Achenbach and Edelbrock Child Behavior Checklist was used to assess children's social competence and behavior problems (Achenbach & Edelbrock, 1983); five scales from the Eder Children's Self-View Questionnaire (Eder, 1990) were used to assess children's self-concepts, and open-ended interview techniques were used to assess preferences associated with sex-role behavior. In this way, the study sought to provide an overview of the children's development.

Results showed that children scored in the normal range for all measures (Patterson, 1994a). On the Child Behavior Checklist, for example, children of lesbian mothers' scores for social competence, internalizing behavior problems, and externalizing behavior problems were lower than the scores for a clinical sample but did not differ from the scores for a large normative sample of American children. Likewise, children of lesbian mothers reported sex-role preferences within the expected normal range for children of this age. On most subscales of the self-concept measure, answers given by children of lesbian mothers did not differ from those given by same-age children of heterosexual mothers studied in a standardization sample (Patterson, 1994a). On two subscales of the self-concept measure, however, Patterson (1994a) found that children of lesbian mothers reported feeling more reactions to stress (e.g., feeling angry, scared, or upset) but a greater sense of well-being (e.g., feeling joyful, content, and comfortable with themselves) than did same-age children of heterosexual mothers in a standardized sample. One possible interpretation of this result is that children of lesbian mothers reported greater reactivity to stress because, in fact, they experienced greater stress in their daily lives than did other children. Another possibility is that, regardless of actual stress levels, children of lesbian mothers were better able to acknowledge both positive and negative aspects of their emotional experience. Although this latter interpretation is perhaps more consistent with the differences in both stress reactions and well-being, clarification of these and other potential interpretations must await the results of further research.

Some additional findings from this study can be mentioned briefly. Contrary to stereotypes of these families as isolated from their families of origin, most reported that children had regular (i.e., at least monthly) contact with one or more grandparents, as well as with other adult friends and relatives of both sexes (Patterson et al., 1998). In families headed by lesbian couples, the parents were likely to maintain egalitarian divisions of labor. When differences occurred, however, biological lesbian mothers were likely to do somewhat more child care and nonbiological lesbian mothers were likely to spend somewhat more time engaged in paid employment (Patterson, 1995d). Even within the relatively restricted range represented in this sample, families in which child care was divided more evenly were also those in which children exhibited the most favorable adjustment (Patterson, 1995d). These results suggest the importance of family process variables as predictors of child adjustment in lesbian as well as heterosexual families.

Chan and his colleagues (Chan, Brooks, Raboy, & Patterson, 1998b; Chan, Raboy, & Patterson, 1998a) studied a group of 80 families formed by lesbian and heterosexual parents via donor insemination and reported that children's overall adjustment was unrelated to parents' sexual orientation. Regardless of parents' sexual orientation or relationship status, parents who were experiencing higher levels of parenting stress, higher levels of interparental conflict, and lower levels of love for each other had children who exhibited more behavior problems. Among lesbian couples, nonbiological mothers' satisfaction with the division of labor, especially in family decision making, was related to better couple adjustment, which was in turn related to children's positive psychological adjustment (Chan et al., 1998a), a result that is consistent with research on heterosexual families (Cowan & Cowan, 1992). Flaks and his colleagues (1995) also compared children from lesbian mother families with those from heterosexual families and found no differences in the children's level of psychological adjustment as a function of the mother's sexual orientation.

In Europe, Brewaeys and her colleagues (1997) studied children's adjustment among a group of 4- to 8-year-old children who were conceived via donor insemination by lesbian and heterosexual

parents and compared them to a group of children who were conceived by heterosexual parents in the conventional way. When
children were asked about their perceptions of parent–child relationships, all children reported positive feelings about their parents;
there were no differences in children's reports as a function of family type. Children's behavior and emotional adjustment were also
assessed. The results indicated that overall, children who were conceived via donor insemination in heterosexual families exhibited
more behavior problems than other children. In particular, girls who
were conceived via donor insemination in heterosexual families
exhibited more behavioral problems than girls from other family
types. Brewaeys et al. concluded that these difference observed in
the heterosexual donor insemination families may be attributable to
issues related to secrecy among such families regarding the origin of
the child. This concern is not relevant to lesbian-parented families,
who generally disclose information about the method of conception. Overall, children of lesbian mothers were developing well.

In another European study, Golombok and her colleagues (1997)
reported on the psychological well-being of children raised since
birth by lesbian mothers and by heterosexual single mothers. These
children were compared with children raised in two-parent heterosexual families. Results indicated that children of lesbian mothers did not show any special emotional or behavior problems (as
reported by parents or by teachers); there were no differences as
a function of family type. In terms of children's attachment relationships to their parents, children from mother-only families (lesbian mothers and heterosexual single mothers) scored higher on
an attachment-related assessment than did children reared by heterosexual couples, suggesting the possibility that children from
mother-only families had more secure attachment relationships
with their mothers – an outcome that would seem to favor development among children of lesbian mothers. With respect to
children's perceived competence, children from mother-only families reported lower perceived cognitive and physical competence
than those children from father-present families. Overall, however,
children born to lesbian mothers appeared to be developing well
(Golombok et al., 1998).

Summary

Despite the sometimes adverse legal climates in which they must live, results of research on children of lesbian and gay parents suggest that they develop in a normal fashion. Certainly the research findings to date provide no justification for limitations on child custody or visitation by lesbian or gay parents. Similarly, results of research do not support the idea that lesbian and gay adults are less likely than others to provide good adoptive or foster homes. The existing research could be augmented in a number of different ways, including studies of children with gay fathers, studies of children growing up in legal jurisdictions that differ in their treatment of lesbian and gay parents and their children, and studies of older children, adolescents, and young adults who have grown up with lesbian and gay parents. Despite the need for further research, however, it remains clear that existing findings on the development of children with lesbian and gay parents provide no warrant for legal discrimination against them or against their parents.

LEGAL AND POLICY RECOMMENDATIONS

Although research to date suggests that children of lesbian and gay parents are developing in a normal fashion, legal discrimination nevertheless persists. Although some headway has been made in breaking down legal barriers to maintenance of parent–child relationships in families headed by lesbian and gay parents, there is still much to be done. In this section, we put forward five recommendations for legal and policy changes that would, we believe, benefit children of lesbian and gay parents and explain why each would have a salutary effect.

Our first recommendation is for the repeal of sodomy laws in the 15 states that still have these laws on the books. If prohibitions against private sexual behavior between consenting adults were removed, then lesbian and gay parents would no longer be viewed as probable criminals on these grounds, and the results for family relationships should be positive. Children of lesbian mothers and gay fathers would be more secure if their parents could not be subject to fines or imprisonment for private sexual behavior. More importantly, children of lesbian and gay parents would no longer be subject to collateral harms such as challenges to child custody and visitation that arise from sodomy laws. Repeal of sodomy laws would leave intact all legal protections against child sexual abuse and would continue the trend of recent years toward eliminating governmental interference in private sexual conduct between two consenting adults.

A second policy innovation that would benefit children of lesbian and gay parents is the legalization of same-sex marriage throughout the United States. The possibility of legal marriage among same-sex couples would benefit society in numerous ways, but here we focus exclusively on the benefits for children of lesbian and gay parents. Some benefits would involve intangible but nevertheless important gains. With their parents' romantic relationships normalized through legal marriage, children of lesbian and gay parents would benefit due to decreased stigmatization of their families. Other benefits, such as access to health insurance through two parents' employment, would be more concrete. Children of heterosexual parents are generally seen as better off if their parents are married, and the same effect should hold for children of lesbian and gay parents. In the event that legalization of same-sex marriage is not attainable, some of the benefits of marriage could also be achieved through legal recognition of domestic partnership agreements or civil unions for same-sex couples.

A third recommendation for policy change that would benefit children of lesbian and gay parents is the legalization of adoption and foster care by lesbian and gay adults (including second-parent adoption) in all the states. In some states, this would involve repeal of the existing antigay adoption statutes. In other states, implementation of this change would be less dramatic, but it should include equal foster care as well as equal adoption opportunities so that lesbian and gay prospective foster or adoptive parents would be allowed to provide homes for waiting children.

Also important here would be the opening up of second-parent adoptions to lesbian and gay couples who seek them. For children of lesbian and gay parents, the opportunity to be adopted by their second parent would provide access to a range of financial benefits such as social security, disability, and inheritance. Adoption would also ensure that, should the parents separate or divorce, the continuity of children's relationships with both parents would be protected by the courts. If one parent should die, the continuity of children's relationships with the surviving parent would be protected if the relationship had been legalized via adoption.

A final recommendation for change derives from a recent legal innovation termed a *pre-birth decree of parenthood*. In a recent San Francisco case (Ness, 1999), a lesbian couple had conceived a child using assisted reproductive technology. One woman's egg was fertilized with sperm from a donor and implanted in the womb of the other woman, who carried the baby until its birth. Because both women could be seen as having a claim to the title of "biological mother," and because both intended to become parents for the child, they petitioned the court for a decree conferring the rights and responsibilities of legal parenthood on them both. The decree was issued on March 1, 1999, in San Francisco's Superior Court, declaring both women to be legal parents of the as yet unborn child. Thus, at his birth on March 20, 1999, this child had two legal parents of the same gender (Ness, 1999).

This case suggests the possibility that, in many nontraditional family situations, it would be useful if parents-to-be could announce their intentions to parent and have their intended parental rights and responsibilities affirmed by a court of law in advance of the birth of a child. In this way, children would be assured of claims to support and supervision from two (or more) parents rather than only one parent. Such an approach would create legal bonds from the announced intentions of prospective parents and obviate the need for cumbersome custody or adoption procedures after the child's birth.

This approach might be known as a *doctrine of intentional parenthood*. Under this doctrine, the adult or adults who intend to take parental responsibility for a child, who are not already named as doing so under current law, and who are nominated for this role by any existing legal parent or parent-to-be could be allowed to declare their intention to parent and have this status affirmed by the court. A declaration of intention to parent, if affirmed by the court, could have the effect of legalizing the parental status of one or more adults, so that from the moment of birth, children could be assured of the care and support due to them by more than one parent. This, of course, is the typical situation of children born to married heterosexual parents, both of whom are presumed in law to become legal parents at the moment of birth. A doctrine of intentional parenthood would extend to children of lesbian and gay parents the possibility of legal bonds from birth with more than one parent. This would open up for lesbian and gay prospective parents the possibility of protection in law for their family relationships, for the state a wider circle of responsibility for the care of minor children, and for children of lesbian and gay parents a more secure future.

A doctrine of intentional parenthood, together with the prebirth decrees of parental status that might embody it, would be valuable for lesbian and gay parents and their children but might also offer benefits for many other kinds of nontraditional families (Ness, 1999). For instance, such prebirth decrees could be useful in sorting out various claims to parental status that arise in other cases of assisted reproductive technology, including egg donation, sperm donation, and surrogacy. Parties to the conception of a child could sort out their intended rights and responsibilities in advance of the child's birth, and have these affirmed by the court, and in this way obviate the need for later legal actions to establish legal parenthood. Such procedures would also benefit the increasing number of children who are born to unmarried parents by establishing from the outset which adults intend to take on the rights and responsibilities of parenthood. Children conceived in these circumstances, as well as society more generally, would be served by ensuring that those adults who intend to parent are legally bound to do so.

In summary, there are many ways in which legal and policy initiatives could benefit lesbian and gay parents and their children even as they also benefit society at large. Among these are repeal of the remaining sodomy laws, legalization of same-sex marriage, legalization of adoption and foster care by lesbian and gay adults, legalization of second-parent adoptions, and use of prebirth declarations of intention to parent and of prebirth decrees of parental status. Together these reforms would extend to lesbian and gay parents and their children the legal protections that are now generally taken for granted by other families. To do so would be, as the

Vermont Supreme Court suggested, "a recognition of our common humanity" (Goldberg, 1999).

References

Achenbach, T. M., & Edelbrock, C. (1983). *Manual for the Child Behavior Check-list and Revised Child Behavior Profile.* Burlington: University of Vermont Department of Psychiatry.

ACLU. (2000). Lesbian and gay rights: Status of the United States sodomy laws. Available electronically at *http://www.aclu.org/issues/gay/sodomy.html.*

ACLU. (2001). A historic victory: Civil unions for same-sex couples. Available electronically at *http://www.aclu.org/issues/gay/civil_union_publ.html*

Adoption of Tammy, 416 Mass. 205, 619 N.E.2d 315 (Mass., 1993).

Adoptions of B.L.V.B. & E.L.V.B., 628 A.2d 1271 (Vt. 1993).

Badgett, M. V. L. (1998). The economic well-being of lesbian, gay and bisexual adults' families. In C. J. Patterson & A. R. D'Augelli (Eds.), *Lesbian, gay and bisexual identities in families: Psychological perspectives* (pp. 231–248). New York: Oxford University Press.

Bailey, J. M., Bobrow, D., Wolfe, M., & Mikach, S. (1995). Sexual orientation of adult sons of gay fathers. *Developmental Psychology, 31*, 124–129.

Bailey, J. M., & Dawood, K. (1998). Behavior genetics, sexual orientation, and the family. In C. J. Patterson & A. R. D'Augelli (Eds.), *Lesbian, gay and bisexual identities in families: Psychological perspectives* (pp. 3–18). New York: Oxford University Press.

Baker et al. v. State of Vermont et al. Supreme Court of Vermont Vt. LEXIS 406 (1999).

Boswell v. Boswell, 352 Md. 204; 721 A.2d 662 (1998).

Bottoms v. Bottoms, No. 941166 (Va. 1995).

Bowers v. Hardwick, 478 U.S. 186 (1986).

Bozett, F. W. (1987). Children of gay fathers. In F. W. Bozett (Ed.), *Gay and lesbian parents* (pp. 39–57). New York: Praeger.

Brantner, P. A. (1992). When mommy or daddy is gay: Developing constitutional standards for custody decisions. *Hastings Women's Law Journal, 3*, 97–121.

Brewaeys, A., Ponjaert, I., Van Hall, E. V., & Golombok, S. (1997). Donor insemination: Child development and family functioning in lesbian mother families. *Human Reproduction, 12*, 1349–1359.

Burgess v. Burgess, 708 N. E. 2d 930; 1999 Ind. App. LEXIS 300.

Chambers, D. L. (1996). What if? The legal consequences of marriage and the legal needs of lesbian and gay male couples. *Michigan Law Review, 95*, 447–491.

Chan, R. W., Brooks, R. C., Raboy, B., & Patterson, C. J. (1998b). Division of labor among lesbian and heterosexual parents: Associations with children's adjustment. *Journal of Family Psychology, 12*, 402–419.

Chan, R. W., Raboy, B., & Patterson, C. J. (1998a). Psychosocial adjustment among children conceived via donor insemination by lesbian and hetero-sexual mothers. *Child Development, 69*, 443–457.

Cowan, C. P., & Cowan, P. A. (1992). *When partners become parents: The big life change for couples.* New York: Basic Books.

Eder, R. A. (1990). Uncovering young children's psychological selves: Individual and developmental differences. *Child Development, 61*, 849–863.

Eskridge, W. N., Jr. (1993). A history of same-sex marriage. *Virginia Law Review, 79*, 1419–1513.

Goldberg, C. (1999, December 21). Vermont's high court extends full rights to same-sex couples. *New York Times*, pp. A1 A23.

Golombok, S., Spencer, A., & Rutter, M. (1983). Children in lesbian and single-parent households: Psychosexual and psychiatric appraisal. *Journal of Child Psychology and Psychiatry, 24*, 551–572.

Golombok, S., & Tasker, F. (1996). Do parents influence the sexual orientation of their children? Findings from a longitudinal study of lesbian families. *Developmental Psychology, 32*, 3–11.

Golombok, S., Tasker, F. L., & Murray, C. (1997). Children raised in fatherless families from infancy: Family relationships and the socioemotional development of children of lesbian and single heterosexual mothers. *Journal of Child Psychology & Psychiatry. 38*, 783–791.

Gottman, J. S. (1990). Children of gay and lesbian parents. In F. W. Bozett & M. B. Sussman (Eds.), *Homosexuality and family relations* (pp. 177–196). New York: Harrington Park Press.

Green, G. D., & Bozett, F. W. (1991). Lesbian mothers and gay fathers. In J. C. Gonsiorek & J. D. Weinrich (Eds.), *Homosexuality: Research implications for public policy* (pp. 197–214). Beverly Hills, CA: Sage.

Green, R. (1978). Sexual identity of 37 children raised by homosexual or transsexual parents. *American Journal of Psychiatry, 135*, 692–697.

Huggins, S. L. (1989). A comparative study of self-esteem of adolescent children of divorced lesbian mothers and divorced heterosexual mothers. In F. W. Bozett (Ed.), *Homosexuality and the family* (pp. 123–135). New York: Harrington Park Press.

In re Adoption of Evan, 583 N.Y.S.2d 997 (Sur. 1992).

Jenny, C., Roesler, T. A., & Poyer, K. L. (1994). Are children at risk for sexual abuse by homosexuals? *Pediatrics, 94*, 41–44.

Kirkpatrick, M. (1996). Lesbians as parents. In R. P. Cabaj & T. S. Stein (Eds.), *Textbook of homosexuality and mental health* (pp. 353–370). Washington, DC: American Psychiatric Press.

Kirkpatrick, M., Smith, C., & Roy, R. (1981). Lesbian mothers and their children: A comparative survey. *American Journal of Orthopsychiatry, 51*, 545–551.

Lambda Legal Defense and Education Fund (1996). *Lesbians and gay men seeking custody and visitation: An overview of the state of the law.* New York: Lambda Legal Defense and Education Fund.

Laumann, E. O., Gagnon, J. H., Michael, R. T., & Michaels, S. (1994). *The social organization of sexuality: Sexual practices in the United States.* Chicago: University of Chicago Press.

Love, N. (1999, May 3). N. H. law repeals ban on gay adoptions. *The Boston Globe*, p. B-5.

Loving v. Virginia, 388 U.S. 1 (1967).

Martin, A. (1993). *The lesbian and gay parenting handbook.* New York: HarperCollins.

McCandlish, B. (1987). Against all odds: Lesbian mother family dynamics. In F. Bozett (Ed.), *Gay and lesbian parents* (pp. 23–38). New York: Praeger.

Meyer v. Nebraska, 262 U.S. 390 (1923).

Michaels, S. (1996). The prevalence of homosexuality in the United States. In R. P. Cabaj & T. S. Stein (Eds.), *Textbook of homosexuality and mental health* (pp. 43–63). Washington, DC: American Psychiatric Press.

Ness, C. (1999, May 2). Lesbian moms gain rights. *San Francisco Examiner*, p. A-1.

Parks, C. A. (1998). Lesbian parenthood: A review of the literature. *American Journal of Orthopsychiatry, 68*, 376–389.

Pattatucci, A. M. L., & Hamer, D. H. (1995). Development and familiality of sexual orientation in females. *Behavior Genetics, 25*, 407–420.

Patterson, C. J. (1992). Children of lesbian and gay parents. *Child Development, 63*, 1025–1042.

Patterson, C. J. (1994a). Children of the lesbian baby boom: Behavioral adjustment, self-concepts, and sex-role identity. In B. Greene & G. M. Herek (Eds.), *Contemporary perspectives on lesbian and gay psychology: Theory, research and applications* (pp. 156–175). Beverly Hills, CA: Sage.

Patterson, C. J. (1994b). Lesbian and gay families. *Current Directions in Psychological Science, 3*, 62–64.

Patterson, C. J. (1995a). Families of the lesbian baby boom: Parents' division of labor and children's adjustment. *Developmental Psychology, 31*, 115–123.

Patterson, C. J. (1995b). Lesbian mothers, gay fathers, and their children. In A. R. D'Augelli & C. J. Patterson (Eds.), *Lesbian, gay and bisexual identities across the lifespan: Psychological perspectives* (pp. 262–290). New York: Oxford University Press.

Patterson, C. J. (1995c). Adoption of minor children by lesbian and gay adults: A social science perspective. *Duke Journal of Gender Law and Policy, 2*, 191–205.

Patterson, C. J. (1995d). Lesbian and gay parenthood. In M. H. Bornstein (Ed.), *Handbook of parenting* (pp. 255–274). Hillsdale, NJ: Erlbaum.

Patterson, C. J. (1997). Children of lesbian and gay parents. In T. Ollendick & R. Prinz (Eds.), *Advances in clinical child psychology* (Vol. 19). New York: Plenum Press.

Patterson, C. J. (1998). Family lives of lesbians and gay men. In A. Bellack & M. Hersen (Eds.), *Comprehensive clinical psychology: Vol. 9. Applications in diverse populations*, N. N. Singh (Vol. Ed.) (pp. 253–273). Oxford: England Elsevier.

Patterson, C. J., Friel, L. V. (2000). Sexual orientation and fertility. In G. Bentley & N. Mascie-Taylor (Eds.), *Infertility in the modern world: Biosocial perspectives* (pp. 238–260). Cambridge: Cambridge University Press.

Patterson, C. J., Hurt, S., & Mason, C. (1998). Families of the lesbian baby boom: Children's contacts with grandparents and other adults. *American Journal of Orthopsychiatry, 68*, 390–399.

Patterson, C. J., & Redding, R. (1996). Lesbian and gay families with children: Public policy implications of social science research. *Journal of Social Issues, 52*, 29–50.

Perrin, E. C. (1998). Children whose parents are lesbian or gay. *Contemporary Pediatrics, 15*, 113–130.

Polikoff, N. (1990). This child does have two mothers: Redefining parenthood to meet the needs of children in lesbian mother and other nontraditional families. *Georgetown Law Journal, 78*, 459–575.

Pollack, S., & Vaughn, J. (1987). *Politics of the heart: A lesbian parenting anthology.* Ithaca, NY: Firebrand Books.

Powell v. State, 510 S. E. 2d 18 (1998).

Pulliam v. Smith, 348 N. C. 616; 501 S. E. 2d 898 (1998).

Rivera, R. R. (1991). Sexual orientation and the law. In J. C. Gonsiorek & J. D. Weinrich (Eds.), *Homosexuality: Research implications for public policy* (pp. 81–100). Newbury Park, CA: Sage.

Roe v. Roe, 324 S.E.2d 691 (Va. 1985).

Rubenstein, W. B. (1991). We are family: A reflection on the search for legal recognition of lesbian and gay relationships. *Journal of Law and Politics, 8*, 89–105.

Rubenstein, W. B. (1996). Lesbians, gay men, and the law. In R. C. Savin-Williams & K. M. Cohen (Eds.), *The lives of lesbians, gays, and bisexuals: Children to adults* (pp. 331–344). New York: Harcourt Brace.

Skinner v. Oklahoma, 316 U.S. 535 (1942).

S.N.E. v. R.L.B., 699 P.2d 875 (Alaska 1985).

Steckel, A. (1987). Psychosocial development of children of lesbian mothers. In F. W. Bozett (Ed.), *Gay and lesbian parents* (pp. 75–85). New York: Praeger.

Tasker, F. L., & Golombok, S. (1991). Children raised by lesbian mothers: The empirical evidence. *Family Law, 21*, 184–187.

Tasker, F. L., & Golombok, S. (1997). *Growing up in a lesbian family: Effects on child development.* New York: Guilford Press.

Thigpen v. Carpenter, 730 S.W.2d 510 (Ark. App. Div. 2 1987).

PART III

JUVENILE AGGRESSION AND JUVENILE JUSTICE

9

Juvenile Transfer to Adult Court

How Can Developmental and Child Psychology Inform Policy Decision Making?

Randall T. Salekin

A wave of youth violence and serious juvenile offending experienced in the mid-eighties and extending to the mid-nineties (Puzzanchera, 1998) left in its path legislation that reflected lawmakers' unwillingness to continue to back the rehabilitative policy of the juvenile justice system. Instead of supporting the rehabilitative model, lawmakers' response to the increase in juvenile violence was to alter the laws for prosecution of cases involving juvenile offenders. The most frequent alteration has been legislation that facilitates adolescents' prosecution under adult criminal laws. The mechanisms that allow for youths to be prosecuted under criminal laws are commonly known as *waiver* or *transfer to adult court*. Although the rates of violent juvenile offending have settled and even declined somewhat in the last few years (Sickmund, Snyder, & Poe-Yamagata, 1997), juveniles are increasingly treated as adults under the recent crime-control model.

Juvenile waiver to adult court has been an option almost since the inception of the juvenile justice system. In the past, however, juvenile transfers to adult court were based primarily on judicial discretion that considered differences in adolescents' dangerousness, sophistication-maturity, and amenability to treatment (Ewing, 1990; Grisso, 1998; Kruh & Brodsky, 1997; Salekin,

Correspondence should be addressed to Randall T. Salekin, Ph.D., Department of Psychology, University of Alabama, P.O. Box 870348, Tuscaloosa, AL 35487-0348. E-mail: rsalekin@bama.ua.edu

Rogers, & Ustad, 2001). As such, juvenile court judges were required to make decisions on a case-by-case basis, considering the individual characteristics of adolescents before transferring youths to adult court. This process has changed substantially over the last decade, and legal reform has resulted in automatic and other transfer mechanisms of adolescents to adult criminal courts. With automatic transfer, judges are unable to use their discretion regarding individual cases, and transfer occurs as a result of the charges alone.

Researchers (e.g., Bishop, Frazier, & Henretta, 1989; Bishop, Frazier, Lanza-Kaduce, & Winner, 1996; Fried & Repucci, this volume; Grisso, 1996, 1998) have argued that empirical and theoretical work in the area of developmental and clinical child psychology indicates that the trend toward more frequent adjudication of children as adults ignores developmental realities. In his seminal article, Grisso (1996) argued that even for the most serious juvenile offenses (including those who commit murder), the fundamental emotional and intellectual differences between juveniles and adults require that differential treatment continue to exist. Nonetheless, some scholars (e.g., Feld, 1999; Grisso, 1996) continue to suggest that there is a small group of juveniles for whom rehabilitation may be unlikely or that their level of dangerousness may warrant transfer to adult court.

Clarifying the constructs of dangerousness, sophistication-maturity, and amenability to treatment and furthering our understanding of youth development may allow for a return to a case-by-case sorting of youth rather than automatic transfers. An individual assessment process may substantially reduce the number of youths who are transferred to adult court and ultimately protect those youth who are unlikely to be chronic offenders, who are, in fact, amenable to treatment, and who are perhaps too immature, developmentally, to fully understand the consequences of their youthful decisions.

In this chapter, I first provide a brief historical overview of juvenile court law and policy. Second, I suggest that there is a need for a clear standard for juvenile waiver to adult court. Third, I outline research that currently exists and that is necessary to clarify the three broad areas thought to be important in the transfer process:

(a) dangerousness, (b) sophistication-maturity, and (c) amenability to treatment. Finally, I provide recommendations for research that is needed to test theoretical arguments that some measurable and meaningful differences exist between juveniles who should be transferred to adult criminal court and those who should remain in juvenile court. For the majority of juveniles, research suggests that these youth are different from adults in substantive ways and thus require differential treatment. I conclude with suggestions for research and policy in this area.

HISTORICAL OVERVIEW OF JUVENILE COURT LAW AND POLICY

Juvenile courts were originally established under the doctrine of *parens patriae*. Historically, the king of England was symbolically the father of the country, and as such, he assumed almost absolute responsibility for all juvenile affairs (Black, 1979). Therefore, the king's chancellors adjudicated all matters involving youths independent of English criminal courts. English common law also established degrees of criminal culpability by age. Children under 18 were considered juveniles because they were not as mature or responsible for their behaviors as adults. Children under 7 were presumed to be incapable of formulating criminal intent, regardless of the seriousness of the offense (Champion & Mays, 1991).

The *parens patriae* doctrine was adopted by the American juvenile justice system in 1899 and has been the foundation for the juvenile courts' intervention with adolescents who violate certain laws (Feld, 1987). Before then, any minor who committed a crime was handled in the adult criminal court. The juvenile courts' guiding principles are rehabilitation and treatment versus the criminal courts' emphasis on punishment and retribution. Despite the early philosophy of *parens patriae* and the rehabilitative focus of the juvenile justice system, most American jurisdictions have enacted laws providing that juveniles charged with serious personal crimes may be prosecuted and punished as adults (Heilbrun, Leheny, Thomas, & Huneycutt, 1997). These laws have (a) relaxed the state's burden of proof in juvenile court transfer hearings, (b) increased the range of offenses for which the transfer is allowed, (c) allowed the

minimum age at which juveniles may be transferred to continually drift downward, and, as mentioned, (d) added different legal
mechanisms for transfer.

There are three ways in which juveniles can be transferred to adult
criminal courts. One method is the judicial waiver, in which a
juvenile judge, often utilizing psychological information, makes a
determination as to whether a juvenile should be transferred to
adult court or remain in juvenile court; this is an option in 47 states.
There are two other, more recent, ways in which youth may be
transferred to criminal court for trial: (a) statutory exclusion and
(b) prosecutorial direct file. Currently, more than half of the states
provide a statutory exclusion. In these states, age and crime types
(often serious offenses such as assault and murder) are automatically outside the jurisdiction of the juvenile court. Therefore, the
charge is originally filed in criminal court, without any input by
juvenile court judges.

The other transfer mechanism recently adopted by some states is
called *prosecutor direct file*. This mechanism, available in just under
one-third of the states, allows prosecutors the discretion to file
charges against youth in either juvenile or adult criminal court for
certain types of offenses. It should be mentioned that even in situations where prosecutorial direct file or automatic transfers occur,
psychological evaluations are still sought in order to assist judges in
making their decisions as to whether youth should remain in adult
court or be returned to the juvenile court (Grisso, 1998). In some
states where criminal courts receive transferred youth via statutory
exclusion or direct file, judges have the option to *reverse transfer*
or *decertify* youth. This process requires a pretrial hearing in criminal court, a procedure similar to a waiver hearing that allows the
criminal court judge to waive jurisdiction. The increase in mechanisms to transfer children and adolescents to adult courts may
be largely responsible for the 71% increase in juvenile delinquency
cases transferred to criminal courts between 1985 and 1994 (Butts,
1997) and for the 100% increase from 1994 to 1998 (Grisso, 1998).

Despite the enactment of laws that allow more youth to be transferred to adult court, there are few meaningful guidelines to suggest which juveniles should be processed in adult versus juvenle courts.

THE NEED FOR A STANDARD FOR TRANSFERRING YOUTH TO ADULT COURT

There is a need for a clear standard that focuses on youth characteristics when considering transfer to adult court. Heilbrun et al. (1997) surveyed the statutes on juvenile transfer and decertification in the U.S. federal and 50 state jurisdictions, as well as the District of Columbia. They found that five criteria relevant to the mental, emotional, and developmental functioning of juveniles are used: (a) treatment needs and amenability, (b) risk assessment of future criminality, (c) sophistication-maturity, (d) the presence of mental retardation or mental illness, and (e) offense characteristics. Most state guidelines for juvenile waiver reflect the factors delineated by the U.S. Supreme Court's landmark decision in *Kent v. United States* (1966).

   The criteria outlined in statutes and *Kent* have generally been distilled to three constructs that are directly related to the juvenile's psychological functioning: (a) potential dangerousness, (b) sophistication-maturity, and (c) amenability to treatment (see Ewing, 1990; Grisso, 1998; Kruh & Brodsky, 1997; Salekin, Rogers, & Ustad, 2001). Based on the psychological nature of these components, the juvenile justice system has relied on forensic psychological and psychiatric assessments of these factors, which are then utilized by judges in the determination of juvenile transfers. Court-ordered evaluations are accorded substantial weight when considering whether to try adolescents as juveniles or adults. However, as greater numbers of youthful offenders are waived to criminal court jurisdiction through direct file or automatic transfer, questions arise about whether all such juveniles truly require transfer and whether such transfers are justifiable. According to many researchers (Beyer, 1999; Champion & Mays, 1991; Feld, 1984; Grisso, 1996), some transferred juveniles are not dangerous, sophisticated-mature, or untreatable.

Developmental and clinical child psychology may offer important information to inform these decisions. Providing clarity on the constructs of dangerousness, sophistication-maturity, and amenability to treatment may assist juvenile waiver decisions and retain many juveniles in rehabilitative settings. In the following sections, theoretical research, primarily from developmental and child psychology, is presented to argue against holding juveniles to the same legal standards as adults. The exceptions are the few adolescents who are high on dangerousness, high on sophistication-maturity, and low on treatment amenability criteria. These individuals would, at the courts' discretion, continue to be transferred to adult criminal court, because keeping them in juvenile court could pose a substantial risk to society.

DANGEROUSNESS AND TRANSFER TO ADULT COURT

Juvenile courts may transfer a youth to adult criminal court if they conclude that the youth is dangerous. The rationale for transfer based on assessment of dangerousness is, arguably, the consideration of community safety. As mentioned earlier, virtually every jurisdiction provides this alternative basis for adult certification, and in many cases, waiver is initially sought and ultimately made because of the threat posed by the youth's serious or persistent criminal misconduct (Grisso, 1998). This factor is often given the most weight and the treatment prognosis is considered to a lessor degree (Grisso, 1998; Salekin, Rogers, & Ustad, 2001). Although it is given considerable weight, our understanding of dangerousness in juveniles is limited. What we do know is that the issue of dangerousness is probably more complex with youth than with adults, who have developed stable and enduring personality styles.

Therefore, the developmental differences between adult and youth dangerousness necessarily challenge the ability of psychologists and the courts to identify personality and/or behavioral characteristics that precede dangerousness and are subsequently predictive of its occurrence in youthful populations. To address this challenge, mental health professionals and the courts should ask themselves, what characteristics are typical or common among dangerous juveniles? In addition, what situational characteristics increase the likelihood of dangerousness in youth? (See Fried &

Reppucci, this volume, for a thorough review of how situational factors relate to violence.) Elucidating such traits, behaviors, and situational factors is likely to improve the classification of youth at high risk for dangerousness. Moreover, such a process will assist in determining which youth are likely to desist from antisocial behavior after engaging in such acts during adolescence, but the issue is complex.

Numerous studies (e.g., Moffitt, 1993) have shown that adolescent antisocial behavior differs in important ways from adult offending; these differences may have implications for justifying differential treatment of adult and juvenile offenders. For instance, there is some support for the notion that antisocial behavior during adolescence is normal (Hirschi, 1969; Moffitt, 1993; Moffitt & Silva, 1988) and that many youth have police contact but are not chronic offenders (Farrington, Ohlin, & Wilson, 1986; Wolfgang, Figlio, & Sellin, 1972). Given this information, how do the courts and clinicians determine which youth are likely to be most dangerous in the future and which youth are engaging in antisocial behavior that is likely to desist?

Over the last decade, violent and antisocial pathways have been conceptualized that may assist in the determination of dangerousness (e.g., Moffitt, 1993). Understanding developmental pathways may assist in the determination of future dangerousness by distinguishing among different types of offenders. Most notably, Moffitt (1993, 1994) proposes two distinct pathways: those of delinquents classified as (a) *adolescent limited* and (b) *life-course persistent*. This model is particularly important because it addresses the issue of why many adolescents engage in antisocial behaviors, including violence, and then desist and live normal adult lives. Moffitt (1993) has suggested that life-course persistent offenders begin their offending well before adolescence, continue well into adulthood, and manifest qualities that seem categorically antisocial. In contrast, adolescent limited delinquents tend to commit their first offense in midadolescence and to desist from illegal behavior as they enter adulthood.

There is some evidence that these distinctions may help to separate dangerous from nondangerous juveniles. This is important when it comes to transfers to adult court because we know that the most persistent 5% or 6% of male offenders are responsible for about 50% of all known crimes (Moffitt, 1993; Wolfgang et al., 1972). Thus, many youth will desist from criminal behavior after their first episodes of delinquency. Table 9.1 provides a summary of several developmental pathways that emphasize different characteristics that can be seen early in childhood, later in adolescence, and finally in adulthood.

These pathways may also shed light on the transfer decision when it comes to specific types of crimes or conduct problems. For instance, Loeber Stouthamer-Loeber (1998) have proposed a triple-pathway model that integrated both predelinquent behavior problems and delinquent acts to describe which youth are at highest risk of becoming chronic and dangerous offenders. This model consists of three developmental pathways: (a) an overt pathway, starting with minor aggression, followed by physical fighting and then violence; (b) a covert pathway, consisting of a sequence of minor covert behaviors, followed by property damage (fire setting or vandalism) and moderate to serious forms of delinquency; and (c) an authority-conflict pathway prior to age 12, consisting of a sequence of stubborn behavior, defiance, and authority avoidance (truancy, running away, staying out late at night). With regard to dangerousness, the violence pathway that has shown developmental ordering with minor aggression (bullying and annoying others) showing the earliest age of onset, followed by physical fighting (including gangs), and finally more serious forms of violence may be particularly informative to the transfer decision. There is preliminary support for their hypotheses in regard to both African American and Caucasian boys in longitudinal data sets (Tolan & Gorman-Smith, 1998).

Psychopathy has recently emerged as a possible developmental pathway that eventually leads to violent behaviors in youthful offenders (Frick, 1998; Lynam, 1996, 1998). The origins of aggression in psychopathy are thought to start early in childhood and to result from callous and unemotional traits (e.g., Frick, 1998; Frick, O'Brien, Wootten & McBurnett, 1994; Lynam, 1996; Moffitt, Caspi, Dickson, Silva, & Stanton, 1996; Thornberry, Huizinga, & Loeber, 1995). Lynam (1998) has suggested that psychopathy predicts not only violent offending but also those who are likely to be the most persistent criminals. Although there is speculation that

TABLE 9.1. *Developmental Models for Antisocial Behavior, Including Violence*

Theorist	Model	Developmental Pathway		
		Childhood	Adolescence	Adulthood
Frick (1998)	Psychopathic conduct problems pathway	Low behavioral inhibition	→ Callous/unemotional traits	→ Conduct problems
	Alternative conduct problems pathway	Poor parental socialization	or Low intelligence	→ Conduct problems
Loeber & Southamer-Loeber (1998)	Authority conflict (earliest)	Stubborn behavior	→ Defiance/disobedience	→ Authority avoidance
	Covert (escalation)	Minor covert behavior	→ Property damage	→ Moderate to serious delinquency
	Overt (increasingly aggressive)	Minor aggression	→ Physical fighting	→ Violence (rape, attack, strongarm tactics)
Lynam (1996)	Psychopathy	Callous/unemotional traits	→ Antisocial behaviors/physical fighting	→ Violence
Moffitt (1993)	Life-course persistent	Antisocial behavior	→ Increase in antisocial behavior	→ Continuation of antisocial behavior including violence
	Adolescent-limited	No antisocial behavior	→ Antisocial behavior in adolescence	→ Discontinuation of antisocial behavior
Patterson (1992)	General pathway	Disobedience, tantrums	→ Physical fighting	→ Stealing
Silverthorn & Frick (1999)	Early-onset pathway for girls	Difficult temperament	→ Failed child–parent encounters prevent child from learning prosocial behavior	→ Antisocial behavior

Note: Specific ages are not provided for each of the stages of these theories. Rather, the developmental models are approximations of how children develop, with the tendency to be violent. In addition, this is not a comprehensive list of developmental pathways.

psychopathy is a predictor of chronic and violent offending, few validation studies have been conducted on this model in relation to dangerousness (see Edens, Skeem, Cruise, & Cauffman, 2001; Salekin, Rogers, & Machin, 2001).

In addition, it is possible that psychopathy, which has been downwardly extended to children and adolescents, may differ in important ways for these two younger populations that have implications for the law (Salekin, Rogers, & Machin, 2001). For instance, it is possible that hallmark symptoms of adult psychopathy that are now being applied to youth may be somewhat less stable in or even inapplicable to children and adolescents. For example, symptoms such as *parasitic lifestyle*, *impulsivity*, and *irresponsibility* are often normal aspects of child and adolescent development. To highlight this point even further, if we consider parasitic lifestyle, most children are dependant on family members and the community for support, yet this would not and should not be viewed as a parasitic lifestyle. Similarly, irresponsibility and impulsivity can be normal developmental stages of childhood and adolescence. Several research studies (e.g., Green, Fry, & Myerson, 1994; Logue, 1988) have shown that children are more impulsive and that they, more often than adults, accept smaller, more immediate rewards including substantially smaller monetary awards compared to their adult counterparts. Even characteristics such as *egocentricity* and *lack of empathy* may not necessarily be signs of severe psychopathology but rather a transient developmental stages. The point here is that although psychopathy may offer psychologists a standard by which to distinguish more serious from less serious juvenile offenders, extending the concept of psychopathy downward to youth is complex, and there are developmental considerations. These developmental diagnostic considerations suggest that at least some juveniles with *psychopathy-like characteristics* might be better handled by the juvenile courts. This may be particularly true if a discerning differential diagnosis indicates that many of the symptoms (e.g., egocentricity) will dissipate with time and/or treatment. Future research will need to focus on determining ways in which distinctions can be made between those who are true psychopaths and those who have *developmental symptoms* that mimic psychopathy and are expected to change over time as they mature.

Aside from developmental pathways and the construct of psychopathy, researchers have also examined individual characteristics of youth to determine their predictive power with regard to dangerousness. Loeber and Stouthamer-Loeber (1988) performed a comprehensive review of predictors in the juvenile delinquency literature. They found that the following predictors of serious delinquency improved classification rates: (a) early conduct problems (e.g., aggression, stealing, truancy, lying, and drug use), (b) continued aggressiveness past early adolescence, (c) the seriousness of the juvenile offense, (d) poor parental supervision and parental rejection of the child, (e) parental criminality and aggressiveness, marital discord, and multiple family handicaps, (f) conduct problems in elementary school, and (g) high aggressiveness as children.

Robins (1966) and Moffitt (1993) have underscored the importance of these findings by asserting that five factors increase the likelihood of persistent antisocial behavior and dangerousness in youth. These factors reflect antisocial behavior with the following features: early onset, high frequency, variety of problem behaviors, and problem behaviors occurring in multiple settings. Salekin, Rogers, and Ustad (2001) specifically addressed the construct of dangerousness in transfer decisions by asking clinical child psychologists to rate the factors that they found to be central to this construct. The following factors received the highest rating, indicating that clinical child psychologists believed them to be central to dangerousness: (a) use of deadly weapons, (b) extreme unprovoked violence, (c) severe antisocial behavior with an early onset, (d) premeditation, (e) violent history, and (f) leadership role in the crime.

The foregoing indicates that theoretical research on the development of antisocial behavior, including violence, in adolescents suggests differential treatment for juveniles is necessary. A better understanding of which youth are likely to persist versus desist in such behavior is paramount. There are at least three avenues that psychologists and the courts can take to advance our understanding of dangerousness in youth. First, knowledge of antisocial pathways and the psychopathy construct may assist mental health professionals and the courts in predicting future criminal and violent behavior. Pathways may allow clinicians to classify those participants who deescalate, maintain a stable adjustment, and escalate to serious

crime and violence. This may then allow for accurate classification of juveniles who should remain in juvenile court. However,
classification estimates will be required before the true efficacy of
this model for juvenile court purposes can be determined. An important step in the process will be sampling community youth (with
no history of violence), nonviolent and violent juvenile offenders,
and juveniles who have been transferred to adult courts to determine their performance (e.g., overall adjustment and antisocial behavior) based on developmental pathway knowledge.

Second, measures of psychopathy may prove useful to risk
assessments of juvenile offenders. Frick and Hare (in press) developed the Psychopathy Screening Device (PSD) for children aged
12 and under, and Lynam (1998) developed the Child Psychopathy
Scale (CPS). Forth, Kosson, and Hare (in press) developed a measure
of psychopathy for adolescents, named the Psychopathy Checklist – Youth Version (PCL-YV). Although the PCL-YV has undergone initial reliability and validity research, data are limited on
this measure as well as on the other childhood measures. Although
there are some data to support the predictive validity of psychopathy in adults (see Salekin, Rogers, & Sewell, 1996), the issue with
children and adolescents is much less clear. Until further research is
conducted, there exists only theoretical (rather than empirical) support for the notion that psychopathy in children and adolescents
is a chronic syndrome with predictive validity (Edens et al., 2001;
Salekin, Rogers, & Machin, 2001).

Third, utilization of specific characteristics such as those put forth
in the Loeber and Stouthamer-Loeber (1998) review may prove
useful. Moreover, combining the approaches may further improve
the courts' ability to make appropriate decisions regarding dangerousness. Specifically, if youth engage in extreme unprovoked
violence, do not express remorse, and are on a life-course persistent antisocial pathway, they may be more dangerous than youth
who do not meet these criteria. In fact, there may be convergence
among the differing conceptualizations that allows the identification of the most dangerous youth. It may be that the psychopathic
young offender fits into Moffitt's (1993) life-course persistent antisocial group, persisting in criminal activity well into adulthood. It
may also be that nonpsychopathic youth are more likely to start

offending in adolescence (adolescent-limited group) and stop shortly thereafter.

Although risk factors are important to our understanding of juvenile waivers, too often the courts and mental health professionals ignore protective factors, psychiatric conditions other than conduct disorder, and developmental realities that may lead to differing conclusions about dangerousness and the related construct of amenability to treatment. As such, any formal testing of these different approaches should consider the possibility that the youth may be suffering from a psychiatric condition such as depression, posttraumatic stress disorder, or even a psychosis that may be fueling antisocial behaviors and conduct problems. In short, the evaluations themselves should be comprehensive and should determine the stability of the dangerousness.

SOPHISTICATION-MATURITY AND TRANSFER TO ADULT COURT

In part, juvenile waiver decisions rest on considerations of the adolescent's level of psychological maturity and sophistication (see Ewing, 1990; Kruh & Brodsky, 1997; Salekin, Rogers, & Ustad, 2001). An element of the juvenile waiver indicates that adolescents who are thought to be mature or sophisticated can be waived to adult criminal courts. Despite the importance of maturity in transfer decisions, it has in the past been a puzzling construct for social scientists and legal scholars. Grisso (1996) has stated that judicial waiver statutes, cast in terms of sophistication-maturity, may in effect be "a broad, somewhat standardless grant of discretion." Moreover, he suggests that the subjectivity inherent in the administration of such waiver statutes "permits inequality among defendants and does not provide a method for external control or any effective check on the courts."

Some of the confusion regarding sophistication-maturity, at least from a psychologist's perspective, has stemmed from attempts to map psychological stage models of maturity onto the legal term of sophistication-maturity. These efforts have been futile because the vast majority of psychological stage models (e.g., Erikson, 1959; Freud, 1958; Piaget, 1972) do not readily lend themselves to the transfer question and, at best, may be only partially related to the legal term of sophistication-maturity. One of the primary reasons that these models have not been applied to youth in contact with the law is that progression through the stages often focuses on the development of prosocial attitudes and behavior without encompassing more fully the developmentally linked traits that may affect decision making and judgment in different contexts.

Sophistication-Maturity: Pursuing Construct Clarity

Several pieces of converging information (e.g., Salekin, Rogers, & Ustad, 2001; Salekin & Yff, 2001) suggest that the legal term and construct of sophistication-maturity may consist of factors that relate to culpability (the ability of youth to formulate criminal intent), criminal sophistication (progressively more involvement in advanced criminality), and, more generally, intellectual and emotional intelligence. In two separate prototypical analyses, both juvenile court judges and clinical child psychologists found these elements to be central to the sophistication-maturity construct. Other factors that juvenile court judges and clinical child psychologists considered central were (a) planned and premeditated crimes, (b) understanding of behavioral norms, (c) ability to identify alternative actions, (d) ability to give thought to the consequences in a larger frame, and (e) decision-making skills (ability to weigh the consequences of different actions before taking action). Unlike other models of maturity, the aforementioned conceptualization does not require the presence of prosocial values. In essence, these factors suggest that the juveniles should be adultlike with regard to their maturity, but they do not necessarily require the juveniles to have made any serious commitments to societal values or mores. Thus, if they are sidestepping societal mores, this does not automatically exclude them from being considered mature.

Clarity on the sophistication-maturity construct may allow for more accurate evaluations of juveniles. Similar to the research on pathways for antisocial behavior (e.g., Moffitt, 1993), different developmental pathways for youth with regard to the sophistication-maturity construct may have utility. For a very small proportion of juveniles, developmentally higher levels of sophistication-maturity may be reached without their having made any serious commitment to the values of society. According to this theory, such individuals would be persistent offenders, and according to the law, culpable actors, who purposefully embark on the commission of a serious crime as central and sophisticated participants. Attention to both intellectual and emotional intelligence as well as moral development may be necessary in determining which youth will persist or desist in criminality. Table 9.2 presents both intellectual/emotional and moral development components of the two pathways that should be tracked when considering sophistication-maturity.

Research on Sophistication-Maturity: Why Most Juveniles Would Not Meet the Threshold

Research by clinical child and developmental psychologists indicates that most youth would not meet the criteria for sophistication-maturity. Several researchers have shed light on ways in which youth differ from adults in important and relevant developmental ways. Perhaps most compelling has been the work of Scott and her colleagues (Scott, 1992; Scott, Reppucci, & Woolard, 1995). Scott (1992) has suggested that youth may differ from adults in their ability to make decisions. Specifically, she suggested that youth generally have difficulty weighing and comparing consequences when making decisions. Moreover, these youth have difficulty contemplating the meaning of long-range consequences that will be realized 5–10 years in the future (see also Woolard, this volume). In part, this difference in the ability to make decisions stems from adolescents' skill level at gathering and organizing information. Scott (1992) suggested that adolescents are generally aware of and use less information than adults. In addition, adolescents are less able to use probability information and give considerably more weight to case study information. Not surprisingly, these differences in the cognitive processes of adolescents also have implications for their ability to be competent defendants in more adversarial "juvenile" atmospheres (see Woolard, this volume).

Other recent reviews have examined the evidence for developmental differences between midadolescents and adults on psychological variables that can influence decision making (Scott et al.,

TABLE 9.2. *Developmental Pathways of Sophistication-Maturity*

Model		Childhood	Developmental Pathway for Sophistication-Maturity			
		Childhood	Early Adolescence	Midadolescence	Late Adolescence	Adulthood
Developmentally immature model	I/E	*Unable* to weigh options and make rational decisions	*Unable* to weigh the risks and long-term consequences of their actions	Choose criminal activities to obtain a desired outcome	Engage in crimes but feel guilt as a consequence of developing morals	As they mature, desist from criminal activities. Intervention and protective factors play a role
	M	adequate moral training from an early age		Temporary experimentation with immoral actions		Return to decision making that incorporates moral thought
Criminal sophistication model	I/E	*Unable* to weigh options and make rational decisions	*Unable* to weigh the risks and long-term consequences of their actions	Choose criminal activities to obtain a desired outcome	Engage in sophisticated crimes because their cognitive maturity allows for advanced crime. No guilt experienced because they are not committed to the mores of society	Continue to mature in a criminological manner as they gain some positive outcomes for criminal behavior
	M	Little or no moral framework		Little to no moral training engage in antisocial acts		No serious commitment to the values of society

Note: I/E = intellectual and emotional intelligence; M = moral development. This model is only theoretical and requires formal testing. Normatively, juveniles are thought to be less mature than adults. Only a small proportion would likely fit the criminal sophistication model. Some youth (likely a very small portion) may be sophisticated in early childhood.

1995; Steinberg & Cauffman, 1996; Woolard, this volume). Factors have included (a) independence and autonomy, (b) emotion and behavior regulation (impulsivity), (c) time perspective, and (d) the framing of problems in a larger context. Researchers have hypothesized that these psychological factors influence adolescents' awareness of alternatives and their potential consequences at the time they are making choices. As well, adolescents' assignment of weight and value to anticipated gains and risks differs from that of adults (Gardner, 1993).

These findings have important implications for juvenile transfer considerations. Remember, only those youth who are advanced in their level of maturity would be waived to adult court. Only a very small proportion of youth would meet this criterion given the developmental differences previously mentioned. If this is the rationale for the sophistication-maturity construct, then it is perhaps one of the more important constructs in the sorting of youth for juvenile versus adult court. Zimring (1982) captured the importance of the sophistication-maturity construct when he described adolescence as a learning period in which young offenders should have the opportunity to proceed through this developmental stage, surviving the legal system, with their "life chances still intact." He suggested that the juvenile justice system acknowledges youths' irresponsibility and sought to protect young offenders from the stigma of conviction and the negative consequences of prolonged incarceration. He also suggested that juveniles could benefit from treatment, supervision, procedural informality, and confidentiality. This ideology echoes early English common law and suggests that except for a small number of juveniles who are sophisticated-mature (as well as meeting dangerousness criteria and recalcitrance to treatment criteria), the majority should remain in juvenile court.

AMENABILITY TO TREATMENT AND TRANSFER TO ADULT COURT

Transfers to adult court requires consideration of whether a juvenile is amenable to treatment. In general, clinical and developmental psychologists have suggested that youth are more malleable than adults and thus more amenable to treatment. In both the medical and psychological literature, there is substantial evidence that the earlier a disease or disorder is detected, the better the prognosis. This notion has been the basis for treating rather than punishing errant youth who may have externalizing disorders such as oppositional defiant disorder, conduct disorder, or other antisocial behavior problems. The principles of early detection and treatment suggest that many youth who come into contact with the law can be redirected toward more prosocial lifestyles. Again, these general theoretical beliefs about the treatment of psychological disorders and syndromes challenge the recent move away from rehabilitative to punishment and crime control models for juveniles. Research on the amenability of both children and adolescents is lacking, however.

Because amenability to treatment is not well defined, prediction of treatment effects with juvenile offenders is thwarted. As it stands, an important step in the amenability-to-treatment construct is understanding client characteristics that predict positive and negative treatment outcomes. Kazdin's (1985, 1987, 1994) successive reviews of interventions with antisocial youth found little research that systematically examined client characteristics in relation to treatment outcome. Although some studies have taken into account demographic variables (e.g., age, ethnicity, and IQ) or behavioral characteristics (e.g., number of convictions), less research has been conducted on attitudinal factors and personality characteristics related to amenability to treatment. The studies that do exist on this issue will now be reviewed.

A meta-analysis by Izzo and Ross (1990) of 46 delinquency intervention studies concluded that factors such as cognition, self-evaluation, expectations, understanding and appraisal of the world, and values are important in treatment. However, Izzo and Ross did not indicate whether these characteristics differentiated amenability to treatment. They recommended that training offenders to think logically, objectively, and rationally without overgeneralization, distorting the facts, or externalizing blame may be an important step toward improving their outcome.

Several other studies provide some information that advances the amenability to treatment construct. Adams (1970) conducted a study of 400 young offenders held by the California Youth Authority in which the clinical staff evaluated the clients with regard to their amenability to treatment. Amenable youth were described as being intelligent, verbal, anxious, insightful, aware of their difficulties, and motivated to change. Carlson, Barr, and Young (1994) investigated 84 youth diagnosed with conduct disorder to determine whether staff assessments of amenability to treatment and other predictors were associated with favorable treatment outcomes. The authors found that amenable clients were cooperative and complied with the rules. Grisso, Tomkins, and Casey (1988) suggested that amenability to treatment in juvenile transfers was most often associated with motivation to change and with prior offenses.

When clinical child psychologists (Salekin, Rogers, & Ustad, 2001) and juvenile court judges (Salekin & Yff, 2001) were asked to rate core characteristics for the amenability to treatment construct as it related to the waiver decision, they found the following factors to be important: (a) motivation to engage in treatment, (b) awareness of difficulties, (c) expectations that treatment would be beneficial, (d) remorse/guilt, (e) empathy, (f) knowledge of right from wrong, and (g) stable and supportive family.

Many of the characteristics listed in the foregoing paragraph have been researched with regard to amenability to treatment in adult populations. For example, the presence of anxiety at the initiation of therapy is a positive prognostic sign in adults (Kernberg et al., 1972; Luborsky, Singer, & Luborsky, 1975; Moras & Strupp, 1982; Smith, Sjoholm, & Nielzen, 1975). Filak, Abeles, and Norquist (1986) investigated whether clients' "affiliation–hostility" dimension would have a significant impact on the outcome of psychotherapy. They found that clients with an affiliative stance often had a highly successful outcome compared to those with a hostile stance. This is a particularly important issue in regard to juveniles, who may have more hostility than those who seek treatment in the community because their treatment is mandated rather than voluntary.

Relatedly, motivation for treatment has been emphasized in terms of both treatment continuation and outcome (Carlson et al., 1994; Grisso et al., 1988; Keithly, Samples, & Strupp, 1980). Frank and his colleagues were among the earliest to call attention to client expectancies and their relation to symptom change (Frank, 1959; Frank, Gliedman, Imber, Stone, & Nash, 1959; Rosenthal & Frank, 1956).

Intelligence and outcome in psychotherapy has also been investigated by numerous researchers. Although no minimum intelligence requirement has been established for successful psychotherapy, certain types of therapy may require more highly intelligent clients. Psychoanalysis is one such example (Garfield, 1994). On the other hand, behavioral therapists have been less concerned with intelligence level. In relation to adolescents being considered for waiver to adult court due to their generally lower level of maturity, the treatment regimen should include behavioral techniques.

At least three other prognostic variables should be investigated in treatment-outcome studies with adolescents who have come into contact with the law: (a) the degree and type of disturbance, (b) family/support system considerations, and (c) protective factors (e.g., hobbies).

Degree of Disturbance and Type of Disorder

In general, because of juveniles' young age, it is likely that they are in the early stages of a disorder. Thus, treatment of that disorder would likely be more effective than the same treatment provided to adults, whose behavioral problems are more enduring. With this premise in mind, most juveniles would likely be more amenable to treatment than adults. Nevertheless, for a small group of juveniles, treatment may be extremely difficult and the prognosis may be generally poor because of the degree of their psychological disturbance. Measures of the degree of disturbance may prove useful to the juvenile justice system in determining which youth are most likely to benefit from treatment.

Family Factors and Amenability to Treatment

Family is a critical component related to how well children and adolescents respond to psychotherapy. Parents' resistance to viewing a youth's problems, at least in part, as a symptom of family difficulties can reduce amenability to treatment. Kazdin (1985) concluded that assessment of parents' expectations of treatment for their adolescent children may be useful clinically in regard to amenability to treatment. Parents' expectations of their children's socialization may also be important. Specifically, some children have never been socialized by their parents to be honest and respect the property of others. This lack of socialization is common among neglectful parents or parents with an indistinct or weak moral stance. The promotion of honesty and respect for others' property can be best instilled by parents' teaching and modeling prosocial alternatives to dishonesty and antisocial behavior.

Protective Factors and Amenability to Treatment

As mentioned in the section on dangerousness, not all individuals at risk for future violence will show later dysfunction. Protective factors are influences that may cancel or attenuate the influence of known risk factors. Researchers have identified protective factors by studying groups known to be at risk because of several "risk factors" and by identifying a subgroup that becomes delinquent later on. For example, in a longitudinal study from birth through young adulthood, youth were identified as at risk for delinquency based on certain risk factors (Werner, 1987; Werner & Smith, 1992). Protective factors for these at-risk youth were (a) being first born, (b) being perceived by their mothers as affectionate, (c) showing high self-esteem and an internal locus of control, (d) having caretakers in the family other than parents, and (e) having a supportive same-sex model who provided structure.

Stouthamer-Loeber, Loeber, Farrington, Zhang, van Kammen, and Maguin (1993) explored a broad range of risk and protective factors in relation to various indices of delinquency in boys between 7 and 14 years of age. Family variables such as supervision/disciplinary practices and parent–child relation factors provided protection for youth at high risk. Other researchers have also examined protective factors and found that some variables such as social competence, intelligence, personality attributes, positive peer relations, positive peer response to authority, good educational performance, and effective use of leisure time can serve as buffers in the presence of risk factors (Hoge, Andrews, & Leschied, 1996; Luthar, 1991; Rae-Grant, Thomas, Offord, & Boyle, 1989).

Taken together, the aforementioned research on amenability to treatment would suggest that prognosis of youth could also be

TABLE 9.3. *Developmental Pathways of Amenability to Treatment*

	Developmental Pathway for Amenability to Treatment		
Model	Childhood	Adolescence	Adulthood
Amenable youth model	Low-moderate degree of psychopathology Parental support Protective factors	→ Motivated to change Early detection Anxiety Shows remorse Shows empathy	→ Good treatment prognosis
Recalcitrant youth model	High-severe degree of psychopathology Difficult-to-treat psychopathology No or few protective factors	→ Lack of motivation to change Late detection Lack of anxiety or concern Lack of remorse for crime Lack of empathy	→ Poor treatment prognosis

Note: This model is only theoretical and requires formal testing. Normatively juveniles are thought to be more amenable to treatment than adults, and only a small proportion would likely be unamenable to treatment.

framed in a developmental pathway. Table 9.3 illustrates two pathways from childhood in which youth are likely to show a better or worse treatment prognosis.

CONCLUDING REMARKS

Juvenile transfers to adult court have serious ramifications for youth including the potential for long-term incarceration and the possibility of the death penalty. However, society's growing concern with the increasing rates of violent juvenile crime has called for more punitive sanctions of adult courts to protect the public. In the last two decades, a shift has occurred from a *parens patriae* model to an emphasis on crime-control models.

However, statutes mandating the prosecution of a youth as an adult on the basis of the offense charged, or the offense history, rather than on the basis of the youth's characteristics, are misguided, according to the developmental and clinical child psychology literatures. The legitimacy of a paternalistic response seems to hinge on the premise that many of the factors that differentiate adolescent decision making from adult decision making are developmental and temporary (Grisso, 1996, 1998). As such, an arbitrary decision to transfer youth to adult courts does not reflect the complexity of the transfer process.

Using a case-by-case evaluative approach to sorting youth will challenge the courts to strike a balance between considerations of punishment, protection of the community, and/or fostering prosocial growth. How much emphasis to place on community safety versus the therapeutic needs of the youth versus providing punishment will depend on the characteristics of the juvenile. Consideration of each element individually will likely reduce the number of youth who are transferred to adult court. These theoretical and to a lesser extent empirical findings have implications for the law. Recommendations for specific policy change will be discussed below.

Reverse the Current Trend to Make Juvenile Courts Increasingly Adversarial and Return to the *Parens Patriae* Philosophy

Although Feld (1981) and other legal scholars have argued for the abolition of the juvenile court in favor of criminal due process protections, the juvenile court's mission is aligned with developmental and clinical child psychology literatures, which elucidate differences between children, adolescents, and adults. Theoretical research with regard to dangerousness, sophistication-maturity, and amenability to treatment justifies the need for a separate court that allows for the rehabilitation of youth. Therefore, the overarching message of this chapter, concurring with Woolard's message (this volume), is that the legal system should increase its sensitivity to the developmental differences between adults and children and adolescents.

Reverse the Ease with Which Youth Can Be Transferred to Adult Courts: Individualized Assessment Remains Key

An attempt to reverse, or at least reduce, the ease with which juveniles can be transferred to adult court is supported by the developmental and clinical child psychology literatures. A need clearly exists for investigation of the characteristics that indicate whether juveniles should be tried in adult court. Specifically, methodologically sophisticated studies of dangerousness, sophistication-maturity, and amenability to treatment as well as treatment effectiveness are required. These studies should have a precise definition of the aforementioned constructs and clear expectations of how juveniles should benefit from treatment. Psychologists' ability to develop meaningful conclusions about the effectiveness of interventions with juveniles and refinements in public policy could be enhanced by replicated findings in regard to juvenile offenders who are most dangerous, most sophisticated, and most recalcitrant to treatment, as well as by identifying promising prevention and intervention programs. We have initiated research on risk, sophistication-maturity, and amenability to treatment in juveniles. Data were collected on 144 juvenile offenders who were assessed at the Court Evaluation Unit in Miami. General psychopathology, interpersonal problems, risk, psychopathy, intelligence, and emotional maturity were measured in interviews and self-report format. Criteria relevant to transfer and juvenile concerns more generally including risk, sophistication-maturity, and amenability to treatment were measured using the Risk, Sophistication-Maturity, and Treatment Amenability-interview (RST-i; Salekin, 1998). Analyses demonstrated significant differences between violent and nonviolent adolescents and distinguished between youth who were thought to be sophisticated versus those who were considered less sophisticated and mature. Analyses also showed significant differences between youth who were transferred to adult court and those who were not, among other findings. It is important to note, however, that there was some overlap among the two groups, which may suggest that some youth are transferred to adult court even though they are not the most dangerous or sophisticated and mature. Clearly, considerable research remains to be conducted on the assessment of these constructs.

Develop More Sophisticated Programs to Improve Socialization in Youth

Perhaps the most urgent policy concern is to provide psychological treatment to all youth who find themselves in contact with the law. Interventions that target severe and violent antisocial behavior would help to shape social policy in a manner that continues to address the problem of youth violence squarely but allows youth to be processed in juvenile courts. Another possibility is to develop school-based interventions that target children in early primary school grades before they come into contact with the law. With regard to prevention interventions, recommendations have been made to invest more in research that aims to reduce aggression in children at an earlier age (Lochman, Whidby, & FitzGerald, 2000).

Sweeping policy changes are unlikely, but efforts to reverse the current direction of the juvenile justice system, which eases the process by which youth can be transferred to adult criminal courts, is necessary. Social scientists often provide theoretical and empirical information to one another in academic settings but have very little political traction. As a result, there is a considerable lag between science and the implementation of that science in practice. Further efforts on the part of social scientists to improve the responsiveness of the justice system are needed. These efforts may be initiated, in part, by providing training for attorneys, judges, mental health professionals, and probation officers on relevant developmental issues related to transfer. Researchers should also provide data that they have obtained, perhaps in the form of small reports, to the judges in their districts, thereby providing them with specific information about the juveniles in their communities and states. Finally, researchers should consider publishing more broadly, outside of the traditional psychological journals, in order to reach beyond academic audiences.

References

Adams, S. (1970). The PICO project. In N. Johnson, L. Savitz, & M. E. Wolfgang (Eds.), *The sociology of punishment and correction* (2nd ed., pp. 548–561). New York: Wiley.

Beyer, M. (1999). Expert evaluations of juveniles at risk of adult sentences. *Child Law Practice, 18*, 17–32.

Bishop, D. M., Frazier, C. E., & Henretta, J. C. (1989). Prosecutorial waiver: Case study of a questionable reform. *Crime and Delinquency, 35*, 179–201.

Bishop, D. M., Frazier, C. E., Lanza-Kaduce, L., & Winner, L. (1996). The transfer of juveniles to criminal court: Does it make a difference? *Crime and Delinquency, 42*, 171–191.

Black, H. C. (1979). *Black's law dictionary.* St. Paul, MN: West.

Butts, J. A. (1997). *Delinquency cases waived to criminal court, 1985–1994. Fact Sheet #52.* Washington, DC: Office of Juvenile Justice and Delinquency Prevention.

Carlson, B. E., Barr, W. B., & Young, K. J. (1994). Factors associated with treatment outcomes of male adolescents. *Residential Treatment for Children and Youth, 12,* 39–58.

Champion, D. J., & Mays, G. L. (1991). *Transferring juveniles to criminal courts: Trends and implications for criminal justice.* New York: Praeger.

Edens, J. F., Skeem, J. L., Cruise, K. R., & Cauffman, E. (2001). Assessment of "juvenile psychopathy" and its association with violence: A critical review. *Behavioral Sciences and the Law, 19,* 53–80.

Erikson, E. H. (1959). *Identity and the life cycle.* New York: International Universities Press.

Ewing, C. P. (1990). Juveniles or adults? Forensic assessment of juveniles considered for trial in criminal court. *Forensic Reports, 3,* 3–13.

Farrington, D., Ohlin, L., & Wilson, J. (1986). *Understanding and controlling crime.* New York: Springer-Verlag.

Feld, B. C. (1981). Legislative policies toward the serious juvenile offender: On the virtues of automatic adulthood. *Crime and Delinquency, 27,* 497–521.

Feld, B. C. (1984). The decision to seek criminal charges: Just deserts and the waiver decision. *Criminal Justice Ethics, 3,* 27–41.

Feld, B. C. (1987). The juvenile court meets the principle of the offense: Legislative changes in juvenile waiver statutes. *Journal of Criminal Law and Criminology, 78,* 471–533.

Feld, B. C. (1999). *Bad kids: Race and the transformation of the juvenile Court.* New York: Oxford University press.

Filak, J., Abeles, N., & Norquist, S. (1986). Client's pretherapy interpersonal attitudes and psychotherapy outcome. *Professional Psychology: Research and Practice, 17,* 217–222.

Forth, A. E., Kosson, D., & Hare, R. D. (in press). The Psychopathy Checklist–Youth Version. Toronto: Multi-Health Systems.

Frank, J. D. (1959). The dynamics of the psychotherapeutic relationship. *Psychiatry, 22,* 17–39.

Frank, J. D., Gliedman, L. H., Imber, S. D., Stone, A. R., & Nash, E. H. (1959). Patients' expectations and relearning as factors determining improvement in psychotherapy. *American Journal of Psychiatry, 115,* 961–968.

Freud, A. (1958). Adolescence. *Psychoanalytic Study of the Child, 13,* 255–278.

Frick, P. J. (1998). Callous-unemotional traits and conduct problems: Applying the two-factor model of psychopathy to children. In D. J. Cooke, A. E. Forth, & R. D. Hare (Eds.), *Psychopathy: Theory, research and implications for society* (pp. 161–188). Dordrecht, the Netherlands: Kluwer.

Frick, P. J., & Hare, R. D. (in press). *The psychopathy screening device-PSD.* Toronto, Ontario: Multi Health Systems.

Frick, P. J., O'Brien, B. S., Wootton, J. M., & McBurnett, K. (1994). Psychopathy and conduct problems in children. *Journal of Abnormal Psychology, 103,* 700–707.

Gardner, W. (1993). A life-span rational choice theory of risk taking. In N. Bell & R. Bell (Eds.), *Adolescent risk taking* (pp. 66–83). Newbury Park, CA: Sage.

Garfield, S. L. (1994). Research on client variables in psychotherapy. In S. L. Garfield & A. E. Bergin (Eds.), *Handbook of psychotherapy and behavior change* (3rd ed., pp. 190–228). New York: Wiley.

Green, L., Fry, A. F., & Myerson, J. (1994). Discounting of delayed rewards: A life-span comparison. *Psychological Science, 5,* 33–36.

Grisso, T. (1996). Society's retributive response to juvenile violence: A developmental perspective. *Law and Human Behavior, 20,* 229–247.

Grisso, T. (1998). *Forensic evaluation of juveniles.* Sarsota, FL: Professional Resource Press.

Grisso, T., Tomkins, A., & Casey, P. (1988). Psychosocial concepts in juvenile law. *Law and Human Behavior, 12,* 403–437.

Heilbrun, K., Leheny, C., Thomas, L., & Huneycutt, D. (1997). A national survey of U.S. statutes of juvenile transfer: Implications for policy and practice. *Behavioral Sciences and the Law, 15,* 125–149.

Hirschi, T. (1969). *Causes of delinquency.* New York: Free Press.

Hoge, R. D., Andrews, D. A., & Leschied, A. W. (1996). *Journal of Child Psychology and Psychiatry, 37,* 419–424.

Izzo, R. L., & Ross, R. R. (1990). Meta-analysis of rehabilitation programs for juvenile delinquents: A brief report. *Criminal Justice and Behavior, 17,* 134–142.

Kazdin, A. E. (1985). Treatment of antisocial behavior in children and adolescents. Homewood, IL: Dorsey Press.

Kazdin, A. E. (1987). Treatment of antisocial behavior in children: Current status and future directions. *Psychological Bulletin, 102,* 187–203.

Kazdin, A. E. (1994). Psychotherapy for children and adolescents. In S. L. Garfield & A. E. Bergin (Eds.), *Handbook of psychotherapy and behavior change* (pp. 543–594). New York: Wiley.

Keithly, L. J., Samples, S. J., & Strupp, H. H. (1980). Patient motivation as a predictor of process and outcome in psychotherapy. *Psychotherapy and Psychosomatics, 33,* 87–97.

Kent v. United States, 383 U.S. 541 (1966).

Kernberg, O. F., Burstein, E. D., Coyne, L., Appelbaum, A., Horwitz, L., & Voth, H. (1972). Psychotherapy and psychoanalysis: Final report on the Meninger Foundation's Psychotherapy Research Project. *Bulletin of the Meninger Clinic, 36,* 1–27.

Kruh, I. P., & Brodsky, S. L. (1997). Clinical evaluations for transfer of juveniles to criminal court: Current practice and future research. *Behavioral Sciences and the Law, 15,* 151–165.

Lochman, J. E., Whidby, J. M., & FitzGerald, D. P. (2000). Cognitive-behavioral assessment and treatment with aggressive children. In P. C. Kendall (Ed.), *Child and adolescent therapy: Cognitive-behavioral procedures* (2nd ed). New York: Guilford Press.

Loeber, R., & Stouthamer-Loeber, M. (1998). Development of juvenile aggression and violence: Some common misconceptions and controversies. *American Psychologist, 53*, 242–259.

Logue, A. W. (1988). Research on self-control: An integrating framework. *Behavioral and Brain Sciences, 11*, 665–679.

Luborsky, L., Singer, B., & Luborsky, L. (1975). Comparative studies of psychotherapies. Is it true that "Everyone has won and all must have prizes"? *Archives of General Psychiatry, 32*, 995–1007.

Luthar, S. S. (1991). Vulnerability and resilience: A study of high risk adolescents. *Child Development, 62*, 600–616.

Lynam, D. R. (1996). The early identification of chronic offenders: Who is the fledgling psychopath? *Psychological Bulletin, 120*, 209–234.

Lynam, D. R. (1998). Early identification of fledgling psychopath: Locating the psychopathic child in the current nomenclature. *Journal of Abnormal Psychology, 107*, 566–576.

Moffitt, T. E. (1993). Adolescence-limited and life-course-persistent antisocial behavior: A developmental taxonomy. *Psychological Review, 100*, 674–701.

Moffitt, T. E. (1994). *Juvenile delinquency: Seed of a career in violent crime, just sowing wild oats – or both?* Washington, DC: Federation of Behavioral, Psychological, and Cognitive Sciences.

Moffitt, T. E., Caspi, A., Dickson, N., Silva, P., & Stanton, W. (1996). Childhood-onset versus adolescent-onset antisocial conduct problems in males: Natural history from ages 3 to 18 years. *Development and Psychopathology, 8*, 399–424.

Moffitt, T. E., & Silva, P. (1988). Self-reported delinquency: Results from an instrument in New Zealand. *Australian and New Zealand Journal of Criminology, 21*, 227–240.

Moras, K., & Strupp, H. H. (1982). Pretherapy interpersonal relations, patients' alliance, and outcome in brief therapy. *Archives of General Psychiatry, 39*, 405–409.

Patterson, G. R. (1992). Developmental changes in antisocial behavior. In R. D. Peters, R. J. McMahon, & V. L. Quinsey (Eds.), *Aggression and violence throughout the life span* (pp. 52–82). Newbury Park, CA: Sage.

Piaget, J. (1972). *The child's conception of the world*. Totowa, NJ: Littlefield, Adams.

Puzzanchera, C. M. (1998). *The youngest offenders, 1996*. Washington, DC: OJJDP.

Rae-Grant, N., Thomas, B. H., Offord, D. R., & Boyle, M. H. (1989). Risk, protective factors, and the prevalence of behavioral and emotional disorders in children and adolescents. *Journal of the American Academy of Child and Adolescent Psychiatry, 28,* 262–268.

Robins, L. N. (1966). *Deviant children grown up: A sociological and psychiatric study of sociopathic personality.* Baltimore: Williams and Wilkins.

Rosenthal, D., & Frank, J. D. (1956). Psychotherapy and the placebo effect. *Psychological Bulletin, 53,* 294–302.

Salekin, R. T. (1998). *A manual for the Risk, Sophistication-maturity, and Treatment Amenability – interview (RST-i).* Unpublished manual.

Salekin, R. T., Rogers, R., & Machin, D. (2001). Psychopathy in youth: Pursuing diagnostic clarity. *Journal of Youth and Adolescence, 30,* 173–195.

Salekin, R. T., Rogers, R., & Sewell, K. W. (1996). A review and meta-analysis of the Psychopathy Checklist and Psychopathy Checklist-Revised: Predictive validity of dangerousness. *Clinical Psychology: Science and Practice, 3,* 203–215.

Salekin, R. T., Rogers, R., & Ustad, K. L. (2001). Juvenile waiver to adult criminal courts: Prototypes for dangerousness, sophistication-maturity, and amenability to treatment. *Psychology, Public Policy, and Law, 7,* 381–480.

Salekin, R. T., & Yff, R. (2001, August). *Criteria for juvenile transfer to adult court: Judges' opinions.* Paper presented at the annual convention of the American Psychological Association, San Francisco.

Scott, E. S. (1992). Judgment and reasoning in adolescent decision-making. *Villanova Law Review, 37,* 1607–1669.

Scott, E. S., Repucci, N. D., & Woolard, J. L. (1995). Evaluating adolescent decision making in legal contexts. *Law and Human Behavior, 19,* 221–244.

Sickmund, M., Snyder H. N., & Poe-Yamagata, E. (1997). *Juvenile offenders and victims: 1997 update on violence.* Washington, DC: Office of Juvenile Justice and Delinquency Prevention.

Silverthorn, P., & Frick, P. J. (1999). Developmental pathways to antisocial behavior: The delayed onset pathway in girls. *Development and Psychopathology, 11,* 101–126.

Smith, G. J., Sjoholm, L., & Nielzen, S. (1975). Individual factors affecting the improvement of anxiety during a therapeutic period of $1^{1}/_{2}$ to 2 years. *Acta Psychiatrica Scandinavica, 52,* 7–22.

Steinberg, L., & Cauffman, E. (1996). Maturity of judgment in adolescence: Psychological factors in adolescent decision making. *Law and Human Behavior, 20,* 249–272.

Stouthamer-Loeber, M., Loeber, R., Farrington, D. P., Zhang, Q., Van Kammen, W. B., & Maguin, E. (1993). The double edge of protective and risk factors for delinquency: Interrelations and developmental patterns. *Development and Psychopathology, 5,* 683–701.

Thornberry, T., Huizinga, D., & Loeber, R. (1995). The prevention of serious delinquency and violence: Implications from the Program of Research on the Causes and Correlates of Delinquency. In J. Howell, B. Krisberg,

D. Hawkins, & J. D. Wilson (Eds.), *Source book on serious, violent and chronic juvenile offenders* (pp. 213–237). Thousand Oaks, CA: Sage.

Tolan, P. H., & Gorman-Smith, D. (1998). Development of serious and violent offender careers. In R. Loeber & D. P. Farrington (Eds.), *Serious and violent juvenile offenders: Risk factors and successful interventions* (pp. 68–85). Thousand Oaks, CA: Sage.

Werner, E. E. (1987). Vulnerability and resiliency in children at risk for delinquency: A longitudinal study from birth to young adulthood. In J. D. Burchard & S. N. Burchard (Eds.), *Prevention of delinquent behavior* (pp. 16–43). Newbury Park, CA: Sage.

Werner, E. E., & Smith, R. S. (1992). *Overcoming the odds: High risk children from birth to adulthood.* Ithaca, NY: Cornell University Press.

Wolfgang, M., Figlio, R., & Sellin, T. (1972). *Delinquency in a birth cohort.* Chicago: University of Chicago Press.

Zimring, F. E. (1982). *The changing legal world of adolescence.* New York: Free Press.

10

Youth Violence

Correlates, Interventions, and Legal Implications

Carrie S. Fried
N. Dickon Reppucci

Although the media spotlight certainly exaggerates the reality, there is no doubt that violence by and against youth is an enormous social problem. Nearly one in six of all violent crime arrests in 1997 involved a juvenile under 18 years of age (FBI, 1997). Arrest rates for violent crimes among juveniles increased 49% between 1988 and 1997 compared with an increase of 19% among persons 18 years of age and over. However, recent data suggest that juvenile arrests for murder and other violent crimes may have peaked in 1994 (Sickmund, Snyder, & Poe-Yamagata, 1997). Moderate decreases in 1995, 1996, and 1997 are evidence of the continuing downward trend in juvenile arrests for violent crimes (FBI, 1996, 1997). Although violence is pervasive in American society, not all groups are equally affected. African American youth are significantly overrepresented among victims and perpetrators of violent crimes (Reiss & Roth, 1993). Arrest data indicate that African American youth account for 52% of youth arrested for violent crimes, even though they make up only 15% of the juvenile population (Dryfoos, 1990). However, data on self-reported violent offenses demonstrate a much narrower difference between the prevalence of violence between Blacks and Whites (Elliot, 1994).

We begin this chapter with a discussion of the difficulties surrounding definitions of violence. Then we review the correlates of youth violence by examining the societal, neighborhood, school, peer, family, and individual factors that predict violent behavior.

Next, we discuss the importance of a developmental perspective in the understanding of violence among youth. Specifically, we focus on the heterogeneity of violence and the various developmental pathways that have been used to explain the development of violence. Then prevention and intervention theories and programs are highlighted, with an emphasis on developmentally appropriate and multifaceted programs. Our ultimate aim, and the focus of the final section, is to incorporate our understanding of violence into a legal framework regarding such issues as amenability to treatment, prediction of violence, and criminal responsibility and culpability.

DEFINITIONAL ISSUES

The difficulty of defining violence complicates the identification of risk factors for violent behavior among youth, as well as efforts to prevent youth violence. The National Center for Health Statistics (1993) defines violence as the threatened or actual use of physical force or power that either results in or has a high likelihood of resulting in death, injury, or deprivation. However, studies of violence tend to employ either an overly broad definition that blurs the distinction between aggression and violence or an overly narrow definition that focuses on specific types of violence, such as murder, rape, robbery, and assault. When researchers rely on the use of official records (e.g., arrests, convictions) to measure outcomes, many violent acts that never lead to an arrest or a conviction are excluded (Farrington, 1997). Due to institutionalized racism and lower-quality legal representation, reliance on official records may exaggerate the relative levels of violence among groups that are more likely to be arrested and convicted (e.g., the poor, Blacks).

The terms *violence* and *aggression* are often used interchangeably because many violent acts are aggressive in nature and vice versa. However, as Megargee (1982) has suggested, aggression refers to the intent to hurt or gain advantage over others, without necessarily involving physical attack, whereas violence involves the use of physical force against another individual. Several researchers have advocated the need to make distinctions among different types of violence and aggression by treating them as heterogeneous categories. This could help move us toward a more heterogeneous treatment of violent youth, which has implications for prevention, treatment, and processing by the legal system. Throughout this chapter we reference mainly studies that have used violence as an outcome variable. However, we have also included several studies of aggression in areas where studies of violence are lacking.

PREDICTORS OF VIOLENCE

Numerous studies of youth violence have examined the predictors or factors that put youth at increased risk of exhibiting violent behavior. These predictors can be categorized using Bronfenbrenner's (1979) ecological model, which distinguishes between factors at the macrosystem/exosystem, microsystem, and individual levels. Macrosystem and exosystem factors are those that relate to cultural and societal level influences (e.g., poverty, media portrayals of violence), whereas the microsystem is made up of family, peer, school, and neighborhood influences. At the individual level, predictors of violence include biological, cognitive, and emotional variables.

Macrosystem/Exosystem Factors

The comparatively high rates of youth violence in the United States compared to other industrialized nations make it difficult to ignore the societal and cultural factors that have contributed to the problem. In this section we briefly explore the role of several societal-level factors – poverty and racism, the media, accessibility of firearms, and societal abuse of drugs and alcohol – in contributing to youth violence.

Poverty and Racism. Poverty is one of the strongest predictors of violence (Centerwall, 1984). Studies that control for socioeconomic status demonstrate that the disparity between the percentage of African Americans and the percentage of the general population who are perpetrators of violence is quite small (Centerwall, 1984; National Research Council, 1993; Reiss & Roth, 1993). However, poverty alone does not account for high rates of violence. It is when poverty is combined with prejudice, discrimination, and structural inequities, resulting in feelings of frustration, deprivation,

injustice, hopelessness, and anger, that violence is likely to occur (Hill, Soriano, Chen, & LaFromboise, 1994). Thus, the effect of
poverty on violence is conditional on multiple other variables, from
parental stress, to the lack of social networks, to joblessness. Shifts
in the American economy resulted in the movement of industry out
of the cities (Wilson, 1987), and African Americans have suffered
disproportionately. Youth who grow up in these communities are
likely to live in impoverished neighborhoods, where parents have
fewer social supports and are more likely to be stressed, impacting
their ability to parent effectively (Hill et al., 1994; McLoyd, 1990).
It has been demonstrated that poverty influences youth aggression
in part through its effect on parenting (Guerra, Huesmann, Tolan,
Van Acker, & Eron, 1995).

The Media. Based on the average number of hours that children
spend watching television and content analyses of the programs
they watch, it is estimated that by the time a child leaves elementary school, he or she would have seen 8,000 murders and more
than 100,000 other acts of violence (Huston et al., 1992). Decades
of research confirm the relationship between exposure to television
violence and levels of childhood and adolescent aggression and violence (Eron, Gentry, & Schlegel, 1994). Although the magnitude of
the effect and the processes by which viewing violent television contributes to violence are disputed, the relationship between exposure
to violent media and aggressive behavior is no longer controversial.
    Evidence of the deleterious influence of media violence on chil-
dren comes from experimental and correlational studies. A recent
meta-analysis (Wood, Wong, & Chachere, 1991) indicates that the
effects of television violence account for about 10% of the variance
in child aggression. The results of hundreds of experimental studies demonstrate that increases in aggressive behavior can be produced by exposing children to either extended or brief amounts
of television violence in either laboratory or natural settings (e.g.,
Bandura, Ross, & Ross, 1963; Berkowitz & Rawlings, 1963; Josephson, 1987). Although correlational studies do not allow determination of the direction of the effect, numerous correlational studies
confirm that more aggressive children watch more violent television (e.g., Huesmann, Lagerspetz, & Eron, 1984; Milavsky, Kessler,

Stipp, & Rubens, 1982). The most fascinating findings come from a classic longitudinal study by Huesmann and Eron (1984) that followed a cohort of 8-year-old children for 22 years. At 30 years of age, those boys who had watched more violent television at age 8 were more likely to have been arrested for a violent crime.

Accessibility of Firearms. Nearly all of the recent increase in homicide among youth has been attributed to the use of firearms (Zimring, 1998). The growth in juvenile homicide between 1987 and 1994 was entirely accounted for by the growth in firearm-related homicides. Likewise, the 17% decline in juvenile homicides in 1995 was accounted for by the decline in homicides committed with a firearm (Sickmund et al., 1997), and decreases in weapons arrests in 1996 and 1997 tend to coincide with decreases in homicides (FBI, 1996, 1997).

Guns are being carried by large numbers of youth. As many as 11.4% of high school boys possess a gun (Callahan & Rivara, 1992), and 15% of high school students carried a handgun to school in the previous year (O'Donnell, 1995). Youth who drop out of school and youth who admitted having been expelled or suspended from school, having sold drugs, and/or having engaged in assault and battery are more likely to own handguns (Callahan & Rivara, 1992). Self-protection is the most commonly cited reason for carrying a weapon (e.g., Sheley & Wright, 1993). Case studies indicate that a desire for respect and power is another reason that youth carry weapons (Wilkinson & Fagan, 1996).

There is a great deal of political debate regarding the ability of tougher gun control laws to control access to firearms. One longitudinal study used a multiple time series design to compare changes in crime rates in countries experiencing the introduction of new gun control legislation to changes in crime rates in neighboring countries where no firearm laws were introduced during the same time period. The results indicate that major legal changes may be effective in reducing certain types of violent crime (e.g., homicide), but minor changes are ineffective in reducing any type of violent crime (Podell & Archer, 1994). Another study compared violent crime rates in Vancouver and Seattle, cities that are similar in many regards but differ in that Vancouver has adopted a more restrictive approach to the regulation of firearms (Sloan et al., 1988). The study found that despite similar overall crime rates, the risk of death from homicide was significantly higher in Seattle. Although rates of homicide by means other than firearms were similar in the two cities, rates of homicide committed with a gun were approximately five times higher in Seattle. Even though this study seems to support the notion that tougher gun control laws can be effective in reducing violence, it does not address the question of whether enacting new laws will lead to changes in rates of violence.

Societal Drug and Alcohol Abuse. Substance abuse is highly correlated with youth violence, but the associations are complicated and a clear causal link has not yet been established. Substance abuse is theorized to have an influence on violent behavior in three ways: (a) the direct effect of alcohol and drugs on an individual's propensity to commit a violent act, (b) the violence that is committed as a result of trying to obtain money to purchase drugs, and (c) the systemic effects related to the violence that arises from the association with drug distribution systems (Goldstein, 1985). The research regarding the direct influence of drugs and alcohol on violent behavior is inconclusive. Although there is a moderately strong correlation between substance use and violence (Elliott, Huizinga, & Ageton, 1985), substance use usually follows the onset of violent behavior (Osgood, 1995; Tolan & Loeber, 1993). One longitudinal study that examined the relationship between substance use and violence demonstrated that aggressive behavior at age 12 predicted alcohol use at age 18, but alcohol use at age 12 did not predict aggression at age 18 (White, Brick, & Hansell, 1993).

Empirical research on the violence resulting from efforts to obtain money to purchase drugs and systemic violence resulting from the sale and distribution of drugs is lacking. Blumstein (1995) suggests that youth violence has increased because youth have been recruited into the drug industry. The picture is complicated by potentially confounding variables (e.g., prior histories of violence, neighborhood factors) that link violence and drug distribution networks (Reiss & Roth, 1993). Despite the intuitive appeal of a theory that links drug trafficking and youth violence, more evidence is needed before a clear connection can be made.

Certainly, the risk factors for both youth violence and substance abuse are similar, and we cannot ignore the high rate of co-occurrence between them. Some researchers believe that both sets of behaviors are caused by the same underlying factors (Snyder & Sickmund, 1995), whereas others believe that substance abuse is a direct risk factor contributing to youth violence (Greenwood, 1995). However, because controlled experimental studies in this area are ethically impossible, it is difficult to determine the causal pathway between substance abuse and violence, although statistical models offer promise in disentangling the relationship.

Microsystem Factors

In this section we briefly review the microsystem factors that are associated with youth violence. The microsystem is made up of the systems with which the individual has direct contact, and include the neighborhood, family, peer group, and school.

Neighborhoods. Poor neighborhoods tend to have higher rates of violence, although not all of them experience high rates of violence. Many economically stressed neighborhoods share other characteristics that make violence more prevalent. Poor neighborhoods tend to be inhabited by a more transient population and also tend to be more disorganized (Hawkins et al., 1998). High levels of mobility make it more difficult for residents to develop support networks and feel a sense of attachment to the community (American Psychological Association Commission on Violence, 1993). Also, the types of public and social services (e.g., recreation programs) that are available in more affluent neighborhoods are often limited in low-income neighborhoods (National Research Council, 1993).

In violent neighborhoods, children witness high levels of shootings, stabbings, and killings (e.g., Jenkins & Bell, 1994), which has an effect on the development of violence and aggression in children (Widom, 1989). A recent study found that exposure to violence was the strongest predictor of adolescents' self-reported use of violence (DuRant, Cadenhead, Pendergrast, Slavens & Linder, 1994). Neighborhoods also appear to affect age of onset. In the most disadvantaged neighborhoods, more 10- to 12-year-old boys were

engaging in acts of violence compared with 10- to 12-year-old boys
from less disadvantaged neighborhoods. Yet, among 13- to 15-year-
old boys, violence was fairly evenly distributed across neighborhoods (Loeber & Wikstrom, 1993).

Family. The family has been cited as the most powerful single influence on the development of aggression and violence
(McGuire, 1997). Family correlates of violence can be classified
into three general categories – demographic and parental characteristics, child-rearing practices, and family functioning (Loeber &
Stouthamer-Loeber, 1986).

Higher levels of aggression and violence are found among children of low socioeconomic status (SES), poorly educated, highly
mobile, single-parent families (Gagnon, Craig, Tremblay, Zhou &
Vitaro, 1995; Kupersmidt, Briesler, DeRosier, Patterson, & Davis,
1995; Saner & Ellickson, 1996; Tremblay, Masse, Kurtz & Vitaro,
1997). However, Kupersmidt and colleagues (1995) note that single parenthood is associated with neighborhood type, and it may
be the interaction between these factors that accounts for some of
the variance in aggression. The criminal behavior of parents is also
strongly and consistently associated with violence in youths (e.g.,
Baker & Mednick, 1984).

The influence of child-rearing practices on the development of
an array of problem behaviors, including violence, has received
considerable attention. Coercive interactions (Capaldi & Patterson,
1996), lax and ineffective parental discipline (Snyder & Patterson,
1987; Weiss, Dodge, Bates, & Pettit, 1992), poor parental monitoring
(Gorman-Smith, Tolan, Zelli, & Huesmann, 1996), physical punishment (Eron, Huesmann, & Zelli, 1991; Farrington, 1978), and child
physical abuse (Manly, Cicchetti, & Barnett, 1994) are all associated
with higher rates of aggression and violence among children. However, it is unclear whether parenting practices cause aggressive and
violent behavior or whether these behaviors lead to harsh and ineffective parenting styles. Longitudinal research seems to indicate
both a reciprocal relationship between child-rearing practices and
child behavior (Vuchinich, Bank, & Patterson, 1992) and an association between poor parental supervision and harsh parenting in
early childhood and later violence (Farrington, 1989).

The effects of parenting strategies appear to be mediated by the quality of the parent–child relationship. Lack of maternal warmth (e.g., Booth, Rose-Krasnor, McKinnon, & Rubin, 1994), insecure attachment (e.g., Erickson, Sroufe, & Egeland, 1985), and parental indifference and rejection (e.g., Farrington, 1991) have all been associated with increased levels of aggression and violence in childhood and adolescence. However, studies examining the link between attachment and later antisocial and violent behavior have produced mixed results (e.g., Bates, Bayles, Bennett, Ridge, & Brown, 1991; Booth et al., 1994). Moreover, maternal warmth seems to play a buffering role in the relationship between harsh discipline and aggression. When harsh discipline is accompanied by close maternal relationships, physical discipline is not correlated with behavior problems (e.g., Deater-Deckard & Dodge, 1997).

Children who grow up in homes characterized by high levels of family conflict and family violence are at increased risk of becoming aggressive and violent. Exposure to parents' marital conflict is predictive of violent criminal convictions (Farrington, 1989; McCord, 1979) and self-reported violence in adolescence (Elliott, 1994). The evidence also seems to indicate that children who have been physically abused or neglected are more likely to be arrested for a violent crime (e.g., Widom, 1989).

Peer Groups. Unlike adults, juveniles commit most violent and serious delinquent acts in the company of peers rather than alone (Zimring, 1998). The process of association with aggressive and antisocial peers begins at a young age with rejection by prosocial peers. There is substantial evidence that aggressive children are likely to be rejected by their peers (for a review see Coie, Dodge, & Kupersmidt, 1990).

Peer rejection leads to increased aggression and antisocial activity and promotes association with antisocial peers (Dishion, Patterson, Stoolmiller, & Skinner, 1991; Dodge, Bates, &, Pettit, 1990; Patterson & Bank, 1989). Deviant, rejected children gravitate to each other and form their own "coercive cliques" (Cairns, Cairns, Neckerman, Gest, & Gariepy, 1988), in which aggression is valued and deviant behaviors are promoted. Other nondeviant adolescents may be attracted to the glamour of these delinquent peer groups, which may contribute to the late onset of aggression in adolescents with no prior history of delinquency or aggression (Moffitt, 1993). Research on delinquency clearly demonstrates that associating with antisocial peers increases the risk of involvement in delinquent behaviors (e.g., Keenan, Loeber, Zhang, Stouthamer-Loeber, & Van Kammen, 1995), but the connection between peer associations and violence is less clear. However, several longitudinal studies have found strong positive correlations between association with delinquent peers in early adolescence and self-reported violence in late adolescence or early adulthood (e.g., Farrington, 1989; Maguin et al., 1995; Saner & Ellickson, 1996). These findings were confirmed by a recent meta-analysis that concluded that lack of positive social ties and association with antisocial peers at ages 12–14 were powerful predictors of later violent or serious delinquency (Lipsey & Derzon, 1998).

Schools. Rates of violence are elevated in schools with higher percentages of students who do not place a high value on good grades, do not believe the curriculum is relevant to their lives, and do not think their school experience will have a positive influence on their lives (National Research Council, 1993). Low student attendance, high student–teacher ratios, instability in the school population, and poor academic quality of the school also characterize schools with higher rates of violence (Hellman & Beaton, 1986). Although violence in schools is a reflection of the community in which the school is located, relations between school characteristics and aggressive behaviors exist even after controlling for neighborhood crime rates. Aggressive and violent behavior is more likely to occur in schools with lax enforcement of rules and undisciplined classrooms (National Research Council, 1993). It is unclear whether high rates of school violence and aggression cause or are caused by the discipline practices of the school. An individual youth's academic achievement and attitude toward school probably interact with the school environment to predict aggression and violence. In a recent meta-analysis of longitudinal research, school attitude and performance from age 6 to age 14 were found to be significant predictors of violence at ages 15 to 25 (Lipsey & Derzon, 1998).

Individual Level Factors

At the individual level, biological, cognitive, and emotional factors contribute to the development of violence and aggression. An accumulation of individual risk factors is presumed to increase the likelihood of eliciting violence or aggression, especially when coupled with multiple microsystem and macro/exosystem risk factors.

Biological Bases of Violence. Although we espouse a social learning theory of the development of violence, which proposes that violent behavior is learned and therefore can be unlearned, we also believe that any discussion of the causes of violence that ignores potential biological influences is incomplete. Although a biological predisposition may make it more or less likely that an individual will exhibit violent behaviors in certain contexts, data suggest that biological factors account for at most a small, inconsistent proportion of the variance in violent behavior (Miczek, Mirsky, Carey, DeBold, & Raine, 1994). Research on heritability, hormones, neurotransmitters, the autonomic nervous system, and neurological functioning has demonstrated some link to violence and aggression. The consensus is that inherited characteristics do not play a direct causal part in the development of violence (McGuire, 1997); rather, genes may influence other physiological processes that may predispose an individual to aggressive behavior (Gottesman & Goldsmith, 1994).

The hormone that is most often implicated in influencing levels of aggression and violence is testosterone. Among adults, substantial evidence links aggression and testosterone levels, although adolescent samples yield mixed results (see Coie & Dodge, 1998). Archer (1994) has suggested that testosterone and aggression influence each other in a reciprocal fashion, such that testosterone could be considered both a cause and a consequence of aggression. One longitudinal study of 15- to 17-year-old boys found that testosterone had a direct effect on aggressive behavior (Olweus, Mattison, Schalling, & Low, 1988). Another more recent longitudinal study examined the effect of aggressive behavior on subsequent testosterone levels (Tremblay et al., 1997). Tremblay and colleagues found that boys who were more aggressive as children had lower testosterone levels at age 13 than less aggressive boys. Between the ages of 15 and 16, however, testosterone levels in the aggressive group had increased sharply, and testosterone levels in the nonaggressive group had declined. The authors offer one particularly compelling explanation for these findings. At age 13, aggressive boys had been rejected by their peers and were not socially dominant. The study also confirmed a concurrent association between social dominance and higher testosterone levels. Then, between the ages of 15 and 16, the more aggressive boys may have become involved in delinquent activities in which aggression enabled them to become socially dominant, increasing their testosterone levels.

Investigations linking autonomic nervous system responses and aggressive behavior have found that a low resting heart rate is consistently related to violent behavior (Farrington, 1997). Raine, Venables, and Williams (1990) used resting heart rate and skin conductance measures of boys at age 15 to predict criminality at age 24. They were able to classify 75 of 101 participants accurately. One of two explanations likely accounts for the strong relationship between resting heart rate and violence. Low resting heart rate may be an indication of fearlessness or autonomic underarousal (Farrington, 1997). Fearless individuals are more likely than fearful individuals to engage in violent behaviors. And autonomic underarousal leads to sensation-seeking and thereby participation in risky behaviors.

Several neurotransmitters have also been linked to the development of aggression. Low levels of serotonin (5-HT) activity have consistently been found to correlate with aggression in both children and adults, especially among high-trait aggressive individuals (e.g., Cleare & Bond, 1995), indicating a causal link. Dopamine and norepinephrine have also been implicated in the development of aggression, but the relationships have not been clearly established.

Studies of neurological functioning have consistently found that violence is related to deficits in the frontal cortex. Raine's (1998) prefrontal dysfunction model posits that damage to the prefrontal cortex results in cognitive, personality, arousal, and anticipatory fear deficits, which in turn predispose individuals to aggressive behavior. Among adolescents, Moffitt and Lynam (1994) found that neurological deficits at age 13 were correlated with delinquency at age 18. Prenatal exposure to toxins (e.g., lead, alcohol, drugs) and complications in childbirth may result in neurological damage that prevents the inhibition of violent behavior (Reiss & Roth, 1993).

Cognitive Factors. Cognitive precursors to aggression and violence include low IQ, reading problems, attention deficits, and hyperactivity. Low IQ is consistently predictive of aggressive and delinquent behavior among adolescents even after controlling for race and SES (Lynam, Moffitt, & Stouthamer-Loeber, 1993). Furthermore, many studies have found that compared to their nondelinquent peers, both nonviolent and violent delinquents demonstrate relatively lower scores on verbal IQ than on performance IQ measures (e.g., Cornell & Wilson, 1992). Cornell and Wilson suggest that the discrepancy is indicative of intellectual deficits among delinquent youth. Lynam and colleagues (1993) examined several theories that have been used to explain the relationship between low IQ and delinquency. The only one to receive support in their study was the indirect effect model, which holds that IQ causes delinquency through its effect on school performance; so, youth with cognitive deficits experience school failure, which in turn contributes to delinquency. Several longitudinal studies demonstrate that childhood hyperactivity and attention deficits are also strongly associated with both self-reported violence and arrests for violent offenses in late adolescence and early adulthood (e.g., Farrington, 1989; Hechtman & Weiss, 1986). Inattention without hyperactivity, however, appears to be only weakly associated with later aggression (Loeber, 1988).

Research also indicates that aggressive delinquent adolescents have more social cognitive deficiencies (e.g., Crick & Dodge, 1994), lower moral reasoning maturity (e.g., Arbuthnot, Gordon, & Jurkovic, 1987), and poorer abstract reasoning and problem-solving skills than nonaggressive youths (e.g., Seguin, Pihl, Harden, Tremblay, & Boulerice, 1995). An individual's cognitive appraisal of an event is a major factor in determining the subsequent behavioral response. Crick and Dodge (1994) elaborated a six-stage information-processing model of social maladjustment and aggression. They found that aggressive children selectively attend to aggressive cues, are more likely to attribute hostile intent to others, generate fewer solutions to problems, and select action-oriented rather than reflective solutions.

Temperament and Emotional Regulation. Based on maternal reports, children who have a difficult temperament as infants are more likely to be aggressive and have other behavior problems in later childhood (e.g., Kingston & Prior, 1995). Maternal reports may be inaccurate, however, because (a) the mother's attitude toward the child, rather than the child's actual behavior, may be driving the reports (e.g., Bates, Maslin & Frankel, 1985) and (b) the interaction between the child's temperament and the quality of the mother–child relationship may be responsible for the correlation between temperament and later aggressive behavior. Individual differences in temperament are present soon after birth and may indicate that temperament is inherited. However, environmental and social factors play a substantial role in the development of aggression in children with difficult temperaments (McGuire, 1997).

Aggressive children are likely to become aggressive and violent adolescents and adults. Longitudinal studies demonstrate consistently high stability in aggression from early childhood into young adulthood (Farrington, 1994; Olweus, 1979) and show that early aggressive behavior is predictive of later arrests for violent crimes. McCord and Ensminger (1995) found that in a Chicago sample nearly half of the boys rated as aggressive by their teachers in first grade had been arrested for a violent crime by age 33 compared with a third of the nonaggressive boys. Early onset of violent behavior and delinquency is also predictive of more serious and chronic violence (Tolan & Thomas, 1995).

DEVELOPMENTAL TRAJECTORIES OF VIOLENCE AND AGGRESSION

Developmental trajectories of violence suggest that behavior develops in a time-ordered fashion. In order to study the developmental pathways of violence and aggression, it is necessary to measure intraindividual change by measuring the same individual repeatedly over time. The ultimate goal is to be able to identify the serious and violent offenders, who make up a small proportion of the popula-tion. Approximately 6–8% of the male population commits about 60–85% of the serious violent crimes (see Tolan & Gorman-Smith, 1998), and among frequent offending juveniles, only 29% have ever been arrested for a violent offense (Snyder, 1998). Even among the most aggressive children, only a small proportion ever become vio-lent offenders. Even though early aggression predicts later violence, these predictions are far from perfect and will yield false positives (youth who are at risk for violence but who are not violent) and false negatives (individuals who were not highly aggressive as children but who become violent) (Loeber & Hay, 1997).

Patterson, Capaldi, and Bank (1991) and Moffitt (1993) have sug-gested that age of onset can be used to distinguish early starters or life-course persistent offenders from late starters or adolescent-limited offenders. Several longitudinal studies indicate that earlier onset and early escalation of offense seriousness seem to be risk fac-tors for serious and violent offending. Aside from age of onset, the other developmental trajectory that has proven to be most effective at categorizing aggressive and delinquent behavior among youths distinguishes between overt and covert behaviors. Loeber and Hay (1994) describe three developmental pathways of delinquency and problem behaviors – the overt pathway, the covert pathway, and the authority conflict pathway (see Salekin, this volume, for de-scriptions of the pathways). Of the three pathways, only the overt pathway leads to violent behaviors, but adolescents can progress along multiple pathways simultaneously. Longitudinal data exist to support the utility of Loeber and Hay's theory in identifying path-ways for violent offending (Tolan & Gorman-Smith, 1998; Tolan, Gorman-Smith, Huesmann, & Zelli, 1997). Meanwhile, Capaldi and Patterson (1996) determined that the violent acts committed by ado-lescents are part of a general involvement in criminal behavior and that distinct pathways for violent versus nonviolent offenders do not exist. Although the Capaldi–Patterson study seems to contra-dict the Loeber–Hay developmental pathways model, it may be that frequent offenders are likely to progress along both the covert and overt pathways simultaneously, ultimately committing both violent and nonviolent offenses.

Understanding the risk factors and the developmental trajectories that lead to violence help to determine the most effective strategies and the most appropriate time for prevention and intervention efforts. Intervention planning should be theory driven and informed by the study of risk factors for violence to ensure that at least one, but preferably multiple, risk factors are targeted (Fried, Reppucci, & Woolard, 2000). The next section provides a brief review of the prevention and intervention programs available to reduce violence among youths.

PREVENTION AND INTERVENTION

Responses to increases in youth violence have generally come in two forms. The first has been an effort to protect society from young "super-predators" by enacting tougher juvenile crime legislation. In the 1990s, most states toughened their juvenile justice systems by enacting laws that make it easier to prosecute juveniles as adults, creating minimum sentencing requirements and blended sentencing provisions, which allow juveniles to be sentenced past the age of 21 (Sickmund et al., 1997). Some proponents of these policies believe that getting tough on crime will have a deterrent effect on potential violent offenders. However, harsher sentences do not appear to be effective in deterring violent criminal behavior (Gottfredson & Hirschi, 1995).

The second response is the prevention of youth violence through interdisciplinary programmatic intervention. Specifically, recent intervention research has focused on the identification of important risk and protective factors, adopted an epidemiological and developmental framework, and targeted interventions at multiple levels (e.g., individual, family, school, neighborhood) (Reppucci, Woolard, & Fried, 1999). Using a public health model, we examine the theory, methodology, and efficacy of prevention and treatment strategies, with an emphasis on multisystemic approaches. Based on the distinctions made by Mulvey, Arthur, and Reppucci (1993), prevention programs target groups of individuals prior to the occurrence of serious violence. Treatment is reserved for individuals already identified as chronically violent and involves strategies to modify behavior.

Prevention Strategies

The identification and amelioration of risks and/or the identification and enhancement of protective factors are the main foci of prevention programs. Prevention programs may target at-risk youth who have already been identified as aggressive or violent, or they may be universally available to all youth. Program components may be targeted to the individual, the family, peers, the school, or the community. Individually based program components might include counseling, medication, social skills training, academic skills training, and anger management. Family-based components include parent training, family therapy, and conflict resolution. Program components that target peers might involve peer leadership and mediation, as well as conflict resolution. School-based components often include education about violence, changes in school organization, behavioral contracting in the classroom, and the addition of safety devices, such as metal detectors. Empowerment initiatives, community organization, and mass media campaigns are examples of community-based program components.

Given the multifaceted nature of the factors that contribute to the development of violence, programs that target multiple domains in a child's life have the greatest chance of being effective. Likewise, interventions that are implemented between the prenatal period and age 6 are more likely to be successful than interventions implemented in later childhood or adolescence, when many of the risk factors for violence may have already accumulated. Because a comprehensive review of violence prevention programs is beyond the scope of this chapter, we briefly highlight one multifaceted program as an exemplar in each of three target groups – infancy through preschool, middle childhood, and adolescence – followed by an overview of community-based interventions. For an excellent, comprehensive review of the prevention of violent juvenile offending, see Wasserman and Miller (1998).

Infancy Through Preschool Exemplar: Prenatal/Early Infancy Project. The Prenatal/Early Infancy Project (Olds, Henderson, Chamberlin, & Tatelbaum, 1986) targets low-income pregnant women bearing their first child. Throughout the course of the

program, which lasts through the second birthday of the woman's
first child, the women receive home visits from a nurse to improve
prenatal health, the care provided to the infants and toddlers, and
the women's own development, especially in the areas of education,
employment, and future pregnancies. A 15-year follow-up with a
sample of 400 low-SES, primarily White women from rural New
York demonstrated 79% fewer verified reports of child abuse and
neglect, 69% fewer maternal arrests, and 56% fewer arrests of the
15-year-old children than a randomly assigned comparison group
(Olds, Hill, Mihalic, & O'Brien, 1998). The program has been expanded to an urban setting in Memphis, Tennessee, with 1,139
African American and White women. Initial results indicate that
the families receiving home visits from a nurse fare better in terms
of maternal and child development than those assigned to a control
group.

***Middle Childhood Exemplar: FAST Track (Families and Schools
Together).*** The FAST Track program provides a good example of a
preventive intervention that targets multiple risk factors and their
interactions in a child's life (Conduct Problems Prevention Research
Group, 1992, 1996). The goals of the program are to increase communication and bonds between the child, the family, and the school;
to improve peer relationships and individual social, cognitive, and
problem-solving skills; and to decrease disruptive behavior in the
home and in the school. The intervention targets kindergarten-age
children scoring in the top 10% of conduct problems through a
two-stage screening process. Program components include parent
training, home visiting/case management, social skills training, academic tutoring, and behavioral classroom management. Analyses
of this longitudinal multisite study are underway, but preliminary
evaluation of three cohorts who have completed first grade indicate that compared to control groups, participants have lower observer ratings of aggressive, disruptive, and oppositional behavior
in the classroom; fewer peer nominations of aggressiveness; more
appropriate parental discipline; and more maternal warmth and involvement. The FAST Track program is an excellent example of a
theory-based approach to preventive intervention that operates in
multiple domains of a child's life.

Adolescent Exemplar: Self-Enhancement, Inc. (SEI). SEI (Gabriel, 1996; Gabriel, Hopson, Haskins, & Powell, 1996) is a Portland, Oregon-based community-service organization that focuses on adolescents in high-risk communities. The SEI program has several components: (a) classroom education, focusing on anger management, conflict resolution, and problem solving; (b) exposure education, consisting of visits to agencies and organizations that deal with the causes and consequences of violence in the community; and (c) proactive education, involving the production of newsletters, assemblies and conferences, and radio and television public service announcements that communicate antiviolence messages. Participants included 102 African American students who were referred by teachers based on poor attendance, academic problems, or behavior problems. After 1 year of participation in the program, participants demonstrated decreases in self-reports of fighting and carrying a weapon, whereas control youth did not demonstrate changes in either behavior.

Community-Based Interventions. Neighborhood organization, gun buybacks, proactive policing, juvenile curfews, and antiviolence mass media campaigns are examples of community-level prevention strategies (Kellermann, Fuqua-Whitley, Rivara, & Mercy, 1998). Evaluations of these strategies suffer from several methodological limitations and most programs are not evaluated with regard to their impact on serious and violent juvenile offenders (Catalano, Arthur, Hawkins, Berglund, & Olson, 1998), so it is not surprising that their utility in preventing violent behavior has yet to be clearly demonstrated. Reviews by Kellermann and colleagues (1998) and Catalano and colleagues (1998) both suggest that curfew programs and proactive policing are promising community strategies for reducing violence. Perhaps the most exciting approach to the prevention of adolescent problem behaviors is the Communities That Care (CTC) program (Hawkins & Catalano, 1992). It is a risk-focused social development strategy that involves representative members from the entire community in creating a program to reduce violence and other adolescent problem behaviors. Community risk and protective factors are identified to help local leaders in planning an intervention strategy to reduce risks and enhance protective factors at multiple levels. Among the 36 community boards that participated in the CTC program, 60% had implemented effective risk reduction strategies at a 1-year follow-up compared with 23% of community teams participating in a different community risk reduction program (Arthur, Ayers, Graham, & Hawkins, 1997).

Treatment

Treatment of offenders may include incarceration, rehabilitation, reintegration into the community following incarceration, and therapy. As was mentioned earlier, incarceration has not been proven to be effective in reducing crime. Based on evaluation data, one of the most effective means of violence prevention may be the use of Multisystemic Therapy (MST) with serious juvenile offenders. MST is a highly individualized family- and community-based therapeutic approach that views behavior as the end product of the interactions between individuals and their interconnected systems (e.g., family, school, community). Treatment plans, developed with the family, integrate family, school, community, peer, and individual interventions (Henggeler, Cunningham, Pickrel, Schoenwald, & Brondino, 1996).

Two studies of MST demonstrate its effectiveness in reducing rearrest rates and out-of-home placement and improving family functioning. A random assignment of 84 serious offenders in Simpsonville, South Carolina – half to usual services and half to MST – found that control group youth were twice as likely to be rearrested as youth in MST (Henggeler, Melton, & Smith, 1992). Another study compared 176 Columbia, Missouri, youth randomly assigned to either MST or individual therapy (Borduin et al., 1995). Results from a 4-year follow-up indicated that rearrest rates among MST completers were 22% compared with 47% for MST dropouts, 71% for individual therapy completers, and 71% for individual therapy dropouts. Results are encouraging from both a treatment and a policy perspective, because the cost of MST is substantially less than the cost of out-of-home placement (Tate, Reppucci, & Mulvey, 1995).

Another promising program for teenagers with histories of chronic and serious criminal behavior, who are at risk of incarceration, is the Multidimensional Treatment Foster Care program

(MTFC; Chamberlain, 1990). The treatment plan combines an interactional family treatment model and a family foster care model. There are four essential components of the program: (a) an individualized behavior management program implemented by the foster parents; (b) a school program monitored by teachers; (c) individual therapy focusing on the youth's maladaptive cognitive-processing patterns; and (d) parent training for the biological family. Typically, the youth stays with the foster family for about 6 months, during which time the biological parents are trained to use the same behavior management program that the foster parents are using. Parents get the opportunity to practice their skills during weekend home visits. Based on a small study of 32 chronic offenders who were placed either in the TFC program or in group homes or residential care, fewer TFC youth were incarcerated at a 1-year follow-up.

Issues in Program Evaluation and Special Considerations of Urban Youth

Although public concern about violence has led to the proliferation of prevention programs, most are unevaluated or poorly evaluated. The tension between the immediate need for action, on the one hand, and the need for time-intensive evaluation, on the other, plagues violence prevention efforts. When programs are evaluated, it is often impossible to distinguish between components that are essential to the success of the program and those that are superfluous or even harmful. In addition, the replication of successful prevention strategies often does not take into account the developmental and cultural differences in target populations. Programs that are successful with White middle-class youth often have no effect, or even deleterious effects, when implemented with poor, urban, minority youth (Guerra, Attar, & Weissberg, 1997). The impact of chronic exposure to poverty and violence needs to be considered in planning violence prevention programs. These conditions of the inner city and the multiple risk factors faced by youth who live in these neighborhoods make it both more difficult to implement intervention programs and less likely that they will be potent enough to produce lasting effects (Guerra, et al., 1997).

YOUTH VIOLENCE AND THE LAW

Increases in juvenile crime, especially violent crime, have raised questions about the adequacy of the juvenile justice system. The juvenile justice system, which was originally established to provide guidance and rehabilitation services to delinquent youth, has become more similar to the adult criminal court over the past two decades. Currently, violent juveniles are likely to be transferred to adult courts or face adultlike punishment if they remain under the jurisdiction of the juvenile court. As mental health professionals and researchers struggle to understand the risk factors for violence and try to prevent and treat violent youth, the legal system struggles to balance community protection with fair treatment of offenders. In this section we address the integration of psychology and law as it relates to the prediction of youth violence, amenability to treatment, and criminal responsibility and culpability. In our discussion, we highlight the legal implications of acknowledging the heterogeneity of violent behavior among youth.

Prediction of Youth Violence

Psychologists are often called upon to determine whether a specific individual is at risk of harming himself or herself or another individual. Two decades ago, Monahan (1981) concluded that when clinician predicted that a person would be violent, they were accurate no more than one in three times. Nonetheless, courts continued to rely on clinicians' assessments. In 1983, the U.S. Supreme Court's decision in *Barefoot v. Estelle* established the admissibility of dangerousness predictions by clinicians. The Court stated that "it makes little sense, if any, to submit that psychiatrists, out of the entire universe of persons who might have an opinion on the issue, would know so little about the subject [prediction of future dangerousness] that they should not be permitted to testify" (p. 897). Recent reviews suggest a more optimistic view of the ability of clinicians to predict violence (e.g., Menzies, Webster, McMain, Staley, & Scaglione, 1994; Monahan, 1992). The use of multiple criterion measures and the focus on short-term predictions are two recent improvements in the research on violence prediction (Monahan, 1996).

Predictions are typically made using one of two methods – clinicians' assessments or actuarial prediction (which provides a statistical probability based on the presence of various risk factors). One of the best recent examples (Lidz, Mulvey, & Gardner, 1993) of clinicians' predictions of violence used a sample of psychiatric emergency room patients assessed by psychiatrists or nurses and followed them for 6 months. Violence was measured using official records, self-report, and a collateral informant report (e.g., a family member). Fifty-three percent of the patients who were predicted to be violent were, in fact, violent. Of the patients who were not predicted to be violent, 36% participated in a violent act in the ensuing 6 months. The accuracy of prediction was much better for male than for female patients. This is likely related to the paucity of information on and lack of understanding about violence among females.

An actuarial study conducted by Harris, Rice, and Quinsey (1993) accurately classified 75% of 618 men who were treated or assessed at a forensic hospital. They used 12 variables, ranging from mental health diagnoses to marital status to a history of elementary school maladjustment, to predict violence over a period of 7 years. The greater prediction accuracy in the Harris et al. study over the Lidz et al. study might be related to the method of prediction (actuarial versus clinical assessment) or the exclusion of women in the actuarial study. Both studies provide evidence of more accurate prediction of future violence than the studies reviewed by Monahan in 1981.

Unfortunately, most of the existing research on the prediction of violence has been conducted with adult samples. What is known about the development of violence suggests that prediction of future violence may be different, and more difficult, for adolescents than for adults (Ewing, 1990). Because most adolescents desist from violent offending before they reach adulthood (i.e., adolescent-limited offenders) and because most studies on the prediction of violence have been conducted only with adults (i.e., life-course persistent offenders), it is unlikely that risk assessment studies of adults would be generalizable to an adolescent population.

Because the life-course persistent offenders pose the greatest threat to society, recent concern has focused on the identification of youths who are at risk for the development of a life-course persistent offender trajectory. The nature of the development of risk factors suggests the need to examine prospectively the predictors of violence in children and adolescents. Such an endeavor is currently underway. The MacArthur Foundation is providing support for a large-scale, longitudinal, prospective study that will follow youth for a 5-year period (E. P. Mulvey, personal communication).

Meanwhile, the courts have the difficult task of balancing community protection with the future of juvenile offenders. Because the courts have no better option than to rely on less than perfect clinician or actuarial predictions, problems associated with predictions yielding false negatives and false positives will continue. If predictions of dangerousness yield too many false negatives (juveniles who are not predicted to be violent but who turn out to engage in later acts of violence), then the judicial system has put the community at risk. On the other hand, if predictions of the risk of violence yield too many false positives (juveniles who are predicted to be violent but who turn out not to engage in later acts of violence), then the judicial system will have imposed unnecessarily harsh punishment on some juveniles.

Effective risk communication is an emerging issue, both with regard to communicating violence risk estimates to the courts (Monahan & Steadman, 1996) and with regard to facilitating clinicians' use of new knowledge in making assessments (Borum, 1996). Borum urges researchers to develop technology that would make their knowledge easily available to clinicians. Monahan and Steadman propose the use of categorical risk communication (e.g., low, moderate, high, very high violence risk categories) rather than communicating risk in terms of probabilities. Categorical risk communication may be preferable in the prediction of rare events, when the probabilities may be misunderstood or misused by mental health professionals and the courts. Reliable prediction and responsible communication of the risk of violence would enable the courts to balance community protection and fair treatment of offenders, arguing for continued research aimed at improving dangerousness prediction for juvenile offenders and methods for communicating the information reliably to courts.

Amenability to Treatment

Determinations of amenability to treatment are central to many decisions made in the juvenile justice system, including the decision to transfer a juvenile to adult court. (See Salekin, this volume, for a more thorough review of assessing amenability to treatment.) Assessment of an individual's amenability to treatment for violence is complex and requires an understanding of the individual's personal characteristics, the context in which the individual is embedded, and the treatments that are available (Mulvey, 1984). With regard to personal characteristics, developmental stage is particularly important to consider in selecting treatment options and determining amenability to treatment. *Developmental stage* refers to both the maturity level of the youth and the progression of violent behavior along developmental trajectories of violence.

The critical role of contextual factors in treatment cannot be overemphasized. Any treatment that relies on addressing the multiple risk factors for violence must consider the amenability of each factor to change. Assessment of amenability to treatment also hinges on the resources that are available to the juvenile. In a community that lacks resources for rehabilitation, a juvenile is less likely to be considered amenable to treatment (Mulvey & Reppucci, 1988). Some believe that it is unethical to find that a juvenile is not amenable to treatment due to a lack of services available in the community (Kruh & Brodsky, 1997). The reality is that evaluations of amenability to treatment reflect not only the juvenile's willingness to change, however, but also the environmental and system-level factors, which are often beyond the juvenile's control (Mulvey & Reppucci, 1988).

The role of mental health professionals in determining amenability to treatment is to help the courts by providing information about programs that are most likely to be successful with a specific individual, taking into account contextual factors along with the juvenile's willingness to change. Once again, it is critical to acknowledge the diversity among violent youth. Motivations for violence and situational antecedents to violence may help inform evaluators about which programs are most likely to be successful and which youth are most likely to be rehabilitated. Determining goodness of fit between the juvenile and possible treatment options is critical to the evaluation of amenability to treatment and should be one of the primary goals of research on amenability to treatment (Kruh & Brodsky, 1997).

Criminal Responsibility and Culpability

A critical premise of the current wave of juvenile justice reform that emphasizes punishment over rehabilitation is that juveniles who commit violent crimes are as culpable as adults for the crimes they commit (Reppucci, 1999). Because our justice system is designed to take intent into account in determining punishment, criminal responsibility (the extent to which individuals choose or cause their own behavior) is closely linked to culpability (the degree to which wrongful behavior merits punishment). So, for adolescents to be deemed as culpable as adults for the crimes they commit, it follows that adolescents and adults are equally responsible for their violent behavior. Is it true that adolescents and adults choose or cause their own behavior to the same extent?

Although this question has not yet been answered, theory and studies of adolescent decision making illustrate some of the differences and similarities between adolescents and adults. The consensus from several studies of adolescent decision making (see Grisso, 1996) is that past the age of 14, the difference in cognitive capacities between adults and adolescents is minimal, as long as they are of at least average intelligence. However, some researchers have suggested that there may be substantial differences between adults and adolescents in their ability to exercise good judgment in decision making in some contexts (see Woolard, this volume). It may be that the accumulation of biological and contextual risk factors is directly associated with violent behavior, or it may be that the risk factors are associated with violent behavior through their influence on maturity and judgment. Empirical research is needed to examine the ways in which development of judgment and psychosocial factors interact with background characteristics to influence decision making in situations that may result in violence.

Recent reforms in the juvenile justice system also have implications for the evaluation of culpability. There is great diversity among adolescents arrested for the same violent crimes, yet several juvenile justice reforms treat them as a homogenous group. Because determination of culpability hinges on an individual's intent in a given criminal situation, the increased use of determinant sentencing and automatic transfer to adult criminal court is inconsistent with the knowledge that individual youth differ in terms of character, offense motivation, and longer-term risk to society (Grisso, 1996; Scott & Grisso, 1997). This is especially troubling in light of the distinction between life-course persistent and adolescent-limited offenders. Increased use of determinant sentencing and automatic transfer to adult criminal court leaves little option for the differential treatment of two juveniles arrested for the same crime – one of whom is an adolescent-limited offender, with no history of violence, whose crime is the result of a lapse in judgment, and the other of whom is a life-course persistent offender, with a history of aggressive behavior, whose crime is the result of an intent to injure or kill another individual. The accuracy with which mental health professionals can make predictions of dangerousness is likely to have an impact on the flexibility of the juvenile justice system in processing cases similar to those just described. If the accuracy of predictions is poor, differential treatment of offenders is more likely to be arbitrary and unfair and to jeopardize public safety.

CONCLUSIONS

Great strides have been made in the enumeration of risk factors for youth violence and the development of programs to prevent and treat violence. Clearly, however, much more needs to be done. Violence is determined by a complex combination of individual, contextual, and societal factors, so it is not likely to be reversed by simplistic, single-faceted fixes. Policy makers, mental health professionals, and researchers must look beyond the individual and develop policies and programs that "address key areas of risk in the youth's life, that seek to strengthen the personal and institutional factors that contribute to healthy adolescent development, that provide adequate support and supervision, and that offer youth a long-term stake in the community" (Office of Juvenile Justice and Delinquency Prevention, 1995, p. 141).

References

American Psychological Association Commission on Violence. (1993). *Violence and youth: Psychology's response* (Vol. 1). Washington, DC: American Psychological Association.

Arbuthnot, J., Gordon, D. A., & Jurkovic, G. J. (1987). Personality. In H. C. Quay (Ed.), *Handbook of juvenile delinquency* (pp. 139–183). New York: Wiley.

Author, M. W., Ayers, C. D., Graham, K. A., & Hawkins, J. D. (1997). *Mobilizing communities to reduce risks for substance abuse: A comparison of two strategies*. Manuscript submitted for publication.

Archer, J. (1994). Testosterone and aggression: A theoretical review. *Journal of Offender Rehabilitation, 21*, 3–39.

Baker, R. L. A., & Mednick, B. R. (1984). *Influences on human development: A longitudinal perspective*. Boston: Kluwer-Nijhoff.

Bandura, A., Ross, D., & Ross, S. H. (1963). Imitation of film-mediated aggressive models. *Journal of Abnormal and Social Psychology, 66*, 3–11.

Barefoot v. Estelle, 463 U.S. 880 (1983).

Bates, J. E., Bayles, K., Bennett, D. S., Ridge, B., & Brown, M. M. (1991). Origins of externalizing behavior problems at eight years of age. In D. J. Pepler & K. H. Rubin (Eds.), *The development and treatment of childhood aggression* (pp. 93–120). Hillsdale, NJ: Erlbaum.

Bates, J. E., Maslin, C. A., & Frankel, K. A. (1985). Attachment security, mother–child interaction, and temperament as predictors of behavior problem ratings at age three years. *Monographs of the Society for Research in Child Development, 50*, 167–193.

Berkowitz, L., & Rawlings, E. (1963). Effects of film violence on inhibitions against subsequent aggression. *Journal of Abnormal and Social Psychology, 66*, 405–412.

Blumstein, A. (1995, August). Violence by young people: Why the deadly nexus? *National Institute of Justice Journal, 229*, 2–9.

Booth, C. L., Rose-Krasnor, L., McKinnon, J., & Rubin, K. H. (1994). Predicting social adjustment in middle childhood: The role of preschool attachment security and maternal style. From family to peer group: Relations between relationship systems [special issue]. *Social Development, 3*, 189–204.

Borduin, C. M., Mann, B. J., Cone, L. T., Henggeler, S. W., Fucci, B. R., Blaske, D. M., & Williams, R. A. (1995). Multisystemic treatment of serious juvenile offenders: Long-term prevention of criminality and violence. *Journal of Consulting and Clinical Psychology, 63*, 569–578.

Borum, R. (1996). Improving the clinical practice of violence risk assessment: Technology, guidelines, and training. *American Psychologist, 51*, 945–956.

Bronfenbrenner, U. (1979). *The ecology of human development*. Cambridge, MA: Harvard University Press.

Cairns, R. B., Cairns, B. D., Neckerman, H. J., Gest, S. D., & Gariepy, J. L. (1988). Social networks and aggressive behavior: Peer support or peer rejection? *Developmental Psychology, 24*, 815–823.

Callahan, C. M., & Rivara, F. P. (1992). Urban high school youth and hand-guns: A school-based survey. *Journal of the American Medical Association, 267*, 3038–3042.

Capaldi, D. M., & Patterson, G. R. (1996). Can violent offenders be distin-guished from frequent offenders?: Prediction from childhood to adoles-cence. *Journal of Research in Crime and Delinquency, 33*, 206–231.

Catalano, R. F., Arthur, M. W., Hawkins, J. D., Berglund, L., & Olson, J. J. (1998). Comprehensive community- and school-based interventions to pre-vent antisocial behavior. In R. Loeber & D. P. Farrington (Eds.), *Serious and violent juvenile offenders: Risk factors and successful interventions* (pp. 248–283). Thousand Oaks, CA: Sage.

Centerwall, B. S. (1984). Race, socioeconomic status, and domestic homicide, Atlanta, 1971–2. *American Journal of Public Health, 74*, 813–815.

Chamberlain, P. (1990). Comparative evaluation of specialized foster care for seriously delinquent youths: A first step. *Community Alternatives: Interna-tional Journal of Family Care, 2*, 21–36.

Cleare, A. J., & Bond, A. J. (1995). The effect of tryptophan depletion and enhancement on subjective and behavioral aggression in normal male sub-jects. *Psychopharmacolgy, 118*, 72–81.

Coie, J. D., & Dodge, K. A. (1998). Aggression and antisocial behavior. In W. Damon & N. Eisenberg (Eds.), *Handbook of child psychology: Vol. 3. Social, emotional and personality development* (pp. 779–862). New York: Wiley.

Coie, J. D., Dodge, K. A., & Kupersmidt, J. (1990). Peer group behavior and social status. In S. R. Asher & J. D. Coie (Eds.), *Peer rejection in childhood* (pp. 17–59). New York: Cambridge University Press.

Conduct Problems Prevention Research Group (Bierman, K., Coie, J., Dodge, K., Greenberg, M., Lochman, J., & McMahon, R.). (1992). A developmental and clinical model for the prevention of conduct disorder: The FAST Track Program. *Development & Psychopathology, 4*, 509–527.

Conduct Problems Prevention Research Group. (1996, May). *An initial evalu-ation of the FAST Track program.* Paper presented at the National Conference on Prevention, Washington, DC.

Cornell, D. G., & Wilson, L. A. (1992). The PIQ > VIQ discrepancy in violent and nonviolent delinquents. *Journal of Clinical Psychology, 48*, 256–261.

Crick, N. R., & Dodge, K. A. (1994). A review and reformulation of social information processing mechanisms in children's social adjustment. *Psy-chological Bulletin, 115*, 74–101.

Deater-Deckard, K., & Dodge, K. A. (1997). Externalizing behavior problems and discipline revisited: Nonlinear effects and variation by culture, context, and gender. *Psychological Inquiry, 8*, 161–175.

Dishion, T. J., Patterson, G. R., Stoolmiller, M., & Skinner, M. L. (1991). Family, school, and behavioral antecedents to early adolescent involvement with antisocial peers. *Developmental Psychology, 27*, 172–180.

Dodge, K. A., Bates, J. E., & Pettit, G. S. (1990). Mechanisms in the cycle of violence. *Science, 250*, 1678–1683.

Dryfoos, J. G. (1990). *Adolescents at risk: Prevalence and prevention.* New York: Oxford University Press.

DuRant, R. H., Cadenhead, C., Pendergrast, R. A., Slavens, G., & Linder, C. W. (1994). Factors associated with the use of violence among urban black adolescents. *American Journal of Public Health, 84*, 612–617.

Elliott, D. S. (1994). Serious violent offenders: Onset, developmental course, and termination: The American Society of Criminology 1993 presidential address. *Criminology, 32*, 1–21.

Elliott, D. S., Huizinga, D., & Ageton, S. S. (1985). *Explaining delinquency and drug use.* New York: Guilford Press.

Erickson, M. F., Sroufe, L. A., & Egeland, B. (1985). The relationship between quality of attachment and behavior problems in preschool in a high-risk sample. *Monographs of the Society for Research in Child Development, 50*, 147–186.

Eron, L. D., Gentry, J. H., & Schlegel, P. (1994). *Reason to hope: A psychosocial perspective on violence and youth.* Washington, DC: American Psychological Association.

Eron, L. D., Huesmann, L. R., & Zelli, A. (1991). The role of parental variables in the learning of aggression. In D. J. Pepler & K. H. Rubin (Eds.), *The development and treatment of childhood aggression* (pp. 169–189). Hillsdale, NJ: Erlbaum.

Ewing, C. P. (1990). Juveniles or adults? Forensic assessment of juveniles considered for trial in criminal court. *Forensic Reports, 3*, 3–13.

Farrington, D. P. (1978). The family background of aggressive youths. In L. A. Hersov, M. Berger, & D. Schaffer (Eds.), *Aggression and antisocial behavior in childhood and adolescence* (pp. 73–93). Oxford: Pergamon.

Farrington, D. P. (1989). Early predictors of adolescent aggression and adult violence. *Violence and Victims, 4*, 79–100.

Farrington, D. P. (1991). Childhood aggression and adult violence: Early precursors and later-life outcomes. In D. J. Pepler & K. H. Rubin (Eds.), *The development and treatment of childhood aggression* (pp. 5–29). Hillsdale, NJ: Erlbaum.

Farrington, D. P. (1994). Childhood, adolescent, and adult features of violent males. In L. R. Huesmann (Ed.), *Aggressive behavior: Current perspectives* (pp. 215–240). New York: Plenum Press.

Farrington, D. P. (1997). The relationship between low resting heart rate and violence. In A. Raine, P. A., Brennan, D. P. Farrington, & S. A. Mednick (Eds.), *Biosocial bases of violence* (pp. 89–105). New York: Plenum Press.

Federal Bureau of Investigation (FBI). (1996). *Uniform crime reports.* Washington, DC: U.S. Department of Justice.

Federal Bureau of Investigation (FBI). (1997). *Uniform crime reports.* Washington, DC: U.S. Department of Justice.

Fried, C. S., Reppucci, N. D., & Woolard, J. L. (2000). Violence prevention. In E. Seidman & J. Rappaport (Eds.), *Handbook of community psychology.* New York: Kluwer Academic/Plenum Press.

Gabriel, R. M. (1996). *Self-enhancement, Inc. violence prevention program.* Portland, OR: RMC Research.

Gabriel, R. M., Hopson, T., Haskins, M., & Powell, K. E. (1996). Building relationships and resilience in the prevention of youth violence. *American Journal of Preventive Medicine, 12* (Suppl. 5), 48–55.

Gagnon, C., Craig, W. M., Tremblay, R. E., Zhou, R. M., & Vitaro, F. (1995). Kindergarten predictors of boys' stable behavior problems at the end of elementary school. *Journal of Abnormal Child Psychology, 23,* 751–766.

Goldstein, P. J. (1985). The drugs/violence nexus: A tripartite conceptual framework. *Journal of Drug Issues, 15,* 493–506.

Gorman-Smith, D., Tolan, P. H., Zelli, A., & Huesmann, L. R. (1996). The relation of family functioning to violence among inner-city minority youth. *Journal of Family Psychology, 10,* 115–129.

Gottesman, I. I., & Goldsmith, H. H. (1994). Developmental psychopathology of antisocial behavior: Inserting genes into its ontogenesis and epigenesis. In C. A. Nelson (Ed.), *Threats to optimal development: Integrating biological, psychological, and social risk factors* (pp. 69–104). Hillsdale, NJ: Erlbaum.

Gottfredson, M. R., & Hirschi, T. (1995). National crime control policies. *Society, 32,* 30–36.

Greenwood, P. (1995). Juvenile crime and juvenile justice. In J. Wilson & J. Petersilia (Eds.), *Crime* (pp. 15–38). San Francisco: ICS.

Grisso, T. (1996). Society's retributive response to juvenile violence: A developmental perspective. *Law and Human Behavior, 20,* 229–247.

Guerra, N. G., Attar, B., & Weissberg, R. P. (1997). Prevention of aggression and violence among inner-city youths. In D. M. Stoff & J. Breiling (Eds.), *Handbook of antisocial behavior* (pp. 375–383). New York: Wiley.

Guerra, N. G., Huesmann, L.R., Tolan, P. H., Van Acker, R., & Eron, L. D. (1995). Stressful events and individual beliefs as correlates of economic disadvantage and aggression among urban children. *Journal of Consulting and Clinical Psychology, 63,* 518–528.

Harris, G. T., Rice, M. E., & Quinsey, V. L. (1993). Violent recidivism of mentally disordered offenders: The development of a statistical prediction instrument. *Criminal Justice & Behavior, 20,* 315–335.

Hawkins, J. D., & Catalano, R. F. (1992). *Communities that care : Action for drug abuse prevention.* San Francisco: Jossey-Bass.

Hawkins, J. D., Herrenkohl, T., Farrington, D. P., Brewer, D., Catalano, R. F., & Garachi, T. W. (1998). A review of predictors of youth violence. In R. Loeber & D. P. Farrington (Eds.), *Serious and violent juvenile offenders: Risk factors and successful interventions* (pp. 106–146). Thousand Oaks, CA: Sage.

Hechtman, L. & Weiss, G. (1986). Controlled prospective fifteen year follow-up of hyperactives as adults: Non-medical drug and alcohol use and anti-social behaviour. *Canadian Journal of Psychiatry, 31,* 557–567.

Hellman, D. A., & Beaton, S. (1986). The pattern of violence in urban public schools: The influence of school and community. *Journal of Research in Crime and Delinquency, 23*, 102–127.

Henggeler, S. W., Cunningham, P. B., Pickrel, S. G., Schoenwald, S. K., & Brondino, M. J. (1996). Multisystemic therapy: An effective violence prevention approach for serious juvenile offenders. *Journal of Adolescence, 19*, 47–61.

Henggeler, S. W., Melton, G. B., & Smith, L. A. (1992). Family preservation using multisystemic therapy: An effective alternative to incarcerating serious juvenile offenders. *Journal of Consulting and Clinical Psychology, 60*, 953–961.

Hill, H. M., Soriano, F. I., Chen, S. A., & LaFromboise, T. D. (1994). Sociocultural factors in the etiology and prevention of violence among ethnic minority youth. In L. D. Eron, J. H. Gentry, & P. Schlegel (Eds.), *Reason to hope: A psychosocial perspective on violence and youth* (pp. 59–97). Washington, DC: American Psychological Association.

Huesmann, L. R., & Eron, L. D. (1984). Cognitive processes and the persistence of aggressive behavior. *Aggressive Behavior, 10*, 243–251.

Huesmann, L. R., Lagerspetz, K., & Eron, L. D. (1984). Intervening variables in the TV violence–aggression relation: Evidence from two countries. *Developmental Psychology, 20*, 746–775.

Huston, A. C., Donnerstein, E., Farichild, H., Feshbach, N. D., Katz, P. A., Murray, J. P., Rubinstein, E. A., Wilcox, B. L., & Zuckerman, D. (1992). *Big world, small screen: The role of television in American society*. Lincoln: University of Nebraska Press.

Jenkins, E. J., & Bell, C. C. (1994). Violence exposure, psychological distress, and high risk behaviors among inner-city high school students. In S. Friedman (Ed.), *Anxiety disorders in African-Americans* (pp. 76–88). New York: Springer.

Josephson, W. L. (1987). Television violence and children's aggression: Testing the priming, social script, and disinhibition predictions. *Journal of Personality and Social Psychology, 53*, 882–890.

Keenan, K., Loeber, R., Zhang, Q., Stouthamer-Loeber, M., & Van Kammen, W. B. (1995). The influence of deviant peers on the development of boys' disruptive and delinquent behavior: A temporal analysis. *Developmental Psychopathology, 7*, 715–726.

Kellermann, A. L., Fuqua-Whitley, D. S., Rivara, F. P., & Mercy, J. (1998). Preventing youth violence: What works? *Annual Review of Public Health, 19*, 271–292.

Kingston, L., & Prior M. (1995). The development of patterns of stable, transient, and school-age aggressive behavior in young children. *Journal of the American Academy of Child and Adolescent Psychiatry, 34*, 348–358.

Kruh, I. P., & Brodsky, S. L. (1997). Clinical evaluations for transfer of juveniles to criminal court: Current practices and future research. *Behavioral Sciences and the Law, 15*, 151–165.

Kupersmidt, J. B., Briesler, P. C., DeRosier, M. E., Patterson, C. J., & Davis, P. W. (1995). Childhood aggression and peer relations in the context of family and neighborhood factors. *Child Development, 66,* 360–375.

Lidz, C., Mulvey, E., & Gardner, W. (1993). The accuracy of predictions of violence to others. *Journal of the American Medical Association, 269,* 1007–1011.

Lipsey, M. W., & Derzon, J. H. (1998). Predictors of violent or serious delinquency in adolescence and early adulthood: A synthesis of longitudinal research. In R. Loeber & D. P. Farrington (Eds.), *Serious and violent juvenile offenders: Risk factors and successful interventions* (pp. 86–105). Thousand Oaks, CA: Sage.

Loeber, R. (1988). Behavioral precursors and accelerators of delinquency. In W. Buikhuisen & S. A. Mednick (Eds.), *Explaining delinquency* (pp. 51–67). Leiden, the Netherlands: Brill.

Loeber, R., & Farrington, D. P. (1998). *Serious and violent juvenile offenders: Risk factors and successful interventions.* Thousand Oaks, CA: Sage.

Loeber, R., & Hay, D. (1994). Developmental approaches to aggression and conduct problems. In M. Rutter & D. F. Hay (Eds.), *Development through life: A handbook for clinicians* (pp. 488–515). Oxford: Blackwell Scientific.

Loeber, R., & Hay, D. (1997). Key issues in the development of aggression and violence from childhood to early adulthood. *Annual Review of Psychology, 48,* 371–410.

Loeber, R., & Stouthamer-Loeber, M. (1986). Family factors as correlates and predictors of juvenile conduct problems and delinquency. In M. Tonry & N. Morris (Eds.), *Crime and justice: An annual review of research* (pp. 219–339). Chicago: University of Chicago Press.

Loeber, R., & Wikstrom, P. (1993). Individual pathways to crime in different types of neighborhoods. In D. P. Farrington, R. J. Sampson, & P. Wikstrom (Eds.), *Integrating individual and ecological aspects of crime* (pp. 169–204). Stockholm: Liber-Verlag.

Lynam, D. R., Moffitt, T. E., & Stouthamer-Loeber, M. (1993). Explaining the relation between IQ and delinquency: Class, race, test motivation, school failure, or self-control? *Journal of Abnormal Psychology, 102,* 187–196.

Maguin, E., Hawkins, J. D., Catalano, R. F., Hill, K., Abbott, R., & Herrenkohl, T. (1995, November). *Risk factors measured at three ages for violence at age 17–18.* Paper presented at the American Society of Criminology, Boston.

Manly, J. T., Cicchetti, D., & Barnett, D. (1994). The impact of subtype, frequency, chronicity, and severity of child maltreatment on social competence and behavior problems. *Developmental Psychology, 7,* 121–143.

McCord, J. (1979). Some child-rearing antecedents of criminal behavior in adult men. *Journal of Personality and Social Psychology, 37,* 1477–1486.

McCord, J., & Ensminger, M. (1995, November). *Pathways from aggressive childhood to criminality.* Paper presented at the meeting of the American Society of Criminology, Boston.

McGuire, J. (1997). Psychosocial approaches to the understanding and reduction of violence in young people. In V. Varma (Ed.), *Violence in children and adolescents* (pp. 65–83). Bristol, PA: Jessica Kingsley.

McLoyd, V. (1990). The impact of economic hardship on black families and children: Psychological distress, parenting, and socioemotional development. *Child Development, 61*, 311–346.

Megargee, E. I. (1982). Psychological determinants and correlates of criminal violence. In M. E. Wolfgang & N. A. Weiner (Eds.), *Criminal violence*. Beverly Hills, CA: Sage.

Menzies, R., Webster, C., McMain, S., Staley, S., & Scaglione, R. (1994). The dimensions of dangerousness revisited: Assessing predictions about violence. *Law and Human Behavior, 18*, 1–28.

Miczek, K. A., Mirsky, A. F., Carey, R., DeBold, J., & Raine A. (1994). An overview of biological influences on violent behavior. In A. J. Reiss, K. A. Miczek, & J. A. Roth (Eds.), *Understanding and preventing violence: Vol. 3. Social influences* (pp. 377–570). Washington, DC: National Academy Press.

Milavsky, J. R., Kessler, R., Stipp, H., & Rubens, W. S. (1982). Television and aggression: Results of a panel study. In D. Pearl, L. Bouthilet, & J. Lazar (Eds.), *Television and behavior: Ten years of scientific progress and implications for the 80's:* (Vol. 2). Washington, DC: U.S. Government Printing Office.

Moffitt, T. E. (1993). Adolescence-limited and life-course persistent antisocial behavior: A developmental taxonomy. *Psychological Review, 100*, 674–701.

Moffitt, T. E., & Lynam, D. R. (1994). Neuropsychological tests predict persistent male delinquency. *Criminology, 32*, 101–124.

Monahan, J. (1981). *The clinical prediction of violent behavior*. Washington, DC: U.S. Government Printing House.

Monahan, J. (1992). Mental disorder and violent behavior: Perceptions and evidence. *American Psychologist, 47*, 511–521.

Monahan, J. (1996). Violence prediction: The past twenty and the next twenty years. *Criminal Justice and Behavior, 23*, 107–120.

Monahan, J., & Steadman, H. (1996). Violent storms and violent people: How meteorology can inform risk communication in mental health law. *American Psychologist, 51*, 931–938.

Mulvey, E. P. (1984). Judging amenability to treatment in juvenile offenders: Theory and practice. In N. D. Reppucci, L. A. Weithorn, E. P. Mulvey, & J. Monahan (Eds.), *Children, mental health, and the law* (pp. 195–210). Beverly Hills, CA: Sage.

Mulvey, E. P., Arthur, M. W., & Reppucci, N. D. (1993). The prevention and treatment of juvenile delinquency: A review of the research. *Clinical Psychology Review, 13*, 133–167.

Mulvey, E. P., & Reppucci, N. D. (1988). The context of clinical judgment: The effect of resource availability on judgments of amenability to treatment in juvenile offenders. *American Journal of Community Psychology, 16*, 525–545.

National Center for Health Statistics. (1993). *Health, United States, 1992.* Hyattsville, MD: U.S. Public Health Service.

National Research Council. (1993). *Losing generations: Adolescents in high-risk settings.* Washington, DC: National Academy Press.

O'Donnell, C. R. (1995). Firearm deaths among children and youth. *American Psychologist, 50,* 771–776.

Office of Juvenile Justice and Delinquency Prevention (OJJDP). (1995). *Guide for implementing the comprehensive strategy for serious, violent, and chronic juvenile offenders.* Washington, DC: U.S. Department of Justice, Office of Juvenile Justice and Delinquency Prevention.

Olds, D. L., Henderson, C. C. R., Chamberlin, R., & Tatelbaum, R. (1986). Preventing child abuse and neglect: A randomized trial of nurse home visitation. *Pediatrics, 78,* 65–78.

Olds, D., Hill, P., Mihalic, S., & O'Brien, R. (1998). *Blueprints for violence prevention, book seven: Prenatal and infancy home visitation by nurses.* Boulder, CO: Center for the Study of Prevention of Violence.

Olweus, D. (1979). Stability of aggressive reaction patterns in males: A review. *Psychological Bulletin, 86,* 852–875.

Olweus, D., Mattsson, A., Schalling, D., & Low, H. (1988). Circulating testosterone levels and aggression in adolescent males: A causal analysis. *Psychosomatic Medicine, 50,* 261–272.

Osgood, D. W. (1995). *Drugs, alcohol, and adolescent violence.* Boulder, CO: Center for the Study and Prevention of Violence.

Patterson, G. R., & Bank, C. L. (1989). Some amplifying mechanisms for pathological processes in families. In M. Gunnar & E. Thelen (Eds.), *Systems and development: Symposia on child psychology* (pp. 167–210). Hillsdale, NJ: Erlbaum.

Patterson, G. R., Capaldi, D., & Bank, L. (1991). An early starter model for predicting delinquency. In D. J. Pepler & K. H. Rubin (Eds.), *The development and treatment of childhood aggression* (pp. 139–168). Hillsdale, NJ: Erlbaum.

Podell, S., & Archer, D. (1994). Do legal changes matter? The case of gun control laws. In M. Costanzo & S. Oskamp (Eds.), *Violence and the law* (pp. 37–60). Thousand Oaks, CA: Sage.

Raine, A. (1998). Antisocial behavior and psychophysiology: A biosocial perspective and a prefrontal dysfunction hypothesis. In D. M. Stoff, J. Breiling, & J. D. Maser (Eds.), *Handbook of antisocial behavior* (pp. 289–304). New York: Wiley.

Raine, A., Venables, P. H., & Williams, M. (1990). Relationships between central and autonomic measures of arousal at age 15 years and criminality at age 24 years. *Archives of General Psychiatry, 47,* 1003–1007.

Reiss, A. J., & Roth, J. A. (1993). *Understanding and preventing violence: Panel on the understanding and control of violent behavior* (Vol. 1). Washington, DC: National Academy Press.

Reppucci, N. D. (1999). Adolescent development and juvenile justice. *American Journal of Community Psychology, 27,* 307–326.

Reppucci, N. D., Woolard, J. L., & Fried, C. S. (1999). Social, community and preventive interventions. *Annual Review of Psychology, 50,* 387–418.

Saner, H., & Ellickson, P. (1996). Concurrent risk factors for adolescent violence. *Journal of Adolescent Health, 19,* 94–103.

Scott, E. S., & Grisso, T. (1997). The evolution of adolescence: A developmental perspective on juvenile justice reform. *Journal of Criminal Law and Criminology, 88,* 137–189.

Seguin, J. R., Pihl, R. O., Harden, P. W., Tremblay, R. E., & Boulerice, B. (1995). Cognitive and neuropsychological characteristics of physically aggressive boys. *Journal of Abnormal Psychology, 104,* 614–624.

Sheley, J. F., & Wright, J. D. (1993). Motivations for gun possession and carrying among serious juvenile offenders. *Behavioral Science Law, 11,* 375–388.

Sickmund, M., Snyder, H. N., & Poe-Yamagata, E. (1997). *Juvenile offenders and victims: 1997 update on violence.* Washington, DC: Office of Juvenile and Delinquency Prevention.

Sloan, J., Kellermann, A., Reay, D., Ferris, J., Koepsell, T., Rivara, F., Rice, C., Gray, L., & LoGerfo, J. (1988). Handgun regulations, crime, assaults, and homicide: A tale of two cities. *New England Journal of Medicine, 319,* 1256–1262.

Snyder, H. N. (1998). Appendix: Serious, violent, and chronic juvenile offenders – An assessment of the extent of and trends in officially recognized serious criminal behavior in a delinquent population. In R. Loeber & D. P. Farrington (Eds.), *Serious and violent juvenile offenders: Risk factors and successful interventions* (pp. 428–444). Thousand Oaks, CA: Sage.

Snyder, H. N., & Sickmund, M. (1995). *Juvenile offenders and victims: 1995 update on violence.* Pittsburgh: U.S. Department of Justice, Office of Juvenile Justice and Delinquency Prevention, National Center for Juvenile Justice.

Snyder, J. N., & Patterson, G. R. (1987). Family interaction and delinquent behavior. In H. C. Quay (Ed.), *Handbook of juvenile delinquency* (pp. 216–243). New York: Wiley.

Tate, D. C., Reppucci, N. D., & Mulvey, E. P. (1995). Violent juvenile delinquents: Treatment effectiveness and implications for future action. *American Psychologist, 50,* 777–781.

Tolan, P. H., & Gorman-Smith, D. (1998). Development of serious and violent offending careers. In R. Loeber & D. P. Farrington (Eds.), *Serious and violent juvenile offenders: Risk factors and successful interventions* (pp. 68–85). Thousand Oaks, CA: Sage.

Tolan, P. H., Gorman-Smith, D., Huesmann, L. R., & Zelli, A. (1997). Assessment of family relationship characteristics: A measure to explain risk for antisocial behavior and depression in youth. *Psychological Assessment, 9,* 212–223.

Tolan, P. H., & Loeber, R. (1993). Antisocial behavior. In P. H. Tolan & B. J. Cohler (Eds.), *Handbook of clinical research and practice* (pp. 307–331). New York: Wiley.

Tolan, P. H., & Thomas, P. (1995). The implications of age of onset for delinquency risk: II. Longitudinal data. *Journal of Abnormal Child Psychology, 23*, 157–181.

Tremblay, R. E., Masse, L. C., Kurtz, L., & Vitaro, F. (1997). From childhood physical aggression to adolescent maladjustment: The Montreal Prevention Experiment. In R. D. Peters & R. J. McMahon (Eds.), *Childhood disorders, substance abuse, and delinquency: Prevention and early intervention approaches* (pp. 1–62). Thousand Oaks, CA: Sage.

Tremblay, R. E., Schaal, B., Boulerice, B., Arseneault, L., Soussignan, R., Perusse, D. (1997). Male physical aggression, social dominance and testosterone levels at puberty: A developmental perspective. In A. Raine, P. A. Brennan, D. P. Farrington, & S. A. Mednick (Eds.), *Biosocial bases of violence* (pp. 271–291). New York: Plenum Press.

Vuchinich, S., Bank, L., & Patterson, G. R. (1992). Parenting, peers, and the stability of antisocial behavior in preadolescent boys. *Developmental Psychology, 28*, 510–521.

Wasserman, G. A., & Miller, L. S. (1998). The prevention of serious and violent juvenile offending. In R. Loeber & D. P. Farrington (Eds.), *Serious and violent juvenile offenders: Risk factors and successful interventions* (pp. 197–247). Thousand Oaks, CA: Sage.

Weiss, B., Dodge, K. A., Bates, J. E., & Pettit, G. S. (1992). Some consequences of early harsh discipline: Child aggression and a maladaptive social information processing style. *Child Development, 63*, 1321–1335.

White, H. R., Brick, J., & Hansell, S. (1993). A longitudinal investigation of alcohol use and aggression in adolescence. *Journal of Studies on Alcohol* (Suppl 11), 62–77.

Widom, C. S. (1989). Does violence beget violence? A critical review of the literature. *Psychological Bulletin, 106*, 4–28.

Wilkinson, D., & Fagan, J. (1996). The role of firearms in violence "scripts": The dynamics of gun events among adolescent males. *Law and Contemporary Problems, 59*, 55–89.

Wilson, W. J. (1987). *The truly disadvantaged.* Chicago: University of Chicago Press.

Wood, W., Wong, F., & Chachere, J. (1991). Effects of media violence on viewer's aggression in unconstrained social interaction. *Psychological Bulletin, 109*, 371–383.

Zimring, F. E. (1998). *American youth violence.* New York: Oxford University Press.

11

Capacity, Competence, and the Juvenile Defendant

Implications for Research and Policy

Jennifer L. Woolard

Some form of delinquent activity is a common aspect of develop-ment for a majority of youth. For many, it appears to represent a time-delimited activity of adolescence that doesn't necessarily come to the attention of a formal system of social control (Moffit, 1993). However, a significant proportion of adolescents comes into con-tact with the justice system as a result of this behavior. In 1994, juvenile courts saw 1.75 million delinquency cases, with approxi-mately 980,000 cases processed formally through a petition for an adjudicatory or waiver hearing (Stahl et al., 1999). For those ado-lescents who do come into contact with it, the justice system can represent a significant intervention in their lives (see Salekin and Fried and Reppucci, this volume, for a discussion of factors that contribute to juvenile violence).

The notion that adolescents are immature, have less decision-making capacity, and therefore should be treated differently than adults has permeated the juvenile justice system since its inception in 1899. Historical differences between the juvenile and adult crimi-nal justice systems have been based on a fundamental notion about adolescent development and the appropriate societal response. In the criminal system, adults are presumed to be autonomous, competent persons who are able to make their own decisions about

Correspondence concerning this chapter should be addressed to Jennifer L. Woolard, Center for Studies in Criminology and Law, University of Florida, PO Box 115950, Gainesville, FL, 32611; e-mail: jwoolard@crim.ufl.edu.

behavior and are held accountable for their choices. Because of their ongoing cognitive and social development, however, juveniles are considered less able to make competent decisions, and therefore are held less culpable and less accountable for their actions. Because it traditionally worked for the benefit of the child through rehabilitation rather than punishment, the juvenile court has the broad discretion to gather all sorts of relevant information about the child's life in order to determine what treatment would work best, activities relatively unconstrained by procedural protections found in the criminal system.

Although the system was intended to act as a benevolent but firm parent, in practice it did not operate that way. In the late 1960s and early 1970s, a significant set of procedural reforms followed several U.S. Supreme Court decisions describing the juvenile justice system as "the worst of both worlds" – failing to provide the promised rehabilitation while simultaneously failing to provide many of the due process protections found in the adversarial adult system (e.g., *Breed v. Jones*, 1975; *In re Gault*, 1967; *In re Winship*, 1970; *Kent v. U.S.*, 1966). This era of reform, particularly the *Gault* decision, was focused on protecting the rights of juveniles as defendants and reducing the discretion and arbitrariness of system processing, extending many (e.g., notice of charges, counsel) but not all (e.g., right to jury trial; *McKeiver v. Pennsylvania*, 1971) of the rights enjoyed by criminal defendants. (See Schmidt & Reppucci, this volume, for a more detailed discussion of the *Gault* decision.)

Many argue that the juvenile justice system is now undergoing another wave of reform based instead on the desire to control what the public perceives, somewhat accurately, as a wave of serious juvenile violence. Although the proportion of murder cases cleared by juvenile arrests have declined since 1994, the 1998 figure of 6.3% is still above the rates in the 1980s (Snyder, 1999). Similarly, juvenile violent crime has declined since 1994 but still represents 12% of the Federal Bureau of Investigation's (FBI) Violent Crime Index offense arrests in 1998 (Snyder, 1999).[1] Even more troubling is the

---

[1] Index offenses refer to the eight offenses used by the FBI's Uniform Crime Reporting Program as a gauge of fluctuation in the amount and rate of crime. These offenses include murder and nonnegligent manslaughter, forcible rape, robbery, aggravated assault, burglary, larceny-theft, motor vehicle theft, and arson.

increasingly younger ages at which juveniles commit serious violent offenses. Thirty-one percent of the juvenile Violent Crime Index arrests in 1998 were committed by juveniles under age 15 (Snyder, 1999).

If *Gault* (1967) heralded the "due process" era of reform of the 1960s and 1970s, in the post-*Gault* era the juvenile court has been moving away from its original rehabilitative model toward a punishment framework in which protection of the community equals or surpasses the traditional goal of acting in the "best interests" of the child (Worrell, 1985). A variety of legislative initiatives in the 1980s and 1990s have created two large categories of change – changes in jurisdiction and changes in sentencing practices. In the past decade, 41 states have altered their jurisdictional authority by removing increasing numbers of "serious and violent" juvenile offenders as young as 10 from the juvenile system to the criminal system through transfer or judicial waiver procedures (Griffin, Torbet, & Szymanski, 1998; Salekin, this volume; Sickmund, Snyder, & Poe-Yamagata, 1997). Although declining since 1994, the number of waived cases in 1997 was 25% higher than in 1988 (Puzzanchera et al., 2000). Twenty-five states have passed laws giving both criminal and juvenile courts new sentencing options, including mandatory minimum terms and determinate sentences (Sickmund et al., 1997).[2]

These legislative changes are based in part on concerns for public safety, but they also represent changing views on how adultlike certain juvenile offenders are. Practically speaking, a segment of the adolescent population has been redefined as adults. Contrary to the rehabilitative approach to the immature or developing adolescent, new policies suggest that, for certain individuals and offenses, the juveniles are by definition *not* immature; or if they are, it is now irrelevant. Changes in the process of crime and punishment suggest that the nature and quality of adolescent participation in the justice system will become a fundamental concern for advocates, policy makers, and scholars alike. In this chapter I examine the developmental implications of adolescents' participation as defendants in the increasingly punitive juvenile and criminal justice systems.

---

[2] Determinate sentences are sentences for a fixed period of time. They contrast with indeterminate sentences, in which a judge has the discretion to impose a sentence that falls between a statutorily specified minimum and maximum length of time.

First, I outline the tasks or expectations of juvenile defendants in terms of the nature of their participation. Then I evaluate the match between adolescents' capacities and the demands of the justice system environment. I highlight several issues that juvenile defendants confront when interacting with two key groups of adults: attorneys and parents. I conclude with suggestions for research and policy in this area.

EXPECTATIONS OF JUVENILE DEFENDANTS

From first contact with law enforcement to decisions about plea agreements, defendants (or suspects) are engaged in a process of protecting their interests. A number of abilities or capacities are needed to operate effectively as a defendant. Recent cases sensationalized in the national media, such as the Chicago-area sexual assault and murder of 11-year-old Ryan Harris and the fatal beating of 5-year-old David Jones, have focused attention on the capacities of younger defendants. In the Harris case, two boys, aged 7 and 8, were interrogated by police without the presence of parents or attorneys and ultimately confessed to the murder (Hanna, 1998; Possley, 1998). Questions about their competence to waive their rights and their competence to stand trial were raised briefly before the charges were dropped because an adult suspect was identified. In the Jones case, controversy arose about the validity of the 9-year-old defendant's waiver of the right to silence and his confession obtained after 6 hours at the police station (Deardorff, 1999; Wilson, 1999).

The U.S. Supreme Court has established some minimal level of capacities that are required of defendants to protect their due process rights. In this section, I review the capacities necessary for the valid waiver of the right against self-incrimination and for competence to stand trial, and a broader concern about effectiveness of participation for juvenile defendants.

Knowing, Voluntary, and Intelligent: The Miranda Waiver

Miranda v. Arizona (1966) established the requirement that adult criminal suspects receive certain warnings prior to custodial interrogation regarding their right to silence, the possible use of their statements in court, and the right to counsel. Defendants' statements, including confessions, can be used in court if the rights enunciated in *Miranda* warnings are waived in a voluntary, knowing, and intelligent manner. Limited to the adjudication phase of juvenile delinquency hearings, the *Gault* decision did not address the extension of *Miranda*'s due process protections to juveniles. But several state and federal court decisions have documented concerns about the voluntariness of confessions by juvenile defendants (e.g., *Gallegos v. Colorado*, 1962; *People v. Lara*, 1967). However, the Supreme Court in *Fare v. Michael C.* (1979) held that the adult "totality of the circumstances" test was appropriate for evaluating the confession of a 16-year-old defendant and that special protections were unnecessary. Even so, the question of some juveniles' capacity to waive their rights remains an ongoing concern (Grisso, 1981; see Schmidt & Reppucci, this volume, for further discussion of children's rights and capacities in this domain). As a matter of policy, some states require law enforcement to notify parents when interrogating a minor.

Understanding, Reasoning, and Appreciation: Adjudicative Competence

Once individuals enter the criminal system, due process and fairness are protected in part by requiring defendants to be competent to stand trial, which generally refers to understanding the process, circumstances, and roles of various legal professionals and assisting counsel in one's defense (*Drope v. Missouri*, 1975; *Dusky v. United States*, 1960). Bonnie (1993) has described two categories of relevant abilities under the organizational framework of adjudicative competence. Abilities needed for *competence to assist counsel* include the capacities to understand the proceedings, appreciate the significance of one's own situation, and communicate relevant information to counsel. Understanding the proceedings includes knowledge of the various actors and procedures involved – for example, the jobs of the defense and prosecuting attorneys, nature of the charges, and the criminal process. Competent defendants must also be able to appreciate the nature of their own particular situations as defendants. Finally, they should be capable of determining relevant information and communicating such information to counsel as part of preparing a defense strategy. *Decisional competence* is composed of the abilities to engage in a reasoning process, thereby weighing the available information in a rational process, and then to make decisions about the defense with input from counsel. These abilities have been summarized as understanding, reasoning, and appreciation, along with a general decisional capacity. Defendants face a number of decisions that vary in their complexity and implications. Many of the decisions about trial strategy and procedure (e.g., filing motions, obtaining discovery) typically do not involve active participation by the defendant, but the decisions to waive the right against self-incrimination, a jury trial, and the rights associated with entering a guilty plea, for example, implicate competence-related abilities (Bonnie, 1993).

Competence to stand trial is a relatively low threshold, and proportionally few adult defendants are so impaired as to warrant a finding of incompetence and treatment for restoration of competence (about 25,000 annually; Steadman & Harstone, 1983). For adults, mental illness and mental retardation, to the degree that they impair relevant abilities, are the primary reasons for incompetence. A host of assessment instruments and forensic practices have been developed for clinical evaluations of competence (e.g., Golding, Roesch, & Schreiber, 1984; Lipsitt, Lelos, & McGarry, 1971; Otto et al., 1998; Wildman, 1978; see Grisso, 1998, for a review of assessment issues specific to juveniles).

Historically, competence in juvenile court was not an issue. In the pre-*Gault* era, the benevolent, rehabilitative ideal focused on treatment for young offenders, not punishment, so the due process protections of competence requirements were not raised. In the post-*Gault* era, however, a significant proportion of states recognized the right to competence in juvenile court proceedings (Grisso, Miller, & Sales, 1987). Consistent with adult proceedings, the issue of competence is most commonly raised because of a defendant's mental illness. Questions about the immaturity of juvenile defendants' capacities have been raised in this context, though. One court case specifically referred to developmental immaturity (*In re Causey*, 1978). Although rare, developmental issues have also been raised in state delinquency statutes. Florida allows questions of competence to be raised at any time during delinquency proceedings, resulting in a mental health evaluation by a minimum of two court-appointed experts and a full-fledged competency hearing (Fla. Stat. §985.223). Like adults, juveniles deemed incompetent due to mental illness or retardation must be committed to the state for treatment.[3] However, a finding of incompetence due to age or immaturity is precluded from state commitment for restoration treatment.

Competence has more often arisen for juveniles processed in criminal court (Grisso, 1997, 1998). Although its use is decreasing, judicial waiver proceedings create an interesting scenario because the juveniles are not yet viewed by the court as adult defendants; as such, the juvenile court's procedures for competence issues probably still apply. One example of an exception occurs in Virginia, where the statute explicitly requires (and presumes) juvenile defendants to be competent for transfer proceedings, but competence is not explicitly addressed for traditional juvenile court proceedings (Va. Code Ann. §16.1–269.1 A(3)). Once in the criminal system, the juveniles are considered legal adults, and it appears that courts have simply used the existing adult standard (*Dusky v. United States*, 1960) that defendants must have a rational and factual understanding of the proceedings as well as the ability to consult with counsel. The same contributors to incompetence, mental illness and mental retardation, would likely also be considered.

Participating Effectively as a Defendant

A narrow focus on competence-related abilities raises broader questions about the nature of juveniles' participation as defendants generally. Effective participation goes beyond constitutional requirements to include those capacities that may affect the nature and quality of a defendant's participation but do not cross the threshold of incompetence to stand trial (Grisso, 2000). Although the substantial majority of defendants meet the requirements of legal competence, they can vary widely in their ability to work actively with counsel, participate meaningfully in the trial process,

---

[3] This commitment for restoration treatment applies only to juveniles facing charges that would be felonies if committed by adults; if the charges would be misdemeanors, the juveniles may not be committed (Fla. Stat. §985.223(2)).

and exhibit appropriate self-presentation skills, among other considerations (Buss, 2000; Grisso, 2000; Tobey, Grisso, & Schwartz, 2000).

Assumptions about adolescents in law and procedure beg the question of whether juvenile defendants possess the same capacities as adult defendants. An increasing body of research has examined the capacity of juvenile defendants to demonstrate the requisite abilities for the waiver of rights and competence to stand trial by operationalizing the adult capacities and testing them in juvenile samples. In the next section, I review the empirical research that has focused on *Miranda* waivers and competence to stand trial in juveniles. Then I outline a recent theoretical and methodological critique of this approach and discuss new theories of adolescent development in legal contexts.

EVALUATING JUVENILE CAPACITIES USING ADULT STANDARDS

Miranda Waivers

To date, research has focused both on the defendant's decision to waive *Miranda* rights and on several factors postulated to influence that decision, including age, IQ, court experience, and other case-related variables. Studies using data from police interrogations (Grisso, 1981; Pearse, Gudjonsson, Clare, & Rutter, 1998) and vignette studies of delinquent and/or nondelinquent youth (Abramovitch, Higgins-Biss, & Biss, 1993; Abramovitch, Peterson-Badali, & Rohan, 1995; Ferguson & Douglas, 1970; Woolard & Reppucci, 1998) indicate that the likelihood of waiving the right to silence decreases with age. However, age variation in *Miranda* waiver does not in itself demonstrate that juveniles are less competent, even though it fuels hypotheses about age-based differences in the abilities associated with a "knowing, voluntary, and intelligent" waiver.

Grisso (1981) evaluated juveniles' legal and psychological competence to waive their right to silence during a police interrogation (see also Schmidt & Reppucci, this volume, for additional discussion of *Miranda* waivers). The series of analyses compared adolescents and adults involved in the legal system on their understanding of

and reasoning about the decision to waive their *Miranda* rights,
among other topics. Seventy-five percent of juveniles aged 12 and
younger and 50% of juveniles aged 13–15 exhibited some comprehension deficits. Less effective reasoning was found in significant
proportions of juveniles aged 14 and under. Based on multiple assessment methods, the author concluded that younger adolescents
(aged 14 and below) were not competent to waive their rights to
silence and counsel. Adolescents aged 15 and older with average
intelligence were able to understand their *Miranda* rights as well as
adults, but Grisso cautioned that understanding may not necessarily translate into assertion of those rights, a concern lent some cre-
dence by the age differences in *Miranda* waiver rates just described.
He also pointed out that the similarities between adolescents and
adults held only for those of average intelligence; adolescents with
below-average IQs did not perform as well as their adult counterparts.

   Other studies using vignette paradigms with community samples have found similar results regarding the effects of age and IQ
on *Miranda* waiver-related capacities. In this type of study, participants respond to questions about a hypothetical story or vignette
in which some factor(s) of interest (e.g., whether the defendant was
actually guilty) are varied. In a study of 12-, 14-, 16-, and 18-year-
olds, Abramovitch and colleagues (Abramovitch et al., 1995) determined that only one-third of 12-year-olds demonstrated adequate
understanding of the right to silence in contrast to 89% of older adolescents. Some juveniles in each age group considered legally relevant variables when making the decision to waive the right against
self-incrimination (e.g., fewer juveniles waived this right when the
evidence was strong). But older adolescents were more savvy regarding the importance of guilt or innocence; compared to younger
adolescents, a greater percentage of the two older groups said they
would remain silent when the vignette character was guilty than
when the character was innocent. Another study established the
link between understanding and the decision to waive rights: 90%
of juveniles who adequately understood the right to silence refused to waive that right in the vignette, whereas only 35% of those
participants with inadequate understanding refused (Abramovitch
et al., 1993).

Competence to Stand Trial

Although the research on adult competence provides a solid foundation for empirical and clinical assessment, the research on juveniles is more tenuous. It has often assessed competence using original or slightly modified versions of adult competence instruments that focus almost exclusively on a defendant's understanding (one prong of competence) based on that defendant's existing knowledge of the legal system. Two commonly used instruments, the Competency Screening Test (CST) and the Georgia Court Competency Test (GCCT), are brief screening instruments with cutoff scores that trigger referral for further clinical assessment (Poythress et al., 1999). Based on test results using these instruments, young adolescents (12 to 13 years old or younger) consistently demonstrate less understanding than older adolescents (15 to 16 years old or older). Cowden and McKee (1995) used the CST in addition to clinical evaluations to assess competence in juvenile detainees referred for competence concerns. Only 17% of juveniles aged 12 or younger were deemed competent compared to over 70% of 15- and 16-year-olds. Cooper (1997) modified the GCCT for use with 100 juveniles aged 13 to 16 experiencing their first institutionalization for delinquency. She found a significant effect of age, with the 13-year-olds scoring significantly more poorly than the other adolescents. In addition, only two adolescents in the *entire* sample scored above a competence cut score determined by forensic experts, an unexpected finding considering that each juvenile had already been adjudicated delinquent. Cooper notes that the modifications for administration with juveniles meant that it was no longer psychometrically equivalent to the original adult version, and new cut scores had to be determined for the study. These changes limit the generalizability to adolescent performance on adult assessment instruments.

Thus, these few studies suggest that age is an important factor in competence assessments of understanding in juveniles. Although the age ranges varied, the previous studies identify important differences between younger adolescents (about age 12 to 13 or less) and older adolescents. These conclusions are constrained by limited sample sizes and the possibility that some of the age-based differences may result from normative increases in cognitive capacity and functioning across development. However, they do underscore the need for further research on the use of adult assessment instruments with juveniles.

Similar age differences in the understanding prong of competence have been found in other studies that used nonstandard assessments of competence-related abilities among offender and community populations. Peterson-Badali and colleagues (Peterson-Badali & Abramovitch, 1993; Peterson-Badali & Koegl, 1998) have conducted a series of studies that tested age differences among community adolescents and adults in their knowledge of legal concepts pertaining to the defense attorney's role, the confidentiality of the attorney–client relationship, entering a plea, and trial procedures. Although some concepts were understood by a majority of all participants, younger adolescents performed more poorly on many, but not all, measures of understanding.

Little research has examined juveniles' capacities for the other two prongs of competence-related abilities, reasoning and appreciation, and none of the studies used delinquent samples. Peterson-Badali and Abramovitch (1993) tested community samples of adolescents and adults on their ability to reason about hypothetical decisions to accept or reject plea agreements. Varying the strength of the evidence held by the police and using recommendations from an expert sample of lawyers as a criterion, the authors concluded that younger adolescents think less strategically (in terms of legal reasoning) than older adolescents and adults about plea agreements.

Although limited in number and scope, the majority of studies of juveniles' capacities relevant to *Miranda* waivers and adjudicative competence suggest that older adolescents, particularly those aged 16 to 17, may have capacities for understanding that are comparable to those of adults when traditional assessment instruments are used. Young adolescents (aged 13 and younger) systematically demonstrate less capacity than adults do. Findings regarding the abilities of middle adolescents (aged 14 and 15) are mixed; generally they fall between those of young and older adolescents, but the differences are not always statistically significant. It is interesting to note that these findings are generally consistent with research on adolescent medical and mental health decision making and informed consent. The informed consent doctrine holds that a competent decision is one that is made in a knowing, voluntary, and competent manner (Appelbaum & Grisso, 1988). Empirical studies of medical (e.g., Ambuel & Rappaport, 1992; Grisso & Vierling, 1978; Lewis, 1980; Weithorn & Campbell, 1982) and mental health (Belter & Grisso, 1984; Kaser-Boyd, Adelman, & Taylor, 1985; Kaser-Boyd, Adelman, Taylor, & Nelson, 1986) decision making suggest that young adolescents do not have adultlike capacity to consent, but that some adolescents over the age of 14 may be able to meet the legal standard of informed consent as well as adults.

As juveniles commit more serious crimes and policy initiatives increasingly treat juvenile defendants as adults, answers to the question "What makes juveniles different?" that supported the creation of the juvenile court have been pushed to the back burner. This chapter argues that juvenile defendants, particularly those in early and midadolescence, are operating in a developmental and contextual environment that differs qualitatively from that of adults. Recent theoretical and empirical work supports the need to examine the differences between adult and adolescent defendants before presuming equivalence in capacity and performance.

CONSIDERING THE IMPACT OF DEVELOPMENT: COMPETENCE
AND JUDGMENT

It is conceivable that the corpus of existing research could be used to support the position that some adolescents, perhaps as young as 14 or 15, can be competent defendants, just as some advocates and researchers have relied on the informed consent research to support policies extending other legal rights to juveniles (e.g., Melton, 1983, 1984). Critics argue that the extant research provides inadequate support for the policy argument that there are no differences between adolescents and adults (Gardner, Scherer, & Tester, 1989; Scott, Reppucci, & Woolard, 1995; Steinberg & Cauffman, 1996). The first group of criticisms identifies the methodological weaknesses in the measurement and evaluation of informed consent tenets. The main concern is that with few exceptions, many studies were laboratory-based self-reports of White middle-class adolescents using hypothetical vignettes. Some studies of juveniles' capacities in the justice system have used more ecologically valid samples (e.g., Grisso, 1981; Woolard & Reppucci, 1998). However, most studies conducted in a structured, unstressful, hypothetical environment may not generalize adequately to the real-life stress of decision making in legal contexts. Although some of these studies do shed light on adolescent and adult performance under certain situational constraints, their data demonstrating "no differences" between adolescents and adults provide a shaky empirical foundation upon which to build policy.

The second concern with the existing literature is primarily conceptual. Even if the methodological weaknesses in the empirical studies were rectified, reliance on the operationalization of adult frameworks regarding cognitive capacity as the ultimate test of adolescent capacity may be unwise. Scott et al. (1995) argue that policy-relevant research must examine additional characteristics and constructs that are relevant to legal decisions because the increasing involvement of juvenile defendants in adult court raises new questions about the presumption of competence and capacity. Although it is important to determine how adolescents compare to adults on measures ordinarily used in adult criminal court, it is imperative that empirical research investigates the developmental implications of extending adult assessment standards to juveniles. In the criminal system, adults are presumed to be mature and to have finished developing their decisional capacities; as such, they are held accountable for their behavior unless severe mental impairment precludes their ability to be competent and they cannot be restored to competence through treatment. However, the juvenile justice system was based not only on ideas about adolescents' cognitive capacities that are traditionally encompassed by competence to stand trial, but also on ideas that their judgment and decision making are less mature. It is quite possible that, for developmental reasons, the nature of juvenile competence may be qualitatively different from that of adults. There may be developmental constructs that are not captured by traditional competence assessments that influence the nature of juveniles' understanding and participation. That is, can a defendant be developmentally incompetent?

Adolescent Judgment

Supporters of an expanded research framework suggest that the juvenile justice system is based not only on assessments of adolescents' cognitive capacities, but also on the notion that, for developmental reasons, adolescents' decisional capacities may differ from those of adults. The judgment model proposed by Scott et al. (1995) is composed of three components that may influence the adolescent decision-making process and outcome differently from those of adults: peer and parental influence, temporal perspective, and risk perception. Their review of developmental research on these three components suggests that each may change across adolescence and may affect the decision-making process and outcome. Adolescents may be more receptive to the influence of peers, which could affect their willingness to participate in delinquent group activity (Berndt, 1979; Steinberg & Silverberg, 1986). The salience of peers during the adolescent years may mean that adolescents' decisions or choices are not always made in the independent, autonomous fashion ascribed to adult decision making. For example, adolescents may be more likely than adults to go along with a group decision to commit a crime, or less likely to provide incriminating information about their friends, because the potential impact of such behavior on peer relationships and group status trumps other concerns. Adolescents also face the developmental tasks of simultaneously maintaining a strong attachment to parents and breaking away from their control. This age-related conflict is related to problem behaviors such as delinquency (Allen, Aber, & Leadbeater, 1990) and could affect legally relevant decisions (e.g., to commit a crime, confess to police) in ways that are largely irrelevant for adults.

Lack of life experience and uncertainty about the future may contribute to an adolescent tendency to focus on short-term consequences to the exclusion of long-term ramifications of decisions (Greene, 1986; Nurmi, 1991). In some situations, adolescents may be relatively uncertain about their own future and thus focus on more imminent consequences (Allen, Leadbeater, & Aber, 1994). Research also indicates that adolescents may have a different risk–benefit calculus than adults in that they focus more on the possibility of gains and pay less attention to potential losses when considering decision options (Benthin, Slovic, & Severson, 1993). Moreover, adolescents may differ from adults in the importance they place on various consequences, such as negative peer reaction (Beyth-Marom, Austin, Fischhoff, Palmgren, & Quadrel, 1992; Furby & Beyth-Marom, 1992).

Building on the judgment framework, Steinberg and Cauffman (1996) concur that judgments are a result of interactions between cognitive and psychosocial factors. They argue that psychosocial factors that emphasize noncognitive effects on decision making fall into three broad categories – responsibility, temperance, and perspective. They also acknowledge, as do Scott et al. (1995), that performance on these three factors may vary according to situational constraints, although developmental trends may still be discernible and useful. Adolescents may differ from adults in their disposition toward responsibility by being less self-reliant and more susceptible to social influence by others, including peers. Temperance relates to research on risk-taking behavior but emphasizes the noncognitive differences between adolescents and adults in increased sensation seeking, greater impulsivity because of hormonal changes, and higher mood volatility. Adolescents probably are less able to control impulses than adults, but research has not clearly linked deficits in impulse control with actual decision-making behavior in simulated or actual legal contexts. Impulsivity could play a role in a variety of situations that could benefit from reflective thought, but research has not linked deficits in impulse control with actual decision-making behavior in legal contexts. Perspective is the third category of factors that distinguish adolescents from adults. Formal reasoning, social perspective taking, and moral reasoning grow throughout early and mid-adolescence. Future time orientation develops throughout adolescence into adulthood. All of these factors could affect legally relevant decision making, such as the ability to take a victim's perspective or consider the long-term consequences of a plea agreement.

Existing developmental studies, although providing evidence that judgment factors may affect adolescent decision making differently than that of adults, suffer from two major weaknesses (Scott et al., 1995; Woolard, Reppucci, & Redding, 1996). First, many studies do not include developmentally relevant and policy-relevant comparison groups. If aspects of adolescent decision making are attributed to the age-related factors that change over time, longitudinal studies and/or comparisons between adolescents of various ages and adults are critical. Age-based sampling techniques should be theoretically driven *and* policy relevant (e.g., distinctions between younger and older adolescents that correspond to juvenile waiver statutes).

Second, existing studies do not adequately examine the role of these factors in legally relevant contexts. A few studies have examined critical legal contexts such as the decision to talk with police (Abramovitch et al., 1993; Grisso, 1981) and to evaluate a plea bargain offer (Peterson-Badali & Abramovitch, 1993), but others remain virtually unexplored (e.g., to consult with an attorney). Context can be critical, both in terms of the types of decisions that adolescents face and in terms of the psychosocial and situational influences that come into play. Comprehensive studies of judgment in the legal context should incorporate both context-specific assessments of judgment and the more general developmental assessments to examine the relationship between noncontextual assessments of judgment and the legally relevant decision process and outcome.

This new theoretical approach to assumptions about adolescent capacities broadens the scope of previous research to include other cognitive and psychosocial factors. The judgment theory hypothesizes that developmental factors excluded from traditional assessments of adjudicative competence (e.g., temporal perspective, risk preference, susceptibility to peers) may be related to decision-making processes and outcomes. Some of these factors may map onto criteria already considered by the justice system in decisions about juveniles (e.g., criteria in transfer decisions).

An Empirical Study of Judgment and Competence

My colleagues and I have initiated research that conceptualizes juvenile defendants' decisions as a function of both judgment and competence, with comparisons between adolescents and adults currently involved in the justice system (Woolard & Reppucci, 1998). Data were collected from 200 juvenile and 100 adult defendants awaiting trial in a secure facility. Measures of adjudicative competence and judgment factors were administered in interview format. Legally relevant decisions and judgment constructs of peer influence, risk perception, perspective, and temperance were measured using a three-part vignette-based interview, the Judgment Assessment Tool for Adolescents (JATA; Woolard, Reppucci, & Scott, 1996), which describes a juvenile facing a series of decisions: (a) talking with police, (b) consulting with an attorney, and (c) considering a plea bargain. Participants responded to a series of questions regarding decision options and consequences that are coded into judgment construct categories. Adjudicative competence was measured by the MacArthur Competence Assessment Tool – Criminal Adjudication (MacCAT-CA; Poythress et al., 1999), which utilizes Bonnie's (1993) tripartite framework to generate scale scores of understanding, reasoning and appreciation. Analyses demonstrated significant differences between adolescents, particularly young adolescents, and adults on questions about reasoning and understanding based on current knowledge about the legal system. Analysis of judgment factors and decision making in the JATA indicated age-based differences in measures of decision choice (e.g., higher proportions of young adolescents recommended waiving the right to silence) and perceptions of others' wishes (e.g., higher proportions of adolescents reported that parents want children to confess to the police), among other findings. The study provides initial support for judgment theory and the notion that age-based differences in judgment constructs relate to decision process and outcome in legally relevant contexts. Demographic factors, adjudicative competence, and judgment all appear to play a role in vignette-based decision processes. Additionally, the role of each of these concepts may vary across legally relevant contexts and the different circumstances that juvenile defendants face.

CONSIDERING CONTEXT: PARENTS AND ATTORNEYS

It is clear from writings in law and psychology that competence in the legal arena is an interactive phenomenon that depends on the defendant's own capacities as well as the context in which they must be exercised (Bonnie & Grisso, 2000; Grisso, 1998). For example, a more complicated decision or one that has more serious consequences, such as pleading guilty to murder and testifying against codefendants, may require more of a defendant than simpler and less serious decisions such as pleading guilty to assault and accepting probation. More broadly defined, the context of a juvenile defendant's participation in the legal system is different from that of adults by virtue of his or her age. Although technically juveniles are viewed as adults when processed in criminal court, it is difficult to escape the fact that they have other special circumstances. Beyond the cognitive and psychosocial factors reviewed earlier, juvenile defendants also face differences in their relationships with two key players: their parents and their attorneys.

Parents

A fundamental organizing principle of the relationship between families and the state is the presumption that parents have their child's best interests at heart. In turn, parents are given the rights and responsibilities of raising children as they see fit, albeit within some broad parameters established by the state. Many perceive parents as serving a protective function for their children who become involved in the legal system by advocating for and advising their children who are faced with dilemmas such as police interrogation or a plea agreement. Grisso (1981) noted that the court presumes that a parent's presence will benefit juveniles at interrogation by reducing fear, providing a supportive presence, and giving advice and information about what is going on in the juvenile's case. The Harris and Jones cases described earlier sparked outrage among family and community members, who complained that the juvenile defendants were taken advantage of by police before their parents became involved (e.g., Deardorff, 1999).

Courts have also recognized, however, that the presumption regarding parents' intent and resulting action is not always accurate. Outside the criminal context, in decisions going back to the dissent in *Wisconsin v. Yoder* (1972), the Supreme Court has acknowledged that parents may not always have an "identity of interests" with, or the same interests as, their children. Within the juvenile justice context, parents' interests may align somewhat with the state for various reasons, including the desire for the child to "do what is right," for the justice system to handle a difficult child, or for a means to access needed services that are otherwise unavailable. These factors may lead parents to encourage their child to confess to the police or accept a plea agreement that, from the child's perspective (or an attorney's), may not be the best decision.

There is little data on the role that parents play in the legal processing of their children. Survey data from the late 1970s reported by Grisso (1981) suggest that a majority of parents do not support a juvenile's protection against self-incrimination. Although two-thirds of those surveyed believed juveniles should have the same rights as adults, over half of the sample felt that juveniles should not be able to withhold incriminating information from the police. Because of the limitations of the sample and the use of hypothetical vignettes, Grisso also reported on an observational study of parental actions during police interrogation conducted by the St. Louis County Juvenile Court. The results documented a consistent pattern of inaction and lack of involvement by parents. Of 390 police interrogations of juveniles, 66% involved no communication between parent and child. Less that 10% of the juveniles asked their parents for advice on how to handle the questioning.

Juveniles' perceptions are a critical link in understanding whether parents could or would serve a beneficial role. In a descriptive study of 25 male Canadian offenders in custody, Koegl (1997) examined the motivational and contextual factors affecting the assertion of various rights. Although Canadian law expressly gives juveniles the right to have a parent present during interrogation, only one juvenile in the sample requested it. When the others were asked why they did not ask for their parents, the main reasons were lack of knowledge concerning the right (33%) and police practices or instructions discouraging it (29%). Interestingly, one-fifth of the participants felt that notifying their parents would have negative effects (e.g., anger, worry) or produce no benefit (25%). Although the small sample size limits generalizability of these results, further research is warranted and should examine how adolescents' perceptions of their parents affects decision making.

Parents are in a position to serve a protective and advocacy function for their children, but several barriers may prevent them from doing so. These include lack of access to their children during legal procedures such as interrogation, their own knowledge or savvy about the legal system, and the juveniles' perceptions of and willingness to utilize their input.

Attorneys

Another interested adult who advocates for the child is the attorney. Issues of competence and effective participation are of critical concern with respect to the attorney–client relationship. Two characteristics distinguish the legal representation of juvenile defendants from that of adults – access to counsel in juvenile court and the nature of the attorney–client relationship in both juvenile and criminal proceedings (see Haralambie, this volume, for a discussion of children's legal representation in civil cases.)

Although *Gault* (1967) established a constitutional right to counsel in juvenile court, researchers and advocates have documented that this right does not necessarily translate into access. Representation rates vary by the stage of proceedings, as well as by geography and individual court characteristics (Caeti, Hemmens, & Burton, 1996; Feld, 1988). Feld's study of representation rates in six states found that in three states, at least half of the delinquency offenders were not represented by counsel. Case factors associated with more severe sanctions were also associated with higher representation rates, but *representation itself* was associated with more severe dispositions independent of other case variables (see also Clarke & Koch, 1980). The significant lack of representation has been attributed to a number of factors, including juveniles' waiver of the right to counsel, influence by court personnel, and parents' financial concerns (Feld, 1988).[4]

There are significant reasons to question the assumption that juvenile defendants have the same capacities as adults to participate with their attorneys as effective defendants. The results of a few studies suggest that juveniles may have misperceptions about the role of counsel and/or may believe that counsel is not helpful to their own situations (American Bar Association Juvenile Justice Center,

---

[4] Feld (1988) indicates that some jurisdictions may require fees for attorneys provided by the state to be reimbursed to the state.

1995; Grisso, 1981; Peterson-Badali, Abramovitch, Koegl, & Ruck, 1997). These attitudes may reduce the effectiveness of juveniles' participation as defendants, but it is not clear whether these findings are age-related or simply reflect the quality of representation of juvenile clients (American Bar Association Juvenile Justice Center, 1995). This difficulty in interpretation results in part from a lack of systematic data on juvenile clients' perceptions of their attorneys and the impact they may have on the effectiveness of the juveniles' participation.

Although adult defendants also manage a lawyer–client relationship, the very *nature* of the juvenile–attorney interaction may be different (Woolard & Reppucci, 2000). The changing landscape of juvenile court has juxtaposed two conflicting models of representation that have been debated in the literature – a paternalistic approach based on analyses of the juvenile client's best interests and an adversarial approach fueled by client-oriented decision making (Davis, 1993–1994; Federle, 1996; Kay & Segal, 1973). Whereas the paternalistic approach places more control in the attorney's hands because the juvenile is not yet adultlike in capacity, the adversarial approach puts the defendant in control of major case decisions. The adversarial approach, endorsed by many in the legal community, presumes some level of competence in its clients, however, and legal commentators have recognized that juvenile clients may have developmental limitations that may preclude full adultlike participation (Buss, 1996, 2000; Federle, 1996; Guggenheim, 1996).

Juveniles may need varying types and levels of skill to operate as effective defendants because the two models require different thresholds of engagement. Attorneys using a client-centered model would expect the juvenile to have a much more active, and in many circumstances controlling, interest in strategy and procedure. Whereas some clients could meet those expectations, perhaps with assistance, the demands might exceed the capacities of many adolescents, those who are younger or have other deficits. Attorneys working from a more paternalistic model may presume incapacity and retain more control; this may ease the burden on juveniles' capacities, but critics argue that it does not always serve the best interests it theoretically promotes, and that a best interests model is clearly inappropriate for those juveniles facing adversarial criminal court proceedings. Attorneys representing juvenile clients must develop their own strategies for working with clients, creating an environment with varied demands on juveniles' abilities. No systematic data exist on the strategies that defense attorneys use with various types of juvenile cases and clients, but the concern about juveniles' capacity to instruct counsel, and about the multiple and sometimes conflicting roles that attorneys adopt, have appeared in the literature for quite some time (e.g., Leon, 1978). Moreover, attorneys not only face the problems of working with potentially immature clients, but they also may be hired by, and pressured to respond to, the client's parents. Depending on the model of representation that is chosen, commentators argue about how much weight the parents' wishes should carry (Hafen, 1993).

IMPLICATIONS FOR RESEARCH AND POLICY

The current research, although limited, suggests that adolescent defendants differ from adults in ways that are important for policy and research. At a broad level, this review argues that the legal system should increase its sensitivity to such developmental differences; the mechanisms by which this can be accomplished vary.

Maintain the differences between juvenile court and adult criminal court. Although some have argued for the abolition of the juvenile court in favor of criminal due process protections, the juvenile court's mission is consistent with recognizable developmental differences between adolescents and adults. This endorsement of juvenile court is often justified on the basis of amenability to treatment, the reduced capacities of defendants, or other arguments (Slobogin, Fondacaro, & Woolard, 1999). At the very least, theory and data call into question the assumption that juvenile defendants operate with adultlike capacities.

Evaluate the efficacy of developmentally sensitive procedural protections. Particularly for young offenders, mechanisms such as a per se rule preventing the waiver of *Miranda* rights (Grisso, 1981), policies requiring the presence of an adult for custodial interrogation, or legally mandated use of competence evaluations can improve the likelihood that adultlike capacities are not presumed. Some law enforcement agencies have moved to videotaped interrogations as one way that questions about the validity of *Miranda* waivers and confessions can be addressed.

Improve the system's responsiveness to the developmental needs of juvenile defendants. Acknowledging developmental differences between adolescents and adults does not automatically eliminate accountability for juvenile offenders. Waiver may still be an important mechanism for removing certain offenders from juvenile court jurisdiction. However, the criminal court should still respond to the cognitive and psychosocial differences between juveniles and adults to ensure that transferred youth can participate effectively as defendants. Training for attorneys, judges, probation officers, and mental health professionals on developmental and forensic issues can be an important step toward that goal.

Continue to develop a base of theoretically driven, policy-relevant empirical research. A number of questions about juveniles' capacities remain unanswered but require an interdisciplinary approach to ensure their utility to both theory and policy (see Woolard & Reppucci, 2000, for a review). For example, research must distinguish between the specific legal definition of adjudicative competence and the broader psychological use of the term to encompass other constructs such as judgment factors. Sampling strategies should be crafted to satisfy theoretical predictions about development and evaluate differential legal processing of offenders in juvenile and criminal courts. The MacArthur Foundation Research Network on Adolescent Development and Juvenile Justice has adopted this interdisciplinary model by bringing together researchers and practitioners to identify gaps in the literature and needs in the justice system that can be addressed through research. Once research has been generated, it is imperative that researchers communicate the findings appropriately to practitioners and policy makers. Publishing in trade journals and providing information at legislative hearings are methods of reaching beyond the traditional academic audiences.

Further work is needed on the capacities that juveniles require to meet legal standards of *Miranda* waiver and adjudicative competence as well as to perform effectively as defendants. However, it is clear that the default extension of adult standards and assessment techniques to juveniles will not capture aspects of development that differentiate adolescents from adults. Continued research with larger and more racially and ethnically diverse samples of both male and female adolescents and adults facing legal decisions will provide a more secure foundation from which policy and practice recommendations can be made. Such research initiatives will have implications for practitioners conducting evaluations of juveniles and the manner in which competence is structured for juveniles in criminal and juvenile courts. Traditionally, within the adult framework, competence and decision making are individual case-by-case matters in which maturity and judgment are rarely considered. A developmental approach broadens the scope of inquiry to examine a class of individuals, adolescents, for whom there may be important developmental differences.

Continued research on issues of competence and effective participation will provide a foundation for designing interventions to improve both adolescents' ability to negotiate the legal system and the system's response to the particular needs of adolescent offenders. Recent legislative initiatives that have redefined adolescent offenders as adults may satisfy the public's desire for punishment, but it is reasonable to expect that the system's process, as well as the outcome, fits both the crime *and* the maturity level of the individual. The research suggests that the differences between adults and adolescents are indeed real, and a more encompassing consideration of defendants' abilities that includes developmental and contextual factors is necessary to understand adolescents' capacities as criminal defendants.

References

Abramovitch, R., Higgins-Biss, K., & Biss, S. (1993). Young persons' comprehension of waivers in criminal proceedings. *Canadian Journal of Criminology, 35,* 309–322.

Abramovitch, R., Peterson-Badali, M., & Rohan, M. (1995). Young people's understanding and assertion of their rights to silence and legal counsel. *Canadian Journal of Criminology, 37,* 1–18.

Allen, J. P., Aber, J. L., & Leadbeater, B. J. (1990). Adolescent problem behaviors: The influence of attachment and autonomy. *Pediatric Clinics of North America, 13,* 455–467.

Allen, J. P., Leadbeater, B. J., & Aber, J. L. (1994). The development of problem behavior syndromes in at-risk adolescents. *Development and Psychopathology, 6,* 323–342.

Ambuel, B., & Rappaport, J. (1992). Developmental trends in adolescents' psychological and legal competence to consent to abortion. *Law and Human Behavior, 16*, 129–154.

American Bar Association Juvenile Justice Center. (1995). *A call for justice: An assessment of access to counsel and quality of representation in delinquency proceedings*. Washington, DC: American Bar Association.

Appelbaum, P. S., & Grisso, T. (1988). Assessing patients' capacities to consent to treatment. *New England Journal of Medicine, 319*, 1635–1638.

Belter, R. W., & Grisso, T. (1984). Children's recognition of rights violations in counseling. *Professional Psychology: Research and Practice, 15*, 899–910.

Benthin, A. C., Slovic, P., & Severson, H. (1993). A psychometric study of adolescent risk perception. *Journal of Adolescence, 16*, 153–168.

Berndt, T. J. (1979). Developmental changes in conformity to peers and parents. *Developmental Psychology, 15*, 608–616.

Beyth-Marom, R., Austin, L., Fischhoff, B., Palmgren, C., & Quadrel, M. J. (1992). Perceived consequences of risky behaviors: Adults and adolescents. *Developmental Psychology, 29*, 549–563.

Bonnie, R. J. (1993). The competence of criminal defendants: Beyond *Dusky* and *Drope*. *University of Miami Law Review, 47*, 540–601.

Bonnie, R. J., & Grisso, R. (2000). Adjudicative competence and youthful offenders. In T. Grisso & R. Schwartz (Eds.), *Youth on trial* (pp. 73–103). Chicago: University of Chicago Press.

Breed v. Jones, 421 U.S. 519 (1975).

Buss, E. (1996). "You're my what?" The problems of children's misperceptions of their lawyers' roles. *Fordham Law Review, 64*, 1699–1762.

Buss, E. (2000). Promoting juveniles' competence as defendants. In T. Grisso & R. Schwartz (Eds.), *Youth on trial* (pp. 243–265). Chicago: University of Chicago Press.

Caeti, T. J., Hemmens, C., & Burton, V. S. (1996). Juvenile right to counsel: A national comparison of state legal codes. *American Journal of Criminal Law, 23*, 611–632.

Clarke, S. H., & Koch, G. (1980). Juvenile court: Therapy or crime control, and do lawyers make a difference? *Law and Society Review, 14*, 263–308.

Cooper, D. K. (1997). Juveniles' understanding of trial-related information: Are they competent defendants? *Behavioral Sciences & the Law, 15*, 167–180.

Cowden, V. L., & McKee, G. R. (1995). Competency to stand trial in juvenile delinquency proceedings: Cognitive maturity and the attorney–client relationship. *University of Louisville Journal of Law, 33*, 629–651.

Davis, S. M. (1993–1994). The role of the attorney in child advocacy. *Journal of Family Law, 32*, 817–831.

Deardorff, J. (1999, April 7). Child's statement on killing disputed: 10-year-old boy allegedly confessed. *Chicago Tribune*, p. 1.

Drope v. Missouri, 420 U.S. 162 (1975).

Dusky v. United States, 362 U.S. 402 (1960).

Fare v. Michael C., 442 U.S. 707 (1979).

Federle, K. H. (1996). The ethics of empowerment: Rethinking the role of lawyers in interviewing and counseling the child client. *Fordham Law Review, 64*, 1655–1697.

Feld, B. C. (1988). *In re Gault* revisited: A cross-state comparison of the right to counsel in juvenile court. *Crime & Delinquency, 34*, 393–424.

Ferguson, A., & Douglas, A. (1970). A study of juvenile waiver. *San Diego Law Review, 7*, 39–54.

Furby, L., & Beyth-Marom, R. (1992). Risk-taking in adolescence: A decision-making perspective. *Developmental Review, 12*, 1–44.

Gallegos v. Colorado, 370 U.S. 49 (1962).

Gardner, W., Scherer, D., & Tester, M. (1989). Asserting scientific authority: Cognitive development and adolescent legal rights. *American Psychologist, 44*, 895–902.

Golding, S., Roesch, R., & & Schreiber, J. (1984). Assessment and conceptualization of competency to stand trial: Preliminary data on the Interdisciplinary Fitness Interview. *Law and Human Behavior, 8*, 321–334.

Greene, A. L. (1986). Future-time perspective in adolescence: The present of things future revisited. *Journal of Youth and Adolescence, 15*, 99–113.

Griffin, P., Torbet, P., & Szymanski, L. (1998). *Trying juveniles as adults in criminal court: An analysis of state transfer provisions*. Washington, DC: U.S. Department of Justice, Office of Justice Programs, Office of Juvenile Justice and Delinquency Prevention.

Grisso, T. (1981). *Juveniles' waiver of rights*. New York: Plenum Press.

Grisso, T. (1997). The competence of adolescents as trial defendants. *Psychology, Public Policy, & Law, 3*, 3–32.

Grisso, T. (1998). *Forensic evaluation of juveniles*. Sarasota, FL: Professional Resource Press.

Grisso, T. (2000). Adolescents' competence in the adjudicative process. In T. Grisso & R. Schwartz (Eds.), *Youth on trial* (pp. 139–171). Chicago: University of Chicago Press.

Grisso, T., Miller, M. O., & Sales, B. (1987). Competency to stand trial in juvenile court. *International Journal of Law and Psychiatry, 10*, 1–20.

Grisso, T., & Vierling, L. (1978). Minors' consent to treatment: A developmental perspective. *Professional Psychology: Research and Practice, 9*, 421–427.

Guggenheim, M. (1996). A paradigm for determining the role of counsel for children. *Fordham Law Review, 64*, 1399–1433.

Hafen, J. O. (1993). Children's rights and legal representation – The proper roles of children, parents, and attorneys. *Notre Dame Journal of Law, Ethics, & Public Policy, 7*, 423–463.

Hanna, J. (1998, August 30). Kids' "competence" a tender issue for courts. *Chicago Tribune*, p. 1.

In re Causey, 363 So. 2d 472 (La. 1978).

In re Gault, 387 U.S. 1 (1967).

In re Winship, 397 U.S. 358 (1970).

Kaser-Boyd, N., Adleman, H. S., & Taylor, L. (1985). Minors' ability to identify risks and benefits of therapy. *Professional Psychology: Research and Practice, 16*, 411–417.

Kaser-Boyd, N., Adelman, H. S., Taylor, L., & Nelson, P. (1986). Children's understanding of risks and benefits of psychotherapy. *Clinical Child Psychology, 15*, 165–171.

Kay, R., & Segal, D. (1973). The role of the attorney in juvenile court proceedings: A non-polar approach. *The Georgetown Law Journal, 61*, 1400–1424.

Kent v. U.S., 383 U.S. 541 (1966).

Koegl, C. J. (1997). *Contextual and motivational factors affecting young offenders' use of legal rights.* Unpublished master's thesis.

Leon, J. S. (1978). Recent developments in legal representation of children: A growing concern with the concept of capacity. *Canadian Journal of Family Law, 1*, 375–434.

Lewis, C. C. (1980). A comparison of minors' and adults' pregnancy decisions. *American Journal of Orthopsychiatry, 50*, 446–453.

Lipsitt, P., Lelos, D., & McGarry, A. L. (1971). Competency for trial: A screening instrument. *American Journal of Psychiatry, 128*, 137–141.

McKeiver v. Pennsylvania, 403 U.S. 528 (1971).

Melton, G. (1983). Toward "personhood" for adolescents: Autonomy and privacy as values in public policy. *American Psychologist, 38*, 99–103.

Melton, G. (1984). Developmental psychology and the law: The state of the art. *Journal of Family Law, 22*, 445–482.

Miranda v. Arizona, 384 U.S. 436 (1966).

Moffitt, T. E. (1993). Adolescence-limited and life-course persistent antisocial behavior: A developmental taxonomy. *Psychological Review, 100*, 674–701.

Nurmi, J. (1991). How do adolescents see their future? A review of the development of future orientation and planning. *Developmental Review, 11*, 1–59.

Otto, R. K., Poythress, N. G., Nicholson, R. A., Edens, J. F., Monahan, J., Bonnie, R. J., Hoge, S. K., & Eisenberg, M. (1998). Psychometric properties of the MacArthur Competence Assessment Tool-Criminal Adjudication (MacCAT-CA). *Psychological Assessment, 10*, 435–443.

Pearse, J., Gudjonsson, G. H., Clare, I. C. H., & Rutter, S. (1998). Police interviewing and psychological vulnerabilities: Predicting the likelihood of a confession. *Journal of Community and Applied Social Psychology, 8*, 1–21.

People v. Lara, 432 P.2d 202 (1967).

Peterson-Badali, M., & Abramovitch, R., (1993). Grade-related changes in young people's reasoning about plea decisions. *Law and Human Behavior, 17*, 537–552.

Peterson-Badali, M., Abramovitch, R., Koegl, C. J., & Ruck, M. D., (1997). Young people's experience of the Canadian youth justice system:

Interacting with police and legal counsel. *Behavioral Sciences and the Law, 17,* 455–465.

Peterson-Badali, M., & Koegl, C. J. (1998). Young people's knowledge of the Young Offenders Act and the youth justice system. *Canadian Journal of Criminology, 40,* 127–152.

Possley, M. (1998, August 30). How cops got boys to talk. *Chicago Tribune,* p. 1.

Poythress, N., Nicholson, R., Otto, R. K., Edens, J. F., Bonnie, R. J., Monahan, J., & Hoge, S. K. (1999). The MacArthur Competence Assessment Tool – Criminal Adjudication: Professional manual. Odessa, FL: Psychological Assessment Resources.

Puzzanchera, C., Stahl, A., Finnegan, T., Snyder, H., Poole, R., & Tierney, N. (2000). *Juvenile court statistics 1997.* Washington, DC: Office of Juvenile Justice and Delinquency Prevention.

Savitsky, J., & Karras, D. (1984). Competency to stand trial among adolescents. *Adolescence, 19,* 349–358.

Scott, E. S., Reppucci, N. D., & Woolard, J. L. (1995). Evaluating adolescent decision making in legal contexts. *Law and Human Behavior, 19,* 221–244.

Sickmund, M., Snyder, H., & Poe-Yamagata, E. (1997). *Juvenile offenders and victims: 1997 update on violence.* Washington, DC: Office of Juvenile Justice and Delinquency Prevention.

Slobogin, C., Fondacaro, M., & Woolard, J. L. (1999). Juvenile justice reform: The promise of *Kansas v. Hendricks* for children. *University of Wisconsin Law Review, 1999,* 186–226.

Snyder, H. N. (1999). *Juvenile arrests 1998.* Washington, DC: Office of Juvenile Justice and Delinquency Prevention.

Stahl, A. L., Sickmund, M., Finnegan, T. A., Snyder, H. N., Poole, R. S., & Tierney, N. (1999). *Juvenile court statistics 1996.* Washington, DC: Office of Juvenile Justice and Delinquency Prevention.

Steadman, H. J., & Hartstone, E. (1983). Defendants incompetent to stand trial. In J. Monahan & H. J. Steadman (Eds.), *Mentally disordered offenders: Perspectives from law and social science* (pp. 39–62). New York: Plenum Press.

Steinberg, L., & Cauffman, E. (1996). Maturity of judgment in adolescence: Psychosocial factors in adolescent decision making. *Law and Human Behavior, 20,* 249–272.

Steinberg, L., & Silverberg, S. B. (1986). The vicissitudes of autonomy in early adolescence. *Child Development, 57,* 841–851.

Tobey, A., Grisso, T., & Schwartz, R. (2000). Youths' trial participation as seen by youths and their attorneys: An exploration of competence based issues. In T. Grisso & R. Schwartz (Eds.), *Youth on trial* (pp. 225–241). Chicago: University of Chicago Press.

Weithorn, L. A., & Campbell, S. A. (1982). The competency of children to make informed treatment decisions. *Child Development, 53,* 1589–1598.

Wildman, R. (1978). The Georgia Court Competency Test (GCCT): *An attempt to develop a rapid, quantitative measure of fitness for trial.* Unpublished manuscript.

Wilson, T. (1999, February 23). Judge to decide whether boy, 10, is fit to stand trial for murder. *Chicago Tribune,* p. 4.

Wisconsin v. Yoder, 406 U.S. 205 (1972).

Woolard, J. L., & Reppucci, N. D. (1998, August). *Juvenile competence: Judgment and decision making in legal contexts.* Paper presented at the American Psychological Association Convention, San Francisco.

Woolard, J. L., & Reppucci, N. D. (2000). Researching juveniles' capacities as defendants. In T. Grisso & R. Schwartz (Eds.), *Youth on trial* (pp. 173–191). Chicago: University of Chicago Press.

Woolard, J. L., Reppucci, N. D., & Redding, R. E. (1996). Theoretical and methodological issues in studying children's capacities in legal contexts. *Law and Human Behavior, 20,* 219–228.

Woolard, J. L., Reppucci, N. D., & Scott, E. S. (1996). *Judgment Assessment Tool – Adolescents.* Unpublished manual.

Worrell, C. (1985). Pretrial detention of juveniles: Denial of equal protection masked by the *parens patriae* doctrine. *Yale Law Journal, 95,* 174–193.

PART IV

CHILDREN AS VICTIMS AND WITNESSES

12

The Effects of Community Violence on Children and Adolescents

Intervention and Social Policy

Steven L. Berman
Wendy K. Silverman
William M. Kurtines

The rate of community violence in the United States has increased dramatically over the past two decades (Osofsky, 1998; Parson, 1997). Although the numbers have begun to decline in recent years (e.g., in 1998, FBI crime statistics indicate that violent acts and property offenses dropped 7% nationwide [Morales & Reisner, 1999]), the rates remain high. For example, Saint Louis, Missouri, the city with the highest crime rate in 1998, had 14,952 crimes per 100,000 people. Miami, Florida, was ranked sixth in the nation in terms of crime, with 12,054 crimes per 100,000 people. The high rate of crime and violence in the country has had a profound impact on youth: The nation's young people, particularly those from low socioeconomic, multiethnic, and urban communities, are increasingly exposed to extreme acts of crime or violence, either as witnesses or as victims (Warner & Weist, 1996). As a consequence of this exposure, young people are at increased risk of experiencing myriad disturbing psychological symptoms.

One main set of problems that results in the aftermath of exposure to crime and violence is the development of distress symptoms, particularly those associated with posttraumatic stress reactions. Because of the high levels of distress experienced by youth who suffer from posttraumatic stress, it is important that interventions

Please address all correspondence to Steven L. Berman, Psychology, Univ. of Central Florida, Daytona Bch, FL 32114 (e-mail: Sberman@mail.ucf.edu) or Wendy K. Silverman, Psychology, Florida International Univ., Miami, FL 33199 (e-mail: Silverw@fiu.edu).

be developed that will help alleviate this distress. It also is important that social policy be formulated and implemented to curb young people's exposure to the trauma of community violence.

In this chapter we focus on these issues. First, we review the research literature on the relation between exposure to crime and violence and the development of posttraumatic stress reactions. Next, we discuss intervention strategies to help alleviate these reactions. We conclude with recommendations for social policy.

EXPOSURE TO CRIME AND VIOLENCE AND THE DEVELOPMENT
OF POSTTRAUMATIC STRESS REACTIONS

Individuals' reactions to exposure to crime and violence are complex and multifaceted. Although exposure to extreme acts of crime and violence places youth at risk for a variety of adverse psychological consequences, distress symptoms of the type associated with posttraumatic stress have emerged as a focal point of recent research (e.g., Davies & Flannery, 1998; Ensink, Robertson, Zissis, & Leger, 1997; Glodich, 1998).

The main symptoms associated with posttraumatic stress reactions include reexperiencing the trauma (e.g., nightmares, flashbacks), avoidance of stimuli associated with the trauma (e.g., thoughts, feelings, conversations, people, places, or things), and increased arousal (e.g., irritability hypervigilance, being easily startled, sleep and/or concentration difficulties). These symptoms became a part of psychiatric nomenclature in the third edition of the *Diagnostic and Statistical Manual of Mental Disorders* (*DSM-III*; American Psychiatric Association, 1980) in the diagnostic category "Posttraumatic Stress Disorder (PTSD)." In some of these studies that we summarize next, some researchers focused on assessing the symptoms of PTSD among child participants, whereas others focused not only on the symptoms, but also on whether full diagnostic criteria have been met to warrant a clinical diagnosis of PTSD among participants.

Studies conducted by Richters and Martinez (1993) were the first systematic attempts to document the link between exposure to crime and violence and symptoms in children. In presenting the rationale for conducting their research, Martinez and Richters (1993) pointed out that although some symptoms (e.g., fear, anxiety, intrusive thoughts) may be viewed as normal reactions to abnormal events and may serve adaptive functions in an objectively dangerous environment, such symptoms also can indicate maladaptive reactions with possible long-term negative consequences for normal social, emotional, and cognitive development. This can happen even when initially adaptive responses become entrenched, resistant to change, and overgeneralized to other situations. Such responses "in the extreme, have come to be associated with posttraumatic stress" (Martinez & Richters, 1993, p. 23).

To examine the relation between children's exposure to crime and violence and distress symptoms, Richters and Martinez (Martinez & Richters, 1993; Richters & Martinez, 1993) assessed 165 children (111 first and second graders and 54 fifth and sixth graders) in a low-income, moderately violent neighborhood in Washington, D.C. Results indicated that among the first and second graders, parents reported that 21% of the children had been victims of at least one violent act. Considerably more children were reported as having been witnesses, with 84% having witnessed at least one violent act. Among the fifth and sixth graders, generally higher rates of exposure were revealed. Parents reported that 35% of the children were victims of at least one violent act, and 90% were witnesses to a violent act. The parents also reported that 3% of the younger children and 4% of the older children had witnessed a murder. For both age groups, parents tended to report lower levels of distress in their children than the children reported themselves. There were no gender differences in terms of exposure to violence or distress symptoms. In terms of the specific symptoms of distress reported by children and parents, anxiety and depression were most pronounced; more specific PTSD symptoms were not assessed.

Another study that documented a relation between exposure to crime and violence and distress symptoms was that of Fitzpatrick and Boldizar (1993). This study, however, involved a sample of not only children but also adolescents. Participants were low-income African American youth who were involved in a federally funded summer camp program a large southern central city. In this sample, more than 70% of the children and adolescents reported

being victims of at least one violent act. Similar to the findings of
Richters and Martinez (1993), participants were more likely to have
witnessed violence than to have been victimized, with close to 85%
having witnessed at least one violent act and 43.4% having witnessed a murder. In addition, of those who had been exposed as
either a witness or a victim, 89% met at least one of the *DSM III-R*
criteria for PTSD (American Psychiatric Association, 1987), with
the average number of symptoms being five. Boys reported significantly more exposure to violence than girls, but girls reported more
PTSD symptoms than boys.

In another study (Jenkins & Bell, 1994), 203 African American
students from a public high school on Chicago's South Side in a high
violent crime district were surveyed. Almost two-thirds of them
indicated that they had seen a shooting, and almost one-half had
been shot at themselves. Forty-five percent reported that they had
seen someone killed. Of those who had witnessed severe violence,
36% reported that the victim was a friend and 34% reported that
the victim was a family member. Although being personally victimized was similarly correlated with psychological distress symptoms
for both boys ($r = .25$) and girls ($r = .22$), witnessing violence was
more highly correlated with psychological distress symptoms for
girls ($r = .33$) than for boys ($r = -.07$). Overall, girls reported more
distress symptoms than boys, and boys reported more high-risk behaviors (e.g., carrying a weapon, substance use, and fighting) than
girls. As Jenkins and Bell pointed out, however, the correlational nature of the data precludes one from concluding whether the boys'
high-risk behaviors represent either reactions to violence exposure
or contributors that lead to exposure.

A large sample of youth ($N = 2,248$; sixth, eight, and tenth
graders) in New Haven, Connecticut, was surveyed by Schwab-
Stone et al. (1995). More than 40% of them reported exposure to a
shooting or stabbing in the past year. Seventy-four percent reported
feeling unsafe in one or more common settings (e.g., home, neighborhood, school). Exposure to violence was found to be associated
with increased willingness to use physical aggression, diminished
perception of risk, lowered personal expectations for the future,
dysphoric mood, antisocial activity, alcohol use, and diminished
academic achievement. This study too was correlational, however.

Also in New Haven, Connecticut, Horowitz, Weine, and Jekel (1995) assessed adolescent girls recruited from a clinic that provided medical and gynecological care to a predominantly urban female adolescent population. The lowest number of violent events experienced by one person was 8 and the highest number was 55, with a mean of 28 violent events across the participants. Approximately 45% of the sample had witnessed a shooting. The mean number of PTSD symptoms for the total sample was 10, and 67% of the participants met the full *DSM-III-R* diagnostic criteria for PTSD.

Berman, Kurtines, Silverman, and Serafini (1996) also examined the relation between exposure and posttraumatic stress symptoms in a sample of students enrolled in an alternative high school aimed at dropout prevention in Miami, Florida. Most of the students in this school came from low-income inner-city neighborhoods where crime and violence are most prevalent. Results indicated that more than 93% of the respondents had witnessed one or more acts of community violence, and 44% reported having been a victim of a violent crime. Similar to the rate reported by Fitzpatrick and Boldizar (1993), 41.6% had witnessed a murder. The results further indicated that 83% of those who had been exposed, either as a witness or a victim, met at least one *DSM-III-R* criterion for PTSD, with the average number of symptoms endorsed being 10 out of a list of 20 symptoms. Using Fredrick's (1985) categorization of level of severity of PTSD, 34% of the participants' symptoms were categorized as mild, 44% as moderate, and 18% as severe. Social support and coping style also were assessed: Higher PTSD scores were found to be related to increased usage of negative coping and the perception of less social support.

In a study conducted in South Africa (Ensink et al., 1997), Xhosa-speaking Black children aged 10 to 16 were recruited from a children's home and a school, both located in a township known for high levels of community violence on the outskirts of Cape Town. All participants had been exposed to community violence, with 56% reporting having been a victim and 45% reporting having been a witness to at least one killing. In terms of the effects of exposure, the most common *DSM-III-R* diagnosis assigned to the children was dysthymia (31.6%), followed by PTSD (21.6%), major depression (6.6%), and conduct disorder (1.6%). Overall, of the

60 participants, 40% were diagnosed with one or more psychiatric disorders, 42% reported psychiatric symptoms but did not meet the criteria for a specific psychiatric disorder, and 18% reported no symptoms.

Kliewer, Lepore, Oskin, and Johnson (1998) recently reported that among children who lived in violent, high-crime areas in Richmond, Virginia, 88% had heard gunfire near their home, 25% had seen someone shot, and 17% had seen someone killed. Based on children's and parents' ratings on several questionnaires, exposure to community violence was found to be significantly associated with internalizing symptoms of depression and anxiety. Social support also was assessed in this study and was found to be inversely related to levels of internalizing symptoms of depression and anxiety. Social support was also found to moderate the relation between exposure to violence and intrusive thoughts.

Overall, the research summarized in this section documents that children and adolescents are significantly exposed to community crime and violence, and that the majority of them experience symptoms associated with posttraumatic stress as a result of this exposure. Many of these children experience the full clinical disorder of PTSD as well. One way to intervene on this problem would be to work toward elimination of crime and violence. Although this is a lofty goal and a worthwhile ideal, concurrent efforts are needed to help those who have already been exposed or soon will be.

INTERVENTIONS FOR YOUTHS' DISTRESS REACTIONS FOLLOWING
EXPOSURE TO CRIME AND VIOLENCE

In light of the high rates of youth exposure to crime and violence and its psychological sequelae, it is important that interventions be developed that can help alleviate the distress and suffering that are likely to ensue. In addition, although children's reactions following exposure to crime and violence have not been followed over extended time periods, research in other areas have shown that a considerable proportion of children continue to display significant posttraumatic stress reactions for as long as 18 months following exposure to traumatic events (e.g., hurricanes: La Greca, Silverman, Vernberg, & Prinstein, 1996). Thus, it seems unlikely that time alone will heal the distress without treatment for all children. And even if it were found that symptoms do abate eventually, the distress associated with symptoms that will be experienced during the interim would be sufficient to justify the need for intervention.

Despite this need for effective interventions that can be used in the aftermath of children's exposure to crime and violence, the research in this area is sparse. For example, we are not aware of any randomized, controlled trials that have been conducted. The literature consists mainly of a small number of studies that have investigated the efficacy of treating PTSD in young people who have been exposed to a variety of traumatic events, not necessarily community violence (e.g., Albano, Miller, Zarate, Cote, & Barlow, 1997; Farrell, Hains, & Davies, 1998; March, Amaya-Jackson, Murray, & Schulte, 1998). March et al. (1998), for example, used a school-based group cognitive behavioral intervention with 17 youth (ages 10 to 15 years) who had been exposed to a single event stressor (types of traumatic stressors varied across participants, though some of the events involved exposure to community violence) and who met *DSM-IV* criteria for PTSD. The treatment took place in 18 weekly sessions. Sessions focused on anxiety and anger management, developing social skills, systematic desensitization to traumatic reminders, and relapse prevention. The study used a single case design to control for extraneous variables rather than a comparison control group. More specifically, intervention start dates were staggered by 4 weeks in two of four schools, thereby generating a multiple baseline across setting and time design. This is an alternative methodology that can be used to demonstrate that changes are due to the treatment and not merely to the passage of time. Results indicated that 57% of the participants no longer met *DSM-IV* criteria for PTSD at posttreatment; 86% were free of PTSD at 6-month follow-up. Significant improvements also were observed in symptoms of depression, anxiety, and anger at posttreatment and follow-up.

In light of the sparse treatment research conducted in this area, there is a clear need for clinical trials to confirm that psychosocial interventions, particularly cognitive behavioral treatments, are safe, acceptable, and effective for children and adolescents who suffer from symptoms of posttraumatic stress and/or PTSD as a result of exposure to community violence (e.g., March et al., 1998).

With this need in mind, in the following section we describe what we believe would be the main elements of an effective intervention. The intervention that we describe draws, in part, on the research findings that have been summarized in this chapter, as well as on research findings obtained in other areas of children's reactions to trauma (e.g., hurricanes: La Greca et al., 1996; Vernberg, La Greca, Silverman, & Prinstein, 1996). The intervention also draws on research findings obtained from clinical trials involving youth with anxiety disorders (e.g., Kendall, 1994; Kendall et al., 1997; Silverman et al., 1999a,b). We stress, however, that the intervention described represents, at this point, a general prototype. Refinement will likely occur as the intervention undergoes empirical scrutiny.

The basic intervention would be group cognitive behavioral treatment (GCBT). Thus, it would involve exposure-based exercises combined with relaxation techniques to decrease anxiety responses to traumatic reminders, as well as techniques to modify negative cognitions. Such techniques have been shown to be effective in treating PTSD for other types of trauma, so they would seem to be the most appropriate place to begin when developing a treatment program specifically for exposure to community violence. The same procedures that we have used in our clinic (Silverman et al., 1999a) could be adapted to a school-based intervention to be implemented by school personnel (e.g., school counselors). Because youth who have been exposed to crime and violence (often in school settings) are not likely to seek help for their distress through traditional modes of intervention, such as mental health clinics or private practice, it makes particular sense to work with them in the schools (Duncan, 1996; Goenjian et al., 1997; Osofsky, 1998; Pynoos & Nader, 1988; Warner & Weist, 1996).

A group format, in particular, also makes a great deal of sense for use in school settings because group treatment is more cost and time efficient than an individual treatment format. A group format also may be especially useful for working with youth who have been witnesses to or victims of crime and violence (Alessi & Hearn, 1984; Frederick, 1985) because group processes can facilitate the discussion of content related to the traumatic event. For example, within the group, discussions of children's reactions can be normalized and universalized (Frederick, 1985). A group format also is consistent with the fact that symptoms associated with posttraumatic stress often result from traumatic events that expose groups of individuals to crime or violence in public places (e.g., shootings in schools, stores, or restaurants; snipers; hostage taking). Thus, even when individuals do not experience exactly the same traumatic event, in cases such as exposure to crime and violence individuals experience very similar events. The group format thus provides a natural setting for individuals to address their shared experience. Other group processes available in GCBT include peer modeling (imitating the successful behavior of peers), peer reinforcement (being congratulated for success by peers), feedback (peer advice), and social comparison (comparing one's progress to that of others). The main foci of GCBT would be the reduction of posttraumatic stress reactions through exposure-based exercises, the enhanced use of adaptive coping responses, and the increase of social support availability and utilization.

Exposure-Based Exercises

There is general consensus that systematic exposure to traumatic cues (reminders) is essential in reducing symptoms associated with PTSD in youth and adults (e.g., Eth & Pynoos, 1985; Fairbank, Schlenger, Caddell, & Woods, 1993; Foa & Kozak, 1986; Keane & Kaloupek, 1982; Lyons, 1987). Although there are varying views among theorists and investigators as to why exposure works (see Barlow, 1988), in their discussion of emotional processing theory, Foa and Kozak (1986) recommended the use of some type of exposure-based procedure to (a) activate the fear memory and (b) provide new information that is incompatible with the current fear structure (also see Litz & Keane, 1989). In this frame, Foa and Kozak (1986) proposed that the use of systematic exposure-based procedures in a safe environment serves to modify the feared memory such that threat cues are reevaluated and habituated. Further, because most individuals who have experienced events as upsetting as crime and violence – either as a witness or as a victim – tend to have oppressive and overpowering emotions, they usually attempt to suppress or avoid these emotions. When they are successful in avoiding these oppressive emotions, individuals have described a complete numbing of affect (Resick & Schnicke, 1992). The use of exposure-based exercises is thereby also designed to encourage individuals' expressions of affect. Indeed, in the absence of such exposure, there is no guarantee that all of these emotions and their related beliefs will be sufficiently elicited so that they can be treated (Resick & Schnicke, 1992).

In working with children and adolescents who have been exposed to community violence, the use of drawing/writing and reading exercises is likely to be particularly useful in GCBT. The participants, for example, might be asked to draw pictures or to write stories about their experiences. These might then be shared with the other members of the group, and similarities and differences in experiences might be elaborated on through group discussion. Not only is this an effective method for helping young children explore their thoughts and feelings, but it is also a means of conducting systematic exposure.

Coping Skills Enhancement

Coping is critical in competency/vulnerability models of child and adolescent psychopathology (Rutter, 1990). In these models, coping is viewed as a process that may serve as a protective factor, helping to buffer individuals' responses to stressful life events. Exposure to crime and violence challenges the victim's or witness's capacity to generate adaptive coping responses, and in the absence of adaptive coping strategies, maladaptive ones may be developed. These might include self-blame, anger, withdrawal, and blaming others (Schepple & Bart, 1983). These maladaptive coping responses, moreover, if sufficiently intense, may facilitate the intrusive memories and avoidance reactions associated with post-traumatic stress (Resick & Schnicke, 1992) and interfere with successful emotional processing during the exposure-based exercise. In GCBT, coping skills enhancement would provide the youth with corrective information as it relates to a particular maladaptive coping response. Thus, coping skills enhancement (e.g., problem solving, cognitive restructuring, emotional regulation) would serve not only to improve the coping responses of the youth but also potentially to moderate the reduction of posttraumatic stress symptoms.

Social Support Availability and Utilization Enhancement

Peers serve as a major source of social support for youth (Levitt, 1991), and traumatic events deplete social support (Kaniasty & Norris, 1992). Existing evidence suggests that the broader and deeper the network of social support, the greater the chance of ameliorating the negative effects of stressful life events (Cohen & Wills, 1985; Kaniasty & Norris, 1992; Keppel-Benson & Ollendick, 1993). In GCBT, a main focus of the social support enhancement component would be on the group itself as a source of social support. In addition, an active effort would be made to enhance external sources of social support, both perceived and received (Kaniasty & Norris, 1992).

Thus, for example, in helping youth to identify support agents, it could be pointed out that they have more support than they think they have (perceived support), and the youth can be taught how to engage outside sources (e.g., parents, siblings, friends) as support agents (received support). To help accomplish this, behavioral strategies such as contingency contracting, modeling, role playing, and feedback can be used. Contingency contracting involves writing a contract that states a specific reward to be earned for successful completion of a specified task (e.g., making a social contact). Modeling involves watching others perform a behavior and then imitating that behavior. Role playing involves practicing the behavior before performing it in the real situation. Feedback involves critiquing the performance of a behavior by pointing out what was done well and how one might improve that which needs improvement. So, for example, if a child is timid and has difficulty asking others for advice (social support), we might start by practicing this behavior in the group (role playing). First, we might have a more extroverted child demonstrate before having the timid child try it (modeling). Members of the group can offer suggestions if the child gets stuck and congratulate the child if he or she does it well (feedback). Finally, the child might make a contract with the group that before the next group session the child will ask his or her teacher for advice. If the child does this, the group will have a pizza party to celebrate (contingency contracting).

IMPLICATIONS FOR SOCIAL POLICY

There are a number of ways that social policy can influence our success in dealing with the effects of community violence on young people. Social policy guides our work in terms of what types of interventions, if any, will be developed, implemented, and supported by our institutions on local, state, and national levels. Interventions can be divided into two types, prevention and treatment. Prevention strategies attempt to head off potential problems before they develop. Treatment strategies attempt to ameliorate the problems after they develop. In addition, both prevention and treatment programs can be aimed at either reducing community violence directly by targeting the perpetrators or reducing the negative effects of violence on young people by targeting the victims. Although our work has focused on the latter population, we advocate both approaches; accordingly, our suggestions for social policy address the need to develop successful prevention and treatment interventions for both victims and perpetrators.

Treatment and Prevention Interventions for Youth Who Have Been Exposed to Community Violence

With the growing recognition of the problem of youth exposure to crime and violence and its aftermath, a number of suggestions have been put forth for shaping social policy to address this problem (e.g., American Psychological Association [APA], 1993; Meyers & Wilcox, 1998; Osofsky, 1998).

One recommendation is to allocate increased funds for research to develop successful interventions for youth who have been exposed to crime and violence and who now suffer from posttraumatic stress reactions as a consequence. As this chapter has shown, there is a paucity of intervention research on both prevention and treatment. As a result, serious consideration of such policy would seem warranted.

Another recommendation is to move intervention efforts out of the clinic and into the schools. The value of conducting school-based interventions to help reduce the distress associated with exposure to crime and violence was mentioned earlier. Certainly, this is another recommendation that warrants serious consideration. Additionally, it has been recommended that attention be paid particularly to developing school-based interventions that target children in the early primary school grades. This recommendation is based on the suggestion that intervention efforts for children who have been exposed to community violence may be more effective with younger children than with older children because the former's exposure is often not as extensive and chronic as the latter's (Guerra & Grotpeter, 1999; Kostelny & Garbarino, 1999).

In terms of prevention interventions, recommendations have been made to invest more in research that aims to increase resilience in children. Garbarino, Dubrow, Kostelny, and Pardo (1992), for example, suggested that schools need to institutionalize caregiving, learning, and mental health as values that will support normal growth and development for children at risk. Garbarino et al. also suggested that teachers be given specific training in child development theory and practice as well as mental health skills. Finally, we note that the same strategies that were recommended in the preceding section for treating children exposed to crime and violence (e.g., enhancing appropriate coping and social support) can be adapted for use in prevention efforts that will enhance children's resilience. In other words, enhancing coping strategies and social support may help young people to deal more effectively with their problems, but in addition, teaching children effective coping strategies and developing their use of social support can stop many problems from developing in the first place.

Treatment and Prevention Interventions for Violent Behavior

Another approach to combating the deleterious effects of youths' exposure to community violence is to attack the problem of violence directly. That is, reduced violence could lead to reductions in the resultant problems of exposure to this violence. One social policy implication, therefore, is to direct increased energy and funding to programs that have the reduction of violence as their main goal. To this end, extensive work has been conducted on children and adolescents who have oppositional and/or conduct disorders (e.g., Dadds & McHugh, 1992; Kazdin 1991; Patterson, Reid, & Dishion, 1992; Webster-Stratton & Hammond, 1990), as these youth are at high risk for engaging in aggressive, violent, and criminal behavior. This work has involved developing and evaluating interventions that target the child as well as key parental and familial factors, such as parenting skills, parents' monitoring of their children, and the parent–child relationship.

In addition, within a transactional, contextual framework (e.g., Bronfenbrenner, 1979), social policy makers need to focus not just on the individual child and his or her family, but also on the school, the neighborhood, and society as a whole. In this frame, similar to the point made with respect to interventions for children who have been exposed to crime and violence, interventions for violent behavior need to be moved out of the clinic and into the schools and other community settings, such as community centers, outreach programs, and juvenile (and adult) correctional facilities. Specifically, schools are excellent sites not only for delivering more accessible services to children and their families, but also for reducing some of the more important correlates of aggression, such as academic failure and peer rejection (Hintze & Shapiro, 1999). Hence, school-based strategies that address children's learning problems, encourage children's success, and foster their social skills may assist in preventing individuals from turning to violence, aggression, and delinquency. For a discussion of individual and community-level precursors to juvenile violence, see the chapters in this volume by Salekin and by Fried and Reppucci.

At the neighborhood level, correlates of community violence include overcrowding, residential instability, poverty, and lack of effective law enforcement. In regard to overcrowding, for example, Mladenka and Hill (1976) reported a correlation of .70 between violence and population density. A high percentage of renters and frequent turnover of residents also are associated with residential instability, which also has been linked to increased rates of crime and violence (Limber & Nation, 1998). Residents in such neighborhoods tend to have less sense of belonging, less commitment, and less involvement in community affairs. Although poorer neighborhoods tend to have much higher rates of community violence than more affluent neighborhoods, unemployment is a better predictor of rates of crime and violence than is poverty alone (i.e., neighborhoods where most residents are "working poor" have much lower rates of crime and violence than neighborhoods that are high in unemployment; Garbarino, Kostelny, & Barry, 1998). A social policy implication of such findings is that community violence can be reduced by building a stronger community. Employment programs, community involvement projects, and zoning laws are just a few examples of how communities can be strengthened. Additionally, effective law enforcement, especially in conjunction with community policing, can help prevent problems rather than just respond to them (APA, 1993).

Finally, at the societal level, the problems of media violence, teen drug and alcohol abuse, availability of guns, and issues of social injustice have all been implicated. In regard to violence on television and in the movies, it has been suggested, for example, that the increase in graphic scenes of violence desensitizes children and encourages callousness, and that exposure to violent role models in action/adventure films affects children's attitudes toward and acceptance of violent behavior (APA, 1993). Abuse of alcohol and drugs also has been linked to violent and criminal behavior. According to Roth (1994), alcohol drinking precedes one-half of all violent crimes, including murder. Firearms have been found to have an even more direct link to violent crime. Over 5,000 children and adolescents died from firearm fatalities in 1991, and the pediatric firearm homicide rate tripled between 1985 and 1992, leading Christoffel (1997) to refer to this problem as an "epidemic phenomenon" (p. 55). In terms of social injustice, the frustrations of ethnic minorities as a result of being victims of discrimination and socioeconomic inequality place them at higher risk for violent behavior (Feshbach & Feshbach, 1998; Slaby, 1998). Alienation and marginalization create an atmosphere of animosity toward the dominant culture and its institutions. Here too, social policy can be used to intervene on these issues. Although there is a great deal of debate and controversy over specific legislation that might reduce the previously mentioned contributors to the increase in violence (e.g., v-chips in televisions, gun control, affirmative action), few would disagree with the need to address these issues at a societal level, as well as for programs that would promote education and public awareness (Meyers & Wilcox, 1998; Osofsky, 1997).

SUMMARY AND CONCLUSION

Although reactions to exposure to crime and violence are complex and multifaceted, distress symptoms associated with posttraumatic stress are a central feature of the distress reaction that youth exhibit when exposed to crime and violence. In addition to the adverse psychological consequences, exposure to crime and violence challenges the victim's and witness's capacity to generate adaptive coping responses and to access and utilize social support. Unfortunately, the population most at risk (i.e., low-socioeconomic multiethnic urban youth) is not likely to seek help for distress symptoms associated with exposure to crime and violence through traditional modes of intervention (e.g., mental health clinics, private practice). In addition, crime and violence have become so much a part of the culture of modern American life that exposure to such traumatic events among many youth has become the norm. Consequently, the effects of exposure to community violence are frequently not recognized by youth as problems in need of mental health services. Thus, the need for development and implementation of community and school-based interventions is considerable. Although the exact nature and content of intervention programs will evolve as empirical research findings in this area become available, basic elements that we outlined in this chapter for such programs include the following: First, it would be a school-based group cognitive behavioral intervention; second, it would use exposure-based exercises; third, it would enhance individuals' use of adaptive coping skills; and fourth, it would enhance the availability and utilization of individuals' social support (both perceived and received).

A number of suggestions have been made in the literature for shaping social policy to address the problem of community violence and its negative psychological consequences. These suggestions have involved developing and evaluating prevention and treatment interventions that target individuals who have been exposed to crime and violence and who now experience symptoms of posttraumatic stress reactions as a result. These suggestions also have involved developing and evaluating prevention and treatment interventions for violent behavior. Because the problem of community violence is embedded in a contextual system, successful interventions would need to intervene at multiple levels: individual, family, school, neighborhood, and society.

The challenges in dealing with community violence and its aftermath are formidable, but we owe it to our nation's youth to meet these challenges. We hope this chapter will stimulate research efforts that will meet these challenges.

References

Albano, A. M., Miller, P. P., Zarate, R., Cote, G., & Barlow, D. H. (1997). Behavioral assessment and treatment of PTSD in prepubertal children: Attention to developmental factors and innovative strategies in the case study of a family. *Cognitive and Behavioral Practice, 4,* 245–262.

Alessi, J. J., & Hearn, K. (1984). Group treatment of children in shelters for battered women. In A. R. Roberts (Ed.), *Battered women and their families: Intervention strategies and treatment programs* (pp. 49–61). New York: Springer.

American Psychiatric Association. (1980). *Diagnostic and statistical manual of mental disorders* (3rd ed.). Washington, DC: Author.

American Psychiatric Association. (1987). *Diagnostic and statistical manual of mental disorders* (3rd ed. revised). Washington, DC: Author.

American Psychological Association. (1993). *Violence and youth: Psychology's response: Vol. I. Summary of the American Psychological Association Commission on Violence and Youth.* Washington, DC: Author.

Barlow, D. H. (1988). *Anxiety and its disorders: The nature and treatment of anxiety and panic.* New York: Guilford Press.

Berman, S. L., Kurtines, W. M., Silverman, W. K., & Serafini, L. T. (1996). The impact of exposure to crime and violence on urban youth. *American Journal of Orthopsychiatry, 66,* 329–336.

Bronfenbrenner, U. (1979). *The ecology of human development: Experiments by nature and design.* Cambridge, MA: Harvard University Press.

Christoffel, K. K. (1997). Firearm injuries affecting U.S. children and adolescents. In J. D. Osofsky (Ed.), *Children in a violent society* (pp. 42–71). New York: Guilford Press.

Cohen, S., & Wills, T. A. (1985). Stress, social support, and the buffering hypothesis. *Psychological Bulletin, 98,* 310–357.

Dadds, M. R., & McHugh, T. A. (1992). Social support and treatment outcome in behavioral family-therapy for child conduct problems. *Journal of Consulting and Clinical Psychology, 60,* 252–259.

Davies, W. H., & Flannery, D. J. (1998). Post-traumatic stress disorder in children and adolescents exposed to violence. *Pediatric Clinics of North America, 45,* 341–353.

Duncan, D. F. (1996). Growing up under the gun: Children and adolescents coping with violent neighborhoods. *The Journal of Primary Prevention, 16,* 343–356.

Ensink, K., Robertson, B. A., Zissis, C., & Leger, P. (1997). Post-traumatic stress disorder in children exposed to violence. *South African Medical Journal, 87,* 1526–1530.

Eth, S., & Pynoos, R. (1985). *Post-traumatic stress disorder in children.* Washington, DC: American Psychiatric Press.

Fairbank, J. A., Schlenger, W. E., Caddell, J. M., & Woods, M. G. (1993). Posttraumatic stress disorder. In P. B. Sutter & H. E. Adams (Eds.), *Comprehensive handbook of psychopathology* (pp. 145–165). New York: Plenum Press.

Farrell, S. P., Hains, A. A., & Davies, W. H. (1998). Cognitive behavioral interventions for sexually abused children exhibiting post-traumatic stress disorder symptomatology. *Behavior Therapy, 29,* 241–255.

Feshbach, N. D., & Feshbach, S. (1998). Aggression in the schools: Toward reducing ethnic conflict and enhancing ethnic understanding. In P. K. Trickett & C. J. Schellenbach (Eds.), *Violence against children in the family and the community* (pp. 269–286). Washington, DC: American Psychological Association.

Fitzpatric, K. M., & Boldizar, J. P. (1993). The prevalence and consequences of exposure to violence among African-American youth. *Journal of the American Academy of Child and Adolescent Psychiatry, 32,* 424–430.

Foa, E. B., & Kozak, M. J. (1986). Emotional processing of fear: Exposure to corrective information. *Psychological Bulletin, 99,* 20–35.

Frederick, C. (1985). Selected foci in the spectrum of post-traumatic stress disorders. In J. Laube & S. Murphy (Eds.), *Perspectives on disaster recovery* (pp. 110–130). East Norwalk, CT: Appleton-Century-Crofts.

Garbarino, J., Dubrow, N., Kostelny, K., & Pardo, C. (1992). *Children in danger: Coping with the consequences of community violence.* San Francisco, CA: Jossey-Bass.

Garbarino, J., Kostelny, K., & Barry, F. (1998). Neighborhood-based programs. In P. K. Trickett & C. J. Schellenbach (Eds.), *Violence against children in the family and the community* (pp. 287–314). Washington, DC: American Psychological Association.

Glodich, A. (1998). Traumatic exposure to violence: A comprehensive review of the child and adolescent literature. *Smith College Studies in Social Work, 68,* 321–345.

Goenjian, A. K., Karayan, I., Pynoos, R. S., Minassian, D., Najarian, L. M., Steinberg, A. M., & Fairbank, J. A. (1997). Outcome of psychotherapy among early adolescents after trauma. *American Journal of Psychiatry, 154,* 536–542.

Guerra, N. G., & Grotpeter, J. K. (1999, April). Long-term impact of violence exposure on behavior and social cognition among inner-city children. In A. Shahinfar & J. B. Kupersmidt (Chairs), *Community violence and its relation to children's cognitions about their social worlds.* Symposium conducted at the biennial meeting of the Society for Research in Child Development, Albuquerque, NM.

Hintze, J. M., & Shapiro, E. S. (1999). School. In W. K. Silverman & T. H. Ollendick (Eds.), *Developmental issues in the clinical treatment of children* (pp. 156–170). Needhom Hts., MA: Allyn and Bacon.

Horowitz, K., Weine, S., & Jekel, J. (1995). PTSD symptoms in urban adolescent girls: Compounded community trauma. *Journal of the American Academy on Child and Adolescent Psychiatry, 34,* 1353–1361.

Jenkins, E. J., & Bell, C. C. (1994). Violence exposure, psychological distress, and high risk behaviors among inner-city high school students. In S. Friedman (Ed.), *Anxiety disorders in African-Americans* (pp. 76–88). New York: Springer.

Kaniasty, K., & Norris, F. (1992). Social support and victims of crime: Matching event, support, and outcome. *American Journal of Community Psychology, 20,* 211–241.

Kazdin, A. E. (1991). Effectiveness of psychotherapy with children and adolescents. *Journal of Consulting and Clinical Psychology, 59,* 785–798.

Keane, T. M., & Kalovpek, D. G. (1982). Imaginal flooding in the treatment of post-traumatic stress disorder. *Journal of Consulting and Clinical Psychology, 50,* 138–140.

Kendall, P. C. (1994). Treating anxiety disorders in children: Results of a randomized clinical trial. *Journal of Consulting and Clinical Psychology, 62,* 200–210.

Kendall, P. C., Flannery-Schroeder, E., Panichelli-Mindel, S. M., Southam-Gerov, M., Henin, A., & Warman, M. (1997). Therapy for youths with anxiety disorders: A second randomized clinical trial. *Journal of Consulting and Clinical Psychology, 65,* 366–380.

Keppel-Benson, J. M., & Ollendick, T. H. (1993). Posttraumatic stress disorder in children and adolescents. In C. F. Saylor (Ed.), *Children and disasters* (pp. 29–43). New York: Plenum Press.

Kliewer, W., Lepore, S. J., Oskin, D., & Johnson, P. D. (1998). The role of social and cognitive processes in children's adjustment to community violence. *Journal of Consulting and Clinical Psychology, 66,* 199–209.

Kostelny, K. L., & Garbarino, J. (1999, April). Perceptions of danger and aggressive behavior in children exposed to family and community violence. In A. Shahinfar & J. B. Kupersmidt (Chairs), *Community violence and its relation to children's cognitions about their social worlds.* Symposium conducted at the biennial meeting of the Society for Research in Child Development, Albuquerque, NM.

La Greca, A. M., Silverman, W. K., Vernberg, E. M., & Prinstein, M. J. (1996). Symptoms of posttraumatic stress in children after hurricane Andrew: A prospective study. *Journal of Consulting and Clinical Psychology, 64,* 712–723.

Levitt, M. J. (1991). Attachment and close relationships: A life-span perspective. In J. L. Gerwitz & W. M. Kurtines (Eds.), *Intersections with attachment* (pp. 183–205). Hillsdale, NJ: Erlbaum.

Limber, S. P., & Nation, M. A. (1998). Violence within the neighborhood and community. In P. K. Trickett & C. J. Schellenbach (Eds.), *Violence against children in the family and the community* (pp. 171–193). Washington, DC: American Psychological Association.

Litz, B. T., & Keane, T. M. (1989). Information processing in anxiety disorders: Application to the understanding of post-traumatic stress disorder. *Clinical Psychology Review, 9,* 243–257.

Lyons, J. A. (1987). Post-traumatic stress disorder in children and adolescents: A review of the literature. *Journal of Developmental and Behavioral Pediatrics, 8,* 349–356.

March, J. S., Amaya-Jackson, L., Murray, M. C., & Schulte, A. (1998). Cognitive-behavioral psychotherapy for children and adolescents with posttraumatic stress disorder after a single-incident stressor. *Journal of the American Academy of Child and Adolescent Psychiatry, 37,* 585–593.

Martinez, P., & Richters, J. E. (1993). The NIMH community violence project: II. Children's distress symptoms associated with violence exposure. *Psychiatry, 56,* 22–35.

Meyers, J. C., & Wilcox, B. L. (1998). Public policy applications of research on violence and children. In P. K. Trickett & C. J. Schellenbach (Eds.), *Violence against children in the family and the community* (pp. 465–478). Washington, DC: American Psychological Association.

Mladenka, K., & Hill, K. (1976). A reexamination of the etiology of urban crime. *Criminology, 13,* 491–506.

Morales, M. A., & Reisner, N. (1999, May 17). Miami, Lauderdale show drop in crime: Cities lower on top 10 list. *The Miami Herald,* pp. 1A, 8A.

Osofsky, J. D. (1997). Prevention and policy: Directions for the future. In J. D. Osofsky (Ed.), *Children in a violent society* (pp. 323–328). New York: Guilford Press.

Osofsky, J. D. (1998). Children exposed to marital violence: Theory, research and applied issues. In G. W. Holden, R. Geffner, & E. N. Jouriles (Eds.), *Children as invisible victims of domestic and community violence* (pp. 95–117). Washington, DC: American Psychological Association.

Parson, E. R. (1997). Posttraumatic child therapy (P-TCT): Assessment and treatment factors in clinical work with inner-city children exposed to catastrophic community violence. *Journal of Interpersonal Violence, 12,* 172–194.

Patterson, G. R., Reid, J. B., & Dishion, T. J. (1992). *Antisocial boys*. Eugene, OR: Castalia.

Pynoos, R. S., & Nader, K. (1988). Psychological first aid and treatment approach to children exposed to community violence: Research implications. *Journal of Traumatic Stress, 1*, 445–473.

Resick, P. A., & Schnicke, M. K. (1992). Cognitive processing therapy for sexual assault victims. *Journal of Consulting and Clinical Psychology, 60*, 748–756.

Richters, J. E., & Martinez, P. (1993). The NIMH community violence project: I. Children as victims of and witnesses to violence. *Psychiatry, 56*, 7–21.

Roth, J. A. (1994). *Psychoactive substances and violence*. Washington, DC: U.S. Government Printing Office.

Rutter, M. (1990). Psychosocial resilience and protective mechanisms. In J. Rolf, A. S. Masten, D. Cicchetti, K. H. Nuechterlein, & S. Weintraub (Eds.), *Risk and protective factors in the development of psychopathology*. New York: Cambridge University Press.

Schepple, K. L., & Bart, P. B. (1983). Through women's eyes: Defining danger in the wake of sexual assault. *Journal of Social Issues, 39*, 63–81.

Schwab-Stone, M. E., Ayers, T. S., Kasprow, W., Voyce, C., Barone, C., Shriver, T., & Weissberg, R. P. (1995). No safe haven: A study of violence exposure in an urban community. *Journal of the American Academy of Child and Adolescent Psychiatry, 34*, 1343–1352.

Silverman, W. K., Kurtines, W. M., Ginsburg, G. S., Weems, C. F., Lumpkin, P. W., & Carmichael, D. H. (1999a). Treating anxiety disorders in children with group cognitive-behavior therapy: A randomized clinical trial. *Journal of Consulting and Clinical Psychology, 67*, 995–1003.

Silverman, W. K., Kurtines, W. M., Ginsburg, G. S., Weems, C. F., Rabian, B., & Serafini, L. T. (1999b). Contingency management, self-control, and education support in the treatment of childhood phobic disorders: A randomized clinical trial. *Journal of Consulting and Clinical Psychology, 67*, 675–687.

Slaby, R. G. (1998). Preventing youth violence through research-guided intervention. In P. K. Trickett & C. J. Schellenbach (Eds.), *Violence against children in the family and the community* (pp. 371–399). Washington, DC: American Psychological Association.

Vernberg, E. M., La Greca, A. M., Silverman, W. K., & Prinstein, M. J. (1996). Prediction of post-traumatic stress symptoms in children after hurricane Andrew. *Journal of Abnormal Psychology, 105*, 237–248.

Warner, B. S., & Weist, M. D. (1996). Urban youth as witness to violence: Beginning assessment and treatment efforts. *Journal of Youth and Adolescence, 25*, 361–377.

Webster-Stratton, C., & Hammond, M. (1990). Predictors of treatment outcome in parent training for families with conduct problem children. *Behavior Therapy, 21*, 319–337.

13

Preventing Child Abuse and Neglect

Mia McFarlane
Howard J. Doueck
Murray Levine

In terms of numbers alone, child maltreatment is a significant social problem. Although recent studies suggest that rates of some types of maltreatment, especially sexual abuse, have decreased markedly in the last decade (Jones & Finkelhor, 2001), overall many children are harmed each year. For example, using a standard of "demonstrable harm as a result of maltreatment," it has been estimated that 1,553,800, or 23.1/1,000 children, were victims of maltreatment during 1993 (U.S. Department of Health and Human Services, 1996, pp. 2–9).

In this chapter, we review some examples of newly developed programs, community-based initiatives, and recent legislation designed and implemented to prevent child maltreatment. In this context, we find that although there have been some successes, such programs and legislation are as likely to have been driven by values, biases, and political considerations as they are to have been driven by a research-based understanding of the problem. Stated differently, there tends to be a gap between what we know empirically about prevention and what ultimately gets implemented. We conclude the chapter with some comments about how social scientists might help bridge this gap.

We gratefully acknowledge the Baldy Center for Law and Social Policy, University at Buffalo, State University of New York, for funding this project and for its continued support of our work.

PREVENTING CHILD ABUSE AND NEGLECT

The U.S. Advisory Board on Child Abuse and Neglect (ABCAN) (1990) described the problem of child maltreatment and the system developed to help solve that problem as a national emergency. In a subsequent report, they called for a preventive strategy that would be "comprehensive, child-centered, family-focused, and neighborhood-based" (U.S. ABCAN, 1993, p. 16; see Small & Limber, this volume).

Consistent with an ecological perspective (see, e.g., Levine & Perkins, 1997), recent federal legislation supports preventive efforts aimed at the community and neighborhood levels (see e.g., 42 U.S.C. §5116 and 42 U.S.C. §5106a(a)(9)). This perspective is based on a focus on the interactions between the individual and his/or her environment, as opposed to a focus either solely on the individual or solely on the environment. In other words, to help individuals, one must build and strengthen the resources within the environment and remove barriers to resource access that may exist in the environment (Barry, 1994). Our research has identified a number of interesting programs that take that approach.

Home Visitation

Olds and his associates have studied prenatal and early childhood home visitation programs for over 20 years (Olds, 1997). Their initial project employed trained nurses and was designed to improve pregnancy outcomes, parental caregiving, and maternal life-course development among low-income Whites. The nurses helped fathers and other relatives to plan for the baby's birth. Visiting regularly after the baby was born, they taught child care and advised about problems with infant and child health and development. In addition, the nurses helped mothers think about birth control and about returning to school or obtaining training. The initial study reported that home visitation significantly reduced subsequent reports of child maltreatment, especially among young mothers, compared to the control group. A 15-year follow-up of the first families indicates that home visitation programs can reduce child maltreatment, other violence, conduct disorders, and prenatal health risks, among other problems. Preliminary findings in Memphis, Tennessee, a city with predominantly low-income African American families, indicated similar positive results.

Hawaii's Healthy Start program, which began in 1985 in Oahu and subsequently expanded statewide between 1988 and 1990 (National Institute of Justice, 1995, pp. 4–5), and Healthy Families America, National Committee to Prevent Child Abuse, with more than 300 programs in 40 states and the District of Columbia (NCPCA, 1998), are two examples of large-scale home visiting programs.

Home visiting is not a panacea; it reduces but does not eliminate child maltreatment (U.S. ABCAN, 1995). However, the Advisory Board considers such programs particularly important in light of studies showing that in 75% or more of child abuse and neglect fatalities, the victim is under the age of 5 and therefore would not be observed in school (U.S. ABCAN, 1995).

Other Programs

The National Center on Child Abuse and Neglect (NCCAN) has funded nine community or neighborhood demonstration projects (NCCAN, n.d.; for a detailed description of two such programs, see Hay & Jones, 1994; Mulroy, 1997). Each of these projects includes public awareness programs and parenting education and support programs, including home visitation and community-based task forces that plan, implement, and supervise the programs (NCCAN, n.d.). However, because of complex community dynamics and other issues, evaluations of neighborhood programs tend to be difficult to carry out, and more rigorous research on the effectiveness of these programs is needed (Korbin & Coulton, 1996).

Challenges to Community-Based Intervention Programs

Given the relationship between poverty and child maltreatment, child abuse prevention programs without an antipoverty component may not be completely effective (Hay & Jones, 1994). Changes to our welfare system may place greater demands on an already overburdened child protection system. Though recent studies indicate no increase in child abuse reports as a result of welfare reform (see Sengupta, 2000), it is probably too soon to determine with much certainty. Regardless, many families may experience increased stress from juggling work requirements and parenting responsibilities while trying to survive on time-limited benefits (Courtney, 1998; see also Wilcox, Colman, & Wyatt, this volume, for an extended discussion of this issue). For example, it is quite probable that some mothers will need to choose between neglecting their children's medical needs or losing pay when they take time off to minister to their children.

PREVENTING CHILD SEXUAL ABUSE

Unlike the programs developed for preventing physical abuse and neglect, the current approach for preventing sexual abuse has not yet evolved into a comprehensive public health strategy (Krugman, 1996). In part this may be because the risk factors associated with identifying potential offenders or victims are less clear for sexual abuse than for physical abuse and neglect and because society tends to be uneasy about issues of sexuality (Daro, 1994). Regardless, prevention of sexual abuse has generally focused on school-based prevention programs or legislative and criminal responses to the offender after abuse has occurred.

School-Based Prevention Programs

School-based sexual abuse prevention programs are not without controversy. They have been criticized as being overly simplistic (Wurtele, 1997), unfair and unrealistic (Melton, 1992), and whose growth has outpaced the evaluation of their effectiveness (U.S. GAO, 1996). Though the results of research on this point are mixed, such programs have also been criticized for possibly increasing children's fears and anxieties (Daro, 1994; U.S. GAO, 1996). Further, because such programs tend to focus on sexual abuse or stranger danger (as opposed to incest and other forms of sexual mistreatment), it is difficult for children to grasp the concept that the abuser may be a family member or another known and trusted adult (Daro, 1994; Finkelhor & Strapko, 1992; U.S. GAO, 1996). Because children are physically smaller and developmentally less mature than adults, they are vulnerable to abuse regardless of program outcomes (Daro, 1994). Despite these reservations, a survey of nearly 400 elementary school districts from 29 randomly selected counties across the nation found that 85% of the districts had at least one school that offered a sexual abuse education program within the year preceding the study, and 64% of the districts had mandated these programs (Daro, 1994).

School-based sexual abuse prevention programs vary in content, teaching methods, and duration. However, most programs address the distinction between a "good touch" and a "bad touch," children's right to control where they are touched and by whom, assertiveness training, the importance of disclosing abuse, and information about where the child can turn for help (Daro, 1994).

Evaluation of these programs has suffered from some of the same design flaws often seen in social research, including lack of a comparison or control group, lack of pretests to determine baseline measures of children's knowledge or skill, and inadequate follow-up (U.S. GAO, 1996).

Regardless, despite serious questions about whether school-based educational programs prevent future abuse, the programs may be useful for other reasons. They may help children to disclose past or current abuse (Finkelhor & Strapko, 1992; U.S. GAO, 1996), and as a result may halt ongoing abuse even if they fail to prevent future abuse (Daro, 1994). Further, a potential offender may be deterred by a child who says that he or she would tell a specific adult (Budin & Johnson, 1989; Conte, Wolf, & Smith, 1989). Finally, these programs may help mitigate some of the trauma of sexual abuse by helping victims feel that they are not alone, that this type of abuse has happened to others (Finkelhor & Strapko, 1992).

School-based sexual abuse prevention programs have been described as the "great social experiment of the 1980s" (Finkelhor & Strapko, 1992, p. 150). The programs began as a quick way to take action against a problem that had been gaining considerable media attention. In California in the early 1980s, a few well-publicized child abductions and the McMartin Preschool case preceded the passage of the state's Child Abuse Prevention Training Act of 1984, which provided for school-based sexual abuse education programs

(Berrick & Gilbert, 1991). The urgent need to do something to prevent sexual abuse led to the implementation of programs that view
all children as potential victims before they could be systematically
evaluated (Finkelhor & Strapko, 1992; Berrick & Gilbert, 1991). Arguably, if policy had followed research or if research about sexual
abuse had kept pace with the public demand for action, the prevention of sexual abuse might have evolved into a system of multiple
approaches rather than a single focus (Daro, 1994).

However, because research on the effectiveness of school-based
sexual abuse prevention programs seems to be lacking, should these
programs be continued? It is possible that the very existence of such
programs may give parents, educators, legislators, and others the
false sense that something is being done to combat sexual abuse
(Berrick & Gilbert, 1991, 1994). This false sense of security coupled
with the sunk costs of programs already in place may reduce the
willingness of community leaders, educators, and researchers to
develop, evaluate, and invest in other potentially more effective
programs. Finally, the existence of a school-based program aimed
at primary prevention may tend to mute the development of a more
comprehensive approach to preventing sexual abuse. As the next
section shows, it may be time to consider school-based programs
as a single component of a comprehensive sexual abuse prevention
strategy.

Community-Based Prevention Programs

School-based sexual abuse programs may be beneficial in some
ways, but they should be only one part of a more comprehensive community effort to prevent abuse (Daro, 1994; Finkelhor &
Strapko, 1992; U.S. GAO, 1996). The prevention of abuse has been
described as a process of altering risk and protective factors in
potential abusers, in potential victims, and in the environment
in which the abuse takes place (Daro, 1994; Wurtele, 1997). Therefore, an effective prevention strategy must include more than programs focused solely on children.

Daro (1994) suggests an interesting approach, including programs aimed at primary, secondary, and tertiary prevention. Such
an approach might include programs of public awareness, parent

education, life skills training for young adults, support groups for vulnerable children and adults, and treatment for offenders. In addition, media campaigns and parent education might emphasize adult responsibility for protecting children. Parent education could emphasize the importance of communication between parents and children so that children feel safe to disclose abuse by other adults. These programs might be linked to the school-based education programs for children or incorporated in home visiting services or other comprehensive efforts that address all forms of maltreatment. In addition to parent education, greater access to quality child care and afterschool programs might also be a priority in any prevention strategy.

Although high-risk groups are not easily identified, there does appear to be an increased risk of sexual abuse, particularly for girls, in troubled families or families in transition (Melton, 1992). Voluntary community-based support groups for adults experiencing separation, divorce, domestic violence, or teenage parenting may be an effective approach to prevention (Daro, 1994).

Because many single teenage mothers have experienced sexual abuse, some sexual abuse prevention programs have been designed especially for this group (Garbarino & Kostelny, 1994). More may be necessary. Young women may need to be taught how to deal with coercion and males to forego coercion.

Perpetrator-Focused Programs

Perpetrators who commit crimes against children should also be the targets of prevention programs. We will describe several approaches – mandating treatment for offenders, community notification of the presence of an offender in a neighborhood, and statutes that incapacitate repeat offenders.

Mandated Treatment. It is difficult to develop voluntary treatment programs for sexual abuse offenders. Even if offenders are willing to participate, the stigma attached to sexual abuse and the fear of criminal prosecution may prevent offenders from coming forward. Research conducted at the Johns Hopkins Sexual Disorders Clinic in Baltimore is illustrative. In 1989, changes in Maryland law mandated psychiatrists to report any disclosures of child sexual abuse by adult patients, including disclosures of all child sexual abuse even if the abuse occurred before the adult entered treatment. A year after this law took effect, the number of self-referrals dropped to zero (Berlin, Malin, & Dean, 1991). This clinic served criminally sophisticated clients. They may have known or were advised of the implications of the law. In contrast, Kalichman (1991) showed there was no change in reporting of sexual abuse statewide in other Maryland clinics after the law changed.

In the absence of public sympathy for offenders, support for publicly funded treatment may only be provided once the perpetrator is incarcerated, and given the criminal justice system's shift away from rehabilitation toward a more "tough on crime" approach, it is unlikely that most offenders will receive treatment when they are behind bars (see U.S. Supreme Court Justice Stephen Breyer's dissent in *Kansas v. Hendricks*, 1997). Tougher criminal laws have been enacted in recent years to address the problem of sexual abuse.

Sex Offender Registration and Community Notification Laws.
Most sex offender registration and community notification legislation has been enacted in a crisis atmosphere in response to highly publicized tragedies. Laws passed in this atmosphere generally do not allow for thoughtful and considered debate or examination of the likely effectiveness or potential unintended consequences of the legislation.

In 1994, the Jacob Wetterling Crimes Against Children and Sexually Violent Offender Registration Act (P.L. 103–322) was enacted. This federal legislation was named after Jacob Wetterling, who was 11 years old when a masked man in St. Joseph, Minnesota, abducted him at gunpoint. Neither Jacob nor the abductor was ever found. Based on a 1990 Department of Justice study, the House of Representatives determined that there are approximately 114,000 nonfamily attempted child abductions each year. Although most attempts are unsuccessful, as many as 4,600 children disappear each year. Two-thirds of these cases involve sexual assault. Child sex offenders are often serial offenders; 74% of imprisoned child sex offenders had one or more prior convictions for a sexual offense against a child (H.R. Rep. 103–392). The Wetterling Act was designed to protect children from abduction and sexual assault by strangers. Though perhaps important, a majority of sexual abuse cases involve perpetrators related or known to the victim.

The Wetterling Act provided for the states to implement systems in which persons who have kidnapped or committed sexual crimes against children must register their address with a state law enforcement agency (P.L. 103–322). The Act was amended in 1996 to require state compliance by 1997 in order to avoid losing federal funds (H.R. 104–555). States now had to release relevant information about sex offenders to protect the public (P.L. 104–145).

When the Wetterling Act was originally passed in 1994, 24 states had already passed sex offender registration statutes (H.R. Rep. 103–392), and some states had adopted community notification laws as well. Like the federal legislation, state laws were passed in response to highly publicized crimes against children. Washington was the first state to enact a community notification law in addition to an offender registration requirement (Matson & Lieb, 1996). Washington's law was passed in 1990 after a 7-year-old boy, lured into a wooded area, was raped and mutilated by a recently released sex offender with an extensive criminal record (Steinbock, 1995).

The name most frequently associated with community notification legislation comes from another tragedy that took place in New Jersey. On July 29, 1994, 7-year-old Megan Kanka was lured to the home of a neighbor who sexually assaulted and killed her. The perpetrator, Jesse Temmendequas, had two previous convictions for child sexual abuse, and he was living with two other previously convicted sex offenders (Steinbock, 1995). "Megan's Law" was passed in New Jersey in response to public outrage that sex offenders could live in their communities without notification of neighbors (Steinbock, 1995). The 1996 amendments to the federal Wetterling Act, adopted the name "Megan's Law" for the federal legislation as well (P.L. 104–145).

Community notification statutes vary in each state. Some provide for broad notification, including releasing information in newspapers and on the Internet; others require notification only to those individuals or organizations at risk, such as neighbors and schools; and still others keep registries at law enforcement agencies that are open for inspection by certain members of the public

(Matson & Lieb, 1997). New York's Sex Offender Registration Act created a board of examiners to provide recommendations regarding an offender's level of risk to the community to a judge prior to the offender's release (N.Y. Corrections § 168–1). The entities notified depend on the board's determination of the risk that the offender will commit another crime. For example, high-risk offenders are given a level three designation and are deemed "sexually violent predators." Information regarding these offenders is maintained in a separate directory and is made available to the general public on request (§ 168–1(6)(c)).

Although sex offender registration and community notification laws have received broad support, some community members have criticized them, mostly on constitutional grounds (e.g., equal protection: why not all offenders, not just sex offenders?; subject to additional loss of liberty and reputation; double jeopardy; ex post facto; cruel and unusual punishment; invasion of privacy; and due process) but also for possible unintended consequences such as vigilante responses to offenders. Perhaps the most unusual case of vigilantism occurred in Wales, where the home of a pediatrician was vandalized because her title was confused with pedophile ("Welsh doctor mistaken," 2000). Megan's laws also frame the issue of protecting the public from sexual abuse as the prevention of stranger danger. These laws may help prevent future abuse by sexually violent predators, although no research has yet made that determination.

Sexual Predator Statutes. Sexual predator statutes presumably prevent sex offenses by incapacitating repeated sex offenders who are considered to have a "mental abnormality." The U.S. Supreme Court in *Kansas v. Hendricks* (1997) upheld a statute that permitted the civil commitment of sexually violent predators after they completed criminal sentences. Leroy Hendricks served 10 years in prison for sexually molesting young boys. Toward the end of his prison sentence, Hendricks was screened by mental health and corrections professionals, who determined that he was a candidate for classification as a sexually violent predator. Under the law, he was then subject to a jury trial to determine if he was a sexual predator. At the trial, he testified that he could not say he would not molest children again if freed. Based on his testimony and expert testimony that he was suffering from the mental abnormality of pedophilia, the jury found he was a sexual predator. Following completion of his criminal sentence, under the law, he was civilly committed to a secure mental health facility outside the prison system. He was no longer being punished for his crime, but he was now subject to treatment for his "mental abnormality." He could be kept in the institution indefinitely if treatment is not effective. The law is justified on the basis that sexual offenders are refractory to rehabilitation efforts and have very high recidivism rates.

The U.S. Supreme Court held that the standard of mental abnormality was sufficient to guard against arbitrary imposition of loss of liberty. The Court was not concerned about the adequacy of treatment nor about the limits of prediction in identifying accurately those who will recidivate and those who will not. Recidivism rates vary with the measure used (self-report of committing another offense, arrest for another offense of any kind, arrest for a sexual offense, conviction of a sexual offense). The best estimate is that the overall recidivism rate (based on a subsequent conviction) for sex offenders averages about 13.4% over a 4- to 5-year follow-up period. That rate rises with increased follow-up periods. Over a 25-year period, the recidivism rate may be 40%. That figure does not tell us how many offenses the perpetrator may have committed without getting caught (Hanson, 1998; also see the entire issue of *Psychology, Public Policy, and Law, 4,* 1998).

We have limited ability to predict which sex offenders will recidivate. The best-validated predictors are static. That is, they are based on factors such as having a history of previous offenses, a diagnosis of antisocial personality disorder, being young at the time of the offense, never having been married, and having molested unrelated or male children. Predictors and recidivism rates may be different for those convicted of child molestation and those convicted of rape.

Using empirically validated predictors, we may be able to identify accurately those few who have the highest risk of reoffending. However, would officials and juries be that selective, admitting only the highest-risk sexual predators to treatment facilities? Would they admit many with a moderate risk and some with a low risk of reoffending because the law is biased toward keeping the community safe from such offenders? We may have some effective treatment techniques (e.g. cognitive behavior approaches; conditioning techniques – Becker & Murphy, 1998). However, we do not have validated measures showing that individuals have indeed overcome their "mental abnormality" and can now be safely released. Release decisions will always pit unchanging predictors based on history (i.e., static factors) against unvalidated measures that purportedly reflect personality and attitude change – for example, a change in sexual orientation, greater compassion for victims, more self control (i.e., dynamic factors). (See Winick & La Fond, 1998, for a thorough discussion of these and related issues.)

Sexual predator statutes were a response to community outrage and to political pressure to incarcerate sexual offenders. If someone is released who then reoffends, the public outcry will be much greater than the outcry about our other failures of prediction, those that result in keeping some persons who would not recidivate incarcerated unnecessarily. The system is inevitably biased toward retention. If we incarcerate at a greater rate than we release, and we do not increase resources to keep up with the increasing prison population, these facilities will quickly become overcrowded. Given that adequately trained personnel to provide treatment are already in short supply, and given the lack of political will to commit resources to a very costly venture (maximum-security incarceration), within a few years these facilities will be subject to charges of scandalous care (La Fond, 1998).

The sexual predator statute is an excellent example of "problem creation through problem solution." We will have solved one problem, that of repeat offenders, but at a high financial price and eventually a great social cost. The problem of protecting society against sexual predators may not be amenable to a technological solution, but it forces us to examine the values that underlie our efforts to solve intractable social problems (Sarason, 1978).

Mandated Reporting

Mandated reporting was another important use of legislation to deal with child abuse and neglect. Although not a primary prevention program, mandated reporting was intended to promote early intervention and thus reduce the worst effects of child maltreatment. The Child Abuse Prevention and Treatment Act of 1974 (CAPTA; P.L. 93–247) provided financial incentives to states to develop mandated reporting laws. The law was intended to lead to "the accurate and relatively complete identification of endangered children" (Hutchison, 1993, p. 58). With good intentions and little research, the bill was overwhelmingly signed into law by a vote of 57 to 7 in the Senate and 354 to 36 in the House.

Under the act, to receive federal funds, states were required to have mandated reporting laws, to investigate reports of suspected abuse or neglect, and to show that administrative procedures were in place to deal effectively with child abuse and neglect (P.L. 93–247). However, mandatory reporting laws provide few guidelines. The statutory definitions of reportable maltreatment are vague and may be culturally biased or ethnically insensitive (National Research Council, 1993). In addition, because such laws are implemented in a complex social environment, they may have unintended or unanticipated consequences (Costin, Karger, & Stoesz, 1996; Levine, 1996).

Few imagined the profound effect mandated reporting would have on the child welfare system and on clinical practice. For example, in 1996 over 2 million reports alleging maltreatment of more than 3 million children were investigated by child protective services agencies. That was three times the number in 1978 (606,000). Approximately 52% were from mandated reporters (U.S. Department of Health and Human Services, 1998). A national study of reporting found that the overwhelming majority of child psychiatrists (90%), clinical psychologists (63%), and social workers (70%) had made one or more reports of suspected child maltreatment during the course of their careers (Zellman & Antler, 1990).

The original intent of mandatory reporting laws was to promote reporting by physicians who might encounter concrete evidence of physical harm to a child (Hutchison, 1993). What began as a response to physicians' reluctance to report led to a vast expansion in the number of professions included as mandated reporters and categories identified as reportable, including physical neglect, emotional maltreatment, and sexual abuse (Small, 1992).

The definitions of child maltreatment in mandated reporting laws were expansive (Besharov, 1985; Stein, 1984). Moreover, the standard for triggering a report, typically some variant of "reasonable cause to suspect" (Besharov, 1985; Hutchison, 1993; Watson & Levine, 1989), has resulted in a high rate of false positives (Kalichman & Brosig, 1992). Far more reports are made to state child protection agencies than are ever investigated or ever substantiated if investigated. Investigations are not benign. They entail social and emotional costs to those who are investigated even if the report is not substantiated.

Underreporting, or the failure to report situations that should have been reported, is also a problem (Besharov, 1990; U.S. Department of Health and Human Services, 1996). Because of both over- and underreporting, critics of the reporting system believe that it is in need of drastic reform (U.S. ABCAN, 1993). Commentators debate about whether the standards in the current laws should be narrowed or remain the same (Barth, 1994; Besharov, 1988, 1990, 1994; Heger, 1994; Hutchison, 1993; Kalichman, 1993; Sullivan, 1994).

During the 1980s, mandatory reporting resulted in an increase in the number of reported cases, but without a commensurate increase in the proportion of maltreatment findings (Besharov, 1990). Although Jones and Finkelhor (2001) recently reported decreasing rates of child sexual abuse case reports and substantiations, the U.S. Department of Health and Human Services (1998) estimated an 18% increase in child protection investigations between 1990 and 1996. The changes ranged from North Dakota, reporting a 91% decrease, to Idaho, reporting a 231% increase. Further, the majority of cases investigated by child protection services are not substantiated, or are closed without a finding, or receive few or no additional services. The very system that was established to prevent harm to children and to provide services to troubled families may have become a victim of the "success" of mandated reporting.

If the goal of mandated reporting was to provide early intervention in an effort to reduce or eliminate child maltreatment, the results are mixed and only recently do statistics appear to be encouraging. Results from studies conducted in the mid-1990s (e.g., the NIS-3 survey, U.S. Department of Health and Human Services 1996) indicated that the rates of all forms of maltreatment per 1,000 children have increased since national data were first collected in 1979 and 1980. The recent Jones and Finkelhor (2001) study brings encouraging news, however, at least concerning reports of child sexual abuse, which declined by 26% from a peak of approximately 429,000 in 1991 to 315,400 in 1998. Child sexual abuse case substantiations have dropped 31% nationwide, from about 150,000 in 1992 to fewer than 104,000 in 1998. Of course, there are myriad possible explanations for these findings. We can only hope that social policies are responsible in part.

CONCLUSION

In this chapter, we examined some programs and legislation designed to prevent child abuse and neglect. We concluded that selected policies, programs, and past legislation may have had some success in preventing child abuse and neglect, although the evidence is far from clear. Home visiting is a promising intervention, though a new vision of broader-based community interventions might be more effective in reducing child abuse and neglect. In regard to school-based sexual abuse prevention programs, we found that despite conceptual problems with such programs and poorly designed evaluations, there may be some other benefits. We need to understand their merits and deficiencies to design better ones. In recent years states have adopted community notification programs, but we have little evidence that these programs are at all successful. We have also relied on the criminal justice system to require sex offenders to take part in treatment and to incarcerate repeat offenders. We have yet to see evidence that such measures will truly protect the community, and they may result in scandalous care in institutions. We have also relied on mandatory reporting of suspicions of child maltreatment by professionals and by the community at large. We have no direct evidence that these programs prevent child abuse and neglect, but they are the best we have at present to call attention to the plight of some children who would otherwise go unprotected.

   If there is an underlying theme to this chapter, it is that a gap currently exists between what we know and can learn from social science and society's need to respond to the very complex issues of child abuse and neglect. However, if social scientists, legislators, and the community continue to attend to the issues and continuously evaluate and make corrections based on good data, there are grounds for optimism that child abuse and neglect can be reduced. Legislative proposals intended to prevent child abuse and neglect are in reality experiments. Social scientists have an obligation and a responsibility to participate in this process, and to inform legislators and the community about current research in the field and the possibilities and challenges inherent in proposed remedies to these problems. One approach would be to encourage support for modest small-scale pilot projects before launching national initiatives that either will do no good or may have unintended negative consequences. Once legislation and programs are in place, there is an obligation to work collaboratively and intensively in evaluating them and fully examining any consequences that may have occurred.

It is likely that legislators will always be inclined to react quickly when there is a highly publicized case, as such reactions are generally driven by political considerations. Such reactions typically take place within a context of highly emotional expressions of community concern. However, even in highly publicized cases where there tends to be an urgent need to "do something," social scientists can influence decisions either through direct communication with legislators or through op-ed pieces in newspapers, appearances on television or radio talk shows, and other means. In addition, researchers can influence the processes by calling attention to research by testifying before legislative committees. Prevention needs to take place at a community level, and that necessarily involves the political system with all that it entails. With collaboration and partnership in the effort, perhaps a more reasoned and successful approach to preventing child abuse and neglect will result.

References

Barry, F. D. (1994). A neighborhood-based approach: What is it? In G. B. Melton & F. D. Barry (Eds.), *Protecting children from abuse and neglect: Foundations for a new national strategy* (pp. 14–39). New York: Guilford Press.

Barth, R. P. (1994). Limiting reporting laws. No. In M. A. Mason & E. Gambrill (Eds.), *Debating children's lives: Current controversies on children and adolescents* (pp. 292–295). Thousand Oaks, CA: Sage.

Becker, J. V., & Murphy, W. D. (1998). What we know and do not know about assessing and treating sex offenders. *Psychology, Public Policy, and Law, 4,* 116–137.

Berlin, F. S., Malin, H. M., & Dean, S. (1991). Effects of statutes requiring psychiatrists to report suspected sexual abuse of children. *American Journal of Psychiatry, 148,* 449–453.

Berrick, J. D., & Gilbert, N. (1991). *With the best of intentions: The child sexual abuse prevention movement.* New York: Guilford Press.

Berrick, J. D., & Gilbert, N. (1994). Mandatory abuse prevention programs in schools. In M. A. Mason & E. Gambrill (Eds.), *Debating children's lives: Current controversies on children and adolescents* (pp. 173–177). Thousand Oaks, CA: Sage.

Besharov, D. (1985). "Doing something" about child abuse: The need to narrow the grounds for state intervention. *Harvard Journal of Law & Public Policy, 8,* 545, 550–558, 567–581.

Besharov, D. J. (1988). The need to narrow the grounds for state interventions. In D. J. Besharov (Ed.), *Protecting children from abuse and neglect. Policy and practice* (pp. 47–90). Springfield, IL: Charles C. Thomas.

Besharov, D. J. (1990). Gaining control over child abuse reports. Public agencies must address both underreporting and overreporting. *Public Welfare, 48,* 34–40.

Besharov, D. J. (1994). Limiting reporting laws. Yes. In M. A. Mason & E. Gambrill (Eds.), *Debating children's lives: Current controversies on children and adolescents* (pp. 287–291, 296–297). Thousand Oaks, CA: Sage.

Budin, L., & Johnson, C. (1989). Sex abuse prevention programs: Offenders' attitudes about their efficacy. *Child Abuse & Neglect, 13,* 77–87.

Child Abuse Prevention and Treatment and Adoption Reform, General Program, Grants to states for child abuse and neglect prevention and treatment programs, 42 U.S.C. §5106a.

Child Abuse Prevention and Treatment and Adoption Reform, Community-Based Family Resource and Support Grants, 42 U.S.C. §5116.

Conte, J., Wolfe, S., & Smith, T. (1989). What sexual offenders tell us about prevention strategies. *Child Abuse & Neglect, 13,* 293–301.

Costin, L. B., Karger, H. J., & Stoesz, D. (1996). *The politics of child abuse in America.* New York: Oxford University Press.

Courtney, M. E. (1998). The costs of child protection in the context of welfare reform. *The Future of Children, 8,* 88–103.

Daro, D. A. (1994). Prevention of child sexual abuse. *The Future of Children, 4*(2), 198–223.

Finkelhor, D., & Strapko, N. (1992). Sexual abuse prevention education: A review of evaluation studies. In D. J. Willis, E. W. Holden, & M. Rosenberg

(Eds.), *Prevention of child maltreatment: Developmental and ecological perspectives* (pp. 150–167). New York: Wiley.

Garbarino, J., & Kostelny, K. (1994). Neighborhood-based programs. In G. B. Melton & F. D. Barry (Eds.), *Protecting children from abuse and neglect: Foundations for a new national strategy* (pp. 304–352). New York: Guilford Press.

Hanson, R. K. (1998). What do we know about sex offender risk assessment? *Psychology, Public Policy and Law, 4,* 50–72.

Hay, T., & Jones, L. (1994). Societal interventions to prevent child abuse and neglect. *Child Welfare, 73,* 379–403.

Heger, R. L. (1994). Are legal definitions of child abuse too broad? Yes. In E. Gambrill and T. J. Stein (Eds.), *Controversial issues in child welfare* (pp. 211–215, 221–222). Boston: Allyn and Bacon.

House Report, Jacob Wetterling Crimes Against Children Registration Act, 103rd Cong., 1st Sess., H.R. Rep. 103–392 (1993, November 20).

House Report, Megan's Law, 104th Cong., 2nd Sess., H.R. Rep 104–555 (1996, May 6).

Hutchison, E. (1993). Mandatory reporting laws: Child protective case finding gone awry? *Social Work, 38*(1), 56–63.

Jacob Wetterling Crimes against Children and Sexually Violent Offender Registration Program, 42 U.S.C. § 14071.

Jones, L., & Finkelhor, D. (2001). *The decline in child sexual abuse cases.* Washington, DC: U.S. Department of Justice, Office of Justice Programs, Office of Juvenile Justice and Delinquency Prevention.

Kalichman, S. C. (1991). Laws on reporting sexual abuse of children. *American Journal of Psychiatry, 148,* 618–619.

Kalichman, S. C. (1993). *Mandated reporting of suspected child abuse. Ethics, law and policy.* Washington, DC: American Psychological Association.

Kalichman, S., & Brosig, C. (1992). The effects of statutory requirements on child maltreatment reporting: a comparison of two state laws. *American Journal of Orthopsychiatry, 62*(2), 284–296.

Kansas v. Hendricks, 117 S. Ct. 2072 (1997).

Korbin, J. E., & Coulton, C. J. (1996). The role of neighbors and the government in neighborhood-based child protection. *Journal of Social Issues, 52,* 163–176.

Krugman, R. D. (1996). Epilogue. In J. Briere, L. Berliner, J. A. Bulkley, C. Jenny, & T. Reid (Eds.), *The APSAC handbook on child maltreatment* (pp. 420–422). Thousand Oaks, CA: Sage.

La Fond, J. Q. (1998). The costs of enacting a sexual predator law. *Psychology, Public Policy, and Law, 4,* 468–504.

Levine, M. (1996). A therapeutic jurisprudence analysis of mandated reporting of child maltreatment by psychotherapists. In D. B. Wexler & B. J. Winick (Eds.), *Law in a therapeutic key* (pp. 323–341). Durham, NC: Carolina Academic Press.

Levine, M., & Perkins, D. V. (1997). *Principles of community psychology* (2nd ed.). New York: Oxford University Press.

Matson, S., & Lieb, R. (1997). *Megan's law: A review of state and federal legislation* (Doc. No. 97-10-1101). Olympia, WA: Washington State Institute for Public Policy.

Melton, G. B. (1992). The improbability of prevention of sexual abuse. In D. J. Willis, E. W. Holden, & M. Rosenberg (Eds.), *Prevention of child maltreatment: Developmental and ecological perspectives* (pp. 168–189). New York: Wiley.

Mulroy, E. A. (1997). Building a neighborhood network: Interorganizational collaboration to prevent child abuse and neglect. *Social Work, 42,* 255–264.

National Clearinghouse on Child Abuse and Neglect. (n.d.). NCCAN lessons learned: The experience of nine child abuse and neglect prevention programs. [Online] Available: http://www.calib.com/nccanch/pubs/lessons/index.htm

National Committee to Prevent Child Abuse. (1998). [Online] Available: http://www.childabuse.org/

National Institute of Justice. (1995). *Helping to prevent child abuse and future criminal consequences: Hawaii Healthy Start* (NCJ 156216). Washington, DC: U.S. Department of Justice.

National Research Council (1993). *Understanding child abuse and neglect.* Washington, DC: National Academy Press.

Olds, D. (1997). The prenatal early infancy project: Preventing child abuse and neglect in the context of promoting maternal and child health. In D. A. Wolfe, R. J. McMahon, & R. D. Peters (Eds.), *Child abuse: New directions in prevention and treatment across the lifespan* (pp. 130–154). Thousand Oaks, CA: Sage.

Sarason, S. B. (1978). The nature of problem solving in social action. *American Psychologist, 33,* 370–380.

Sengupta, S. (2000, August 5). No rise in child abuse seen in welfare shift. *New York Times,* pp. A1, A20.

Sex Offender Registration Act, New York Corrections Law §168.

Small, M.A. (1992). Policy review of child abuse and neglect reporting statutes, *Law & Policy, 14,* 129–152.

Stein, T. (1984). The Child Abuse Prevention and Treatment Act. *Social Services Review, 58*(2), 302–314.

Steinbock, B. (1995). A policy perspective. *Criminal Justice Ethics, 14,* 4–9.

Sullivan, R. (1994). Are legal definitions of child abuse too broad? In E. Gambrill & T. J. Stein (Eds.), *Controversial issues in child welfare* (pp. 215–221). Boston: Allyn and Bacon.

U.S. Advisory Board on Child Abuse and Neglect. (1990). *Child abuse and neglect: Critical first steps in response to a national emergency.* Washington, DC: U.S. Government Printing Office.

U.S. Advisory Board on Child Abuse and Neglect. (1993). *The continuing child protection emergency: Challenge to the nation.* Washington, DC: U.S. Government Printing Office.

U.S. Advisory Board on Child Abuse and Neglect. (1995). *A nation's shame: Fatal child abuse and neglect in the United States.* Washington, DC: U.S. Government Printing Office.

U.S. Department of Health and Human Services. (1996). *Third national incidence study of child abuse and neglect: Final report.* Washington, DC: U.S. Department of Health and Human Services, Administration for Children and Families.

U.S. Department of Health and Human Services, Children's Bureau. (1998). *Child maltreatment 1996: Reports from the states to the National Child Abuse and Neglect Data System.* Washington, DC: U.S. Government Printing Office.

U.S. General Accounting Office. (1996). *Preventing child sexual abuse: Research inconclusive about effectiveness of child education programs* (GAO/GGD-96–156). Washington, DC: U.S. General Accounting Office.

Watson, H., & Levine, M. (1989). Psychotherapy and mandated reporting of child abuse. *American Journal of Orthopsychiatry, 59*(2), 246–256.

Welsh doctor mistaken for pedophile. (2000, August 21). *The Buffalo News,* p. A4.

Winick, B. J., & La Fond, J. Q. (Eds.). (1998). Special theme. Sex offenders: Scientific, legal, and policy perspectives. *Psychology, Public Policy and Law, 4,* 1–570.

Wurtele, S. K. (1997). Sexual abuse. In R. T. Ammerman & M. Hersen (Eds.), *Handbook of prevention and treatment with children and adolescents: Intervention in the real world context* (pp. 357–384). New York: Wiley.

Zellman, G., & Antler, S. (1990). Mandated reporters and CPS: A study in frustration. *Public Welfare, 48,* 30–3.

14

Children's Eyewitness Memory

True Disclosures and False Reports

Jennifer M. Schaaf, Kristen Weede Alexander,
Gail S. Goodman, Simona Ghetti,
Robin S. Edelstein, Paola Castelli

Hand in hand with society's increased awareness of the problem of child abuse has come an increased presence of children as eyewitnesses in the legal system. Whether testifying as victims in open court or providing bystander eyewitness reports in a forensic interview, children have a good deal of valuable information to give the justice system, and in cases that rely largely on eyewitness evidence, a just outcome may rest on the testimony of a child. Despite children's strengths and abilities as eyewitnesses, children's memory, like that of adults, is not infallible, and children in some situations may be more susceptible to minor and serious error than adults. In this chapter, we overview how children perform when called on to provide eyewitness information about experienced events and also how they perform when questioned about never-experienced events. The chapter is divided into four main sections: disclosure of abuse, trauma and memory, false memory, and current trends in legal and research arenas. Overall, we argue that (a) children are often, although not always hesitant to disclose abuse; (b) children have the capacity for accurate memories of abusive experiences; (c) many children can, to a certain degree, resist suggestive questions about abuse, although some children (especially preschoolers) are more

Correspondence concerning this chapter should be addressed to Dr. Gail S. Goodman, Department of Psychology, University of California, One Shields Avenue, Davis, CA 95616 (e-mail: ggoodman@ucdavis.edu).

prone to false report, especially in multiply suggestive contexts; and (d) the current focus on false reports and false memory, although clearly important, often overstates the problem of children's suggestibility about abuse and risks disbelief of child witnesses when belief is justified (for discussion, see also Lyon, this volume).

DISCLOSURE OF ABUSE

Disclosure of abuse by a child is the starting point for many child abuse investigations. The timeliness and completeness of the disclosure often guide the ensuing investigation and subsequent interviews. Therefore, before examining the reliability and veracity of children's eyewitness memory, we discuss children's willingness to disclose and talk about abuse experiences. Although children may be expected to provide information of an intimate nature in forensic interviews or in court, they may be unwilling to do so. Children are often reluctant to disclose abuse, especially sexual abuse, and may not do so for weeks, months, or years after it has occurred (Farrell, 1988; Sauzier, 1989; Smith et al., 2000). In fact, the number of sexually abused children who never disclose the abuse until adulthood is quite large, often estimated to be around 70% of abuse victims (e.g., Arata, 1998; Roesler, 1994). If children do not disclose abuse, the assaults may continue undetected and additional victims may be involved. At the same time, however, it is also essential to minimize the risk of eliciting false allegations from children. For these reasons, it is imperative to understand the factors that influence or inhibit children's disclosure.

The Process of Children's Disclosure

Most child victims initially disclose sexual abuse to their parents or close friends (Berliner & Conte, 1995; Roesler & Wind, 1994; Smith et al., 2000). In only a small percentage of sexual abuse cases are the authorities ever contacted (Russell, 1986). Nevertheless, most studies of the disclosure process concern disclosure to authorities. These studies suffer from several methodological difficulties. For instance, there is rarely independent validation of the abuse, so the accuracy of disclosures often cannot be evaluated. Moreover, in retrospective studies that ask adults to report on their past experiences, some participants who had suffered abuse may deny it simply because they are unwilling to reveal their abuse to researchers. Despite these obstacles, research on disclosure is accumulating, but the findings are mixed.

One line of thought, based on clinical observations of intrafamilial abuse cases in therapeutic settings, is that children's disclosure may be characterized by a series of stages that children pass through before they ultimately disclose abuse. In a frequently cited paper, Summit (1983) proposed a "child sexual abuse accommodation syndrome" consisting of five stages characterizing children's disclosure of sexual abuse: (a) secrecy, unwillingness to disclose information about the abuse, (b) helplessness, the feeling of being unable to alter the situation, (c) entrapment and accommodation, adjustment to the abuse, (d) delayed, conflicted, and unconvincing disclosure, and (e) retraction. Attempting to test this model, Sorenson and Snow (1991) examined 116 cases from a larger sample of children who had received therapy for sexual abuse. Their qualitative analyses suggest a similar four-stage model of the disclosure process in children: denial, disclosure, recantation, and affirmation. Although 96% of the children in this sample eventually disclosed some form of abuse, only 11% of the children made disclosures at the initial interview and almost 25% recanted their later allegations at some point (see also Gonzalez, Waterman, Kelly, McCord, & Oliveri, 1993). These results should be interpreted with caution. The children's disclosures were obtained in a therapeutic context, and disclosures may have been the result of suggestive interviewing techniques. However, experimental and "scientific case studies" also offer support for part of the disclosure process specified in these models, including secrecy (Bidrose & Goodman, 2000) and inconsistency. For instance, children tend to be inconsistent in their reports of body touch (Quas, Denton, Goodman, & Myers, 1996), even when they have no motivation to conceal such touch, and some children do not readily report genital touch in open-ended interviews (Saywitz, Goodman, Nicholas, & Moan, 1991).

Other research has not supported the disclosure process as depicted by Summit (1983) and Sorenson and Snow (1991). Bradley and Wood (1996), for example, examined disclosure in 234 validated sexual abuse cases and found that only 6% of the children initially denied abuse. Additionally, only 3% of the children in Bradley and Wood's (1996) sample recanted their initial allegations, with half of them recanting in response to a caretaker's pressure. Jones and McGraw (1987) similarly found a low recantation rate. These results have led some scholars to argue that children are not prone to deny or conceal abuse when asked directly about it (Bruck, 1999).

As previously noted, Sorenson and Snow (1991) examined children's disclosure in a therapeutic setting, while Bradley and Wood (1996) and Jones and McGraw (1987) examined the same process in a more formal child protection services setting. Regardless of the context, however, the discrepancy between their findings has significant implications for interviewing children about abuse. If hesitancy or denial are frequent characteristics of children's disclosure, the use of leading questions may be considered justified at times to encourage disclosure from children who have suffered abuse. There is reason to believe that leading questioning is needed to obtain embarrassing or secret information from children (Bottoms, Goodman, Schwartz-Kenney, & Thomas, in press; Bruck, Ceci, & Hembrooke, 1998). In fact, some children fail to disclose abuse when questioned even in the face of medical evidence confirming the sexual activity (Lawson & Chaffin, 1992) and fail to reveal secrets even when asked leading questions (Bottoms et al., in press), highlighting the fact that some children do not disclose readily. In contrast, if denial and recantation are falsely believed to be normal stages in the process of disclosure, interviewers may discount children's denials and question children repeatedly and suggestively in pursuit of disclosures (Bruck, 1999; Bruck & Ceci, 1998). If in fact the majority of children do not initially deny abuse or later recant, as suggested by Bradley and Wood (1996), the risk of false reports that may be incurred by repeated suggestive interviewing may become unacceptably high (Poole & Lindsay, 2002). Next, we discuss specific individual and situational factors that affect children's disclosure.

Developmental Factors

Developmental factors affect disclosure in children (De Young, 1987). Young children are generally less likely to disclose abuse to adults in a formal setting even when they have made an initial disclosure to a parent or other adult (Keary & Fitzpatrick, 1994). In general, it has been noted that many of the disclosures children do make are accidental, without a clear intention of revealing the abuse; this is particularly likely for younger rather than older children (Campis, Hebden-Curtis, & DeMaso, 1993; Mian, Wehrspann, Klajner-Diamond, LeBaron, & Winder, 1986). This may be due to younger children's difficulties inhibiting their speech and behavior, resulting in spontaneous, unplanned disclosures.

Further, young children's lack of knowledge of social norms concerning sexual behavior may influence their disclosure of sexual abuse (Goldman & Goldman, 1984). They may not have sufficient understanding to recognize the inappropriateness of sexual activity and therefore may not report it to adults. Thus, sexual abuse prevention programs that educate children about what is and is not appropriate touch may result in disclosures of child abuse (see MacFarlane, Doueck, & Levine, this volume). More often, as children approach puberty and obtain knowledge of appropriate and inappropriate sexual behavior, they tend to make more self-disclosures of sexual abuse (Farrell, 1988). At the same time, however, a limited understanding of sexuality may also inadvertently facilitate disclosure of sexual abuse. Because younger children may not appreciate the taboo nature of sexuality, they may be more willing to discuss topics and acts that might embarrass older children. Saywitz et al. (1991) found that although older children generally reported more information and were more accurate than young children when interviewed about a medical examination involving genital and other touch, older children were more reluctant to report genital touch.

Factors such as the abuse victim's IQ, race, socioeconomic status, and level of education have not generally been related to children's patterns of disclosure (e.g., Mian et al., 1986). However, developmental differences in children's understanding of others' dispositional characteristics may impede young children's disclosure of abuse. Rholes and Ruble (1984) found that unlike older children and adults, young children do not regard others' dispositional characteristics as stable and thus do not expect cross-situational consistency of behavior. They also do not expect negative behaviors to reoccur. Young children who are abused may therefore have difficulty making global inferences about an abuser or even predicting that the abusive behavior will continue. Older children, realizing the taboo nature of the acts and their own involvement, may try to talk the abuser out of continuing but may still not report the acts voluntarily to their parents (Bidrose & Goodman, 2000). In either case, children may be unlikely to disclose the abuse and thus end it.

Taken as a whole, these findings have implications for forensic interviews of children, suggesting that young children may be particularly difficult to interview about abuse in a formal setting and that they may disclose abuse unpredictably in other contexts. Compared to younger children, older children's greater cognitive sophistication makes them more capable of disclosing abuse in a formal interview, but it also provides them with an understanding of social norms and taboos that may inhibit disclosure. Still, many children who have disclosed abuse previously will disclose it again in the forensic context.

Characteristics of the Abuse

Along with age, characteristics of the abuse situation can also influence children's willingness to disclose. Sauzier (1989) examined 156 children referred to a sexual abuse program and found that children allegedly abused by a natural parent or another family member were particularly reluctant to disclose the abuse, whereas alleged victims of extrafamiliar abuse tended to reveal the abuse sooner after the incident occurred. Children abused by a family member may feel more loyalty toward the perpetrator and thus more ambivalence about disclosing the abuse (Mian et al., 1986). They may also have more difficulty understanding that the abuse is wrong when the perpetrator is a trusted adult in a position of authority than when the adult is a stranger or someone not in a position of authority over the child.

Sauzier (1989) also found that the methods used by perpetrators to obtain victim compliance were related to the timing of the children's disclosures; only about 25% of children who had been psychologically manipulated and/or threatened by their abuser reported the abuse immediately. Psychologically manipulated children may accept some of the blame for their abuse, inhibiting

348 Schaaf et al.

their motivation to report it, and threatened children may under-standably be too frightened. In a study of a prosecution sample, Goodman-Brown (1994) reported that children who feared negative consequences to others were least likely to readily disclose sexual abuse. Findings are mixed concerning how the severity of abuse affects disclosure (Arata, 1998; Farrell, 1988; Roesler, 1994; Sauzier, 1989).

Overall, research indicates that loyalties and fears inhibit children's disclosures. These socioemotional forces, which take effect in early years (Bottoms et al., in press; Bussey, Lee, & Grimbeek, 1993), may need to be overcome in a forensic interview about abuse. Even leading questions may not pry secret information from children.

Parents' Questioning and Reports of Children's Disclosures

Although most children disclose sexual abuse to a parent or friend, how these initial disclosures are elicited is largely unknown. Some children disclose spontaneously, but others disclose in response to parental questioning once suspicion arises (Berliner & Conte, 1995). Given that children often disclose to parents, particularly mothers, it is important to examine the effects of parental questioning on children's accuracy. Recent research suggests that children may be less suggestible when asked misleading questions by their mothers compared to unknown female interviewers (Goodman, Sharma, Thomas, & Considine, 1995). Nevertheless, misinformation from parents can, under certain circumstances, distort children's memory reports (Poole & Lindsay, 2001).

In real cases, after interviewing their children, parents often tell investigators what their children disclosed. Absent malice or the like, mothers' reports have been found to be accurate regarding the gist of what the child said but imprecise about the exact questions asked and whether the questions were open-ended or somewhat leading (Bruck, Ceci, & Francoeur, 1999). This imprecision is not specific to mothers (Warren & Woodall, 1999). In general, laypersons and many professionals often lack a clear understanding of the distinction between open-ended and leading questions (Goodman, Batterman-Faunce, Schaaf, & Kenney, in press). Fortunately, laypersons (and, it is hoped, most professionals) do distinguish between highly leading and less leading questions (Castelli, Goodman, & Ghetti, 2000).

In a number of the sensational preschool cases of the past (e.g., *State of New Jersey v. Michaels*, 1994), children's *initial* disclosures of abuse were first made to parents rather than to the interviewers, who employed notoriously leading questioning. Because memory researchers (and perhaps jurors as well) consider the conditions under which children's initial reports are made to be of special importance, additional research is needed on children's disclosures to parents.

Summary and Implications

The reliability and veracity of children's eyewitness testimony are important considerations in child abuse investigations. Children may be hesitant to recount their experiences even when they are capable of doing so. Age, relationship to the perpetrator, fear of negative consequences, and identity of the initial interviewer may all affect the likelihood and process of disclosure. Thus these factors need to be considered when interviewing children about traumatic experiences such as sexual abuse. It is premature to conclude from the research base that most children readily disclose when questioned about abuse, and premature to assume that a sequence of denial, disclosure, and recantation is typical, although there is reason to believe that some children disclose in each of these ways.

TRAUMA AND MEMORY

Children interviewed in forensic situations often must recount personal experiences that were highly stressful or traumatic. Emotion and cognition are inextricably linked in the ongoing process of child development (Fischer & Bidell, 1998). Because of the emotion-laden content of traumatic events, qualitative differences may exist in memory for such events compared to more emotionally neutral events. Trauma also affects concurrent and later mental health and cognitive processing, consequently influencing how events are processed, stored, and retrieved (Azarian, Miller, & Skriptchenko-Gregorian, 1996; Spaccarelli, 1994). It is vital to examine children's statements regarding stressful events to obtain a complete picture of children's memory capabilities in the context of forensic interviews and testifying in court.

Research on Stress and Memory

The accuracy and durability of children's memory for stressful experiences is a controversial topic. Some researchers argue that memory for stressful events may be similar to memory for other events imbued with great personal significance (e.g., Howe, 1997). According to this view, emotion directs attention to significant aspects of unique events and maintains higher levels of cognitive activation for important features of the event (Bower, 1992). Others, however, argue that inescapable stress may overwhelm children's coping mechanisms and lead to less efficient memory processing (van der Kolk, 1996). According to the latter view, traumatic memories may be encoded differently from other types of memories and lead to extremes of retention or forgetting. Unfortunately, it is difficult to conduct ethical and scientifically sound research to test these provocative theoretical ideas. Nevertheless, researchers have employed a number of methodologies to study the relations between stress and memory, with both theoretical and applied issues in mind.

Naturally occurring highly stressful events allow for examination of the association between trauma and memory. Researchers have examined children's memory for disasters such as earthquakes (Azarian, Lipsitt, Miller, & Skriptchenko-Gregorian, 1999), hurricanes (Bahrick, Parker, Fivush, & Levitt, 1998), and sniper attacks (Pynoos & Nader, 1989). It is often difficult to assess children's accuracy for specific details of such traumas because researchers may be unable to obtain objective records of the initial event. For example, Bahrick and colleagues (1998) studied children's memory for a major hurricane. One hundred 3- and 4-year-old children were interviewed 2 to 6 months following the hurricane. Stress was operationally defined as the degree of damage that occurred to the child's home. Although there was an apparent small drop in recall at the highest level of stress, significance tests were not performed on the means for the medium- and high-stress-level groups. Therefore, it is not known whether a significant decrease in recall at the highest stress level occurred. Children recalled impressive *amounts* of detail (especially at the medium and high stress levels), but accuracy could not be definitively determined.

To overcome the problem of lack of verifiability, some researchers have studied children's memory for naturally occurring yet more verifiable stressors. These studies include testing children's memory for documented medical experiences such as catheterization (Goodman, Quas, Batterman-Faunce, Riddlesberger, & Kuhn, 1994), inoculations (Goodman, Hirschman, Hepps, & Rudy, 1991), and emergency room experiences (e.g., Peterson, 1999; Peterson & Bell, 1996). For example, Goodman et al. (1994) investigated children's memory for a highly stressful medical procedure called *voiding cystourethrogram fluoroscopy* (VCUG). This procedure is performed by doctors on children who are experiencing urinary tract problems. During the procedure, which was videotaped to permit later coding for memory accuracy, children were held down or strapped to a table and then catheterized by a nurse. They were then told to urinate on the table, and x-rays were taken. In addition, Peterson and colleagues (e.g., Peterson & Bell, 1996) have investigated children's memory for stressful hospital emergency room experiences. They documented children's experiences in the emergency room and later asked children about the details. Studies such as those conducted by Goodman et al. and Peterson and Bell, which verified (through objective records or parental report) children's accuracy in recalling naturally occurring stressful events, show that children's memory can be highly accurate for the central details of a stressful event. Memory for central details is also well retained over time (e.g., 2 years), with some increase in error overall, but mainly among only a few children (Peterson, 1999).

Age differences exist, however, in children's ability to recount stressful experiences. Children who are older at the time of their traumatic experience tend to recall that experience explicitly more often than do younger children (Azarian et al., 1999; Quas, Goodman, Bidrose, Pipe, Craw, & Ablin, 1999; Williams, 1994) and recall more information than younger children (Bahrick et al., 1998). Further, children who are older at the time of the event remember central details more accurately than do younger children

(Peterson & Bell, 1996). Two-year-olds, the youngest children tested, are particularly helped in maintaining their memories by repeated interviews (Peterson, 1999).

In addition to age, other child characteristics influence children's ability to report stressful incidents. Children's prior knowledge and expectations influence memory and commission errors in recounting stressful experiences (Ornstein et al., 1998). The attachment style of parents and children may also affect children's ability to remember stressful events. A secure attachment style is characterized by a tendency to seek relationships and a lack of anxiety about relationships. Children whose parents form secure adult attachments tend to be less suggestible about stressful events (Goodman et al., 1994). In addition, children who themselves have a secure attachment may be better able to organize and integrate memory for negative affect than children who have insecure attachments (Kirsh & Cassidy, 1997).

Thus, studies investigating children's reports about traumatic events reveal that many children, even 3- and 4-year-olds, have the ability to be largely accurate about the central features of a stressful event, such as the main actions involved, but may not give complete reports. Whether memory may be compromised at some very high levels of stress is still debated (Christianson, 1992). Preschool and early elementary school children, however, may still have some (fragmented) memories of stressful events that occurred when they were toddlers (see also Pillemer, Picariello, & Pruett, 1994; Quas et al., 1999). Although studies of stressful experiences can provide valuable data about children's memory, the ecological validity of such studies as applied to children's memory of abuse experiences can always be challenged. It is therefore important to conduct studies of memory for actual abuse experiences.

Abuse and Memory

There is reason to believe that past abuse might make children's memory less accurate, but there is also reason to believe it would make facets of their memory more accurate. Regarding the first possibility, repeated abuse is a chronic stressor for children. Recent physiological evidence, based on animal studies, suggests that chronic stress may have long-term negative influences on memory. Although the release of epinephrine that accompanies stressful experiences can have positive effects on memory in the short run (Gold & McCarty, 1995), in the long run this epinephrine release during severe or chronic stress may damage brain areas that consolidate memory (Sapolsky, 1992). Thus, children who are maltreated, especially if the maltreatment is severe and protracted, may show deficits in memory. This could account in part for lost memories of abuse (Williams, 1994). Alternatively, abused children may be particularly vigilant and attentive to situations that might cause harm and show especially detailed memory. Finally, it is also possible that past abuse has little effect on basic eyewitness memory abilities.

Reliable records of children's experiences are often unavailable to verify what children report in the forensic context about past abuse. Anecdotal accounts indicate that some children who experienced sexual abuse at barely verbal ages can provide vivid accounts of the abuse later in childhood (Hewitt, 1994). For example, a preverbal child who was sexually abused by her male cousin when she was 22 months old was able to report specific central details to her mother at age 4 years. (Other studies suggest that infantile amnesia effects would eventually block access to early abuse memories; Terr, 1988). Anecdotal reports hint at children's accuracy in reporting abuse, but are not definitive for lack of an objective record against which to evaluate children's memory reports. In a few recent studies, however, researchers have taken advantage of corroborating evidence to examine children's accuracy in reporting abuse experiences.

Bidrose and Goodman (2000) conducted a "scientific case study" of children's memory for sexual abuse. The legal case involved several girls, aged 8 to 14 years at the time of disclosure, who had responded to a "help-wanted" advertisement to clean a disabled man's apartment. These girls were subsequently involved in sexual activity with this man and several of his male friends. During these times, pornographic photographs and audiotapes were made of the children. After the sexual abuse was discovered, four of the girls were interviewed by police and testified in deposition hearings about their sexual experiences with the defendants. The oldest abuse victim had first been abused almost a year earlier, but the others had been involved for only a few months. The researchers compared the girls' reports with the photographic and audiotaped evidence to determine the accuracy of their eyewitness reports. Results revealed that of the girls' 246 allegations, 194 (79%) were corroborated by photographs, audiotapes, or both. Of the remaining 21% of allegations that were not corroborated by available evidence, it is not definitively known whether the act occurred and went un- recorded (which was likely given the perpetrators' tendencies) or whether the girls reported events that did not happen. In any case, many of the uncorroborated allegations concerned arrangements for the sex sessions rather than sexual acts themselves. In addition, the uncorroborated sexual acts were consistent with the corrobo- rated abuse. Further, there was photographic or audiotaped evi- dence for 318 sexual acts, of which only 194 (64%) were reported by the girls when interviewed. This represents a rather large omission error rate of 36%. Thus, although the girls' reports of abuse were quite accurate, they also made a sizable number of omission errors.

In another case study, Orbach and Lamb (1999) examined a single child's accuracy in recalling a sexual abuse incident. They analyzed the content of an investigative interview of a 13-year-old victim by comparing it with an audiotaped record of the abuse incident, the perpetrator's account of the incident, and the victim's sister's ac- count of what happened immediately prior to and after the abuse. The victim had audiotaped the abuse herself in an attempt to con- vince her mother that the abuse she had alleged in the past was ac- tually occurring. The victim reported primarily on details that were central to the event. Over 50% of the reported details were corrob- orated by the audiotaped evidence. Other details could be neither corroborated nor contradicted because of the nature of the details and lack of pictorial evidence. Additional details were confirmed by the perpetrator's and sister's reports. Orbach and Lamb con- cluded that the child's report was highly accurate. Thus, although this study included only one child, it strengthens the evidence for children's eyewitness memory being quite accurate for abuse expe- riences (see also Jones & Krugman, 1986).

In summary, although few studies exist in which a record of ac- tual abuse exists for comparison to children's reports, extant studies suggest that children's reports of abuse are quite accurate, although omission errors are frequent. Infantile amnesia, the phenomenon whereby individuals are unable to report memories from early childhood, may explain loss of memory for abuse that occurs early in life, as found by Terr (1988).

Abused Children's Memory for Nonabusive Experiences

Abused children may be interviewed by authorities not only about abuse they actually experienced, but also about events they did not experience. In the past, fears were raised that a history of abuse would predispose children to make false reports (e.g., that past abuse experiences would intrude into children's reports of nonabusive events, possibly leading to arrest of an innocent person). What are the effects of abuse on children's memory for nonabusive events? Does it cause them to remember nonabusive actions as abusive? This question is relevant to false reports of abuse. Although we discuss the issue of false reports in greater detail in the next section of this chapter, particularly in regard to "false memory," here we mention research on the effects of abuse on eyewitness memory for nonabusive events more generally.

Controlled research on eyewitness memory in abused children is relatively new but suggests that abused children's memory is comparable to that of nonabused children. Eisen, Goodman, Qin, and Davis (1998; Eisen, Goodman, Davis, & Qin, 1999) studied maltreated children's memory and suggestibility for a medical exam. Abused children, like nonabused children, reported quite accurately stressful but nonabusive events (an anogenital examination and venipuncture). As expected, there were age differences in the abused sample, as has been demonstrated in samples of nonabused children. Younger children had less complete memory and were more easily misled than older children. Of importance, in this sample of maltreated children, those with more psychopathology as well as those with lower intellectual ability performed more poorly during the memory interview. Thus, it is possible that, short of physiological damage, abuse per se does not directly have adverse effects on memory, but rather has indirect effects to the extent that abuse is associated with poor mental health and poor intellectual functioning (which may also be related to dysfunctional families).

Some researchers suggest that maltreated children are at risk of developing negatively biased social information processing tendencies (Dodge, Bates, & Pettit, 1990; Pollak, Ciccetti, & Klorman, 1998), causing them to falsely infer negative intentions of others or to process negative information preferentially. In a study comparing abused and nonabused children's memory for a neutral play event, Goodman, Bottoms, Rudy, Davis, and Schwartz-Kenney (2001) found that abused children responded with similar accuracy (in comparison to age-, gender-, and socioeconomically matched nonabused children) to questions related to abuse, including false suggestions about abuse. However, individual-difference variables, some often cited as influential for memory and suggestibility, were found to differ significantly between the abused and nonabused groups: IQ (the abused group scored lower) and internalizing and externalizing behavior problems (the abused group scored higher). Interestingly, these individual-difference variables did not mediate the abuse effects, contrary to Eisen et al.'s (1998) findings.

Overall, to date, research does not support the contention that abused children's eyewitness memory is any more problematic than that of nonabused children of the same age and socioeconomic status, except perhaps to the extent that some abused children may evince greater psychopathology and lower intellectual ability. Few studies on this important issue exist, however, and future studies may reveal important differences, perhaps particularly when chronic stress (e.g., repeated abuse, exposure to community violence) has been experienced. (For a discussion of the impact of community violence on children, see Berman, Silverman, & Kurtines, this volume.) Additional research is needed to determine other possible factors that may influence memory of abuse, such as social support for the victim, posttraumatic stress symptoms, and dissociative tendencies (Carter, Bottoms, & Levine, 1996; Davis & Bottoms, 2002; Eisen et al., 1998).

CHILDREN'S FALSE REPORTS

During the past two decades, a number of legal cases in which young children made sexual abuse claims were brought to the attention of scholars and laypeople by the mass media (e.g., *State of*

New Jersey v. Michaels, 1994; *State v. Amirault LeFave*, 1985). Common among these cases was the alleged involvement of multiple perpetrators and multiple victims, and, at times, the presence of unrealistic allegations describing bizarre events including satanic ritualistic abuse (Bottoms, Shaver, & Goodman, 1996). Also similar in these cases was a lack of corroborating adult eyewitnesses and a dearth of medical evidence despite the violence of the alleged crimes. Children's statements were therefore the main evidence on which prosecutors built these criminal cases. Prosecutors typically argued that young children's lack of knowledge about sexual matters would make it unlikely that children would fabricate sexually explicit accounts (Ceci & Bruck, 1995). Defense attorneys commonly contended that allegations had been elicited through insistent questioning by parents, social workers, therapists, and law enforcement professionals.

A large number of recent studies have helped to clarify the situations in which children can provide accurate reports (e.g., Goodman, Bottoms, Schwartz-Kenney, & Rudy, 1991; Saywitz, 1995; Warren & Lane, 1995). These studies reveal that many children, at least by about 4 to 5 years of age, can be surprisingly resistant to false suggestions of abuse in single or even multiple interviews that are otherwise relatively neutral or even that contain some negative implications (e.g., that someone might have done something wrong: Goodman, Bottoms, et al., 1991; Rudy & Goodman, 1991; Tobey & Goodman, 1992). Moreover, recent research indicates that children are less suggestible about repeated events, for which their memory may be strong, than about nonrepeated events (Connolly & Lindsay, 1998; Pezdek & Roe, 1995; Powell, Roberts, Ceci, & Hembrooke, 1999). Empirical evidence is also available on the factors that may reduce children's accuracy (e.g., Bruck, 1999; Bruck et al., 1998; Pezdek & Hodge, 1999; Poole & Lindsay, 1995). Next, we discuss findings that advance our understanding of the factors that reduce children's report accuracy and that may ultimately contribute to young children's production of false allegations. These studies generally concern the issue of false memory in children. It should be noted that a number of methodological issues and problems of generalization are inherent in many of the false memory studies conducted to date. We discuss these issues and problems after we review the studies.

Repeated Suggestions and Interviewer Bias

Question repetition per se does not necessarily jeopardize children's accuracy; it also has the potential of consolidating and facilitating children's eyewitness memory (Brainerd & Ornstein, 1991). However, the use of repeated suggestive questions, especially in the context of other suggestive influences (e.g., an accusatory context, previous stereotypes, instructions to pretend), can create inaccuracies in children's reports (Bruck & Ceci, 1999). Even in a single interview, substantial false information can be obtained when multiply suggestive techniques are employed (Lepore & Sesco, 1994). Repeated multiply misleading interviews can further compromise children's accuracy. When children were asked in repeated interviews about events that they had not experienced (e.g., "Did your finger ever get caught in a mouse trap?"), about 30–40% of young preschoolers (3-year-olds) affirmed such events. The affirmation rate did not significantly differ from the first to the last interview (Ceci, Huffman, Smith, & Loftus, 1994). In a related study, preschoolers were asked repeatedly about an event they had not experienced, were told that their mothers had verified that the child had experienced the event, and were instructed to imagine it in their heads (that is, given multiple sources of suggestion). In this study, false affirmations of the event increased over trials (Ceci, Loftus, Leichtman, & Bruck, 1994). It is of interest that the adverse effects in this latter study were more pronounced for positive events (e.g., a hot air balloon ride) and neutral events (e.g., waiting for a bus) than for negative events (e.g., falling off a tricycle and getting stitches). These results imply that it would be more difficult to create false affirmations or false memories for abusive (negative) events than for many other types of events. Overall, these results indicate that the multiply suggestive nature of the interview is more important than repeated interviewing per se (Quas, 1998).

This conclusion is reinforced by a recent study by Garven, Wood, Malpass, and Shaw (1998). These researchers were able to obtain false allegations from 3- to 6-year-olds against a classroom visitor in a single multiply suggestive interview. The interview factors that seemed particularly important to the high error rates were social influence and reinforcement, such as implying that positive or negative consequences would follow an accusation and asking the child questions that she or he had just unambiguously answered. Such factors resulted in a 58% error rate, whereas suggestive questions alone resulted in a 17% error rate.

To the extent that false reports or false memories are created in such studies, an important question concerns how long such falsehoods last in children's eyewitness accounts. Two years after being repeatedly interviewed in a false memory study, relatively few children claimed to have experienced the false events (Huffman, Crossman, & Ceci, 1997). Thus, if false memories were formed, they tended not to endure. (Nevertheless, in some real cases, what may well have been false memories have endured.)

Such false memories are more readily obtained with 3- and 4-year-olds than with older children, but even within this young age group, false reports are related to individual differences among children in cognitive abilities and social influences (see Quas, Qin, Schaaf, & Goodman, 1997, for a review). For instance, in regard to cognitive abilities, a measure of inhibition that taps executive functioning (higher-order, goal-oriented cognitive behaviors) in children predicts how readily young children assent to suggestions of false events (Schaaf, Goodman, & Alexander, 1999). In regard to social factors, children who have high self-esteem are more likely to resist false suggestions than children with low self-esteem (Howie & Dowd, 1996; Vrij & Bush, 1998). Creativity has also been found to be positively related to children's increased false reports (Brown et al., 1999). Some of these findings are sporadic, however.

In forensic situations, interviewers may persistently ask leading questions in an attempt to confirm a previously held belief about what happened to a child, although typical forensic interviews do not appear to be tainted in this way (Lyon, 1999). Because of these expectations, interviewers may seek only confirmatory information and then neglect to explore other possibilities. (For a discussion of the social psychological literature on confirmatory hypothesis-testing biases, see Bottoms & Davis, 1997.) Studies on effects of interviewer bias either directly employ standardized biased interviews (Thompson, Clarke-Stewart, & Lepore, 1997) or provide interviewers with a set of beliefs that they can either confirm or disconfirm during the interview (Bruck, 1999; Goodman et al., 1995; White,

Leichtman, & Ceci, 1997). Results of studies using both types of paradigms indicate that children at times conform to interviewers' expectations even if conforming decreases children's accuracy. For example, Ceci and Huffman (1997) manipulated interviewers' beliefs about what preschoolers and kindergartners had done during a play session. Experienced social workers interviewed children after 1 month's delay. Across age groups, when the social workers were given accurate information prior to the interview, children provided little inaccurate information, whereas when the social workers received inaccurate information, the percentage of inaccurate information provided by the children increased. These effects were replicated in a subsequent interview 2 months later.

Clearly, there are situations in which children can be led to make false statements, including bizarre reports of satanic ritualistic abuse (Bottoms et al., 1996; Bottoms & Davis, 1997). The risks are especially apparent with 3-year-olds and then taper off, but do not disappear, at older ages. (In fact, adults are also subject to false reports and false memory effects: Bottoms et al., 1996; Loftus & Pickrell, 1995; Qin & Goodman, 1999). The false reports vary from children simply nodding their heads to providing elaborate false details. Even in a single interview, however, children may at one point confirm experiencing a false event and then later indicate that they did not experience it. Children's tendency to alternate between accurate and inaccurate answers makes claims of false memory less likely because a stable false memory should not lead to such variability in children's reports (Quas et al., 1999).

Critique of False Memory Research

Research on false memory and suggestibility in children remains controversial. Many types of memories, including memories of abuse or violence, cannot ethically be suggested to children (e.g., see Goodman, Quas, & Redlich, 1998; Herrmann & Yoder, 1998). Additionally, it is not always easy to verify that a supposedly false event never really occurred. Researchers typically question a participant's family members to determine whether the participant experienced a target event (such as being lost in a mall). But the verification of a family member is not proof positive that the event never happened; the questioned family member may be unaware of an experience of being lost that actually did occur. A further limitation is that ecological validity is often lacking in these studies in regard to the events being discussed. This leads to questions about how applicable this body of research is to the forensic setting, where it is often applied. This subsection of our chapter focuses on the limitations of false memory research and suggests that false reports of abuse, which clearly do occur in a certain subset of children and adults, may be more difficult to obtain than is implied by false memory research.

Pezdek and Hinz (in press) describe two specific shortcomings of false memory research. First, there is no clear operational definition of what a false memory is. Specifically, researchers often do not differentiate between false reporting and false memory. When children are interviewed, they may assent to a false event because they feel socially obligated to agree or because they believe the interviewer knows more than they do and thus must be correct. Although both cases might lead to false reports, in neither case would the child's memory have been altered by the questioning. Second, Pezdek and Hinz point out that false memory research is limited by its method of gathering true and false information. In a number of false memory studies (e.g., Ceci, Huffman, Smith, & Loftus, 1994; Loftus & Pickrell, 1995), researchers are forced to rely on family members' memory for these events. Their memories may be no more reliable than the child's in some situations.

Studies on false memory in children often deal with events that are not representative of abuse situations about which children would be interviewed in the forensic setting (Saywitz & Lyon, 2001). For example, certain events may be more or less plausible than others, and children are more likely to be susceptible to suggestions about more plausible events (Pezdek, Finger, & Hodge, 1997; but see Ornstein, Gordon, & Larus, 1992). In addition, revealing abuse (true or false) often involves a high price for the child, including betraying a loved one and discussing personal and embarrassing information with strangers (Lyon, 1999; but see Ceci & Friedman, 2000). Situations in which children provide false details about a man visiting their day-care center (e.g., Leichtman & Ceci, 1995) may not be comparable to situations more typical of forensic interviews about abuse. Although the false memory studies have scientific value in furthering theory and research, the events used and the content discussed often differ in important ways from those of interest in abuse investigations and thus may not always or easily generalize to forensic settings.

Finally, some false memory researchers, in their attempts to right the wrongs of egregious interviewing seen in several sensational day-care cases of the past, have used scoring techniques that make children look particularly inaccurate. For instance, in studies by Leichtman and Ceci (1995) on the effects of stereotypes and suggestion on preschoolers' memory and by Poole and Lindsay (1995) on the effects of repeated parent-provided misinformation, data were scored and analyzed in terms of children who make "one or more incorrect answers." Specifically, if children were asked 10 questions and each child incorrectly answered only 1 of them, the data would normally be scored as showing the children to be 90% correct; however, when children's data are scored as wrong if they make one or more incorrect answers, the same children are portrayed as being 100% incorrect. This unorthodox scoring system heightens the impression of inaccuracy.

It is important to clarify the limitations of false memory research because of reliance on false memory studies in the legal system. This research is increasingly cited in courts of law to provide scientific evidence to decision makers about the veracity of children's testimony (e.g., see Bruck, 1999). Thus, in the long term, this body of research has the potential to influence life-changing decisions for victims and defendants alike. Consequently, false memory research should be held to the highest scientific standards (Pezdek & Hinz, in press), critically examined to determine its relevance in any given case, and balanced to meet the needs of both science and the legal system (Saywitz & Lyon, 2002; see Lyon, this volume, for discussion).

It is sometimes asked if the recent flood of false memory research has returned us to a time when children's testimony is overly doubted. The answer to this question may be a qualified "yes." Over the years, in conducting numerous studies of mock jurors' reactions to child witnesses (e.g., Bottoms & Goodman, 1994; Goodman, Golding, Helgeson, Haith, & Michelli, 1987; Goodman,

Tobey, Batterman-Faunce, Orcutt, Thomas, & Sachsenmaier, 1998; Goodman et al., 1996), we have noted an increase in jurors' doubting children's testimony. Mock jurors have commented during deliberations on false memory studies (as depicted in the media) and have used these studies as a basis for not believing children who are telling the truth. In these cases, it was known that the children were telling the truth because an objective record of the events in question was made as part of the studies. False memory studies may have affected the public generally by creating or increasing skepticism about children's statements. To the extent that false reports exist, such skepticism is appropriate. To the extent that false memory studies overstate the suggestibility of children and are inappropriately applied, children who are accurate may not be believed.

Summary and Implications

Multiply suggestive questioning (e.g., combinations of misleading suggestions, social reinforcement, interviewer bias, stereotypes, instructions to pretend) can adversely influence children's eyewitness memory reports, leading to greater error than less suggestive questioning. Individual differences in children's false memory creation also play an important role. When children are questioned in a forensic interview or required to provide testimony, they are not simply asked to perform a memory test but also to handle a complex situation in which many social pressures come to bear. Although children may sometimes make false statements, it is far less clear that forensic interviewers *often* create false memories. False memory research has limitations and must be evaluated cautiously when applied to forensic settings.

FUTURE DIRECTIONS FOR RESEARCH AND LEGAL TRENDS

As researchers answer more and more questions about children's capabilities as eyewitnesses, they will be able to provide more information to those in the justice and social service systems, allowing children's testimony to be elicited and evaluated in the best manner possible. Studies of children's eyewitness memory also provide valuable information relevant to basic theory concerning children's memory and cognitive development. In this section, we address several current trends in both the legal and research arenas.

Legal Trends

A current trend in the legal arena concerns taint hearings. Some argue that such proceedings in effect replace competence hearings of the past, but with a specific focus on children's suggestibility. Taint hearings were prompted by the decision in *State of New Jersey v. Michaels* (1994). In this case, it was ruled on appeal that children were subjected to such egregiously suggestive interview techniques that their reports had become "tainted" and their statements were therefore suspect. The conviction was overturned, and the court took the unprecedented step of requiring that taint hearings be held before the children were allowed to testify at trial. Based on this ruling, attorneys in New Jersey (and, based on other state court rulings, attorneys in a few other states as well) can request taint hearings when concerned about the interviewing practices used with children, which is a typical challenge to children's credibility in child sexual abuse cases (Goodman, Quas, Bulkley, & Shapiro, 1999). Taint hearings are held to determine whether children's allegations of abuse are the result of overly zealous questioning rather than based on fact. If the results of the hearing cause a judge to determine that children's testimony was tainted by pretrial suggestion, the children would be barred from testifying. The concept of the taint hearing assumes that once a child is exposed to overly suggestive questioning, his or her testimony becomes "forever tainted" (Lyon, 1999) and therefore cannot be admissible in court. Interestingly, one of the lead authors (Ceci) of an *amicus* brief that was written in part to convince the *Michaels* appeal court to institute taint hearings has recently argued against such hearings (see Ceci & Friedman, 2000), presenting a position consistent with that of one of the lead authors (Goodman) of the present chapter when she declined to endorse the *amicus* brief.

The assumptions on which the concept of taint hearings rest are generally not agreed on but are open to empirical investigation. Although research has indicated that suggestive questioning, especially multiply misleading questioning, can cause children to give false reports, the degree to which children come to believe in the veracity of those reports is still debated (Bjorklund et al., 1997; Papierno, Hembrooke, & Ceci, 1998). As mentioned earlier, one study that investigated the long-term effects of false memory reports revealed that for most children, false memories do not endure (Huffman et al., 1997). In fact, many of those children recalled much of the true detail from 2 years before and denied most of the false information presented. Similarly, in a study that investigated children's memories for science demonstrations, Poole and Lindsay (1997) found that although children's false reporting rates were elevated immediately after the presentation of the misleading information, their accuracy rebounded at a later interview. Additionally, Quas et al. (1999) found that false reports decreased in response to more detailed questioning. Nevertheless, for some children, false memories may endure.

Many children can provide accurate reports, especially of central actions, even after the acceptance and earlier reporting of misinformation and certainly after mere exposure to misinformation (e.g., Schwartz-Kenney & Goodman, 1999). Consequently, the assumption that improper questioning renders children incapable of remembering and reporting the truth at a later time in a different situation is not fully supported by research, and deserves further investigation with carefully controlled studies to help inform legal practice in the future.

Another important legal trend is the use of child advocacy centers. These centers are designed to help investigators maximize the amount and accuracy of information elicited from children while minimizing the negative aspects of children's legal involvement, such as multiple interviews (Goodman et al., 1992; Tedesco & Schnell, 1987). Many jurisdictions across the nation are now establishing these multidisciplinary interviewing centers to improve the fact-finding process with child victims. Goals include reducing the number of interviews, promoting interagency cooperation, providing a child-friendly environment for forensic interviews, and maximizing valid and reliable information obtained from children by using forensically sound, developmentally appropriate interviewing techniques (Myers et al., 1994). These centers can help to ensure that problematic interviewing practices by legal agencies are a thing of the past.

Benefits derived from such centers are demonstrated in a final report to the California attorney general's office (Myers et al., 1994). This report was based on a project that established several multidisciplinary interviewing centers in California. The goals of the project, namely to increase the accuracy and completeness of children's reports and decrease stress for children in the legal system, were achieved because of highly trained interviewers who were made aware of the needs of the various agencies involved and of sound interviewing practices based on scientific research.

Research Trends

In the research arena, a number of new trends have emerged, but we focus on only two here. First, there has been growing interest in research on individual differences in children's eyewitness capabilities. It is important to come to a greater understanding of the characteristics that make children more or less prone to suggestion and misleading questions. Such individual differences are of interest because research on group differences offers limited information about how a certain child will react under particular circumstances, which is the main concern of the legal system. With increased knowledge about the circumstances under which individual children may be more or less prone to error, interviews could be designed for specific children, taking their individual characteristics into consideration. In addition, increased knowledge would enable courts to make better evaluations of children's testimony.

A number of individual differences are being investigated for their role in children's eyewitness testimony (Quas et al., 1997). These include cognitive factors such as children's ability to maintain simultaneously two representations of a single object (dual object representation; Welch-Ross, Diecidue, & Miller, 1997), ability to inhibit irrelevant information and inappropriate responses (inhibition; Schaaf et al., 1999), and ability to distinguish between different sources of information (source monitoring; Poole & Lindsay, 1995). Social factors such as attachment (Goodman et al., 1997) and parent–child communication (Tessler & Nelson, 1994) also affect children's eyewitness reports. Although some of these individual differences are of interest primarily for theoretical reasons, others are potentially important for the development of interview and courtroom techniques to increase children's accuracy and effectiveness.

A second new direction concerns the development and testing of interviewing techniques for use with children. Primary examples include the cognitive interview, narrative elaboration, the stepwise interview, and structured interview protocols (Camparo et al., 1999; McCauley & Fisher, 1995; Saywitz, Geiselman, & Bornstein, 1992; Saywitz & Snyder, 1996; Sternberg, Lamb, Esplin, & Baradaran, 1999; Yuille, 1988). Although the methods vary and have somewhat different theoretical underpinnings, similarities do exist. Interviewers are taught to pay special attention to building rapport with the child, assess the child's developmental level and linguistic abilities, familiarize the child with the format of the interview, and avoid leading and suggestive questions when possible. Extensive use of open-ended questions instead of specific or "yes-no" questions is advocated (Fisher & McCauley, 1995; Geiselman, Saywitz, & Bornstein, 1993; Poole & Lamb, 1998; Yuille, Hunter, Joffe, & Zaparniuk, 1993). The benefits of these interviewing techniques need to be evaluated further and individual differences explored to develop optimal ways to interview children. Interviewers would best be served by having a variety of empirically validated techniques at hand, along with knowledge about which is best for a particular child in a certain case.

Also recognized as important by researchers is the benefit of training interviewers. Despite the existence of thoughtful guidelines and relatively nonleading interviewing protocols, interviewers do not always utilize them. Training programs have therefore been developed to improve the quality of interviewing techniques, although they may not always be successful (Aldridge & Cameron, 1999; Warren et al., 1999). Some studies, however, do indicate that training can be effective (Lindberg, Chapman, & Thomas, 1999; Orbach, Lamb, & Sternberg, 1999). Training programs that provide opportunities for practice and critical feedback may be particularly useful in training interviewers, and efforts in this direction have begun (Orbach et al., 1999).

CONCLUSION

Research and legal landscapes both constantly change. By being responsive to each other, legal professionals and social science researchers can work in tandem to increase the benefits to society.

In the case of child abuse, the possible benefits to society are considerable. Reducing child abuse serves the twin goals of justice and child protection. Society faces two serious dangers in dealing with child eyewitnesses: the problem of underreporting of abuse and the danger of false reports. With careful research and prudent application in policy and law, these twin dangers may be minimized to the benefit of all.

References

Aldridge, J., & Cameron, S. (1999). Interviewing child witnesses: Questioning techniques and the role of training. *Applied Developmental Science,* *3*, 136–147.

Arata, C. M. (1998). To tell or not to tell: Current functioning of child sexual abuse survivors who disclosed their victimization. *Child Maltreatment, 3*, 63–71.

Azarian, A.G., Lipsitt, L. P., Miller, T. W., & Skriptchenko-Gregorian, V. G. (1999). Toddlers remember quake trauma. In L. M. Williams & V. L. Banyard (Eds.), *Trauma and memory* (pp. 299–309). Thousand Oaks, CA: Sage.

Azarian, A., Miller, T. W., & Skriptchenko-Gregorian, V. (1996). Baseline assessment of children traumatized by the Armenian earthquake. *Child Psychiatry and Human Development, 27*, 29–41.

Bahrick, L. E., Parker, J. F., Fivush, R., & Levitt, M. (1998). The effects of stress on young children's memory for a natural disaster. *Journal of Experimental Psychology: Applied, 4*, 308–331.

Berliner, L., & Conte, J. R. (1995). The effects of disclosure and intervention on sexually abused children. *Child Abuse and Neglect, 19*, 371–384.

Bidrose, S., & Goodman, G. S. (2000). Testimony and evidence: A scientific case study of memory for child sexual abuse. *Applied Cognitive Psychology, 14*, 197–213.

Bjorklund, B. R., Douglas, R. N., Park, C. L., Nelson, L. K., Sanders, L., Gache, J., Cassel, W. S., & Bjorklund, D. F. (1997, April). *When does misleading questioning cause children to change their minds as well as their answers?* Poster presented at the biennial meeting of the Society for Research in Child Development, Washington, DC.

Bottoms, B. L., & Davis, S. L. (1997). The creation of satanic ritual abuse. *Journal of Social and Clinical Psychology, 16*, 112–132.

Bottoms, B. L., & Goodman, G. S. (1994). Evaluation of children's testimony: Factors influencing the jury. *Journal of Applied Social Psychology, 24,* 702–732.

Bottoms, B. L., Goodman, G. S., Schwartz-Kenney, B., & Thomas, S. (in press). Keeping secrets. *Law and Human Behavior.*

Bottoms, B. L., Shaver, P. R., & Goodman, G. S. (1996). Allegations of ritualistic and religion-related child abuse. *Law and Human Behavior, 20,* 1–34.

Bower, G. H. (1992). How might emotions affect learning? In S. A. Christianson (Ed.), *Handbook of emotion and memory: Research and theory* (pp. 3–31). Hillsdale, NJ: Erlbaum.

Bradley, A. R., & Wood, J. M. (1996). How do children tell? The disclosure process in child sexual abuse. *Child Abuse and Neglect, 20,* 881–891.

Brainerd, C., & Ornstein, P. A. (1991). Children's memory for witnessed events: The developmental backdrop. In J. Doris (Ed.), *The suggestibility of children's recollections* (pp. 10–20). Washington, DC: American Psychological Association.

Brown, R. D., Bjorklund, D. F., Singer, K., Muller, K., Sheridan, T., & Reiss, T. (1999, April). *Individual differences in cognitive factors related to children's false memory creation.* Poster presented at the biennial meeting of the Society for Research in Child Development, Albuquerque, NM.

Bruck, M. (1999). A summary of an affidavit prepared for the case of *Commonwealth of Massachussets v. Cheryl Amirault LeFave. Applied Developmental Sciences, 3,* 110–127.

Bruck, M., & Ceci, S. (1998). Reliability and credibility of young children's reports: From research to policy and practice. *American Psychologist, 53,* 136–151.

Bruck, M., & Ceci, S. J. (1999). The suggestibility of children's memory. *Annual Review of Psychology, 50,* 419–439.

Bruck, M., Ceci, S. J., & Francoeur, E. (1999). The accuracy of mothers' memories of conversations with their preschool children. *Journal of Experimental Psychology: Applied, 5,* 89–106.

Bruck, M., Ceci, S. J., Francouer, E., & Renick, A. (1995). Anatomically detailed dolls do not facilitate preschoolers' reports of a pediatric examination involving genital touching. *Journal of Experimental Psychology: Applied, 1,* 95–109.

Bruck, M., Ceci, S. J., & Hembrooke, H. (1998). Reliability and credibility of young children's reports. *American Psychologist, 53,* 136–151.

Bussey, K., Lee, K., & Grimbeek, E. J. (1993). Lies and secrets: Implications for children's reporting of sexual abuse. In G. S. Goodman & B. L. Bottoms (Eds.), *Child victims, child witnesses: Understanding and improving testimony* (pp. 147–168). New York: Guilford Press.

Camparo, L. B., Wagner, J. T., Saywitz, K. J., Jawad, M., Fregoso-Graciano, N., Brown, A., & Medina, C. (1999, April). *Interviewing children about real and fictitious events: Revisiting the narrative elaboration procedure.* Poster presented at the biennial meeting of the Society for Research in Child Development, Albuquerque, NM.

Campis, L. B., Hebden-Curtis, J., & DeMaso, D. R. (1993). Developmental differences in detection and disclosure of sexual abuse. *Journal of the American Academy of Child and Adolescent Psychiatry, 3,* 920–924.

Carter, C. A., Bottoms, B. L., & Levine, M. (1996). Linguistic and socioemotional influences on the accuracy of children's reports. *Law and Human Behavior, 20,* 335–358.

Castelli, P., Goodman, G. S., & Ghetti, S. (2000, March). Jurors' reactions to leading questioning in child sexual abuse cases. In B. L. Bottoms & M. B. Kovera (Chairs), *Juror decision making in cases involving child witnesses.* Symposium conducted at the biennial meeting of the American Psychology–Law Society, New Orleans.

Ceci, S. J., & Bruck, M. (1995). *Jeopardy in the courtroom: A scientific analysis of children's testimony.* Washington, DC: American Psychological Association.

Ceci, S. P., & Friedman, R. D. (2000). The suggestibility of children: Scientific research and legal implications. *Cornell Law Review, 86,* 33–108.

Ceci, S. J., & Huffman, M. L. C. (1997). How suggestible are preschool children? Cognitive and social factors. *Journal of the American Academy of Child and Adolescent Psychiatry, 36,* 948–958.

Ceci, S. J., Huffman, M. L. C., Smith, E., & Loftus, E. F. (1994). Repeatedly thinking about a non-event: Source misattribution among preschoolers. *Consciousness and Cognition, 3,* 388–407.

Ceci, S. J., Loftus, E. F., Leichtman, M., & Bruck, M. (1994) The role of source misattributions in the creation of false beliefs among preschoolers. *International Journal of Clinical and Experimental Hypnosis, 62,* 304–320.

Christianson, S. A. (1992). Emotional stress and eyewitness memory: A critical review. *Psychological Bulletin, 112,* 284–309.

Connolly, D. A., & Lindsay, D. S. (2001). The influence of suggestions on children's reports of a unique event versus an instance of a repeated event. *Applied Cognitive Psychology, 15,* 205–223.

Davis, S., & Bottoms, B. L. (2002). The effects of social support on the accuracy of children's statements: Implications for the forensic interview. In M. Eisen, J. A. Quas, & G. S. Goodman (Eds.), *Memory and suggestibility in the forensic interview* (pp. 437–476). Mahwah, NJ: Erlbaum.

De Young, M. (1987). Disclosing sexual abuse: The impact of developmental variables. *Child Welfare League of America, 66,* 217–223.

Dodge, K., Bates, J., & Pettit, G. S. (1990). Mechanisms in the cycle of violence. *Science, 250,* 1678–1683.

Eisen, M. L., Goodman, G. S., Davis, S. L., & Qin, J. (1999). Individual differences in maltreated children's memory and suggestibility. In L. M. Williams & V. L. Banyard (Eds.), *Trauma and memory* (pp. 31–46). Thousand Oaks, CA: Sage.

Eisen, M. L., Goodman, G. S., Qin, J., & Davis, S. L. (1998). Memory and suggestibility in maltreated children: New research relevant to evaluating allegations of abuse. In S. J. Lynn & K. M. McConkey (Eds.), *Truth in memory* (pp. 163–189). New York: Guilford Press.

Farrell, L. T. (1988). Factors that affect a victim's self-disclosure in father–daughter incest. *Child Welfare League of America, 57,* 462–468.

Fischer, K. W., & Bidell, T. R. (1998). Dynamic development of psychological structures in action and thought. In W. Damon & R. M. Lerner (Eds.), *Handbook of child psychology: Vol. 1. Theoretical models of human development* (pp. 467–561). New York: Wiley.

Fisher, R. P., & McCauley, M. R. (1995). Improving eyewitness testimony with the cognitive interview. In M. S. Zaragoza, J. R. Graham, G. Hall, R. Hirschman, & Y. S. Ben-Porath (Eds.), *Memory and testimony in the child witness* (pp. 141–159). Thousand Oaks, CA: Sage.

Garven, S., Wood, J. M., Malpass, R. S., & Shaw, J. S. (1998). More than suggestion: The effect of interviewing techniques from the McMartin Preschool case. *Journal of Applied Psychology, 83,* 347–359.

Geiselman, R. E., Saywitz, K. J., & Bornstein, G. K. (1993). Effects of cognitive questioning techniques on children's recall performance. In G. S. Goodman & B. L. Bottoms (Eds.), *Child victims, child witnesses: Understanding and improving testimony* (pp. 71–93). New York: Guilford Press.

Gold, P. E., & McCarty, R. C. (1995). Stress regulation of memory processes: Role of peripheral catecholamines and glucose. In M. J. Friedman, D. S. Charney, & A. Y. Deutch (Eds.), *Neurobiological and clinical consequences of stress: From normal adaptation to post-traumatic stress disorder* (pp. 151–162). Philadelphia: Lippincott-Raven.

Goldman, R., & Goldman, J. (1984). Perception of sexual experience in childhood: Relating normal development to incest. *Australian Journal of Sex, Marriage and Family, 5,* 159–166.

Gonzalez, L. S., Waterman, J., Kelly, R. J., McCord, J., & Oliveri, M. K. (1993). Children's patterns of disclosures and recantations of sexual and ritualistic abuse allegations in psychotherapy. *Child Abuse and Neglect, 17,* 81–89.

Goodman, G. S., Batterman-Faunce, J., Schaaf, J. M., & Kenney, R. (in press). Nearly four years after an event: Professionals' and nonprofessionals' assessments of accuracy. *Child Abuse and Neglect.*

Goodman, G. S., Bottoms, B. L., Rudy, L., Davis, S. L., & Schwartz-Kenney, B. M. (2001). Effects of past abuse experiences on children's eyewitness memory. *Law and Human Behavior, 25,* 269–298.

Goodman, G. S., Bottoms, B. L., Schwartz-Kenney, B, M., & Rudy, L. (1991). Children's testimony about a stressful event: Improving children's reports. *Journal of Narrative and Life History, 1,* 69–99.

Goodman, G. S., Golding, J., Helgeson, V., Haith, M. M., & Michelli, J. (1987). When a child takes the stand: Jurors' perceptions of children's eyewitness testimony. *Law and Human Behavior, 11,* 27–40.

Goodman, G. S., Hirschman, J. E., Hepps, D., & Rudy, L. (1991). Children's memory for stressful events. *Merrill-Palmer Quarterly, 37,* 109–157.

Goodman, G. S., Myers, J., Qin, J. J., Quas, J., Schuder, M., Rogers, L., & Redlich, A. (1996, February). Should interviews of children be videotaped or adults testify in children's place?: Effects of hearsay on jurors' decisions. In B. L. Bottoms (Chair), *Jurors' reactions to child witnesses.* Symposium presented at the American Psychology and Law Society meetings, Hilton Head, SC.

Goodman, G. S., Quas, J. A., Batterman-Faunce, J. M., Riddlesberger, M. M., & Kuhn, J. (1994). Predictors of accurate and inaccurate memories of traumatic events experienced in childhood. *Consciousness and Cognition, 3,* 269–294.

Goodman, G. S., Quas, J. A., Batterman-Faunce, J. M., Riddlesberger, M. M., & Kuhn, J. (1997). Children's reactions to and memory for a stressful event: Influences of age, anatomical dolls, knowledge, and parental attachment. *Applied Developmental Science, 1,* 54–75.

Goodman, G. S., Quas, J., Bulkley, J., & Shapiro, C. (1999). Innovations for child witnesses: A national survey. *Psychology, Public Policy, and Law, 5,* 255–281.

Goodman, G. S., Quas, J., & Redlich, A. D. (1998). The ethics of conducting "false memory" studies with children: A reply to Herrmann and Yoder. *Applied Cognitive Psychology, 12,* 207–217.

Goodman, G. S., Sharma, A, Thomas, S. F., & Considine, M. G. (1995). Mother knows best: Effects of relationship status and interviewer bias on children's memory. *Journal of Experimental Child Psychology, 60,* 195–228.

Goodman, G. S., Taub, E. P., Jones, D. P., England, P., Port, R. L., & Prado, L. (1992). Testifying in criminal court: Emotional effects on child sexual assault victims. *Monographs of the Society for Research in Child Development, 57,* Serial No. 229.

Goodman, G. S., Tobey, A., Batterman-Faunce, J., Orcutt, H., Thomas, S., Shapiro, C., & Sachsenmaier, T. (1998). Face-to-face confrontation: Effects of closed-circuit technology on children's eyewitness testimony and jurors' decisions. *Law and Human Behavior, 22,* 165–203.

Goodman-Brown, T. B. (1994). *Why children tell: A model of children's disclosure of sexual abuse.* Unpublished doctoral dissertation, California School of Professional Psychology, Los Angeles.

Herrmann, D., & Yoder, C. (1998). The potential effects of the implanted memory paradigm on child subjects. *Applied Cognitive Psychology, 12,* 198–206.

Hewitt, S. K. (1994). Preverbal sexual abuse: What two children report in later years. *Child Abuse and Neglect, 18,* 821–826.

Howe, M. L. (1997). Children's memory for traumatic experiences. *Learning and Individual Differences, 9,* 153–174.

Howie, P. M., & Dowd, H. J. (1996). Self-esteem and the perceived obligation to respond: Effects on children's testimony. *Legal and Criminological Psychology, 1,* 197–209.

Huffman, M. L., Crossman, A. M., & Ceci, S. J. (1997). Are false memories permanent? An investigation of the long-term effects of source misattributions. *Consciousness and Cognition, 6,* 482–490.

Jones, D. P. H., & Krugman, R. (1986). Can a 3-year-old child bear witness to her sexual assault and attempted murder? *Child Abuse and Neglect, 10,* 253–258.

Jones, D. P. H., & McGraw, J. M. (1987). Reliable and fictitious account of sexual abuse in children. *Journal of Interpersonal Violence, 2,* 27–45.

Keary, K., & Fitzpatrick, C. (1994). Children's disclosure of sexual abuse during formal investigation. *Child Abuse and Neglect, 18,* 543–548.

Kirsh, S. J., & Cassidy, J. (1997). Preschoolers' attention to and memory for attachment-relevant information. *Child Development, 68,* 1143–1153.

Lawson, L., & Chaffin, M. (1992). False negatives in sexual abuse disclosure interviews: Incidence and influence of caretaker's belief in abuse cases of accidental abuse discovery by diagnosis of STD. *Journal of Interpersonal Violence, 7,* 532–542.

Leichtman, M. D., & Ceci, S. J. (1995). The effects of stereotypes and suggestions on preschoolers' reports. *Developmental Psychology, 31,* 568–578.

Lepore, S. J., & Sesco, B. (1994). Distorting children's reports and interpretations of events through suggestion. *Journal of Applied Psychology, 79,* 108–120.

Lindberg, M. A., Chapman, M. T., & Thomas, S. W. (1999, April). *Tests of three approaches to interviewing child witnesses.* Paper presented at the biennial meeting of the Society for Research in Child Development, Albuquerque, NM.

Loftus, E. F., & Pickrell, J. E. (1995). The formation of false memories. *Psychiatric Annals, 25,* 720–725.

Lyon, T. D. (1999). The new wave in children's suggestibility research: A critique. *Cornell Law Review, 84,* 1004–1087.

McCauley, M. R., & Fisher, R. P. (1995). Enhancing children's eyewitness testimony with the Cognitive Interview. In G. Davies & S. Lloyd-Bostock (Eds.). *Psychology, law, and criminal justice: International developments in research and practice* (pp. 127–134). Berlin: Walter De Gruyter.

Mian, M., Wehrspann, W., Klajner-Diamond, J., LeBaron, D., & Winder, C. (1986). Review of 15 children 6 years of age and under who were sexually abused. *Child Abuse and Neglect, 10,* 223–229.

Myers, J. E. B., Saywitz, K., Gordon, S. M., Stewart, D. C., Pizzini, S., & Walton, T. (1994). *Child victim witness investigative pilot projects: Research and evaluation final report.* Sacramento: California Attorney General's Office.

Orbach, Y., & Lamb, M. E. (1999). Assessing the accuracy of a child's account of sexual abuse: A case study. *Child Abuse and Neglect, 23,* 91–98.

Orbach, Y., Lamb, M. E., & Sternberg, K. J. (1999, August). Enhancing the quality of forensic interviews in field settings by implementing interview protocols. In M. E. Lamb & D. Poole (Chairs), *Interviewing children in the legal context*. Symposium conducted at the annual meeting of the American Psychological Association Conference, Boston.

Ornstein, P. A., Gordon, B. N., & Larus, D. M. (1992). Children's memory for a personally experienced event: Implications for testimony. *Applied Cognitive Psychology, 6*, 49–60.

Ornstein, P. A., Merritt, K. A., Baker-Ward, L., Furtado, E., Gordon, B. N., & Principe, G. (1998). Children's knowledge, expectation, and long-term retention. *Applied Cognitive Psychology, 12*, 387–405.

Papierno, P., Hembrooke, H., & Ceci, S. J. (1998, March). *The role of saliency in children's source misattribution for experienced and nonexperienced events*. Poster presented at the biennial meeting of the American Psychology and Law Society, Redondo Beach, CA.

Peterson, C. (1999). Children's memory for medical emergencies: Two years later. *Developmental Psychology, 35*, 1493–1506.

Peterson, C., & Bell, M. (1996). Children's memory for traumatic injury. *Child Development, 67*, 3045–3070.

Pezdek, K., Finger, K., & Hodge, D. (1997). Planting false childhood memories: The role of event plausibility. *Psychological Science, 8*, 437–441.

Pezdek, K., & Hinz, T. (in press). The construction of false events in memory. In H. Westcott, G. Davies, & R. Bull (Eds.), *Children's testimony in context*. London: Wiley.

Pezdek, K., & Hodge, D. (1999). Planting false childhood memories in children: The role of event plausibility. *Child Development, 70*, 887–895.

Pezdek, K., & Roe, C. (1995). The effect of memory trace strength on suggestibility. *Journal of Experimental Child Psychology, 60*, 116–128.

Pillemer, D. B., Picariello, M. L., & Pruett, J. C. (1994). Very long-term memories of a salient preschool event. *Applied Cognitive Psychology, 8*, 95–106.

Pollak, S., Cicchetti, D., & Klorman, R. (1998). Stress, memory, and emotion: Developmental considerations from the study of child maltreatment. *Development and Psychopathology, 10*, 811–828.

Poole, D. A., & Lamb, M. E. (1998). *Investigative interviews of children: A guide for helping professionals*. Washington, DC: American Psychological Association.

Poole, D. A., & Lindsay, D. S. (1995). Interviewing preschoolers: Effects of nonsuggestive techniques, parental coaching, and leading questions on reports of nonexperienced events. *Journal of Experimental Child Psychology, 60*, 129–154.

Poole, D. A., & Lindsay, D. S. (1997, April). *Misinformation from parents and children's source monitoring: Implications for testimony*. Paper presented at the biennial meeting of the Society for Research in Child Development, Washington, DC.

Poole, D., A., & Lindsay, D. S. (2002). Children's suggestibility. In M. Eisen, J. A. Quas, & G. S. Goodman (Eds.), *Memory and suggestibility in the forensic interview* (pp. 355–382). Mahwah, NJ: Erlbaum.

Powell, M. B., Roberts, K., Ceci, S., & Hembrooke, H. (1999). The effects of repeated experience on children's suggestibility. *Developmental Psychology, 35*, 1462–1477.

Pynoos, R. S., & Nader, K. (1989). Children's memory and proximity to violence. *Journal of the American Academy of Child and Adolescent Psychiatry, 28*, 236–241.

Qin, J., & Goodman, G. S. (1999, November). *Individual differences and characteristics of false memory.* Paper presented at the annual meeting of the Psychonomics Society, Los Angeles.

Quas, J. A. (1998). *Children's memory of experienced and non-experienced events across repeated interviews.* Unpublished doctoral dissertation, University of California, Davis.

Quas, J. A., Denton, M., Goodman, G. S., & Myers, J. (1996, February). Consistency in children's true and false reports. In J. Quas & G. S. Goodman (Chairs), *Children's eyewitness memory: True and false reports.* Symposium presented at the biennial meeting of the American Psychology and Law Society, Hilton Head, SC.

Quas, J. A., Goodman, G. S., Bidrose, S., Pipe, M-E., Craw, S., & Ablin, D. (1999). Emotion and memory: Children's remembering, forgetting, and suggestibility. *Journal of Experimental Child Psychology, 72*, 235–270.

Quas, J. A., Qin, J., Schaaf, J. M., & Goodman, G. S. (1997). Individual differences in children's and adults' suggestibility and false event memory. *Learning and Individual Differences, 9*, 359–390.

Rholes, W. S., & Ruble, D. N. (1984). Children's understanding of dispositional characteristics of others. *Child Development, 55*, 550–560.

Roesler, T. A. (1994). Reactions to disclosure of childhood sexual abuse: The effect on adult symptoms. *Journal of Nervous and Mental Disease, 182*, 618–624.

Roesler, T. A., & Wind, T. W. (1994). Telling the secret: Adult women describe their disclosures of incest. *Journal of Interpersonal Violence, 9*, 327–338.

Rudy, L., & Goodman, G. S. (1991). Effects of participation on children's reports: Implications for children's testimony. *Developmental Psychology, 27*, 1–26.

Russell, D. E. H. (1986). *The secret trauma: Incest in the lives of girls and women.* New York: Basic Books.

Sapolsky, R. M. (1992). *Stress, the aging brain, and the mechanisms of neuron death.* Cambridge, MA: MIT Press.

Sauzier, M. (1989). Disclosure of child sexual abuse: For better or for worse. *Psychiatric Clinics of North America, 12*, 455–469.

Saywitz, K. J. (1995). Improving children's testimony: The question, the answer, and the environment. In M. S. Zaragoza, J. R. Graham, G. Hall, R. Hirschman, & Y. S. Ben-Porath (Eds.), *Memory and testimony in the child witness* (pp. 113–140). Thousand Oaks, CA: Sage.

Saywitz, K. J., Geiselman, R. E., & Bornstein, G. K. (1992). Effects of cognitive interviewing and practice on children's recall performance. *Journal of Applied Psychology, 77,* 744–756.

Saywitz, K. J., Goodman, G. S., Nicholas, E., & Moan, S. F. (1991). Children's memories of a physical examination involving genital touch: Implications for reports of child sexual abuse. *Journal of Consulting and Clinical Psychology, 59,* 682–691.

Saywitz, K., & Lyon, T. (2002). Coming to grips with children's suggestibility. In M. Eisen, J. A. Quas, & G. S. Goodman (Eds.), *Memory and suggestibility in the forensic interview* (pp. 85–114). Mahwah, NJ: Erlbaum.

Saywitz, K. J., & Snyder, L. (1996). Narrative elaboration: Test of a new procedure for interviewing children. *Journal of Consulting and Clinical Psychology, 64,* 1347–1357.

Schaaf, J. M., Goodman, G. S., & Alexander, K. W. (1999). *Effects of repeated questions on children's memory and suggestibility about true and false events.* Paper presented at the biennial meeting of the Society for Research in Child Development, Albuquerque, NM.

Schwartz-Kenney, B. M., & Goodman, G. S. (1999). Children's memory of a naturalistic event following misinformation. *Applied Developmental Sciences, 3,* 34–46.

Smith, D. W., Letourneau, E. J., Saunders, B. E., Kilpatrick, D. G., Resnick, H. S., & Best, C. L. (2000). Delay in disclosure of childhood rape: Results from a national survey. *Child Abuse and Neglect, 2,* 273–287.

Sorenson, T., & Snow, B. (1991). How children tell: The process of disclosure in child sexual abuse. *Child Welfare League of America, 70,* 3–15.

Spaccarelli, S. (1994). Stress, appraisal, and coping in child sexual abuse: A theoretical and empirical review. *Psychological Bulletin, 116,* 340–362.

State v. Amirault LeFave, Middlesex S. Ct. 8563 (MA., 1985).

State of New Jersey v. Michaels, 136 N. J. 299, 642 A.2d 1372 (N. J., 1994).

Sternberg, K. J., Lamb, M. E., Esplin, P. W., & Baradaran, L. P. (1999). Using a scripted protocol in investigative interviews: A pilot study. *Applied Developmental Science, 3,* 70–76.

Summit, R. (1983). The child sexual abuse accommodation syndrome. *Child Abuse and Neglect, 7,* 177–193.

Tedesco, J., & Schnell, S. (1987). Children's reactions to sex abuse investigation and litigation. *Child Abuse and Neglect, 11,* 267–272.

Terr, L. (1988). What happens to early memories of trauma? A study of 20 children under age 5 at the time of the documented traumatic events. *Journal of the American Academy of Child and Adolescent Psychiatry, 27,* 96–104.

Tessler, M., & Nelson, K. (1994). Making memories: The influence of joint encoding on later recall by young children. *Consciousness and Cognition, 3,* 307–326.

Thompson, W. C., Clarke-Stewart, K. A., & Lepore, S. J. (1997). What did the janitor do? Suggestive interviewing and the accuracy of children's accounts. *Law and Human Behavior, 21,* 405–426.

Tobey, A. E., & Goodman, G. S. (1992). Children's eyewitness memory: Effects of participation and forensic context. *Child Abuse and Neglect, 16,* 779–796.

van der Kolk, B. A. (1996). Trauma and memory. In B. A. van der Kolk & A. C. McFarlane (Eds.), *Traumatic stress: The effects of overwhelming experience on mind, body, and society* (pp. 279–302). New York: Guilford Press.

Vrij, A., & Bush, N. (1998, March). *Differences in suggestibility between 5–6 and 10–11 year olds.* Paper presented at the biennial meeting of the American Psychology–Law Society, Redondo Beach, CA.

Warren, A. R., & Lane, P. (1995). Effects of timing and type of questioning on eyewitness accuracy and suggestibility. In M. S. Zaragoza, J. R. Graham, G. C. N. Hall, R. Hirschman, & Y. S. Ben-Porath (Eds.), *Memory and testimony in the child witness* (pp. 44–60). Thousand Oaks, CA: Sage.

Warren, A. R., & Woodall, C. E. (1999). The reliability of hearsay testimony: How well do interviewers recall their interviews with children? *Psychology, Public Policy, and Law, 5,* 355–371.

Warren, A. R., Woodall, C. E., Thomas, M., Nunno, M., Keeney, J. M., Larson, S. M., & Stadfeld, J. A. (1999). Assessing the effectiveness of a training program for interviewing child witnesses. *Applied Developmental Science, 3,* 128–135.

Welch-Ross, M. K., Diecidue, K., & Miller, S. A. (1997). Young children's understanding of conflicting mental representation predicts suggestibility. *Developmental Psychology, 33,* 43–53.

White, T. L., Leichtman, M. D., & Ceci, S. J. (1997). The good, the bad, and the ugly: Accuracy, inaccuracy, and elaboration in preschoolers' reports about a past event. *Applied Cognitive Psychology, 11,* 37–54.

Williams, L. M. (1994). Recall of childhood trauma: A prospective study of women's memories of child sexual abuse. *Journal of Consulting and Clinical Psychology, 62,* 1167–1176.

Yuille, J. C. (1988). The systematic assessment of children's testimony. *Canadian Psychology, 29,* 247–262.

Yuille, J. C., Hunter, R., Joffe, R., & Zaparniuk, J. (1993). Interviewing children in sexual abuse cases. In G. S. Goodman, & B. L. Bottoms (Eds.), *Child victims, child witnesses: Understanding and improving testimony* (pp. 95–115). New York: Guilford Press.

15

Expert Testimony on the Suggestibility of Children

Does It Fit?

Thomas D. Lyon

State v. Sloan (1995 [Mo. Ct. App.]) was a criminal case of child sexual abuse. A.D., the 6-year-old alleged victim, was dropped off on Friday by her mother at her grandmother's house, where the child's aunt Evelyn and the defendant also resided. Two days later, on Sunday, the child's aunt Anita phoned the child's mother and told her that something was wrong. A.D. then told her mother that the defendant had sexually assaulted her the day before. The mother called the child abuse hot line. On Thursday, 5 days after the alleged abuse, a social worker and a police detective interviewed the child at her school. A.D. reported that her aunt Evelyn had allowed her to get into bed with the defendant and had then left the house. She stated that defendant had "placed his finger in her punkie," that she had touched his "wiener," and that defendant "had placed her on his wiener." Approximately 3 weeks later, the police detective reinterviewed the child, and she gave a similar report. The child testified at the trial, and her testimony was consistent with the testimony of her mother, the social worker, and the detective. The testimony of the child's aunt Evelyn and her grandmother (who both testified for the defense) as to the events subsequent to the alleged abuse was consistent with the child's.

Thanks to Geoff Deboskey and to Hazel Lord and her staff for research assistance. Thanks to John Myers and Brian Holmgren for their help in identifying appellate cases. Author's address: University of Southern California Law School, 699 Exposition Blvd., Los Angeles, CA 90089-0071. E-mail: tlyon@law.usc.edu.

The defendant was convicted, but the conviction was overturned on appeal. The Missouri appellate court[1] held that the defendant should have been allowed to present the testimony of an expert witness that the social worker and the detective questioned the child in a manner that was "unreasonably suggestive" and "not probative of guilt" (*State v. Sloan*, 1995, p. 596). The expert would have testified that the use of such questions as "Where did he touch you ?" was inappropriately leading, that one should not use "repeats," which the expert defined as "questions that take the end of an answer and feed it back to the child in the beginning of the next question," "affirms," which are questions indicating that the child is "on the right track," or yes/no questions, because "you cannot judge the validity of the response" to questions that can be answered "yes" or "no" (p. 597). The appellate court opinion had two effects. First, the defendant was entitled to a retrial, at which the expert testimony on suggestibility would be admissible. Second, future trial courts reading the opinion would be more inclined to admit this kind of expert testimony.

Sloan reflects a new trend among American courts toward admitting defense expert testimony on the suggestibility of children (Myers, 1997). Traditionally, psychological experts in child abuse cases have been clinical psychologists retained by the prosecution to explain the dynamics of child sexual abuse (Lyon & Koehler, 1998) or, more recently, to lay the foundation for special courtroom procedures designed to minimize the trauma of testifying (McAuliff & Kovera, this volume). Of late, experimental psychologists have entered the fray to explain how children may be led astray by leading and coercive questioning. Typically, these experts are retained by the defense, but prosecutors have also presented their own suggestibility experts to rebut the claims of defense experts.

The courts' receptivity to expert testimony provides researchers with a distinct opportunity to educate and influence legal decision makers. At the same time, researchers' new-found influence brings with it additional responsibilities, which require careful

[1] As a general rule, the state trial courts' decisions are appealed to the state appellate courts and then to the state supreme courts. The decisions of federal trial courts (which are called *district courts*) are appealed to the circuit court of appeals and then to the U.S. Supreme Court.

examination of both science and law. Consider the facts of *Sloan*. The case is quite unlike the multivictim ritual abuse day-care cases that have caught the public's eye and inspired a rash of research on young children's suggestibility. In some of these cases, large numbers of asymptomatic children were repeatedly questioned in highly coercive ways months after their last contact with the day-care providers (Ceci & Bruck, 1995). In contrast, in *Sloan* the child reported abuse shortly after the alleged event. The first investigative interview occurred shortly thereafter. There was nothing bizarre about the child's allegations. There was no evidence of incessant interviews, repeated questions, or bad-mouthing of the defendant. The defendant was someone very familiar to the child. The interviewers did not tell the child that she was abused or that other children had been abused. The child was not asked to imagine abuse or to pretend that it had occurred; she was not even shown anatomically detailed dolls. In short, the case was an unexceptional, routine sexual abuse case that criminal attorneys see every day. Nevertheless, an expert agreed to testify for the defense, and the conviction was overturned because the trial court did not allow the expert to testify.

Whether the courts ought to admit defense expert testimony on suggestibility raises issues regarding the law of expert testimony and the psychology of children. Commentators have argued that because most experts agree on the factors that influence children's suggestibility, and because the research on suggestibility is scientific, expert testimony on suggestibility is scientifically valid and therefore admissible (Kovera & Borgida, 1998). Their argument is based on two cases regulating the admissibility of expert testimony: *Frye v. United States* (1923 [D.C.Cir.]) and *Daubert v. Merrell-Dow Pharmaceuticals* (1994). Under *Frye*, scientific expert testimony is admissible if the expert's methodology is generally accepted by other scientists in the field. Under *Daubert*, expert testimony is admissible if it is scientifically valid. *Frye* is the rule in many states and, until *Daubert* was decided, the rule in many federal courts (Mueller & Kirkpatrick, 2000). *Daubert* is now the rule in federal courts, but it incorporates the "general acceptance" test from *Frye* as part of its inquiry into what is scientifically valid. Under either standard, the goal of the courts is to admit good science and exclude junk science.

However, the more general rules regarding the admissibility of expert testimony, the relevance of evidence, and the exclusion of evidence that misleads the jury are at least as important as the definitions of good science in *Frye* and *Daubert*. These rules continue to apply whether a court follows *Frye* or *Daubert*. In assessing expert testimony on suggestibility, perhaps the most important consideration is *fit*: a rule of relevance whereby the expert's testimony must fit the facts of the case. Expert testimony is prone to influence jurors even if the testimony is inapplicable to the facts of the case (Kovera, Gresham, Borgida, Gray, & Regan, 1997). The courts are appropriately cautious because of the risk that jurors may defer too much to experts and because jurors lack the skills to appraise expert testimony critically. Social scientists have raised concerns regarding the applicability of suggestibility research findings to typical cases of abuse (e.g., Garven, Wood, Malpass, & Shaw, 1998; Goodman, Emery, & Haugaard, 1998; Lyon, 1999; Saywitz & Lyon, 2002; Westcott, 1998). Much of the research both uses suggestive techniques that are atypical of investigative interviews and fails to take account of factors – such as fear, loyalty, and embarrassment – that make false allegations of abuse less likely to occur (Lyon, 1999). Attention to fit requires experts to tailor their testimony to match the facts of the case at bar.

In this chapter, I outline what I believe are the most useful means by which the courts should evaluate expert testimony on suggestibility. I will describe the various legal objections and note their limitations. First, I consider the traditional objection that expert testimony regarding suggestibility invades the province of the jury to assess witness' credibility. Appellate courts have chipped away at this objection, and the resulting rules may actually encourage expert testimony that is less helpful and more misleading. Second, I discuss the objection that expert testimony regarding suggestibility is not helpful to the jury because the testimony does not tell the jury anything that they do not already know. Because laypeople probably understand that young children are suggestible, this objection has some force, but it is limited by the fact that expert testimony can almost always be packaged so as to transmit information of which the average juror is unaware. Third, I discuss the concern that expert testimony be scientifically valid, a requirement highlighted by the Supreme Court in *Daubert*. Given the quality of the scientific research on this topic, the courts have been surprisingly reluctant to admit expert testimony as scientifically valid. I argue that this situation will likely change. At the same time, *Daubert* provides a useful framework for requiring experts to describe the research on which they rely in greater detail so that the courts can assess admissibility intelligently. Finally, I consider the objection that expert testimony on suggestibility often does not fit the facts of the individual case, which is derived from the rules of relevance and helpfulness. I argue that this is the most important and compelling objection to some types of expert testimony. Experts who misapply research or assert facts beyond what research supports should not be permitted to testify.

THE RULE AGAINST INVADING THE PROVINCE OF THE JURY TO ASSESS CREDIBILITY

One objection against expert testimony on suggestibility is that it concerns the credibility of witnesses, and expert testimony on credibility invades the province of the jury to assess the veracity of witnesses. The "province of the jury" objection has had an uneasy history. The argument was criticized long ago by the renowned evidence scholar John Henry Wigmore. Calling it a "mere bit of empty rhetoric," Wigmore noted that the jury is always free to reject an expert's opinion and thus retains the right to assess the credibility of witnesses (Wigmore, 1904, p. 18). Wigmore's argument was endorsed by the California Supreme Court in *People v. McDonald* (1984), an influential opinion supporting the admissibility of expert testimony on the difficulties of adult eyewitness identification.

Recently, the argument that expert testimony commenting on the credibility of witnesses invades the province of the jury was considered by the U.S. Supreme Court in assessing the constitutionality of an evidentiary rule barring the results of polygraph tests (*United States v. Scheffer*, 1998). Although the majority opinion upheld the rule, only four of the justices accepted the argument that expert testimony would "diminish the jury's role in making credibility determinations" (p. 1266), whereas the other five (four concurring in the judgment and one dissenting) believed that such an argument

"demeans and mistakes the role and competence of jurors in deciding the factual question of guilt or innocence" (id., p. 1269 [Kennedy,
J., concurring]). Hence, a majority of the Supreme Court would
reject the argument that expert testimony on credibility invades the
province of the jury.

Nevertheless, the rule continues to exert some force. In spite of
Scheffer, the Seventh Circuit Court of Appeals recently upheld the
exclusion of expert testimony on the failings of eyewitnesses in
part on the grounds that "the credibility of eyewitness testimony
is generally not an appropriate subject matter for expert testimony
because it influences a critical function of the jury – determining the
credibility of witnesses" (*United States v. Hall*, 1999, p. 1107). State
courts, which are not bound by federal cases interpreting the rules of
evidence, have sometimes rejected expert testimony in child sexual
abuse cases on similar grounds (e.g., *Commonwealth v. Ianello*, 1987
[Mass.]).

Limitations on the Rule Against Invading the Province of the Jury to Assess Credibility

On the federal level, several circuit courts of appeal have acknowledged an "increasing hospitality" toward the testimony of experts
on adult eyewitness identification (*United States v. Brien*, 1995 [1st
Cir.]; *United States v. George*, 1992, p. 1432 [9th Cir.]; *United States v.
Harris*, 1993 [4th Cir.]). In part, this reflects a distinction that some
courts have drawn between expert testimony that a *particular* witness is or is not credible (inadmissible) and expert testimony about
the unreliability of eyewitnesses more generally (admissible). Specific opinions may invade the jury's province, but generalities are
admitted.[2]

In addition to allowing a large amount of expert testimony, this
exception to the province of the jury objection creates line-drawing
difficulties for the courts. As the Eighth Circuit Court of Appeals
has queried, "as the expert applies his or her general opinions to the

---

[2] Of course, this distinction does not survive *Scheffer* (1998), because the expert in that
case would have testified that a specific witness was being truthful in his responses
to the polygraph. Nevertheless, the Court did not believe that the expert's testimony
would have invaded the jury's province.

case at hand, at what point does this more specific opinion testimony become an undisguised, impermissible comment on a child victim's veracity?" (*United States v. Rouse*, 1997, p. 571). The difficulty of drawing such lines is illustrated by the expert's opinions at issue in *Rouse*. The trial court would not allow the expert to express an opinion on whether the child witness's report was believable. This holding was not challenged on appeal. The trial court allowed the expert to testify about "practices of suggestibility" that produce unreliable child testimony and to opine that suggestive questioning can create false memories. These were sufficiently general to be unobjectionable. However, the trial court did not allow the expert to criticize the practices used by the interviewer in the particular case. This holding was challenged on appeal, and the appellate court held that this was a error: Future experts can criticize methods of interviewing both in general terms and with respect to the case at bar. Contrast this to an Eighth Circuit Court of Appeals case decided one year previously, *United States v. Kime* (1996). In that case, the appellate court upheld the exclusion of an expert opinion criticizing the manner in which an in-court identification was made. The puzzle for future trial courts is this: How is testimony regarding an in-court identification more specific than testimony regarding an interview? Why does the former invade the province of the jury but not the latter? The state courts have had similar difficulty in deciding whether experts can specifically criticize the interviewing practices used in the individual case. Some say they can (*State v. Erickson*, 1990 [Minn. Ct. App.]; *State v. Kirschbaum*, 1995 [Wis. Ct. App.]; *State v. Malarney*, 1993 [Fla. Ct. App.]). Some say they cannot (*Commonwealth v. Allen*, 1996 [Mass. Ct. App.]; *State v. Steffes*, 1994 [Mont.]).

   A few courts have attempted to avoid the specific–general distinction altogether by reasoning that the expert can testify as to the actions of the interviewer without thereby commenting on the credibility of the child (*Barlow v. State*, 1998 [Ga.]; *State v. Sloan*, 1995 [Mo. Ct. App.]). For example, the court in *Sloan* explained that expert testimony that the interviewers used methods that "were unreasonably suggestive" was not "particularized testimony concerning the victim's credibility" because "it [was] directed at the activities of the witness" (p. 596). This position is problematic. Whether an interviewer's questions are unreasonably suggestive depends to a large extent on the suggestibility of the child. The court's distinction would mean that experts can testify to outside influences on a witness but not on equally important endogenous factors that affect the perception, memory, and sincerity of a child witness, both directly and in interaction with outside influences.

The rule against commenting on a child's credibility appears to have been all but swallowed by the exception in several cases in which the courts have allowed experts to testify to everything short of whether they believed the child. In *Schutz v. State* (1997), the Court of Criminal Appeals of Texas held that the expert's testimony "that the complainant did not exhibit the traits of manipulation did not constitute a direct comment upon the truth of the complainant's allegation" (p. 73). In *United States v. Cacy* (1995), the Court of Appeals for the Armed Forces held that an expert could testify that a child "did not appear rehearsed" but not that "she in fact believed the victim" (p. 218). The distinctions are very fine: One can testify whether the child has the traits or characteristics of a inaccurate witness but not that she is, indeed, inaccurate. One can testify that the child's story is not believable but not whether one believes the child. Even these distinctions are hard to maintain in *Doe v. Johnson* (1995), a case in which the Seventh Circuit Court of Appeals held that an expert's testimony that "he believed that [the child's] allegations were the product of parental suggestion" (p. 1563) was admissible because it was not an opinion "as to the [child's] credibility" (id.).

Prosecutors who challenge testimony on the grounds that such distinctions are artificial must tread carefully lest they appear hypocritical, because the distinctions are largely the product of prosecutorial efforts to introduce expert testimony that children's behavioral symptoms are proof that they were sexually abused. In order to overcome the objection that such testimony vouched for the credibility of the child witness, prosecutors have argued that experts could properly testify as to the characteristics of sexually abused children in general, or testify that a particular child's behavior was "consistent with sexual abuse," without testifying that they in fact believed that the child had been sexually abused. In states where experts can go so far for the prosecution, defense attorneys can legitimately argue that their experts ought to be able to testify that a child's behavior is consistent with a false allegation of sexual abuse.

The way in which prosecutors are hamstrung by their own distinctions is illustrated by *Commonwealth v. Allen* (1996 [Mass. Ct. App.]), a Massachusetts case in which the defendant was convicted of sexually abusing his 8-year-old daughter and 9-year-old son. Prior to *Allen*, the Supreme Court of Massachusetts had held that an expert for the prosecution may testify on the "general behavioral characteristics of sexually abused children" but that a comparison of a particular child to those characteristics "impermissibly intrudes on the jury's province to assess the credibility of the witness," thus establishing the distinction between general and specific expert testimony (*Commonwealth v. Trowbridge,* 1995, p. 420 [Mass.]). Following the logic of *Trowbridge,* the trial court in *Allen* allowed the defense expert to testify "generally about proper and improper interview techniques," to testify that children are more suggestible than adults, and to assert that the use of anatomically detailed dolls "suggest[s] to the complainant that the interviewer wants to hear about genitalia or sexual acts," but the court did *not* allow the expert to "comment specifically on the questions employed in the videotape itself" (*Commonwealth v. Allen,* 1996, p. 109).

The facts of *Allen* raise the question of why *any* expert testimony on the suggestibility of children was justified. In upholding the trial court's exclusion of testimony specific to the case, the appellate court noted that the questions that the expert was prepared to criticize "were not particularly leading, nor were they coercive. . . . [T]here was no vilification of the defendant, no incessant questioning, no references to statements made by the other complainant, and no use of threats, bribes, or cajoling" (p. 108). The trial court's focus on distinguishing between specific and general testimony obscured an inquiry as to what general testimony would tell the jury.

In states where the distinction between general and specific expert testimony on credibility has essentially disappeared, defense experts are now being given the same latitude. In *State v. Malarney* (1993), a Florida appellate court overturned a sexual abuse conviction on the grounds that the defendant should have been allowed to introduce expert testimony that "the techniques used in interviewing the alleged victim were unreasonably suggestive and that the victim's 'affect' was inconsistent with sexual abuse" (pp. 740–741). The dissenting judge argued that the expert's opinion invaded the province of the jury, but the force of his argument was limited by the fact that the Florida Supreme Court had held that an interviewer could testify that she believed the child had been abused (*Glendening v. State*, 1988). Recognizing this problem, the dissenter suggested that "perhaps the supreme court should revisit the Glendening opinion" and assess whether expert testimony on the credibility of child witnesses satisfies the prerequisites for scientific expert testimony (*State v. Malarney*, 1993, p. 742 (Dimitrouleas, J., dissenting [Fla. Ct. App.]). Once the invading the province argument is dispensed with, the courts may recognize the need to regulate expert testimony on credibility through other rules.

In sum, the argument that expert testimony on credibility invades the province of the jury has been weakened by distinctions between specific and general testimony, between the suggestiveness of the interviewer and the suggestibility of the interviewee, and between the believability of the child and the beliefs of the expert. Rather than serve as a means of ensuring that expert testimony is helpful to the jury, the presumptive admissibility of testimony couched in general terms may make it easier to introduce testimony that is of little relevance to a particular case. Yet even when such testimony does not match the facts of the case, jurors are likely to be influenced by the expert's implicit opinion that the child should not be believed.

THE RULE AGAINST TELLING THE JURY WHAT THEY ALREADY KNOW

In order to reach the jury, an expert must be prepared to tell the jurors something they do not already know. This requirement is derived from the rules regarding the admissibility of expert testimony and the exclusion of prejudicial evidence. Under Rule 702 of the Federal Rules of Evidence (2001), expert testimony must "assist the trier of fact to understand the evidence or to determine a fact in issue." Assessing the admissibility of expert opinion on the accuracy of adult eyewitnesses, the Fourth Circuit Court of Appeals explained that "the court should consider whether the testimony is within the common knowledge of the jurors. This type of evidence, almost by definition, can be of no assistance to a jury" (*United States v. Harris*, 1993, p. 534). The *Harris* court and a number of other courts have upheld the exclusion of expert testimony on the grounds that jurors are already generally aware of the dangers of misidentification (*United States v. Daniels*, 1995 [7th Cir.]; *United States v. Kime*, 1996 [8th Cir.]; *United States V. Larkin*, 1992 [7th Cir.]; *United States v. Sha*yn 1995 [1st Cir.]). Most state courts follow a similar rule for admitting expert testimony, and many state appellate courts have similarly upheld the exclusion of expert testimony on eyewitness identification (*People v. Gibbs*, 1990 [N.Y.]; *State v. Long*, 1990 [N.J.]; *Utley v. State*, 1992 [Ark.]).

Another basis for excluding expert testimony that fails to teach the jurors what they do not already know is that it will mislead or confuse the jury or that it is simply a waste of time, rendering it inadmissible under Federal Rule of Evidence 403 (2001). As the helpfulness of the expert decreases, the potential to mislead the jury looms large. Jurors may infer that the expert is testifying on behalf of the defense because the expert believes that the eyewitness is mistaken. Indeed, this is precisely what a good defense attorney offering an expert on behalf of his or her client hopes will happen. Therefore, the Seventh Circuit Court of Appeals has held that a trial court's decision to bar expert testimony on adult eyewitness identification on the grounds that the jury was already generally aware of the dangers of misidentification was justified under either Rule 702 (assisting the jury) or Rule 403 (misleading the jury) (*United States v. Curry*, 1992, p. 1051).

Some state appellate courts have upheld exclusion of expert testimony on children's suggestibility on the grounds that jurors already believe that young children are suggestible (*State v. Ellis*, 1996 [Me.]; *State v. James*, 1989 [Conn.]; *State v. Swan*, 1990 [Wash.]). Ironically, expert testimony that is framed in generalities so as to avoid the challenge that it invades the province of the jury is especially susceptible to the claim that the expert is not telling the jury anything new. For example, in *State v. Ellis* the proffered expert was prepared to inform the jury that "young children are more susceptible to suggestions than older children or adults, that children will sometimes give an answer they think is expected, and that leading questions increase the possibility of suggestion" (p. 753). The Supreme Court of Maine upheld exclusion of the testimony on the grounds that this is common knowledge.

If experts can identify a misconception common among laypeople regarding credibility, their testimony is more likely to be admitted. Courts that have approved the admissibility of expert testimony on adult eyewitness identification have emphasized the extent to which some research findings regarding eyewitness accuracy "contradict the expectations of the average juror" (*People v. McDonald*, 1984, p. 721 [Cal.]; see also *United States v. Smith*, 1984, p. 1106 [6th Cir.] [expert testimony helpful because it would "question common-sense evaluation"]). For example, in allowing Professor Michael Leippe to testify regarding the potential errors of adult eyewitnesses, the federal district court in *United States v. Norwood*, 1996 (D.N.J.) emphasized that the research findings ran counter to what jurors usually believe: Leippe discussed studies finding that the presence of weapons reduces eyewitness accuracy (rather than increases it), that extreme stress impairs memory (rather than enhances it), and that increased confidence does not increase accuracy (contrary to jurors' heavy reliance on confidence as a measure of veracity).[3]

In contrast to experts in adult eyewitness cases, experts on children's suggestibility have rarely if ever argued that jurors harbor misconceptions about children's reliability. Laypeople intuit that children are more suggestible than adults (Leippe & Romanczyk, 1987; McAuliff & Kovera, 1998, Ross, Dunning, Toglia, & Ceci, 1989; Yarmey & Jones, 1979).[4] Experimental psychologists often attack "myths" regarding children's suggestibility (e.g., *State v. Sloan*, 1995 [Mo. Ct. App.]), but these are beliefs about children espoused by social workers and clinical psychologists, who are themselves challenging commonsensical skepticism of young children's reports.

---

[3] Even some of the most often repeated assertions about eyewitness identification are subject to question. For a recent criticism of the assertion that confidence is unrelated to accuracy, see Lindsay, Reed, and Sharma (1998).

[4] This need not translate into a greater reluctance to convict when the witness is a child, because there are factors other than suggestibility that affect the decision to convict. Jurors may be more inclined to convict when the victim is a child because they believe that children are less likely to lie (Leippe & Romanczyk, 1987) or less likely to have consented to the abuse (Isquith, Levine, & Scheiner, 1993).

Some experts have emphasized that highly suggestive and repeated questioning can create false reports that may fool a jury. However, the admissibility question is not whether convincing false narratives can be created, but whether jurors believe they cannot be created. If jurors are aware of the possibility of a false story that rings true, this is often as much as an expert can offer. The argument that expert testimony on children's suggestibility is not helpful to the jury thus has some force; indeed, it appears to have greater empirical support than a similar argument against expert testimony on inaccuracies in adult eyewitnesses.

Limitations on the Rule against Telling the Jury What They Already Know

However, there are a number of reasons why the argument that jurors already understand the suggestibility of children will not stop courts predisposed to admitting expert testimony from doing so. First, the courts' assertions regarding what jurors know about children are rarely if ever backed up by empirical research. This makes it easy for courts favoring the admissibility of such testimony to simply assert that jurors do not already know what suggestibility experts have to offer (*State v. Gersin,* 1996 [Ohio]; *State v. Kirschbaum,* 1995 [Wis. Ct. App.]; *State v. Sloan,* 1995 [Mo. Ct. App.]).

Second, expert testimony is more or less obvious depending on the way in which it is characterized. Expert testimony sounds less obvious when it is couched in terms of commentary on professional standards of interviewing rather than lay beliefs about suggestibility. In *State v. Gersin* (1996), an Ohio supreme court case in which the court upheld the admissibility of expert testimony on children's suggestibility, the majority asserted that "most jurors lack the knowledge of accepted practices in interviewing child victims" (p. 494), whereas the dissent argued that "specialized knowledge" was unnecessary "to identify when an interview might have been overly suggestive" (p. 498). Recall that attacks on the interviewer rather than on the credibility of the witness also appear less invasive of the jurors' province. Expert testimony that criticizes interviewers rather than interviewees thus moves from the jury's province to the experts'.

In jurisdictions where specific discussion of the particular case is forbidden, experts may find it more difficult to avoid discussing the obvious generalities, but they can frame their discussion as a description of specific research rather than as a summary of general conclusions. Jurors may understand that younger children are more suggestible than older children but may be unable to predict the outcome of specific studies examining age effects. Similarly, experts could discuss factors influencing suggestibility and accuracy that jurors are either ignorant of or undervalue. Some factors understood by psychologists as influencing children's reliability do not appear to be understood by laypeople, such as the centrality of details, the participation of the witness, and the prestige of the source (McAuliff & Kovera, 1998).

Third, it is unclear just how much jurors must understand in order for an expert's testimony to be characterized as unhelpful. The drafters of the Federal Rules of Evidence suggest that expert testimony is unhelpful only if the "untrained layman" could determine the issue "to the best degree" without the help of the expert (Advisory Committee Notes Rule 702, Federal Rules of Evidence, 2001). Certainly the average expert on suggestibility can tell jurors *something* they did not fully understand. In *People v. McDonald* (1984), the California Supreme Court case that looked favorably on expert testimony on eyewitness identification, the court approved discussion of facts that "may be known only to some jurors, or may be imperfectly understood by many, or may be contrary to the intuitive beliefs of most" (p. 720). Certainly there are *some* jurors who harbor misconceptions about child witnesses.

Prosecutors opposing expert testimony on suggestibility are unlikely to push too hard on the issue of what jurors already know lest their own experts be barred from testifying. At least one court has criticized expert testimony regarding the behavioral consequences of sexual abuse on the grounds that jurors already understand that sexual abuse has negative behavioral consequences (*People v. Dunkle*, 1992 [Pa.]). Mason (1995) has made the same argument with respect to rehabilitative expert testimony, which rebuts defense arguments that factors such as delays in reporting prove allegations false (Mason, 1995). Although there is some empirical support for the belief that jurors have misconceptions about sexual abuse

(Morison & Greene, 1992), as experts qualify their statements to characterize the available research accurately (Lyon, 2002), their testimony sounds more like the average juror's understanding. That is, when an expert conservatively states that "many" (rather than "most") victims delay, his or her testimony comes close to merely affirming what a layperson might intuit about sexual abuse. A stringent standard for when expert testimony tells the jury something new would equally limit the prosecution and defense.

THE RULE THAT EXPERT TESTIMONY BE SCIENTIFICALLY VALID

In *Daubert v. Merrell-Dow Pharmaceuticals* (1993), the U.S. Supreme Court held that in order for scientific expert testimony to be admissible under the Federal Rules of Evidence, the theory or technique on which the expert's testimony is based must be *reliable*. To be reliable (scientists would prefer the term *valid*), the expert's testimony must be grounded in the methods and procedures of science. Specifically, the Court set out a nonexhaustive list of factors for the trial court to consider: whether the expert's theory or technique can be (or has been) tested, whether it has been subjected to peer review and publication, its rate of error, and its general acceptance within the relevant scientific community. Under the *Frye* standard (*Frye v. United States*, 1923), which had been adopted by most federal courts prior to *Daubert* and remains the standard in many states (Mueller & Kirkpatrick, 2000), a court simply considers the last of the *Daubert* factors – the "general acceptance" of the theory or technique – in deciding whether to admit scientific expert testimony. *Daubert* requires judges to defer less to experts' professional peers and act more like "amateur scientists" in evaluating the admissibility of expert testimony (*Daubert v. Merrell-Dow Pharmaceuticals*, 1993, p. 600 (Rehnquist, C.J., dissenting in part).

This opinion has enabled the courts to take a closer look at proffered expert testimony, and with a longer list of factors, any of which can lead to exclusion of the expert's testimony. The Supreme Court's opinion in *General Electric Co. v. Joiner* (1997) illustrates such an approach. The trial court excluded the expert's testimony after considering the applicability of the expert's studies to the facts of the case. The court of appeals rejected the trial court's approach, holding that the court should not "make independent scientific judgments on the basis of individual studies" (*Joiner v. General Electric.*, 1996, p. 532 [11th Cir.]). The Supreme Court held that the appellate court was not sufficiently deferential to the trial court's judgment and approved the trial court's study-by-study analysis.

Testimony on suggestibility would appear to be based on reliable scientific knowledge. Kovera and Borgida (1998) have argued that "expert evidence on child witness memory probably would be admissible under Daubert" because "the psychological research on this topic is reliable: it is grounded in scientific methods, has been subjected to peer review, and is generally accepted by the relevant scientific community" (p. 189). Suggestibility research has been conducted by extremely well respected research psychologists, has been published in the highest-quality peer-reviewed psychological journals, and has been summarized in several influential books published by the American Psychological Association (Ceci & Bruck, 1995; Poole & Lamb, 1998). Social scientists since the turn of the 20th century have generally agreed that young children are suggestible (Ceci & Bruck, 1993), and surveys of research psychologists confirm this long-standing view (McAuliff & Kovera, 1998; Yarmey & Jones, 1979). More recently, in at least two high-profile child sexual abuse cases, dozens of research psychologists signed on to summaries of the suggestibility research designed to inform the courts of the danger that coercive interviewing may elicit false allegations of abuse (Committee of Concerned Social Scientists, 1993, reprinted in Ceci & Bruck, 1995; Scientists for the Accurate Communication of Data, 1998). Although it is notable that several prominent suggestibility researchers refused to sign, this would not preclude a judicial finding that the briefs' conclusions are "generally accepted" by the research community (cf. *People v. McDonald*, 1984).

Despite this long-standing consensus, there is little case law upholding the scientific reliability of suggestibility testimony. The Washington Supreme Court held that a suggestibility expert's opinion was not supported by the scientific community (*State v. Swan*, 1990). The Supreme Court of Maine rejected a suggestibility expert's testimony on the grounds that there was a lack of "valid empirical research establishing a causal relationship . . . between particular techniques . . . and inaccuracies in reporting" (*State v. Gordius*, 1988, p. 8).

Given the rapid growth of suggestibility research in the 1990s, these cases may be out of date. As the Scientists for the Accurate Communication of Data (SACD) informed the Supreme Court of Massachusetts in 1998, "[i]t was only at the beginning of the 1990s that researchers in the field of children's suggestibility began to systematically examine the effects of interview bias, repeated questions, repeated interviews, stereotype induction, anatomically detailed dolls, peer pressure, and selective reinforcement on the accuracy of young children's reports" (SACD, 1999, p. 6).

A more recent case – the Eighth Circuit Court of Appeals's original opinion in *United States v. Rouse* (1996) – has been cited as supporting the admissibility of suggestibility testimony (Bruck, Ceci, & Hembrooke, 1998; Kovera & Borgida, 1998). However, the opinion is a mixed blessing for defendants. The original opinion referred to the general acceptability of research by Ceci, Bruck, and others, but was vacated and a rehearing was held. On rehearing, the appellate court upheld the trial court's ruling that the testifying expert (Dr. Ralph Underwager) "should not embellish his own research and opinions by telling the jury about the research and writing of other psychologists because these works have not produced a consistent body of scientific knowledge" (*United States v. Rouse*, 1997, p. 571).[5] It is therefore unlikely that *Rouse*'s holding will facilitate the admissibility of expert testimony on suggestibility research.

Despite the lack of case support thus far, it is likely that future cases will hold that suggestibility research qualifies as scientific knowledge, if only because courts in general are exhibiting increased receptivity to expert testimony on children's suggestibility. Courts that have held that such testimony ought to be admitted have simply not considered whether it meets the requirement of

---

[5] What is unclear is why the court would allow an expert to discuss any research at all if there was no "consistent body of scientific knowledge." One could speculate that the trial court did not perceive the expert's description of his own findings as "scientific," and therefore believed them exempt from *Daubert*. Such an approach has now been rejected by the Court, which recently held that no expert testimony is categorically exempt from *Daubert*'s requirements (*Kumho Tire Co., Ltd. v. Carmichael*, 1999).

scientific expert testimony. When they do, it will not be difficult for them to justify a finding that much of the testimony is based on scientific knowledge. This is currently the case with expert testimony on adult eyewitnesses. Courts that admit such testimony can emphasize the fact that the expert was able to "determine that each study scrupulously adhered to scientifically valid methodologies, was capable of replication and objective measurement, and was subjected to discriminating peer review prior to publication" (*United States v. Norwood*, 1996, p. 1136 [D.N.J.]). In some cases, prosecutors have simply conceded that eyewitness research is scientific knowledge (*United States v. Hall*, 1999 [7th Cir.]).

Once the courts hold that suggestibility research is scientific knowledge, this does not make the *Daubert* analysis superfluous. *Daubert* provides a foundational prerequisite for the admissibility of expert testimony on issues that have been the subjects of scientific research. Experts who seek to testify on children's suggestibility must provide a scientific basis for their testimony before they will be allowed to take the stand. As Ceci and Bruck (1995) note, ethical experts should be cognizant of the relevant research in their area of expertise. Ignorance of the research will be a basis for exclusion.

Details of the research, rather than summary conclusions, are a necessary prerequisite to admissibility. The research itself must be described in sufficient detail for the court to do more than blindly defer to the expert's credentials. In *United States v. Kime* (1996), the Eighth Circuit Court of Appeals held that a review of eyewitness research that supported its conclusions with summary citations to the original research said "nothing whatsoever to the district judge attempting to assess the credibility of the research underlying [the expert's] opinions" (p. 883). Other courts have similarly barred eyewitness experts from testifying when they could not describe the methodology of the research underlying their assertions (*United States v. Brien*, 1995 [1st. Cir.]; *United States v. Downing*, 1985 [E.D. Pa.]).

Research details are essential for a court to perform the next steps in the *Daubert* analysis. The court will determine whether the research constitutes scientific knowledge *and* whether the research provides a sufficient foundation for the expert's conclusions. Suggestibility research is undoubtedly scientific, but experts may

nevertheless make excessive claims about the implications of research, either because of their own predilections because of the
pressures of testifying for one side in an adversarial dispute. As social scientists recognize, there are two kinds of validity: internal and
external. A study may be scientifically sound on its own terms, and
thus be internally valid, but be inapplicable to a particular situation
or individuals, and thus be externally invalid as applied. External validity is likely to be particularly important in assessing suggestibility research, because judges are poor at assessing internal
validity (Kovera & McAuliff, 2000) and because the major concerns
regarding suggestibility research involve their applicability to real-
world cases (e.g., Goodman et al., 1998).

In *Joiner*, the studies on which the experts relied for their conclusions were clearly scientific; they were published, peer-reviewed
articles utilizing well-respected methods. However, the trial court
barred the experts from testifying – both as to the research they
cited and the conclusions they reached – because it believed that
their conclusions could not be extrapolated from the research they
offered. Because *Daubert* had warned that the courts are expected to
analyze scientific experts' methodology and not their conclusions,
the Eleventh Circuit Court of Appeals in *Joiner* criticized the trial
court's willingness to second-guess the conclusions drawn by the
proffered experts. However, the Supreme Court approved the trial
court's actions, noting that "conclusions and methodology are not
entirely distinct from one another" (*General Electric Co. v. Joiner*,
1997, p. 519). Sometimes the method by which an expert reaches
his or her conclusions is invalid. As the Supreme Court explained:
"Trained experts commonly extrapolate from existing data. But
nothing in either *Daubert* or the Federal Rules of Evidence requires a
district court to admit opinion evidence which is connected to existing data only by the ipse dixit of the expert. A court may conclude
that there is simply too great an analytical gap between the data
and the opinion offered" (id.). Without using the term *external validity*, the Court recognized that prudent extrapolation is an aspect
of appropriate scientific methodology. As of 2001, the Federal Rules
of Evidence (2001) explicitly require that the court determine if the
proffered expert "has applied the principles and methods reliably
to the facts of the case."

Perhaps experts could evade findings that their extrapolations were unscientific if they simply refrained from extrapolating from the research to the particular case. They could offer to discuss the research and let the jury draw its own conclusions. Such an approach has been advocated by some experts for other reasons. It allows experts to avoid the presumptive inadmissibility of specific commentary on credibility (the first objection discussed in this chapter). It allows experts to participate in cases with which they are relatively unfamiliar, enabling them to remain objective (and certainly increases the appearance that they are not taking sides). Finally, it acknowledges the difficulty that to draw conclusions, the expert must inject his or her own standards of proof. For example, the conclusion that a child's statements are unreliable relies on a subjective judgment regarding the likelihood that a statement must be true in order to be judged as true.

THE RULE THAT EXPERT TESTIMONY FITS THE FACTS OF THE CASE

The expert who avoids excessive extrapolation, however, may run afoul of a different requirement for expert testimony to be admissible. In addition to qualifying as scientific knowledge, the information offered by the expert must assist the jury (Federal Rule of Evidence 702, 2001). And although assisting the jury has long been recognized as a prerequisite to admitting expert testimony, the opinion in *Daubert* helped to elaborate on the helpfulness inquiry. *Daubert* described the assistance standard in terms of fit: whether the proffered expert testimony "is sufficiently tied to the facts of the case that it will aid the jury in resolving a factual dispute" (*Daubert v. Merrell-Dow Pharmaceuticals*, 1993, pp. 2795–2796). If the research that the expert describes cannot be appropriately applied by the jury to the particular case, the expert's testimony fails to fit and should be excluded.[6] One cannot rely on jurors to detect a mismatch; jurors

---

[6] It is sometimes said that fit is essentially synonymous with relevance, which concerns the tendency of a piece of evidence to make a matter in issue more probable or less probable than it would be without the evidence (Federal Rules of Evidence 402, 2001). I believe it is useful to refer to the issue as *fit* rather than *relevance*, however, because of the higher standards established for the admissibility of expert testimony than for evidence more generally. An expert's testimony might be marginally relevant but

are persuaded by expert testimony despite its lack of fit (Kovera et al., 1997).

The external validity problem thus persists even if the expert refrains from drawing conclusions; it simply changes from a scientific reliability problem to a fit or relevance problem. If the expert draws an inappropriate conclusion from the research, the testimony is excluded as unscientific. If the expert's testimony would lead the jury to draw an inappropriate conclusion, the testimony is excluded for its lack of fit.

Whereas the reliability question focuses the court's attention on the research, the fit question focuses the court on the facts. The expert must not only provide the necessary research, but also be able to link the research to facts in the case. In a leading federal case on the admissibility of expert testimony on eyewitness identification, the Third Circuit Court of Appeals held that "A defendant who seeks the admission of expert testimony must make an on-the-record detailed proffer to the court, including an explanation of precisely how the expert's testimony is relevant to the eyewitness identifications under consideration. The offer of proof should establish the presence of factors (e.g., stress, or difference in race or age as between the eyewitness and the defendant) which have been found by researchers to impair the accuracy of eyewitness identification" (*United States v. Downing*, 1985, p. 1242 [3rd. Cir.]). The court noted that a "[f]ailure to make such a detailed proffer is sufficient grounds to exclude the expert's testimony" (id.).

The inquiry into fit is a searching one. In a number of federal cases dealing with exposure to toxic substances and subsequent injuries, appellate courts have upheld the exclusion of expert testimony when the experts assumed facts that were not supported by the record. An expert cannot testify that a particular amount of chemical A causes disease B unless there is evidence that the plaintiff ingested chemical A (*Sorensen v. Shaklee Corp.*, 1994, p. 648 [8th Cir.]), evidence that the plaintiff ingested the particular amount of A necessary to cause B (*Moore v. Ashland Chemical, Inc.*, 1998, p. 278

---

nevertheless might be excluded as insufficiently fitting the facts to be helpful to the jury.

[5th Cir.]), and evidence that the plaintiff ingested chemical A before contracting disease B (*Heller v. Shaw Industries, Inc.*, 1999, pp. 149–150 [3rd Cir.]); *Porter v. Whitehall Laboratories, Inc.*, 1993, p. 616 [7th Cir.]). In the context of children's suggestibility, these decisions suggest that to testify that various types of suggestive techniques lead to false responding, there must be evidence that the suggestive techniques were indeed used, that they were used in sufficient amounts to lead to false responding, and that the suggestive techniques predated the child's initial allegations of abuse.

In several state appellate cases, courts have upheld the exclusion of expert testimony when the proffered experts could only speculate that inappropriate questions were asked (*State v. Kirschbaum*, 1995 [Wis. Ct. App.]; *State v. Mazerolle*, 1992 [Me.]; *State v. Russell*, 1990 [Me.]; *Stringer v. Commonwealth*, 1997 [Ky.]). An adequate assessment of fit would go still further: The types of inappropriate questions asked in the case must match the types of suggestive questions asked in the research.

If there is no factual basis for asserting that interviews were suggestive, experts might resort to commenting on the "typical" interview. What is typical is itself a factual issue, however, requiring reference to the observational research on forensic interviewing. Because observational research has failed to find that the use of pretense and guided imagery, stereotype induction, and a number of other suggestive methods are as prevalent in real-world interviews as in suggestibility research, research on these issues would not be admissible (Lyon, 1999). Moreover, generalizations about the typical interview should not be allowed when interviews are available. In *State v. Hulbert* (1992 [Iowa]), after hearing a fourth-grade program on "good, bad, and confusing touches," a 10-year-old girl told her school counselor that her custodial father had abused her on several occasions. Shortly thereafter, she was interviewed on videotape by a social worker. At trial, the court allowed the expert testifying for the defense (Dr. Ralph Underwager) to testify as to "techniques generally employed by child abuse investigators," including their "tendency . . . to interview children in a way that confirms the investigator's own hypothesis as to what occurred" (p. 334). What is particularly troubling about the expert's testimony is that the videotape was available and offered into evidence but was excluded due to the objections of the *defendant*. If specific assertions about inappropriate interviewing are barred by the jury's inability to see the interview for themselves, then generalizations about interviewing ought to be barred as well.

Whereas the party offering the expert testimony must provide a foundation for fit, the party opposing the expert may argue that other facts lead to a lack of fit. In *United States v. Nguyen* (1992 [D.N.J.]), the court excluded expert testimony on errors in cross-racial identification despite the fact that the eyewitness and the defendant were of different races. The court did so on the grounds that the research on cross-racial identification failed to fit the facts of the case, given the witness's greater exposure to and familiarity with the defendant's race, the witness's attentiveness to the defendant's features (knowing that he would have to identify him later), and the length of exposure (see also *United States v. Downing*, 1985 [E.D. Pa.], where the court excluded expert testimony on eyewitnesses on similar grounds).

There are a number of grounds on which research on children's suggestibility will fail to fit individual cases. Most of the recent research on children's suggestibility has focused on the preschool child. Given the "dramatic developmental trends" often found within age ranges from 3 to 6 years (Leichtman & Ceci, 1995, p. 568), much of the research is inapplicable to the older child. For example, special attention should be paid to the age of the child when an expert hopes to criticize the use of anatomically detailed dolls, because the critical research has focused on preschool children (Bruck, Ceci, & Francouer, 2000; Bruck, Ceci, Francouer, & Renick, 1995; Deloache & Marzolf, 1995), whereas research examining 5-year-old and older children has found substantially lower rates of error (Saywitz, Goodman, Nicholas, & Moan, 1991). Indeed, the lead author of much of the most critical research has emphasized the importance of age differences in reconciling otherwise inconsistent findings on the rates of false positive reporting by children interviewed with the dolls (*Commonwealth v. Cheryl Amirault LeFave*, 1998 [testimony of Maggie Bruck]). Expert testimony that the use of dolls with 8-year-old and older children is unreasonably suggestive (*Commonwealth v. Allen*, 1996 [Mass. Ct. App.]; *State v. Erickson*,

1990 [Minn. Ct. App.]) is simply not supported by the available research.

One court that has recognized the lack of fit between expert testimony and cases with older children is *State v. Biezer* (1997 [Mo. Ct. App.]), in which the defendant was convicted of sexually assaulting his 11-year-old grandniece and two of her friends, who were 11 and 17 years old. The court was confronted with the same expert whose proffered testimony was the basis for reversal in *Sloan* and was bound by *Sloan's* holding that the expert's opinion regarding the appropriateness of questions asked by investigative interviews is "evidence only an expert could give on matters not within the knowledge of a juror" (*State v. Sloan*, 1995, p. 597 [Mo. Ct. App.]). Nevertheless, the court upheld exclusion of the expert testimony, emphasizing that the victims were older than the 6-year-old child in *Sloan*.

Another important factor is whether the interviewers encouraged children to pretend or imagine that the events in question had occurred. Some of the most impressive demonstrations of suggestibility in young children were in studies that encouraged children to fantasize about fictitious events over multiple interviews (among other suggestive techniques) (Bruck, Hembrooke, & Ceci, 1997; Ceci, Loftus, Leichtman, & Bruck, 1994). In contrast, Ceci and SACD (1998) have noted that if there is an "air of seriousness" in the interviews it is "very difficult to elicit consistent false reports from young children" (p. 24). The SACD cites a study by Shyamalan and Lamb (1995), who found virtually no false reporting among preschoolers who were asked whether a man who had visited their classroom 4 months prior to the interview had gotten angry and yelled at them (he had not). Only 1 child out of 24 ever made a false claim; he did so at the first interview and consistently denied it in subsequent interviews. Shyamalan and Lamb and the SACD emphasize that at the outset of each interview, the interviewer told the child to "[t]ry to remember if it REALLY happened to you" and that "I need to make sure that you tell me the truth" (SACD, 1998, p. 24; see also Myers, Saywitz, & Goodman, 1996, for a similar discussion of Shyamalan and Lamb's study). Other factors that are important in assessing the fit of suggestibility research are discussed elsewhere (Ceci & Bruck, 1995; Holmgren, 1997; Lyon, 1999; Westcott, 1998;

for a review of the literature on children's eyewitness testimony, see Schaaff, Alexander, Goodman, Ghetti, Edelstein, & Castelli, this volume).

Limitations on the Rule That Expert Testimony Be Scientifically Valid and Fit the Facts of the Case

The state courts are free to reject the *Daubert* standards, because the case interprets the Federal Rules of Evidence and the states have their own rules. The reception has been mixed: Some states have in fact rejected *Daubert*; others have found it persuasive (Faigman, Kaye, Saks, & Sanders, 1997). However, rejection of *Daubert* should not stop the state courts from considering the reliability and relevance of expert testimony on suggestibility, because the same approach discussed here under *Daubert* is applicable under universally accepted rules of evidence. State courts can exclude expert testimony on suggestibility that fails to fit the facts of the case because it does not assist the jury, because expert's testimony has "little relevance or probative value" (*State v. Mazerolle*, 1992, p. 72 [Me. 1992]), or because it would confuse or mislead the jury (*State v. Biezer*, 1997 [Mo. Ct. App.]; *State v. Russell*, 1990 [Me.]). The specifics of *Daubert* may not be universally adopted by the states, but rules requiring that expert testimony assist the jury, be relevant, and not be misleading are ubiquitous.

As with the other objections to expert testimony discussed in this chapter, the *Daubert* inquiry is limited by the fact that issues such as reliability and fit are matters of degree without bright lines. Courts that are eager to admit expert testimony can justify findings that expert testimony is sufficiently scientifically reliable and fits well enough to reach the jury. They can emphasize language in the case law that these standards are "not that high" (*In re Paoli Railroad Yard PCB Litigation*, 1994, p. 745 [3rd Cir.]) and note *Daubert*'s admonition that expert testimony can always be tested through cross-examination and the other traditional tools of the adversary process. Nevertheless, there are some bright lines in *Daubert* and its progeny. The cases establish clear procedural guidelines that must be followed before the court can even consider admitting expert testimony on suggestibility: The research must be provided, and the fit between the research and the facts of the case must be specified. With the research in front of it, the court can see for itself the suggestive methods employed, the age of the subjects, and the inclusion of factors important in understanding the dynamics of sexual abuse allegations (such as fear, loyalty, and embarrassment). The well-informed court can overcome predispositions to admit testimony based on popularly held intuitions about children's suggestibility or popularly received impressions of recent research. The court's analysis will thus match what Bruck and Ceci call on practitioners to do: to make "certain that the studies they call upon resemble the case in terms of the types of acts, the severity of suggestions, and so on. Failure to do this could lead to miscarriages of justice" (Bruck & Ceci, 1999, pp. 436–437).

CONCLUSION

Recent developments in the law indicate that expert testimony on suggestibility can no longer be blocked by outdated assertions about the province of the jury, and that an increasing number of courts are receptive to such testimony. Increasing receptivity to such testimony requires increased scrutiny of the scientific basis for the testimony and the applicability of the testimony to the individual case.

Juries likely understand that young children are susceptible to coercive and suggestive questions. Experts who can offer more than platitudes may assist the jury, assuming that there is a sound scientific basis for going beyond the obvious. As an example of the way in which the standards outlined here could be applied, consider the case discussed in the introduction: *State v. Sloan* (1995 [Mo. Ct. App.]).

Under the analysis outlined here, the party offering the expert must provide the court with the research underlying the expert's conclusions. Most of the best-known research on suggestibility in the past decade is simply inapplicable to the facts of *Sloan*, in which the child disclosed shortly after the alleged abuse occurred and repeated her allegation when questioned shortly thereafter. It would be misleading to discuss research in which children are told to pretend or imagine how events occurred, are repeatedly reminded that the events did in fact occur, are told that other children have revealed wrongdoing, and are informed of other misdeeds by the alleged wrongdoers (see Bruck & Ceci, 1999, for a review of much of this research).

The expert's condemnation of affirms (questions that inform the child that he or she is on the right track) and repeats (questions that repeat back to the child information from the previous question) must be clarified and supported. The scientific basis for such a classification and criticism of these types of questions is unclear. Perhaps the expert intended to criticize the use of selective reinforcement or bribery for particular responses; this assertion conforms with intuition, and with basic principles of reward and punishment, and has some recent empirical support (Garven, Wood, & Malpass, 2000). On the other hand, if the expert intended to criticize reinforcement generally, there is some evidence that supportiveness may *increase* children's accuracy and resistance to suggestion (Carter, Bottoms, & Levine, 1996; Davis & Bottoms, 2002). Perhaps the expert intended to refer to the literature on repeated questions (e.g., Poole & White, 1991, 1993), though the point of that literature is that repetition of questions implicitly tells the child that his or her initial response is incorrect, which is the opposite of the supposed effect of a repeat. Indeed, the structured protocol designed by Michael Lamb, Kathleen Sternberg, and others in their laboratory at the National Institute of Child Health and Development (Sternberg, Lamb, Esplin, Orbach, & Hershkowitz, 2002) *recommends* that interviewers repeat information the child provides in order to cue further recall. Only attention to the research on which the expert relies and the specifics of the interview enable the court to assess adequately the usefulness of the expert's testimony.

The expert in *Sloan* also criticized the use of questions like "Where did he touch you" (a wh- question) and questions that can be answered "yes" or "no" (yes/no questions). Psychologists have long recognized that as one moves from open-ended questions (questions that require more than one word to answer) to specific questions (which include wh- questions and yes/no questions) the proportion of errors increases. However, they emphasize that the total amount of information obtained also increases, particularly when young children are questioned (Ceci & Bruck, 1993). Hence, interviewers must balance "the need for a full and detailed account against the need to minimize the potential for error" (Ceci, Powell, &

Crossman, 1999, p. 56). To the extent that some psychologists argue that specific questions should never be asked, this reflects a subjective value judgment regarding the appropriate trade-off between false disclosures and false denials.

The expert's labeling a wh-question as inappropriately leading appears to express a value judgment. On the other hand, her assertion that one cannot judge the validity of children's answers to yes/no questions is expressed as a factual claim. Note that this claim is much different than the well-supported argument that yes/no questions increase the number of errors. Rather, the claim asserts that children's answers to yes/no questions are uninformative. I know of no evidence to support such a claim. It is clearly unsupportable given the child's age (6 years) and the length of time between the alleged event and her first report of abuse (1 day, with interviews 5 days and 3 weeks later). The literature on yes/no questions is too large to review here. A fairly representative study, however, and one that is referenced by other reviews of the literature (Bruck & Ceci, 1999), is Carole Peterson's work on children's memories of traumatic injuries resulting in an emergency room visit. Peterson and her colleagues have calculated the relative accuracy of responses to free recall questions, wh- questions, and yes/no questions (Peterson & Bell, 1996; Peterson & Biggs, 1997). They find the usual pattern: Free recall is most accurate, whereas wh- questions increase the rate of error and yes/no questions elicit the highest number of errors. However, also consistent with other research, supplementing free recall questions with wh-questions increases the completeness of information children provide.

Among the 5-year-olds (the group closest in age to the 6-year-old child in *Sloan*), children were almost 100% accurate in responding to free recall questions (Peterson & Bell, 1996), 97% accurate in responding to wh- questions, and 80% accurate in responding to yes/no questions (Peterson & Biggs, 1997). Children's accuracy improved appreciably with age, highlighting the limited applicability of work on preschoolers to school-age children.

Careful review of the suggestibility research thus has a number of advantages in assessing the admissibility of expert testimony. First, experts must tone down their conclusions: Here, the most an expert could say is that answers to yes/no questions are "less accurate" than answers to free recall or wh- questions. It is clearly not justifiable to claim that answers to wh- questions and yes/no questions are invalid. Value judgments disguised as scientific opinion can be excluded.

Second, my scrutiny of the research on wh- and yes/no questions highlights the need for the courts to require that the foundation for expert testimony consist of the original research rather than summaries of the research (*United States v. Brien*, 1995 [1st Cir.]; *United States v. Downing*, 1985 [E.D. Penn.]; *United States v. Kime*, 1996 [8th Cir.]). In a review of the suggestibility research published in the *Annual Review of Psychology*, Bruck and Ceci (1999) highlight Peterson's work when discussing the increased error associated with specific questions. Their discussion contains an unfortunate error: They assert that the children in Peterson's sample were only 45% accurate when responding to wh- and yes/no questions (compared to 91% for free recall questions). The mistake exaggerates the unreliability of specific questions and could lead courts unfamiliar with the original research to allow experts to condemn the use of such questions when questioning children in abuse cases.

Research on the suggestibility of children will continue to be a popular subject for scientific research. It has generated an enormous amount of useful information that should be disseminated to policy makers and professionals who question children. Researchers have generated means by which suggestibility can be reduced (Saywitz & Lyon, 2002; Sternberg et al., 2002) and by which courtroom procedures can be less traumatic for child witnesses (McAuliff & Kovera, this volume). Nevertheless, trials will continue to function as adversarial battles that polarize positions and potentially distort scientific findings. Expert testimony on suggestibility may inform, but it can easily mislead. The courts must take seriously their role as gatekeepers.

References

Barlow v. State, 507 S.E.2d 416 (Ga. 1998).
Bruck, M., & Ceci, S. J. (1999). The suggestibility of children's memory. *Annual Review of Psychology, 50,* 419–439.

Bruck, M., Ceci, S. J., & Francoeur, E. (2000). Children's use of anatomically detailed dolls to report genital touching in a medical examination: Developmental and gender comparisons. *Journal of Experimental Psychology: Applied, 6,* 74–83.

Bruck, M., Ceci, S. J., Francouer, E., & Renick, A. (1995). Anatomically detailed dolls do not facilitate preschoolers' reports of a pediatric examination involving genital touching. *Journal of Experimental Psychology: Applied, 1,* 95–109.

Bruck, M., Ceci, S. J., & Hembrooke, H. (1998). Reliability and credibility of young children's reports: From research to policy and practice. *American Psychologist, 53,* 136–151.

Bruck, M., Hembrooke, H., & Ceci, S. J. (1997). Children's reports of pleasant and unpleasant events. In D. Read & S. Lindsay (Eds.), *Recollections of trauma: Scientific research and clinical practice* (pp. 199–213). New York: Plenum Press.

Carter, C., Bottoms, B., & Levine, M. (1996). Linguistic and socio-emotional influences on the accuracy of children's reports. *Law & Human Behavior, 20,* 335–358.

Ceci, S. J., & Bruck, M. (1993). Suggestibility of the child witness: A historical review and synthesis. *Psychological Bulletin, 113,* 403–439.

Ceci, S. J., & Bruck, M. (1995). *Jeopardy in the courtroom: A scientific analysis of children's testimony.* Washington, DC: American Psychological Association.

Ceci, S. J., Loftus, E. F., Leichtman, M. D., & Bruck, M. (1994). The possible role of source misattribution in the creation of false beliefs among preschoolers. *International Journal of Clinical and Experimental Hypnosis, 62,* 304–320.

Ceci, S. J., Powell, M. B., & Crossman, A. M. (1999). The scientific status of children's memory and testimony. In D. L. Faigman, D. H. Kaye, M. J. Saks, & J. Sanders (Eds.), *Modern scientific evidence: Supplemental Vol. 3* (pp. 40–69). St. Paul, MN: West.

Committee of Concerned Social Scientists. (1993). Reprinted in M. Bruck & S. J. Ceci (1995). Amicus brief for the case of *State of New Jersey v. Michaels* presented by committee of concerned social scientists. *Psychology, Public Policy, and Law, 1,* 272–322.

Commonwealth v. Allen, 665 N.E.2d 105 (Ct. App. Mass. 1996).

Commonwealth v. Cheryl Amirault LeFave, Middlesex S.S., Superior Court, Criminal Action Nos. 85–63, 66, 67; 85–2678–2680 (1998).

Commonwealth v. Ianello, 515 N.E.2d 1181 (Mass. 1987).

Commonwealth v. Trowbridge, 647 N.E.2d 413 (Mass. 1995).

Daubert v. Merrell-Dow Pharmaceuticals, 509 U.S. 579 (1993).

Davis, S. L., & Bottoms, B. L. (1998, March). *Effects of social support on children's eyewitness reports.* Paper presented at the biennial meeting of the American Psychology–Law Society, Redondo Beach, CA.

Davis, S. L., & Bottoms, B. L. (2001). Social support and children's eyewitness memory. In M. L. Eisen, G. S. Goodman, & J. A. Quas (Eds.), *Memory and suggestibility in the forensic interview*. Mahwah, NJ: Erlbaum.

Deloache, J. S., & Marzolf, D. P. (1995). The use of dolls to interview young children: Issues of symbolic representation. *Journal of Experimental Child Psychology, 60*, 155–173.

Doe v. Johnson, 52 F.3d 1448 (7th Cir. 1995).

Faigman, D. L., Kaye, D. H., Saks, M. J., & Sanders, J. (1997). *Modern scientific evidence: The law and science of expert testimony* (Vol. 1). St. Paul, MN: West.

Federal Rules of Evidence (2001).

Frye v. United States, 293 F. 1013 (D.C. Cir. 1923).

Garven, S., Wood, J. M., & Malpass, R. S. (2000). Allegations of wrongdoing: The effects of reinforcement on children's mundane and fantastic claims. *Journal of Applied Psychology, 85*, 38–49.

Garven, S., Wood, J. M., Malpass, R. S., & Shaw, J. S. (1998). More than suggestion: The effect of interviewing techniques from the McMartin preschool case. *Journal of Applied Psychology, 83*, 347–359.

General Electric Co. v. Joiner, 522 U.S. 136 (1997).

Glendening v. State, 536 So.2d 212 (Fla. 1988).

Goodman, G. S., Emery, R. E., & Haugaard, J. J. (1998). Developmental psychology and law: Divorce, child maltreatment, foster care, and adoption. In W. Damon (Series Ed.), D. Kuhn, & R. S. Siegler (Vol. Eds.), *Handbook of child psychology: Vol. 2. Cognition, perception, and language* (5th ed., pp. 775–874). New York: Wiley.

Heller v. Shaw Industries, Inc. 167 F.3d 146 (3d Cir. 1999).

Holmgren, B. K. (1997). Expert testimony on children's suggestibility: Should it be admitted? *APSAC Advisor, 10*(1), 10–14.

In re Paoli Railroad Yard PCB Litigation, 35 F.3d 717 (3rd Cir. 1994).

Isquith, P. K., Levine, M., & Scheiner, J. (1993). Blaming the child: Attribution of responsibility to victims of child sexual abuse. In G. S. Goodman & B. L. Bottoms (Eds.), *Child victims, child witnesses: Understanding and improving testimony* (pp. 203–228). New York: Guilford Press.

Joiner v. General Electric Co., 78 F.3d 524 (11th Cir. 1996).

Kovera, M. B., & Borgida, E. (1998). Expert scientific testimony on child witnesses in the age of Daubert. In S. J. Ceci & H. Hembrooke (Eds.), *Expert witnesses in child abuse cases: What can and should be said in court* (pp. 185–215). Washington, DC: American Psychological Association.

Kovera, M. B., Gresham, A. W., Borgida, E., Gray, E., & Regan, P. C. (1997). Does expert psychological testimony inform or influence juror decision making? A social cognitive analysis. *Journal of Applied Psychology, 82*, 178–191.

Kovera, M. B., & McAuliff, B. D. (2000). The effects of peer review and evidence quality on judge evaluations of psychological science: Are judges effective gatekeepers? *Journal of Applied Psychology, 85*, 574–586.

Kumho Tire Co., Ltd., v. Carmichael, 119 S.Ct. 1167 (1999).

Leichtman, M. D., & Ceci, S. J. (1995). The effects of stereotypes and suggestions on preschoolers' reports. *Developmental Psychology, 31*, 568–578.

Leippe, M. R., & Romanczyk, A. (1987). Children on the witness stand: A communication/persuasion analysis of jurors' reactions to child witnesses. In S. J. Ceci, M. P. Toglia, & D. F. Ross (Eds.), *Children's eyewitness memory* (pp. 155–177). New York: Springer-Verlag.

Lindsay, D. S., Read, J. D., & Sharma, K. (1998). Accuracy and confidence in person identification: The relationship is strong when witnessing conditions vary widely. *Psychological Science, 9*, 215–218.

Lyon, T. D. (1999). The new wave in children's suggestibility research: A critique. *Cornell Law Review, 84*, 1004–1087.

Lyon, T. D. (2002). Scientific support for child sexual abuse accommodation syndrome. In J. Conte (Ed.), *Critical issues in child sexual abuse* (pp. 107–138). Thousand Oaks, CA: Sage.

Lyon, T. D., & Koehler, J. J. (1998). Where researchers fear to tread: Interpretive differences among testifying experts in child sexual abuse cases. In S. J. Ceci & H. Hembrooke (Eds.), *Expert witnesses in child abuse cases: What can and should be said in court* (pp. 249–263). Washington, DC: American Psychological Association.

Mason, M. A. (1995). The child sex abuse syndrome: The other major issue in *State of New Jersey v. Margaret Kelly Michaels. Psychology, Public Policy, and Law, 1*, 399–410.

McAuliff, B. D., & Kovera, M. B. (1998, August). *Are layperson's beliefs about suggestibility consistent with expert opinion?* Poster presented at the annual meeting of the American Psychological Association, San Francisco.

Moore v. Ashland Chemical, Inc., 151 F.3d 269 (5th Cir. 1998).

Morison, S., & Greene, E. (1992). Juror and expert knowledge of child sexual abuse. *Child Abuse and Neglect, 16*, 595–613.

Mueller, C. B., & Kirkpatrick, L. C. (2000). *Evidence under the rules: Text, cases, and problems*. Gaithersburg, NY: Aspen.

Myers, J. E. B. (1997). *Evidence in child abuse and neglect cases* (Vol. 1, 3rd ed.). New York: Wiley.

Myers, J. E. B., Saywitz, K. J., & Goodman, G. S. (1996). Psychological research on children as witnesses: Practical implications for forensic interviews and courtroom testimony. *Pacific Law Journal, 28*, 3–91.

People v. Dunkle, 602 A.2d 830 (Pa. 1992).

People v. Gibbs, 550 N.Y.S.2d 400 (1990).

People v. McDonald, 690 P.2d 709 (Cal. 1984).

Peterson, C., & Bell, M. (1996). Children's memory for traumatic injury. *Child Development 67*, 3045–3070.

Peterson, C., & Biggs, M. (1997). Interviewing children about trauma: Problems with "specific" questions. *Journal of Traumatic Stress, 10*, 279–290.

Poole, D. A., & Lamb, M. E. (1998). *Investigative interviews of children: A guide for helping professionals.* Washington, DC: American Psychological Association.

Poole, D. A., & White, L. T. (1991). Effects of question repetition on the eyewitness testimony of children and adults. *Developmental Psychology, 27,* 975–986.

Poole, D. A., & White, L. T. (1993). Two years later: Effects of question repetition and retention interval on the eyewitness memory of children and adults. *Developmental Psychology, 29,* 844–853.

Porter v. Whitehall Laboratories, Inc., 9 F.3d 607 (7th Cir. 1993).

Ross, D. F., Dunning, D., Toglia, M. P., & Ceci, S. J. (1989). Age stereotypes, communication modality, and mock jurors' perceptions of the child witness. In S. J. Ceci, D. F. Ross, & M. P. Toglia, *Perspectives on children's testimony* (pp. 37–56). New York: Springer-Verlag.

Saywitz, K. J., Goodman, G. S., Nicholas, E., & Moan, S. F. (1991). Children's memories of a physical examination involving genital touch: Implications for reports of child sexual abuse. *Journal of Consulting and Clinical Psychology, 59,* 682–691.

Saywitz, K. J., & Lyon, T. D. (2002). Coming to grips with children's suggestibility. In M. Eisen, G. Goodman, & J. Quas (Eds.), *Memory and suggestibility in the forensic interview* (pp. 85–113). Hillsdale, NJ: Erlbaum.

Schutz v. State, 957 S.W.2d 52 (Ct. Crim. App. Tex. 1997).

Scientists for the Accurate Communication of Data. (1998). Amicus Curiae brief in *Commonwealth of Massachusetts v. Cheryl Amirault LeFave,* Middlesex S.S., Supreme Judicial Court, No. SJC-7529.

Shyamalan, B., & Lamb, S. (1995, August). *The effects of repeated questioning on preschoolers reports of abusive behavior.* Poster presented at the annual meeting of the American Psychological Association.

Sorensen v. Shaklee Corp., 31 F.3d 638 (8th Cir. 1994).

State v. Biezer, 947 S.W.2d 540 (Mo. Ct. App. 1997).

State v. Ellis, 669 A.2d 752 (Me. 1996).

State v. Erickson, 454 N.W.2d 624 (Minn. Ct. App. 1990).

State v. Gersin, 668 N.E.2d 486 (Ohio 1996).

State v. Gordius, 544 A.2d 309 (Me. 1988).

State v. Hulbert, 481 N.W.2d 329 (Iowa 1992).

State v. James, 560 A.2d 426 (Conn. 1989).

State v. Kirschbaum, 535 N.W.2d 462 (Wis. Ct. App. 1995).

State v. Long, 575 A.2d 435 (N.J. 1990).

State v. Malarney, 617 So.2d 739 (Fl. Ct. App. 1993).

State v. Mazerolle, 614 A.2d 68 (Me. 1992).

State v. Russell, 571 A.2d 229 (Me. 1990).

State v. Sloan, 912 S.W.2d 592 (Mo. Ct. App. 1995).

State v. Steffes, 887 P.2d 1196 (Mont. 1994).

State v. Swan, 790 P.2d 610 (Wash. 1990).

Sternberg, K. J., Lamb, M. E., Esplin, P. W., Orbach, Y., & Hershkowitz, I. (2002). Using a structured protocol to improve the quality of investigative interviews. In M. Eisen, G. Goodman, & J. Quas (Eds.), *Memory and suggestibility in the forensic interview* (pp. 409–436). Mahwah, NJ: Erlbaum.

Stringer v. Commonwealth, 956 S.W.2d 883 (Ky. 1997).

United States v. Brien, 59 F.3d 274 (1st Cir. 1995).

United States v. Cacy, 43 M.J. 214 (1995).

United States v. Curry, 977 F.2d 1042 (7th Cir. 1992).

United States v. Daniels, 64 F.3d 311 (7th Cir. 1995).

United States v. Downing, 609 F.Supp. 784 (E.D. Penn. 1985).

United States v. Downing, 753 F.2d 1224 (3rd Cir. 1985).

United States v. George, 975 F.2d 1431 (9th Cir. 1992).

United States v. Hall, 165 F.3d 1095 (7th Cir. 1999).

United States v. Harris, 995 F.2d 532 (4th Cir. 1993).

United States v. Kime, 99 F.3d 870 (8th Cir. 1996).

United States v. Larkin, 978 F.2d 964 (7th Cir. 1992).

United States v. Nguyen, 793 F.Supp. 497 (D.N.J. 1992).

United States v. Norwood, 939 F.Supp. 1132 (D.N.J. 1996).

United States v. Rouse, 100 F.3d 560 (8th Cir. 1996).

United States v. Rouse, 111 F.3d 561 (8th Cir. 1997).

United States v. Scheffer, 118 S.Ct. 1261 (1998).

United States v. Shay, 57 F.3d 126 (1st Cir. 1995).

United States v. Smith, 736 F.2d 1103 (6thCir. 1984).

Utley v. State, 826 S.W.2d 268 (Ark. 1992).

Westcott, H. (1998). Jeopardy in the courtroom. [Review of the book *Jeopardy in the courtroom: A scientific analysis of children's testimony*]. *British Journal of Psychology, 89,* 525.

Wigmore, J. H. (1904). A treatise on the system of evidence in trials at common law (Vol. 3). Boston: Little, Brown.

Yarmey, A. D., & Jones, H. P. T. (1979). Is the psychology of eyewitness identification a matter of common sense? In S. M. A. Lloyd-Bostock & B. R. Clifford (Eds.), *Evaluating witness evidence: Recent psychological research and new perspectives* (pp. 13–40). Chichester, UK: Wiley.

16

The Status of Evidentiary and Procedural Innovations in Child Abuse Proceedings

Bradley D. McAuliff
Margaret Bull Kovera

Prosecuting physical and sexual crimes allegedly perpetrated against children is a complex and difficult task. Often the sole eyewitness to the crime is the abused child. As a result, the successful prosecution of many child abuse cases hinges on the child victim's account of the crime. Testifying in court can be stressful for any witness, particularly for child victims of physical or sexual abuse (Goodman et al., 1992). Several features of traditional trial proceedings, such as facing the accused or describing the details of the alleged crime in open court, may make children reluctant to testify about their abuse (Sas, 1991) and may decrease the accuracy of their testimony (Saywitz & Nathanson, 1993).

Various evidentiary and procedural innovations have been introduced over the past decade to help enable victims to testify

We would like to thank the jury administration staff and personnel at Broward County Courthouse, Seventeenth Judicial District, Fort Lauderdale, Florida, for making the research reported in this chapter possible. In particular, we are grateful for the continued assistance and support of the Honorable Robert L. Andrews, Dolly Gibson, Norman Houghtaling, Pat Todaro, Lisa Muggeo, Audrey Edwards, Marvin Edelstein, and Allison Mitchel. We also thank Galit Geiger, Juliette Kelly, and Steffi Roedenbeck for their data entry assistance.

Correspondence concerning this chapter should be addressed to the first author at the Department of Psychology, University of Nebraska-Lincoln, 238 Burnett Hall, Lincoln, NE 68588-0308 or the second author at the Department of Psychology, Florida International University, 3000 NE 151st Street, North Miami, FL 33181-3600. Electronic mail may be sent via the Internet to bmcaulif@unlserve.unl.edu or koveram@fiu.edu in child abuse proceedings. At the federal level, for example, the Victims of Child Abuse Act of 1990 (§3266) amended the Federal Rules of Criminal Procedure, extending special accommodations to children such as allowing the presence of a support person during the child's testimony and closing the courtroom to the public (Whitcomb, 1992). Many states have enacted statutes permitting the use of innovative procedures, such as videotaped or closed-circuit television (CCTV) testimony, in trials involving alleged child abuse victims. Those innovations are examples of a broad spectrum of alternatives to traditional testimony that were designed to reduce the stress associated with appearing in court and to increase the accuracy of children's testimony.

The purpose of our chapter is to provide an overview of recent evidentiary and procedural innovations designed to accommodate children in criminal abuse proceedings. We begin by describing various innovations and discussing their availability and use in the United States. We then review the empirical literature examining legal professionals' views regarding the presence of alternative testimonial procedures in court. Do judges and attorneys view innovative procedures favorably? Next, we discuss studies investigating the effectiveness of child witness accommodations. Do children who use innovative procedures experience less stress and provide more accurate testimony than children who testify in a traditional manner? We then review several studies investigating the effects of various accommodations on lay and professional perceptions of defendants and child witnesses. Do jurors, judges, and attorneys evaluate defendants more negatively when courts accommodate child witnesses? Do those individuals view accommodated children more positively than they do children who provide traditional testimony? We conclude by discussing the results from a recent study that we conducted to learn more about jurors' expectancies for children's physical and emotional demeanor when courts use alternative testimonial procedures.

EVIDENTIARY AND PROCEDURAL INNOVATIONS IN CHILD
ABUSE PROCEEDINGS

What Alternatives to Traditional Testimony Exist for Children in the United States?

As Table 16.1 illustrates, a variety of evidentiary and procedural innovations is available to accommodate children in criminal proceedings involving child abuse in the United States (U.S. Department of Health and Human Services, 2000). Those innovations all share the common goal of reducing children's stress and enabling them to provide accurate evidence at trial; however, they vary in several key regards. First, the innovations differ in the degree to which they alter traditional trial practice. Permitting the use of leading questions requires less procedural modification than does allowing the child to testify outside the courtroom. Second, the resources required and the practical ease with which the various innovations are introduced into traditional trial practice also differ. Certain modifications, such as limiting the duration of a child's testimony, are relatively easy to implement at trial and

TABLE 16.1. *Evidentiary and Procedural Innovations Currently Available in Criminal Child Abuse Proceedings in the United States*

Type of Innovation	Number of States with Legislation Permitting the Innovation
Child presumed competent to testify	50
Videotaped testimony and/or depositions	37
Closed-circuit television testimony	37
Hearsay testimony exception	33
Speedy disposition of case	24
Videotaped interviews or statements	16
Appointment of special support person	16
Closed courtrooms	18
Anatomically detailed dolls	9
Leading questions	3
Limitations on the duration of child's testimony	3

Note: Adapted with permission from Child Abuse and Neglect State Statute Series, Vol. 4, No. 20–8. U.S. Department of Health and Human Services (2000).

require few additional resources. In contrast, the use of CCTV or videotaped testimony may require physical alteration of the courtroom environment and additional equipment such as television monitors to transmit the child's testimony to jurors. Finally, accommodations vary in the degree to which they potentially infringe on the constitutional rights of defendants. Certain alternative procedures, such as those that deny a defendant the right to confront his or her accuser, are more likely than other procedures to serve as the basis for a subsequent appeal on constitutional grounds.

Videotaped Testimony. Looking more closely at some of the accommodations most readily available in criminal child abuse proceedings, we see that at least 37 states permit children to testify using some form of videotape. Videotaped evidence can be presented in the form of an interview, deposition, or testimony, and the exact nature of each varies from state to state. In some states, for example, the child witness is deposed in the presence of both attorneys prior to trial, and a videotape of the child's deposition is later admitted at trial. In other states, a child's grand jury or preliminary hearing testimony is presented at the subsequent trial. Far fewer states permit a videotape of a previously conducted interview with the child to be admitted at trial. Statutes in those states generally require the child to be available for cross-examination or require a showing that the child's statements are trustworthy if the child is unavailable to testify. State statutes also vary in the degree of requisite trauma that must be demonstrated before a child's videotaped evidence can be shown to jurors in lieu of the child's live, in-court testimony.

CCTV. Thirty-seven states have enacted legislation permitting the use of CCTV in criminal child abuse proceedings. Although the Supreme Court approved the conditional use of CCTV in *Maryland v. Craig* (1990), it remains one of the most controversial forms of alternative testimony available to child witnesses. Courts generally use two forms of CCTV: one- and two-way CCTV. Two-way CCTV allows live images of the child to be broadcast from a remote location to the courtroom while select images from the courtroom (e.g., a judge or an attorney posing questions) are broadcast simultaneously to the child. When one-way CCTV procedures are used, only the image of the child and others present with the child (e.g., the attorneys or a support person) is transmitted to the courtroom. CCTV transmissions are both visual and aural in nature. CCTV statutes vary on several dimensions from state to state. Some states, for example, allow the attorneys and the defendant to be present with the child in the testimonial room while the judge and jury remain in the courtroom. Other states allow only the attorneys to be present in the testimonial room to question the child. In still other states, all participants (except the child) remain in the courtroom, and the attorneys conduct direct and cross-examination via CCTV. State statutes also vary in the degree of child victim trauma that prosecutors must demonstrate before CCTV testimony can replace a child's live testimony in court. Some statutes presume that any testimony in open court is traumatic for child victims, whereas others limit the use of CCTV to cases in which the defendant actually harmed or violently threatened the child (Whitcomb, 1992).

Hearsay Testimony. Thirty-three states have legislation allowing the use of special hearsay exceptions in criminal child abuse cases. As set forth in Rule 801 of the Federal Rules of Evidence, hearsay consists of any out-of-court statement offered into evidence to prove the truth of the matter asserted. Hearsay evidence typically is inadmissible at trial because it is not subject to cross-examination. To be admissible, such evidence must fall under one of many traditional hearsay exceptions (e.g., a dying declarant's last words). Because out-of-court statements made by child abuse victims often do not fall within traditional hearsay exceptions, some states have created special hearsay exceptions to permit children's out-of-court statements in certain circumstances. Most states, for example, require that the trustworthiness of a child's out-of-court statements be demonstrated and require additional live, in-court testimony from the child unless he or she is declared unavailable by the court (e.g., unable to testify). (For more thorough discussions of hearsay testimony and traditional hearsay exceptions, see McGough, 1994, and Myers, 1992.)

Support Person. At least 16 states permit the appointment of special support persons in criminal cases involving child abuse. Trial judges generally have a fair amount of discretion when determining who is qualified to serve as a support person. In some states, the support person is an attorney appointed by the state to represent the child's interests (i.e., guardian *ad litem;* see Haralambie & Nysse-Carris, this volume, for a discussion), whereas in other states a friend, family member, or any individual who contributes to the well-being of the child can serve as the support person. State statutes also vary in the degree to which they specify the exact nature of the support person's role in the trial proceedings. Some states, such as Hawaii, restrict the level of communication between the support person and the child during the child's testimony. Other states, such as Idaho and California, specify that the support person can accompany the child witness to the stand or remain in close proximity to the child during his or her testimony.

Pretrial Preparation. Although we are unaware of any state statutes that specifically provide for the pretrial preparation of child witnesses, many courts have adopted programs designed to prepare children for their day in court. Pretrial preparation programs vary in their formality and foci. Less formal preparation may consist of an attorney providing a child with a tour of the courtroom and cursory review of the case facts (Saywitz & Snyder, 1993). More formal programs may focus on increasing the accuracy of children's testimony (Saywitz & Snyder, 1996) or increasing children's knowledge of the court's professionals and procedures and reducing the stress created by testifying in open court (Sas, 1991). One preparation program in Huntsville, Alabama (Keeney, Amacher, & Kastanakis, 1992), uses a series of structured sessions to address children's fears and uncertainties about their involvement in criminal proceedings, including confronting the defendant, testifying on direct and cross-examination, expecting retaliation by the defendant, and their lack of familiarity with the judge, jury, and courtroom. Sessions incorporate tours of the courthouse and courtroom, art and Gestalt techniques, and role-playing activities to help minimize children's stress attendant to their impending court appearance. (See also Lipovsky & Stern,

1997, for interdisciplinary recommendations to prepare children for court.)

Tendency for Courts to Use Alternatives to Traditional Testimony in the United States

Researchers in several studies have examined the frequency with which children testify using various evidentiary and procedural innovations in the United States. Researchers in one of the earliest studies surveyed Alabama judges and prosecutors regarding their use of accommodations in domestic child abuse cases (Sigler, Crowley, & Johnson, 1990). Sixty-six percent of respondents reported that the use of hearsay testimony at preliminary hearings was a common practice, whereas just over half (52%) stated that children commonly testified while being accompanied by a friend or toy. Fewer (37%) indicated that the use of videotaped testimony was a common practice. The Sigler et al. study provided important preliminary data regarding the use of evidentiary and procedural innovations; however, the vague and subjective nature of respondents' classifications of each procedure as a "common practice" limits our ability to determine how frequently Alabama courts actually used innovative procedures.

A subsequent field study by Goodman and her colleagues (1992) improved on the limitations of the Sigler et al. (1990) survey. Goodman et al. spent over 2 years following a group of 218 children in Denver, Colorado, through criminal court and documenting their trial-related experiences. They found that courts infrequently accommodated child witnesses, despite the existence of legislation permitting various accommodations in Colorado at that time. When courts elected to accommodate children, they tended to close the courtroom during the child's testimony or to allow a support person (e.g., a parent or victim advocate) to remain in the audience. With the exception of allowing a victim advocate to be present during the child's testimony, the use of those accommodations was more common during preliminary hearings than during actual trials. Interestingly, no children in that sample provided videotaped testimony and only one used CCTV.

One potential explanation for the low rates of videotape and CCTV use that Goodman et al. and Sigler et al. observed is that both studies were conducted prior to the Supreme Court's landmark decision in *Craig*. In that decision, the Supreme Court upheld the use of alternative testimonial procedures that allow children to testify outside the defendant's presence if certain conditions are met (i.e., the procedure is necessary to protect the child, the child is traumatized by the defendant's presence specifically, and the child's emotional distress is more than a general nervousness or reluctance to testify). Prior to *Craig*, judges and prosecutors may have feared that higher courts would deem certain features of those procedures (e.g., not allowing the defendant to view the child while testifying) unconstitutional. However, only 9 out of 134 (7%) prosecuting attorneys who responded to a recent survey believed that the *Craig* ruling had affected their use of innovative procedures (Goodman, Quas, Bulkley, & Shapiro, 1999).

Unlike the Sigler et al. (1990) and Goodman et al. (1992) studies, which each assessed the use of innovative evidentiary procedures within a specific state, the focus of two recent studies was national in scope. In a national survey of state trial court judges, Hafemeister (1996) found that the most commonly reported approach to minimizing trauma for the child or to reducing evidentiary barriers to accurate testimony was to ensure that members of the court posed age-appropriate questions to the child (88%). Seventy-two percent of the judges reported using the hearsay exception to admit children's out-of-court statements of abuse, whereas only 27% had encountered videotaped testimony and 11% had used CCTV in sexual abuse cases involving children.

Goodman et al. (1999) surveyed U.S. prosecutors about their attitudes toward and experiences with courtroom innovations designed to decrease children's testimonial stress. These researchers observed a great deal of variability in the reported use of alternatives to traditional testimony. Over 90% of the respondents indicated that they always or frequently used pretrial preparation and the presence of a support person in cases involving children. Forty-nine percent reported they had used hearsay testimony, but fewer than 3% reported they had used some form of videotaped testimony or CCTV (as reported in Quas, DeCicco, Bulkley, & Goodman,

1996). When asked why hearsay, videotape, or CCTV innovations were used infrequently or discontinued, prosecutors indicated that they feared these procedures would harm the case or provide grounds for a defense challenge or appeal.

In summary, extant research indicates that U.S. courts use most evidentiary and procedural innovations on a relatively infrequent basis despite their widespread availability. Not surprisingly, courts seem to prefer accommodations that are the easiest to implement and the least disruptive to the traditional practice of law. Examples include the presence of a support person, pretrial preparation of the child, and posing age-appropriate questions to the child. Moreover, courts appear to be more likely to implement these innovations in the early stages of the judicial process, such as during a child's preliminary hearing or grand jury testimony, compared to the later stages such as the actual trial. This trend may be due in part to the less formal nature of grand jury or preliminary hearing testimony and judges' tendency to relax evidentiary and procedural rules early in proceedings involving children.

Do Alternative Testimonial Procedures Reduce Children's Stress and Increase their Accuracy?

Survey Research. One approach to determining whether accommodations effectively reduce children's stress and increase their accuracy is to survey the opinions and observations of legal professionals. One recent study asked state court judges to rate the effectiveness and fairness of 22 accommodations designed to minimize children's trauma when testifying (Hafemeister, 1996). Ninety-five percent or more of respondents believed that posing questions at the child's comprehension level, closing the courtroom, consulting an expert, modifying the court schedule, permitting leading questions, and permitting hearsay statements were effective in reducing children's court-related stress. Fewer judges believed that videotape and CCTV testimony (83% and 79%, respectively) minimized children's trauma. Goodman et al. (1999) observed similar findings in their national survey of district attorneys. Respondents in that study believed that certain procedures, such as preparing children to testify, allowing a support person to be present, and giving children a tour of the courtroom, were most effective in reducing trauma. Attorneys believed that innovative procedures such as the use of expert testimony, one-way mirrors, and videotaped interviews were least effective in reducing children's stress.

The Hafemeister (1996) and Goodman et al. (1999) surveys provide important information regarding whether legal professionals believe that various accommodations serve their intended purpose. Yet certain factors, such as response bias, may limit the generalizability of those findings. For example, legal professionals who viewed innovative procedures favorably or who used them on a regular basis may have been more likely to return a survey on those issues than were professionals who held different beliefs. If that were the case, the surveys may overestimate the optimistic nature of judges' and attorneys' evaluations of child witness accommodations. Also, measuring the *perceived* benefits of innovative procedures on children's stress is not equivalent to measuring the *actual* benefits that children may or may not experience. Based on the Hafemeister and Goodman et al. surveys, it remains unclear whether innovations actually reduced children's stress or whether they merely appeared to do so.

Quasi-Experimental Research. Social scientists also have assessed the efficacy of innovative procedures by examining the relation between traditional/alternative testimony and positive/negative outcomes for children in actual trials. In the United States, Goodman et al. (1992) used this quasi-experimental approach to examine whether certain innovative testimonial procedures were associated with children's decreased stress and increased accuracy. Results indicated that children who testified in the presence of a nonoffending parent/loved one were less frightened and less likely to give inconsistent testimony regarding peripheral crime details. When a victim advocate was present during the child's testimony, children were less likely to recant their identifications of the perpetrators and their descriptions of the abuse during defense questioning. Finally, children who testified in closed courtrooms were less likely to cry during defense questioning.

Researchers abroad have conducted additional quasi-experimental research where CCTV technology is used routinely to accommodate child witnesses. Davies and Noon (1991) conducted a multifaceted study evaluating the use of the Live link (i.e., the British equivalent of two-way CCTV) for the first 2 years after its introduction in England and Wales. Seventy-four percent of judges, 83% of barristers, and 93% of court clerks who had recently participated in Live link cases had a "favorable" or "very favorable" impression of the Live link. Further, compared to 89 children who testified in open court in Scotland, 150 children testifying via Live link in England were judged to be less stressed and to give more complete, consistent testimony. Moreover, Live link children were more resistant to leading questions and less likely to give inconsistent testimony about the main actions of the accused than were their Scottish counterparts. Davies and Noon qualified their findings by noting that in addition to the format of children's testimony, other differences existed between the English and Scottish samples, such as the nature of the reported offense (sexual versus physical abuse) and the child's role (victim versus witness). Those differences may also explain the variance in children's perceived stress when testifying in open court or via Live link.

Cashmore (1992) conducted a similar study in Australia. Legal professionals, law enforcement personnel, families of the victims, and victims generally expressed the belief that CCTV achieved its objective of reducing stress and facilitating testimony for children, and that CCTV did not create unfair prejudice against defendants. A minority of respondents, however, expressed concern that testifying via CCTV might make it easier for children to lie and more difficult for viewers to detect dishonesty. Murray (1995) evaluated the introduction of the Live link during the first 27 months of its use in Scottish criminal trials. The majority of parents who had been part of the Live link experience believed that their children's evidence would not have reached the trial at all without the use of the Live link. During posttrial interviews, 94% of the children who testified via Live link believed it to be easier and less distressing than traditional courtroom testimony, citing reasons such as testifying outside the presence of the defendant and the crowded courtroom.

Overall, quasi-experimental studies conducted in the United States and abroad offer the following generalized findings regarding the effectiveness of innovative testimonial procedures in cases involving children. In the United States, certain accommodations were associated with positive outcomes. Children testifying in the presence of a support person were less likely to be frightened, less likely to give inconsistent testimony, and less likely to recant their accusations than children providing traditional testimony. In England, Wales, Australia, and Scotland, the vast majority of legal professionals who directly experienced the courtroom use of CCTV believed that CCTV reduced stress and improved the testimony of child witnesses. Moreover, both parents and judges in those studies agreed that in many instances the use of CCTV enabled children to give evidence who would have been unable or unwilling to do so without the use of the alternative procedure. Children also had favorable impressions of testifying via CCTV, frequently preferring it to courtroom testimony. Researchers did, however, note some negative effects associated with CCTV testimony as well. Respondents in all three studies reported that the court experienced technical difficulties with the equipment at some point that rendered the child's testimony inaudible. Many judges and attorneys also expressed concern regarding the diminished impact of children's testimony when it appeared on the television monitor.

As with any type of research, certain caveats govern our interpretation of the findings observed in these quasi-experimental studies. In particular, the researchers' inability to manipulate the variable of interest and to assign participants randomly to different testimonial conditions limits the internal validity of these studies. For example, although judges reported that children appeared less stressed when using certain accommodations, we cannot conclude that the use of such accommodations *caused* children to be less stressed. We only know that an outcome (the appearance of decreased stress) was associated with or related to a particular variable (use of accommodations). Moreover, because researchers in those studies did not assign children randomly to each testimonial condition (traditional versus innovative), we cannot rule out the possible influence of confounding or extraneous variables. Other variables, such as the nature or degree of abuse experienced by the child witness, may serve as rival explanations for any emerging differences in these studies (if researchers did not statistically control or account for the influence of such variables). It seems reasonable to expect, for example, that the children who used alternative testimonial procedures had experienced more severe or extended abuse than the children who testified in court. Those differences at the outset could also explain the variation in stress and accuracy attributed to the use of innovative procedures.

Experimental Research. In response to the aforementioned criticisms, social scientists have begun to study the effects of alternative versus traditional testimony on children in more controlled laboratory settings. Although real-world studies possess increased ecological validity, that benefit often comes at the cost of decreased internal validity. Experimental research possesses certain characteristics that are difficult to obtain in real-world settings, including the ability to manipulate experimentally the variable of interest and the ability to assign participants randomly to each experimental condition. These characteristics afford researchers a certain degree of control over variables that is not present in real-world settings, thereby increasing their ability to attribute any emerging differences between conditions to the experimentally manipulated variable. Recent experimental studies have evaluated the accuracy and stress-reducing potential of CCTV testimony, pretrial preparation, and hearsay testimony.

CCTV. In an elaborate study by Goodman et al. (1998), children of various ages participated in a play session with an unfamiliar male confederate who encouraged them to place stickers either on their exposed body parts (e.g., children's arms, toes, and navels) or on their clothing. Two weeks later, children testified about the play session at a mock trial in a downtown courthouse, providing either traditional in-court testimony or testimony outside the courtroom that was transmitted to mock jurors via CCTV. Results showed that when responding to misleading questions, younger children who testified in the open court condition made more errors of omission than their peers who testified in the CCTV condition. Goodman et al. also observed a small but statistically significant positive effect of CCTV on children's ability to answer direct questions overall. Children who expected to testify live in court indicated higher levels of pretrial stress than children who expected to testify via CCTV. Finally, jurors rated children testifying via CCTV as being less stressed during their testimony than those children testifying in open court.

PRETRIAL PREPARATION. CCTV is a rather invasive accommodation that may help alleviate the stress experienced by young children who testify in court proceedings. Some courts and agencies have developed a less intrusive accommodation that may also minimize the stressfulness of a child's courtroom experience: child witness preparation (Aldridge & Freshwater, 1993; Keeney et al., 1992; Melton, Limber, Jacobs, & Oberlander, 1992; Sas, 1992). One preparation program in Canada helps to prepare children for their day in court by having the children learn about courtroom participants, tour a courtroom, practice speaking in court, and learn relaxation techniques to reduce their stress. A field study found that children who completed this program and then testified in court were better adjusted psychologically than those who did not complete the program (Sas, 1991). Moreover, attorneys who interacted with the prepared children found them to be better witnesses than those children whom they had previously encountered in court.

Although the attorneys in the Sas (1991) study believed that the prepared children were better witnesses than the unprepared children, it is impossible to determine whether these prepared children were more accurate witnesses because there is no record of the actual events to which the children testified. To assess the effects of preparation on the accuracy of children's memories, it is necessary to have such a record. Therefore, laboratory studies in which the experimenter creates and records the event to be remembered are needed to address this question.

Saywitz and her colleagues have conducted several laboratory studies examining the effects of a particular type of preparation on the accuracy of children's testimony. These researchers have focused on testing the efficacy of preparation programs designed to augment children's abilities to comprehend and answer accurately questions posed during forensic interviews and trial. Their research suggests that children can provide more correct information about witnessed events if they are trained to describe different characteristics of the event, such as the participants, setting, actions, and dialogue (Saywitz & Snyder, 1996; Saywitz, Snyder, & Lamphear, 1996). This procedure did not increase the amount of incorrect information recalled by children.

Other research has examined whether preparation programs that teach children to monitor their comprehension of difficult questions increase the accuracy of children's reports. In one such study, children witnessed a staged event and subsequently answered questions about that event (Saywitz, Snyder, & Nathanson, 1999). Saywitz et al. instructed one group of children to alert the interviewer whenever they did not understand a question. Another group participated in more intensive training for the comprehension monitoring skill. Specifically, the second group watched videotaped vignettes in which children experienced negative consequences when they answered questions that they did not understand. Further, the trained group practiced identifying misleading or difficult questions, and they were rewarded when they told the adult interviewer that they did not understand questions. Compared to a control group that received neither instruction nor training, the prepared children provided more accurate information and less inaccurate information about the witnessed event. Moreover, the children who had practiced comprehension monitoring performed better than the children who were merely instructed to identify confusing questions. Most preparation programs merely provide children with information about the courtroom, about the people with whom they will interact in court, and about the types of tasks they will perform while testifying. However, recent research suggests that preparation programs that provide comprehension monitoring training in addition to this task-demand training will produce children who are capable of providing more accurate testimony than programs providing task-demand training alone (Peters & Nunez, 1999).

HEARSAY TESTIMONY. In addition to CCTV and pretrial preparation, researchers have evaluated the effectiveness of hearsay evidence as an alternative to children's live, in-court testimony. Certain characteristics of hearsay testimony pose unique challenges to researchers studying that innovative form of evidence in experimental settings. First, unlike other alternatives to traditional testimony, hearsay testimony entails a second witness communicating the child's testimony to the triers of fact instead of the child. Given the imperfect nature of human memory (Schacter, 1999), one could argue that hearsay testimony doubly increases the potential for error in the testimony that finally reaches the court. A hearsay witness could provide very accurate testimony about a child's inaccurate account of the original crime or vice versa; therefore, jurors must not only consider the accuracy of the child's account of the crime but also the accuracy of the hearsay witness.

Second, because hearsay testimony is communicated to the court via a hearsay witness and not the child, the behavior and personal characteristics of the hearsay witness may influence jurors' judgments regarding the credibility of the child witness's testimony. In essence, hearsay testimony denies jurors traditional cues used to assess directly the accuracy and truthfulness of a child's testimony. Instead, jurors must base their judgments on cues related to the hearsay witness. Jurors, for example, may not believe an accurate (but nervous and hesitant) hearsay witness testifying about a child's accurate account of the crime. Or jurors may believe a confident and nonhesitant hearsay witness testifying about a child's inaccurate account of the crime. For these reasons, studies examining the effectiveness of hearsay evidence ideally should take into account the child's accuracy, the hearsay witness's accuracy, and jurors' perceptions of both the child and the hearsay witness.

Research has shown that interviewers' hearsay accounts are in-complete compared to their original conversations with children but that the accuracy of the information contained in their hearsay accounts can be high. Mothers questioned approximately 3 days after interviewing their children about a play session recalled 66% of the primary event activities and 35% of the details that their chil-dren had reported to them (Bruck, Ceci, & Francoeur, 1999). The accuracy of the mothers' gist (i.e., general content) and verbatim (i.e., surface structure) information was quite high (88% and 74%, respectively). Forewarning mothers that they would be asked to recall their conversations with children did not affect the accuracy of mothers' gist or verbatim memory. Trained professionals who interviewed children about a past event in a study by Warren and Woodall (1999) recounted 83% of the major event activities, 65% of the event details, and 60% of the errors that children had reported. In both studies, however, interviewers had difficulty recalling the exact questions they had asked children (only 17% in Bruck et al. and 20% in Warren & Woodall). Finally, a recent study revealed that investigators' notes misrepresented the information elicited from child interviewees and the methods used to elicit that information (Lamb, Orbach, Sternberg, Hershkowitz, & Horowitz, 2000). Investigators failed to record 25% of the total incident-relevant details and more than half of the utterances used to elicit information from the children.

In summary, the studies reviewed show that CCTV and pretrial preparation can decrease children's stress and increase their accuracy in certain circumstances. The emerging literature on hearsay testimony, however, indicates that legal professionals and jurors should approach hearsay testimony with caution due to the incomplete and sometimes inaccurate nature of that form of alternative testimony.

How Do Jurors View the Use of Alternative Testimonial Procedures?

Research documenting that children are less stressed and more accurate when testifying using accommodations is relevant to legal settings only insofar as jurors are able to recognize children's heightened accuracy and incorporate that factor appropriately into their decision-making processes. In addition to evaluating children's accuracy at trial, jurors are inundated with a flood of cues and information that may affect their perceptions and decision making. Jurors may assume, for example, that a defendant is guilty when courts accommodate a child witness. They may reason that the only logical explanation for the child's trauma and need for accommodation is that the defendant actually abused the child. If this were the case, such procedures should not be allowed on the grounds that they violate defendants' constitutional right to a fair trial and due process. Similarly, if jurors are more skeptical of children's accounts when courts accommodate children (despite their increased accuracy), we must question the utility of accommodating children at trial. Thus, it behooves us to consider whether the use of innovative testimonial procedures influences jurors' perceptions of defendants and child witnesses.

Videotaped Testimony. In one of the first studies of its kind, Swim, Borgida, and McCoy (1993) presented undergraduates with a video-taped child sexual abuse trial in which the child testified live in court or via videotaped deposition. Compared to the live testimony con-dition, participants believed that the child was better able to tes-tify via videotape and that such testimony was less harmful to the child's psychological well-being. Swim et al. did not observe any differences between participants' perceptions of the defendant or any other witness (including the child) in the live and videotaped deposition conditions. Overall, undergraduates believed both trials were equally fair; however, analyses of on-line response data indicated that participants who viewed the child's videotaped deposition harbored a pro-prosecution bias at several points throughout the trial. Despite this apparent pro-prosecution bias, however, participants were less likely to find the defendant guilty of first-degree sexual assault in the videotaped deposition condition (30%) compared to the live testimony condition (48%).

Hearsay Testimony. Golding and his colleagues conducted three studies examining the effects of hearsay testimony in child sex-ual abuse cases (Golding, Alexander, & Stewart, 1999; Golding, Sanchez, & Sego, 1997). Undergraduate mock jurors read fictional trial summaries containing testimony from several witnesses, in-cluding an alleged child victim, a hearsay witness, both, or neither, depending on the study. The general trend in results across these three studies was that mock jurors believed the hearsay testimony whether it was presented by an adult or a young sibling of the al-leged child victim and whether it appeared alone or was accompa-nied by the child victim's testimony. Mock jurors were more likely to find the defendant guilty, to believe the prosecution's witnesses, and to think that the abuse actually occurred when they viewed the child victim's testimony, the hearsay witness's testimony, or both compared to when neither witness testified. Differences between ju-rors' responses in the former three conditions were nonsignificant, however. That is, juror judgments did not differ when the child victim, hearsay witness, or both testified.

Another recent study used a more realistic trial stimulus than Golding et al.'s written summaries and found evidence that jurors may react differently to traditional versus hearsay testimony in child abuse cases (Ross, Lindsay, & Marsil, 1999). Psychology under-graduates viewed two versions of a videotaped trial simulation. An alleged 10-year-old victim testified in one version, and the child's mother testified as a hearsay witness on the child's behalf in the other. The content of the abuse allegation remained constant across conditions. Students who viewed the mother's hearsay testimony were less likely to convict the defendant and found the child witness to be less credible than those who viewed the child's testimony (24% and 53% guilty verdicts, respectively). With one exception, view-ing the child's testimony or the mother's hearsay testimony did not influence mock jurors' credibility ratings of the mother or the defendant. Mock jurors in the child testimony condition rated the defendant's claim that he was helping his daughter dry off after her bath as more credible than did mock jurors in the hearsay testimony condition.

Ross et al. (1999) varied the identity of the hearsay witness (the alleged child victim's mother, doctor, teacher, or neighbor) in a second study and found that the child victim's testimony re-sulted in fewer guilty verdicts than the hearsay testimony of the doctor, teacher, or mother. Mock jurors also perceived the child and her mother to be less credible than the doctor, teacher, and neighbor, and found the defendant to be more credible when the child testified compared to when either the doctor or teacher testified.

Redlich, Myers, Goodman, and Qin (1999) explored mock jurors' perceptions of two forms of hearsay evidence in a child sexual abuse case. In that study, jury-eligible citizens viewed videotaped forensic interviews of an alleged child victim or the live testimony of a police officer who repeated the child's statements from the forensic interview. Jurors who viewed the police officer's hearsay testimony were more doubtful that the child fully disclosed crime-relevant details during the forensic interview compared to mock jurors who saw the videotaped forensic interviews themselves. Jurors in the police officer condition also rated certain aspects of the forensic interview (e.g., whether the interviewer used suggestive questions or whether the child was coached before the interview) as less important to their determination of whether the officer's tes-timony was believable than did jurors in the videotaped condition.

Path analyses also revealed an indirect effect of the testimonial condition on jurors' conviction rates; jurors were more likely to acquit the defendant when they viewed the police officer's hearsay testimony than when they viewed the videotaped interviews.

CCTV. Similar to Swim et al. (1993), Ross et al. (1994) presented participants with a videotaped simulation of a child sexual abuse trial in which the victim testified in open court, in open court from behind a protective screen that shielded the defendant from the witness's view, or outside the courtroom via one-way CCTV. Neither participants' guilty verdicts nor their ratings of the defendant's and child's credibility and trial fairness differed across the three testimonial conditions. In a second study, Ross et al. concluded the trial simulation immediately after the child's testimony. Results were similar except that undergraduates were less likely to convict the defendant when the child used alternative testimonial procedures rather than testifying in court.

Results of a study by Lindsay, Ross, Lee, and Carr (1995) mirrored those of the Ross et al. (1994) study. Neither mock jurors' verdicts nor credibility ratings of a defendant and a child witness in a child sexual abuse case differed when the child testified in court, in court from behind a protective screen, or from outside the courtroom via CCTV. Lindsay et al. also included a judicial instruction manipulation in which undergraduates either heard or did not hear an instruction to not draw inferences of any kind from the use of the alternative testimonial procedure. Mock jurors were more likely to find the defendant guilty when they received a warning in the protective shield and CCTV condition than when they did not. Those conviction rates, however, were not significantly different from that obtained in the live testimony condition. Warned participants evaluated the child's credibility more positively and found the trial fairer than did nonwarned participants. The judicial instruction manipulation had no effects on the defendant's perceived credibility.

Conclusions and Caveats about Previous Research

Overall, it appears that the use of alternative testimonial procedures has little if any effect on jurors' evaluations of defendants and child witnesses. In the studies we reviewed, mock jurors did not evaluate defendants and children more negatively when children testified via alternative versus traditional means. We should note some exceptions to this general conclusion. Ross et al. (1994) found evidence that children's accommodated testimony may bias jurors against the defendant. Mock jurors in that study were less likely to convict the defendant when the child testified outside the courtroom via CCTV than in open court; however, that outcome occurred only when Ross et al. concluded the trial immediately after the child's testimony. The first of two subsequent studies by Ross et al. (1999) found that mock jurors who viewed hearsay testimony were less likely to convict the defendant and provided lower credibility ratings for the child victim than mock jurors who viewed the child's traditional testimony. In the second study, hearsay testimony from the child victim's doctor, teacher, or mother resulted in more guilty verdicts than did the child's traditional testimony (the exact opposite of the effect obtained in the first study), and mock jurors provided higher defendant credibility ratings when the child testified than they did when either the doctor or teacher hearsay witnesses testified. Finally, Redlich et al. (1999) observed that jurors were more skeptical of the completeness of a child's report when relayed by an adult hearsay witness than when the child described the event.

Certain characteristics of the studies evaluating the effects of accommodations on jurors' perceptions qualify the conclusions we can draw based on that work. First, many of the studies relied on samples of undergraduate students to play the role of mock jurors. Whether college students' responses to accommodations are similar to or different from those provided by jury-eligible community members remains an unanswered empirical question (see Bornstein, 1999, summarizing the results of jury simulations that directly compared student and nonstudent samples). Second and more important, researchers in several studies presented each of the various testimonial conditions to jurors on videotape. Consequently, those studies may have overlooked additional variables that covary with the format of the child's testimony that could influence jurors' attitudes and perceptions. For example, findings from the studies conducted in actual trials in England, Wales, Australia, and

Scotland indicated that differences in the audibility of children's testimony existed when children testified outside the courtroom. Children's audibility or other variables may affect jurors' evaluations of the evidence and their perceptions of the trial participants. Third, researchers in many studies held the child's demeanor and testimony constant across the various testimonial conditions. As demonstrated in the research evaluating the efficacy of innovative procedures, we should expect differences in children's behavior and the quality of their accounts when providing traditional versus accommodated testimony. From this perspective, one could argue that the lack of differences observed in those studies is not particularly surprising because researchers did not take into account critical differences in the child's demeanor and testimony that result from the use of accommodations.

To our knowledge, only two studies have overcome the aforementioned limitations of previous research on jurors' perceptions of defendant and child witness credibility in trials containing traditional versus alternative forms of testimony. In one recent hearsay study, researchers collected data from actual jurors participating in child sexual abuse trials in California and Arizona (Myers, Redlich, Goodman, Prizmich, & Imwinkelried, 1999). After deliberating in cases that contained child victim and adult hearsay testimony, jurors completed a survey concerning their perceptions of both witnesses (all analyses were conducted at the jury level, however, because jurors completed the questionnaires after deliberations; therefore, their responses were not independent). Jurors reported no differences in perceptions of the demeanor and appearance of children and adult hearsay witnesses, and they thought that children's in-court testimony was more complete and more important than their pretrial statements. Jurors also thought that adult hearsay witnesses were more complete, less suggestible, and less likely to have made up things than the children who provided pretrial and in-court testimony. Interestingly, however, jurors indicated that the adults' hearsay testimony was less important than the children's pretrial and in-court statements. Overall, jurors also found adult hearsay witnesses to be more accurate, more consistent, more confident, and less attractive than child witnesses.

Goodman et al. (1998) conducted a CCTV study and, as we previously described, children interacted with a confederate and later testified about their experience in a downtown courthouse. Children either testified live in court or via CCTV. Mock jurors rendered verdicts to a fictitious charge against the confederate and evaluated the trial participants on several dimensions. In contrast to the earlier studies in which college students viewed the videotaped, scripted testimony of a child actor, in the Goodman et al. study jury-eligible community members viewed the live, unrehearsed testimony of a child witness who was assigned randomly to testify in court or via CCTV. Therefore, jurors observed not only children testifying in different testimonial conditions, but also children's *reactions* to testifying in different testimonial conditions.

Similar to earlier researchers, Goodman et al. (1998) failed to find any evidence that the use of CCTV biased jurors against the defendant. Overall, jurors who viewed CCTV testimony were no more likely to find the defendant guilty than were those who viewed in-court testimony. The format of the children's testimony also did not affect jurors' ratings of trial fairness for the defendant. More striking, however, were the results pertaining to jurors' impressions of children testifying in court or via CCTV (reported in Tobey, Goodman, Batterman-Faunce, Orcutt, & Sachsenmaier, 1995). Jurors who viewed CCTV testimony evaluated child witnesses more negatively on several dimensions compared to jurors who viewed children's live, in-court testimony. Specifically, jurors perceived children testifying via CCTV to be less believable, less accurate (during both direct and cross-examination), less accurate in recalling the event, more likely to have made up the story, less likely to have based their testimony on fact than fiction, less attractive, less intelligent, less confident, but less stressed than jurors who viewed children's traditional testimony. Path analyses confirmed that jurors found children who testified live in court to be more accurate and believable than their CCTV counterparts. However, Goodman et al. also noted an indirect effect of the testimonial condition. When CCTV children were more accurate in answering direct questions than those testifying in court, jurors recognized CCTV children's increased accuracy and rated them as more accurate and believable.

The findings reported by Goodman et al. (1998) and Tobey et al. (1995) illustrate a perplexing dilemma that faces courts and professionals who contemplate the use of alternative testimonial procedures with children. Despite the documented ability of certain accommodations to reduce children's stress and increase their accuracy, jurors tend to evaluate accommodated children more negatively on a variety of dimensions. Although Goodman et al. noted an indirect effect of CCTV (increased response accuracy to direct questions) on jurors' perceptions of accuracy, results also indicated that jurors' evaluations of children's accuracy and believability tended to be based more on other factors (such as children's perceived confidence and consistency) than on children's *actual* accuracy. Thus, in addition to the actual accuracy of children's testimony, other verbal and nonverbal cues exhibited by child witnesses influenced jurors' perceptions of children's credibility. Perhaps accommodating children leads to changes in their verbal and nonverbal behavior that negatively affect jurors' perceptions.

Previous research provides little insight into how variations in children's behavior resulting from accommodation might influence jurors' perceptions of child witnesses. In the only study on this topic, Kovera, Gresham, Borgida, Gray, and Regan (1997) asked a sample of attorneys to report which behaviors are typically exhibited by prepared child witnesses and which behaviors are typically exhibited by unprepared child witnesses. Based on those attorneys' beliefs about the effects of preparation on child witness behavior, Kovera et al. constructed a trial simulation in which an actress portrayed the child witness as either prepared (e.g., the child made eye contact, sat still, and responded confidently) or unprepared (e.g., the child looked down, fidgeted, and responded hesitantly). When jurors were reminded (via effective expert testimony) that children who are abused might be confused and uncertain, they judged the unprepared child to be more credible than the prepared child.

Based on the extant research indicating that jurors may evaluate children more negatively when courts accommodate children and that jurors' evaluations may be related to changes in children's behavior resulting from the use of accommodations, we were interested in providing a theoretical explanation for why this outcome may occur. We decided to investigate one potential variable that may shed light on these findings: juror expectancies for child witness behavior.

EXPECTANCY VIOLATION THEORY AND RELEVANT PSYCHOLEGAL RESEARCH

Expectancy violation theory (EVT; Burgoon & Hale, 1988) posits that people approach social interactions expecting others to engage in certain verbal and nonverbal behaviors. Expectancies are based largely on social norms and past experience, but they also include the known idiosyncrasies of others. In essence, people expect behaviors that they consider to be typical and feasible for a particular setting, purpose, and set of participants. Expectancy violations attract attention and result in an interpretation/evaluation process in which people assess the meaning of the expectancy violation, assign it a positive or negative valence, and react accordingly. Based on that process, people render judgments regarding the positive or negative nature of expectancy violations. People consider an expectancy violation to be positive if they assign a valence to the violation that is more positive than the valence of the original behavioral expectancy. Similarly, people consider an expectancy violation to be negative if they assign a valence to the violation that is more negative than the valence of the originally expected behavior.

What effects do positive or negative expectancy violations have on people's cognitive and behavioral reactions? EVT predicts that people will react more favorably to positive expectancy violations than they will to negative expectancy violations. Indeed, findings from studies by Burgoon and her colleagues (Burgoon, 1993; Burgoon & Hale, 1988; Burgoon & LePoire, 1993; Burgoon & Walther, 1990) have supported this prediction. Additional psycholegal research has demonstrated that expectancy violations can affect people's attitudes and decision-making processes in legal settings as well. In one of the earliest studies of its kind, Hemsley and Doob (1978) hypothesized that jurors expect witnesses to maintain high levels of eye contact while testifying and that any deviation from this norm could lead jurors to evaluate witnesses negatively. Jurors in that study believed that a witness who avoided eye contact was lying. Feldman and Chesley (1984) conducted a trial simulation in which the defendant displayed a high or low rate of behaviors commonly associated with deception (e.g., shifting in his seat, fidgeting, speaking hesitantly). Jurors found the defendant accused of a minor crime (but not a major crime) less believable when he displayed a high rate of deceptive-like behavior. Feldman and Chesley reasoned that jurors expected the defendant to be nervous when he was accused of the major crime; however, the defendant's nervous behavior in the minor crime condition violated jurors' expectancies and resulted in lower believability ratings. Researchers in another study found that extreme violations of jurors' expectancies for the emotional expression of a female defendant (either extremely flat or high affect) resulted in higher guilt ratings than when the defendant displayed moderate (i.e., expected) levels of emotion (Salekin, Ogloff, McFarland, & Rogers, 1995). Thus, at least in studies involving adults, it appears that negative expectancy violations committed by defendants and witnesses can adversely impact jurors' attitudes and decisions.

Do jurors also doubt the credibility of child witnesses who negatively violate jurors' expectancies for their behavior? To our knowledge, only one study to date has examined the effects of expectancy violations committed by a child witness on jurors' perceptions (Schmidt & Brigham, 1996). Those researchers reasoned that jurors would react unfavorably when a child used a communication style that violated their age-appropriate stereotypes. In that study, undergraduates playing the role of mock jurors viewed a child witness of various ages (5, 10, or 15 years old) who used a powerful or powerless communication style when testifying. The child's powerful communication style was characterized by confident responses, direct eye contact, and a lack of hesitancy when answering questions. In contrast, children displaying the powerless communication style were more fidgety, maintained lower levels of eye contact, and used more nonfluencies and hesitations. Schmidt and Brigham hypothesized that jurors would rate younger children who displayed the powerful communication style more positively than older children using the same style. They also predicted that jurors would rate older children who used the powerless communication style more negatively. Results supported Schmidt and Brigham's hypotheses;

jurors rated the powerless 15-year-old witness as the least truthful and least intelligent of all the child witnesses. Jurors also rated the powerful 5-year-old more positively than the child witnesses in any other condition.

In light of Schmidt and Brigham's (1996) findings, we were interested in exploring the role of EVT in explaining why jurors evaluate children more negatively when they provide alternative versus traditional forms of testimony. Unlike others (e.g., Salekin et al., 1995; Schmidt & Brigham, 1996) who have assumed that jurors hold certain expectancies for trial participants (e.g., a powerful 15-year-old witness or a moderately emotional defendant), we wanted to determine the exact nature of jurors' *actual* expectancies for a child's testimonial behavior. We did just that by measuring jurors' expectancies for the verbal and nonverbal behavior of a child witness testifying in a criminal abuse trial. In the next section, we present preliminary results from this investigation.

PRESENT STUDY

We designed a study to address two primary research questions. First, what types of verbal and nonverbal behavior do jurors expect child witnesses to exhibit when testifying? Second, do jurors' expectancies vary as a function of the means by which children provide testimony? To answer those questions, we constructed a survey in which we asked jurors to use a series of bipolar adjective scales to describe their beliefs regarding how a child alleging sexual abuse would appear in five different testimonial conditions: traditional live testimony, support person present during testimony, prepared testimony, videotaped testimony, and CCTV testimony.

We generated two potential hypotheses based on EVT to help explain why jurors may evaluate child witnesses more negatively when courts accommodate children. The first hypothesis was that children's behavior might exceed jurors' expectancies, causing jurors to become more suspicious and skeptical of a child's testimony. Jurors may expect children to lack confidence, to be inconsistent, and to provide little detail when testifying; however, the use of accommodations may result in more confident, consistent, and detailed witnesses, thus violating jurors' expectancies. A second hypothesis was that perhaps jurors overestimate the effects that accommodations have on children and their testimony. That is, jurors may expect accommodated children to be more confident, consistent, and detailed than children who are not accommodated. If accommodated children fail to meet jurors' expectancies (i.e., they still lack confidence, consistency, and detail), jurors also may react negatively. Jurors may in fact react more negatively if the latter is true because accommodation may attenuate or eliminate one potential explanation for children's observed behavior. That is, jurors who view traditional testimony may attribute the child's stress or impaired testimonial performance to situational factors (e.g., testifying in court or having to face the defendant), whereas it is more difficult for them to do so when accommodations are used because those factors are attenuated (e.g., preparation or support) or do not exist (e.g., CCTV).

In testing our hypotheses, the first step was to determine what expectancies jurors hold regarding children's verbal and nonverbal behavior when providing different forms of testimony. We found that jurors' expectancies of children's behavior did in fact vary as a function of the testimonial conditions included in our study. Jurors thought that children using the alternative forms of testimony would be more confident, provide more consistent and detailed testimony, and maintain greater eye contact with the questioner than children testifying in a traditional manner. Jurors also believed that children testifying live in court would have a much slower rate of speech than prepared children. Finally, jurors expected that prepared children or those accompanied by a support person would appear more rehearsed and less spontaneous than children testifying via CCTV.

Additional research is necessary to evaluate our hypotheses and the role that expectancies play when jurors evaluate child witnesses. In particular, many of the studies we reviewed lacked specific and objective measures of children's traditional and accommodated behavior. Such measures are critical in evaluating our hypotheses because they allow us to determine whether children's behavior varies in a manner that is consistent or inconsistent with jurors' expectancies. Previous studies, however, have included general and subjective measures of children's traditional and accommodated behavior (e.g., observer ratings of children's stress, confidence, and happiness), which provide at least some reference point for comparing jurors' expectancies to children's testimonial behavior.

Our findings appear to provide some initial evidence that jurors hold expectancies that may be violated when courts use alternative procedures. Researchers, legal professionals, law enforcement personnel, and families of the victims who saw children testify in court or via CCTV in one study indicated that children's behavior changed very little as a function of CCTV use (Cashmore, 1992). CCTV children appeared less anxious during their direct examination than children who did not use CCTV. During cross-examination, CCTV children appeared more fluent than children in one of the samples in which CCTV was not used (two non-CCTV samples were included in this study, one from the Australian Capital Territory and the other from New South Wales). However, children's confidence, cooperativeness, ability to answer questions, amount of detail provided, or concentration during direct or cross-examination did not differ as a function of testimonial condition. Trained observers in a similar study by Murray (1995) also observed few differences in the behavior of accommodated versus nonaccommodated child witnesses. The only difference to reach traditional levels of statistical significance was the observers' ratings of children's crying behavior. Children who testified using CCTV were less tearful during cross-examination than children who testified in court. Again, observers did not note any differences in composure, confidence, concentration, cooperation, or fluency in children who testified in open court compared to those who did not.

Contrary to the observations noted by Cashmore (1992) and Murray (1995), jurors in our study expected accommodated children to appear more confident, more consistent, more fluent, and more detailed than children providing traditional testimony. Thus, children's behavior when using CCTV (at least as measured in the Cashmore and Murray studies) may violate jurors' expectancies. This evidence appears to provide at least partial support for our second hypothesis, which stated that jurors may expect changes in children's behavior due to accommodation that simply do not occur.

Our findings also support the assertion that when courts use accommodations with children, jurors' expectancies may be violated on a more intuitive level as well. Jurors in our study did not expect accommodated children to appear any more rehearsed or less spontaneous than children testifying in a traditional manner. When courts use accommodations, attorneys or other court personnel help familiarize the child with the alternative procedures. That process varies greatly from one jurisdiction to the next, ranging from a simple explanation of the alternative procedure to a more detailed demonstration in which children practice using the alternative procedure. Efforts to familiarize children with accommodations may lead children to appear more rehearsed and less spontaneous than those who do not use accommodations. This especially may be the case when children receive more extensive forms of preparation such as those that involve comprehension monitoring and task demand training. By practicing these techniques and simulating the question/answer format of courtroom testimony, children may become more rehearsed and violate jurors' expectancies.

Like others in the field (e.g., Schmidt & Brigham, 1996), we believe jurors' expectancies for children's behavior play an important role in understanding jurors' evaluations of children and their testimony. Clearly, accommodations are widely available and can lead to beneficial effects in abuse cases by reducing children's stress and increasing their accuracy. However, researchers must continue to explore how accommodating children may lead to changes in children's verbal and nonverbal behavior that violate jurors' expectancies because such violations may cause jurors to evaluate children more negatively, thus diminishing the impact of children's testimony at trial.

References

Aldridge, J., & Freshwater, K. (1993). The preparation of child witnesses. *Journal of Child Law, 5*, 25–27.

Bornstein, B. H. (1999). The ecological validity of jury simulations: Is the jury still out? *Law and Human Behavior, 23*, 75–91.

Bruck, M., Ceci, S. J., & Francoeur, E. (1999). The accuracy of mothers' memories of conversations with their preschool children. *Journal of Experimental Psychology: Applied, 5*, 89–106.

Burgoon, J. K. (1993). Interpersonal expectations, expectancy violations, and emotional communication. *Journal of Language and Social Psychology, 12*, 30–48.

Burgoon, J. K., & Hale, J. L. (1988). Nonverbal expectancy violations: Model elaboration and application to immediacy behaviors. *Communication Monographs, 55*, 58–79.

Burgoon, J. K., & LePoire, B. A. (1993). Effects of communication expectancies, actual communication, and expectancy disconfirmation on evaluations of communicators and their communication behavior. *Human Communication Research, 20*, 67–96.

Burgoon, J. K., & Walther, J. B. (1990). Nonverbal expectancies and the evaluative consequences of violations. *Human Communication Research, 17*, 232–265.

Cashmore, J. (1992). *The use of closed-circuit television for child witnesses in the ACT.* Sydney, New South Wales: Australian Law Reform Commission.

Davies, G., & Noon, E. (1991). *An evaluation of the live link for child witnesses.* London: Home Office.

Feldman, R. S., & Chesley, R. B. (1984). Who is lying, who is not: An attributional analysis of the effects of nonverbal behavior on judgments of defendant believability. *Behavioral Sciences and the Law, 2*, 451–461.

Golding, J. M., Alexander, M. C., & Stewart, T. L. (1999). The effect of hearsay witness age in a child sexual assault trial. *Psychology, Public Policy, and Law, 5*, 420–438.

Golding, J. M., Sanchez, R. P., & Sego, S. A. (1997). The believability of hearsay testimony in a child sexual assault trial. *Law and Human Behavior, 21*, 299–325.

Goodman, G. S., Quas, J. A., Bulkley, J., & Shapiro, C. (1999). Innovations for child witnesses: A national survey. *Psychology, Public Policy, and Law, 5*, 255–281.

Goodman, G. S., Taub, E. P., Jones, D. P. H., England, P., Port, L. K., Rudy, L., & Prado, L. (1992). Testifying in criminal court: Emotional effects on child sexual assault victims. *Monographs of the Society for Research in Child Development, 57* (Serial No. 229).

Goodman, G. S., Tobey, A. E., Batterman-Faunce, J. M., Orcutt, H., Thomas, S., Shapiro, C., & Sachsenmaier, T. (1998). Face-to-face confrontation: Effects of closed-circuit technology on children's eyewitness testimony and jurors' decisions. *Law and Human Behavior, 22*, 165–203.

Hafemeister, T. L. (1996). Protecting child witnesses: Judicial efforts to minimize trauma and reduce evidentiary barriers. *Violence and Victims, 11*, 71–92.

Hemsley, G., & Doob, A. (1978). The effect of looking behavior on perceptions of a communicator's credibility. *Journal of Applied Social Psychology, 8*, 136–144.

Keeney, K. S., Amacher, E., & Kastanakis, J. A. (1992). The court prep group: A vital part of the court process. In H. Dent & R. Flin (Eds.), *Children as witnesses* (pp. 201–209). Chichester, U.K.: Wiley.

Kovera, M. B., Gresham, A. W., Borgida, E., Gray, E., & Regan, P. C. (1997). Does expert testimony inform or influence juror decision-making? A social cognitive analysis. *Journal of Applied Psychology, 82,* 178–191.

Lamb, M. E., Orbach, Y., Sternberg, K. J., Hershkowitz, I., & Horowitz, D. (2000). Accuracy of investigators' verbatim notes of their interviews with alleged child abuse victims. *Law and Human Behavior, 24,* 699–708.

Lindsay, R. C. L., Ross, D. F., Lea, J. A., & Carr, C. (1995). What's fair when a child testifies? *Journal of Applied Social Psychology, 25,* 870–888.

Lipovsky, J., & Stern, P. (1997). Preparing children for court: An interdisciplinary view. *Child Maltreatment, 2,* 150–163.

Maryland v. Craig, 497 U.S. 836 (1990).

McGough, L. S. (1994). *Child witnesses: Fragile voices in the American legal system.* New Haven, CT: Yale University Press.

Melton, G. B., Limber, S. P., Jacobs, J. E., & Oberlander, L. B. (1992). *Preparing sexually abused children for testimony: Children's perceptions of the legal process* (Final Report to the National Center on Child Abuse and Neglect, Grant No. 90-CA-1274). Lincoln: University of Nebraska-Lincoln.

Murray, K. (1995). *Live television link: An evaluation of its use by child witnesses in Scottish criminal trials.* Edinburgh: Scottish Office, Central Research Unit.

Myers, J. E. B. (1992). *Legal issues in child abuse and neglect.* Beverly Hills, CA: Sage.

Myers, J. E. B., Redlich, A. D., Goodman, G. S., Prizmich, L. P., & Imwinkelried, E. (1999). Jurors' perceptions of hearsay in child sexual abuse cases. *Psychology, Public Policy, and Law, 5,* 388–419.

Peters, W. W., & Nunez, N. (1999). Complex language and comprehension monitoring: Teaching child witnesses to recognize linguistic confusion. *Journal of Applied Psychology, 84,* 661–669.

Quas, J. A., DeCicco, V., Bulkley, J., & Goodman, G. S. (1996). District attorneys' views of legal innovations for child witnesses. *American Psychology-Law Society Newsletter, 16,* 5–8.

Redlich, A. D., Myers, J. E. B., Goodman, G. S., & Qin, J. (1999). *A comparison of two forms of hearsay in child sexual abuse cases.* Manuscript submitted for publication.

Ross, D. F., Hopkins, S., Hanson, E., Lindsay, R. C. L., Hazen, K., & Eslinger, T. (1994). The impact of protective shields and videotape testimony on conviction rates in a simulated trial of child sexual abuse. *Law and Human Behavior, 18,* 553–566.

Ross, D. F., Lindsay, R. C. L., & Marsil, D. F. (1999). The impact of hearsay testimony on conviction rates in trials of child sexual abuse: Toward balancing the rights of defendants and child witnesses. *Psychology, Public Policy, and Law, 5,* 439–455.

Salekin, R. T., Ogloff, J. R. P., McFarland, C., & Rogers, R. (1995). Influencing jurors' perceptions of guilt: Expression of emotionality during testimony. *Behavioral Sciences and the Law, 13,* 293–305.

Sas, L. D. (1991). *Reducing the system-induced trauma for child sexual abuse victims through court preparation, assessment and follow-up* (Final Report, Project No. 4555-1-125, National Welfare Grants Division, Health and Welfare Canada). London, Ontario: London Family Court Clinic.

Sas, L. D. (1992). Empowering child witnesses for sexual abuse prosecution. In H. Dent & R. Flin (Eds.), *Children as witnesses* (pp. 181–199). Chichester, U.K.: Wiley.

Saywitz, K. J., & Nathanson, R. (1993). Children's testimony and their perceptions of stress in and out of the courtroom. *Child Abuse and Neglect, 17,* 613–622.

Saywitz, K. J., & Snyder, L. (1993). Improving children's testimony with preparation. In G. S. Goodman & B. L. Bottoms (Eds.), *Child victims, child witnesses: Understanding and improving testimony* (pp. 117–146). New York: Guilford Press.

Saywitz, K. J., & Snyder, L. (1996). Narrative elaboration: Test of a new procedure for interviewing children. *Journal of Consulting and Clinical Psychology, 64,* 1347–1357.

Saywitz, K. J., Snyder, L., & Lamphear, V. (1996). Helping children tell what happened: A follow-up study of the narrative elaboration procedure. *Child Maltreatment, 1,* 200–212.

Saywitz, K. J., Snyder, L., & Nathanson, R. (1999). Facilitating the communicative competence of the child witness. *Applied Developmental Science, 3,* 58–68.

Schacter, D. L. (1999). The seven sins of memory: Insights from psychology and cognitive neuroscience. *American Psychologist, 54,* 182–203.

Schmidt, C. W., & Brigham, J. C. (1996). Jurors' perceptions of child victim-witnesses in a simulated sexual abuse trial. *Law and Human Behavior, 20,* 581–606.

Sigler, R. T., Crowley, J. M., & Johnson, I. (1990). Judicial and prosecutorial endorsement of innovative techniques in the trial of domestic abuse cases. *Journal of Criminal Justice, 18,* 443–453.

Swim, J. K., Borgida, E., & McCoy, K. (1993). Videotaped versus in-court witness testimony: Does protecting the child witness jeopardize due process? *Journal of Applied Social Psychology, 23,* 603–631.

Tobey, A. E., Goodman, G. S., Batterman-Faunce, J. M., Orcutt, H. K., & Sachsenmaier, T. (1995). Balancing the rights of children and defendants: Effects of closed-circuit television on children's accuracy and jurors' perceptions. In M. S. Zaragoza, J. R. Graham, G. C. N. Hall, R. Hirschman, &

Y. S. Ben-Porath (Eds.), *Memory and testimony in the child witness* (pp. 214–239). Thousand Oaks, CA: Sage.

U.S. Department of Health and Human Services. (2000). *Child Abuse and Neglect State Statute Series, 4.* Washington DC: National Clearinghouse on Child Abuse and Neglect Information.

Warren, A. R., & Woodall, C. E. (1999). The reliability of hearsay testimony: How well do interviewers recall their interviews with children? *Psychology, Public Policy, and Law, 5,* 355–371.

Whitcomb, D. (1992). *When the victim is a child* (2nd ed.). Washington, DC: U.S. Department of Justice.

PART V

CONCLUSIONS AND FUTURE DIRECTIONS

17

Starting a New Generation of Research

Gary B. Melton

Bottoms, Kovera, and McAuliff have composed their book *Children, Social Science, and the Law* at a propitious time. We are at a natural point to look back at the ups and downs of interaction between the social sciences and the juvenile justice system. It has been a century since the establishment of the juvenile court and a generation since the Supreme Court's affirmation of the personhood of children and its command that juvenile courts follow the rudiments of due process (*In re Gault*, 1967).

The juvenile court began as the paradigmatic invention of the legal realists. The court was the entry point into a distinctive system designed to match the realities of life for wayward children and troubled families. Not only were the court's own procedures supposed to reflect knowledge about child development, but the court also acted as creator of new settings for family support, such as child guidance centers (Levine & Levine, 1992). Further, as the import of *Gault* became clear more than a half-century later, use of social science was a common feature in the panoply of children's cases in the appellate courts, whether testing the limits of autonomy for children on the one hand or applying special entitlements on the other (Mnookin, 1985). Indeed, the ostensible reliance on social science in children's cases has become so widely accepted

Send correspondence to Gary B. Melton, Institute on Family and Neighborhood Life, Clemson University, 158 Poole Agricultural Center, Clemson, SC 29634-0132. Telephone: 864 656 6271. Fax: 864 656 6281. E-mail: gmelton@clemson.edu that whether such work is cited no longer has much to do with judges' ideology (Hafemeister & Melton, 1987).

At the same time, the marriage between law and social science relating to children has been ambivalent at best. The juvenile court was – and to a large extent still is – based on erroneous assumptions, whether about youth themselves, the treatment system, or the effects of adversary procedures (Melton, 1984). In part because of this errant policy making, the court has long attracted the disdain of scholars and policy makers on both the left (for offering neither effective treatment nor fair procedures) and the right (for failing to hold wayward juveniles sufficiently accountable). Researchers have documented that mental health professionals have often contributed to these problems by offering opinions that have little grounding in science and that step into moral and legal domains that properly should be reserved for the courts themselves (Melton, Petrila, Poythress, & Slobogin, 1997; Morse & Whitebread, 1982; Weithorn, 1987). In short, the juvenile court's approach to individual cases often has been marked by an uneasy alliance between legal and mental health professionals and a lackluster performance on both sides.

This general picture has been matched in cases of substantive law in the appellate courts. As noted earlier, social science has been unusually welcome in such cases. Indeed, it is not accidental that a children's case was the focus for the first use by the Supreme Court of social science evidence in deciding that a state law was unconstitutional (the famous footnote 11 in *Brown v. Board of Education*, 1954). Nonetheless, the general (although not universal) practice has been an approach to such evidence that has been less well reasoned than many would expect (for a contrary example, see *Maryland v. Craig*, 1990, and the American Psychological Association's brief filed in that case; i.e., Goodman, Levine, Melton, & Ogden, 1991). Even in the case of *Brown*, the research cited was methodologically weak, and the predictions made in the brief filed by a distinguished group of social scientists turned out to be largely inaccurate (Stephan, 1978).

Although lawyers apparently typically believe that they need to introduce *some* social science evidence in any test case involving children, whatever the legal issue at stake, that evidence has often not been closely linked to the legal arguments being made, even in the U.S. Supreme Court (Mnookin, 1985). Moreover, the Court itself has often found the "pages of human experience" – an intuitive assessment of social reality based on the way that the Court believes that the world *ought* to be ordered – to be more persuasive than empirical research in drawing factual conclusions to underlie its reasoning about matters pertaining to children and families (Melton, 1987; see, e.g., Melton, Lyons, & Spaulding, 1998, and Perry & Melton, 1984, discussing *Parham v. J.R.*, 1979, and related cases).

Moreover, as in other areas of law, social scientists have tended to focus their research on questions that easily fit their research methods and professional concerns and to ignore other, more fundamental questions. Research on legal issues related to child abuse and neglect is clearly illustrative. Although a huge body of research has developed on the factors affecting the quality of children's testimony and on the likelihood of mental health professionals' filing reports of suspected child maltreatment, most of the fundamental assumptions underlying child protection policy have been largely unexplored (Melton, Goodman, Kalichman, Levine, & Koocher, 1995). Even in the domains that have been studied, the policy utility of the research has been limited. Relatively little research has been conducted on ways to facilitate children's involvement in the legal process and to mitigate the adverse effects of reporting of child abuse and neglect on the mental health system.

There is evidence, however, that we may be entering a new and more positive era in the interaction between law and social science research on issues involving children. First, the overall quality of scholarship on such matters has improved substantially. This book is illustrative. The chapters still vary in how closely they address assumptions in the law. Nonetheless, perhaps reflecting the influence of the *social science in law* movement (Monahan & Walker, 1998), most chapters do include a thoughtful legal analysis accompanied by a comprehensive review of research on the empirical assumptions identified. Moreover, every chapter is a gem of scholarship on a legally relevant phenomenon, even if not always a particular set of assumptions in the substantive law. The contributors consistently provide careful and detailed reviews of law, empirical research, or both. *Children, Social Science, and the Law* is a useful and comprehensive reference to psycholegal child research, which has burgeoned in both quality and influence in the generation since *Gault*.

Second, there are glimmers that the law itself may be entering a new day in regard to the status of children – a change that poses a new agenda for the social sciences. Notably, as Small and Limber discuss in their chapter in this book, the nearly universal adoption of the Convention on the Rights of the Child (1989) represents a remarkable global advance in children's legal status. With a unifying focus on the dignity of children, the Convention offers a comprehensive child-centered framework for legal policy affecting children.

In making this claim, I am aware, of course, that the United States stands alone among fully functioning national governments in its failure to ratify (see Kimbrough-Melton & Melton, 1999; Limber & Wilcox, 1996). Someday, however, the composition of the Senate Foreign Relations Committee will change, and the United States will join the global community and ratify the Convention. Until then, the United States is arguably bound by the Convention as a matter of customary international law, and it is obligated in any event as a signatory (but not a party) to the Convention not to adopt policies contrary to it.

Until then, careful study of the Convention offers the opportunity to build a new body of developmental research that examines the significance of the law in children's everyday lives (cf. Melton, 1988) and that explores potential legal mechanisms to create social structures compatible with children's sense of dignity. In so doing, researchers may elucidate the meaning of the fundamental legal constructs in children's lives. This is a noble goal, and this volume may represent the transition to that new generation of research.

References

Brown v. Board of Education, 347 U.S. 483 (1954).
Convention on the Rights of the Child, U.N. Doc. A/Res/44/25 (1989).
Goodman, G. S., Levine, M., Melton, G. B., & Ogden, D. W. (1991). Child witnesses and the confrontation clause: The American Psychological Association brief in *Maryland v. Craig. Law and Human Behavior, 15*, 13–29.

Hafemeister, T. L., & Melton, G. B. (1987). The impact of social science research on the judiciary. In G. B. Melton (Ed.), *Reforming the law: Impact of child development research* (pp. 27–59). New York: Guilford.

In re Gault, 387 U.S. 1 (1967).

Kimbrough-Melton, R., & Melton, G. B. (1999, November). The politics of children's rights: The influence of the Religious Right on U.S. policy. Paper presented at the conference on *Entering the New Millennium: Children's Rights and Religion at the Crossroads*, Nazareth, Israel.

Levine, M., & Levine, A. (1992). *Helping children: A social history*. New York: Oxford University Press.

Limber, S. P., & Wilcox, B. L. (1996). Application of the U.N. Convention on the Rights of the Child. *American Psychologist, 51*, 1246–1250.

Maryland v. Craig, 497 U.S. 836 (1990).

Melton, G. B. (1984). Developmental psychology and the law: The state of the art. *Journal of Family Law, 22*, 445–482.

Melton, G. B. (1988). The significance of law in the everyday lives of children and families. *Georgia Law Review, 22*, 851–895.

Melton, G. B. (1987). The clashing of symbols: Prelude to child and family policy. *American Psychologist, 42*, 345–354.

Melton, G. B., Goodman, G. S., Kalichman, S. C., Levine, M., & Koocher, G. P. (1995). Empirical research on child maltreatment and the law (Report of the American Psychological Association Working Group on Legal Issues Related to Child Abuse and Neglect). *Journal of Clinical Child Psychology, 24*(Suppl.), 47–77.

Melton, G. B., Lyons, P. M., Jr., & Spaulding, W. J. (1998). *No place to go: The civil commitment of minors*. Lincoln: University of Nebraska Press.

Melton, G. B., Petrila, J., Poythress, N. G., & Slobogin, C. (1997). *Psychological evaluations for the courts: A handbook for mental health professionals and lawyers* (2nd ed.). New York: Guilford Press.

Mnookin, R. H. (Ed.). (1985). *In the interest of children: Advocacy, law reform, and public policy*. San Francisco: W. H. Freeman.

Monahan, J., & Walker, L. (1998). *Social science in law: Cases and materials* (4th ed.). New York: Foundation Press.

Morse, S. J., & Whitebread, C. H., II. (1982). Mental health implications of the Juvenile Justice Standards. In G. B. Melton (Ed.), *Legal reforms affecting child and youth services* (pp. 5–27). New York: Haworth.

Parham v. J. R., 442 U.S. 584 (1979).

Perry, G. S., & Melton, G. B. (1984). Precedential value of judicial notice of social facts: *Parham* as an example. *Journal of Family Law, 22*, 633–676.

Stephan, W. G. (1978). School desegregation: An evaluation of predictions made in *Brown v. Board of Education*. *Psychological Bulletin, 85*, 217–238.

Weithorn, L. A. (Ed.). (1987). *Psychology and child custody determinations: Roles, knowledge, and expertise*. Lincoln: University of Nebraska Press.

18

What It Will Take to Bring Child-Focused Law, Policy, and Research into the 21st Century?

Concluding Thoughts

Howard Davidson

If you've read *Children, Social Science, and the Law* thus far, you might share my belief that the fiscal and legislative reforms needed to remedy the problems noted by the distinguished authors of these chapters are quite formidable – especially given contemporary political trends. The more we know (and this book has provided a wealth of research synthesis information), the *less* it seems that critical laws, policies, and practices conform to what, in so many ways, is best for children and their families. Our public systems of intervention for some very vulnerable populations – children in high-conflict parental custody disputes, in abuse/neglect cases, and in the juvenile delinquency arena – continue to fail far too many of them. And we simply have *no coherent unifying national children's policies* through which proposed new legislation and practice reforms can be evaluated.

In reading these chapters, I sense that we are destined to continue having fragmented, underfunded, and politically expedient approaches to governmental intervention with children and their families (including some poorly thought out laws opportunistically named for deceased children) unless:

1. Policy makers step back before passing new child-related legislation and take time to learn from the experts what has worked and what has not;

The views expressed herein are my own and do not, unless otherwise indicated, represent the policies or positions of the American Bar Association.

2. Program models are adequately funded and evaluated; and
3. Information on successful programs is more widely disseminated so that there can be stronger support for expanding them to serve far more children and families in need.

So many policies or court practices explored herein – affecting juvenile waiver of rights, roles of children's attorneys, interventions for children exposed to violence, prevention of delinquency, responses to child sexual abuse, child witness credibility challenges, transfer of delinquents to adult court, termination of parental rights, resolution of child custody conflicts (including those affecting children of gay and lesbian parents) – have been insufficiently guided by research findings, have lacked scientific evaluations altogether, or have (as noted by Patterson, Fulcher, and Wainright) virtually ignored the findings of scientific studies. It may thus be time for child advocates to go beyond calling for new laws and to start focusing on legislative oversight, fiscal accountability, outcome measurement, and other strategies through which current child-related legal and judicial practices can be tested.

Although this book includes chapters on children's rights, there really is no American *child rights jurisprudence*. A few isolated child-focused U.S. Supreme Court cases (well described by Schmidt and Reppucci) have been cited throughout, but most frequently when the Court has addressed an issue, it has decided cases without any discussion of children's rights per se. American legislatures, courts, and administrative agencies are afraid to use the term *children's rights*. It seldom appears in laws, regulations, or cases.

Unlike in other countries, the topic of children's rights is rarely addressed in the media or in public discourse. And symbolic of our apprehension, the U.S. Senate has not ratified the Convention on the Rights of the Child (CRC), making the United States the world's only recognized government not to have embraced it. We cannot do so because no president in the last decade was willing to advocate courageously for its approval or to submit the CRC to the Senate so that it could be considered for ratification (Cohen and Davidson, 1990). There are apparently no political "points" to be scored for publicly supporting this international treaty on children's rights, and kowtowing to CRC opposition from arch conservatives has been a weakness of not only several presidents but also cabinet members and congressional leaders.

In the remainder of this chapter, I share my thoughts about the public policy implications of specific topics addressed in this book.

REVERSING INEFFECTIVE, AND INAPPROPRIATELY PUNITIVE, POLICIES AFFECTING JUVENILE OFFENDERS

Several authors (Fried and Reppucci, Woolard, Salekin) have noted policy shifts away from the rehabilitative model on which the American juvenile court movement was founded about 100 years ago. America has moved far toward a punitive model characterized by legislative actions that permit increasingly younger children to be tried as adults for their criminal acts. Fried and Reppucci have expressed justifiable concern that so-called juvenile justice reforms are addressing greater numbers of juvenile offenders homogeneously, even though there is great variation among them. Examples of the punitive, retributive focus taken by juvenile laws include increasing use of determinate (including mandatory minimum) sentencing by juvenile court judges, extending juvenile jurisdiction to permit longer incarceration periods, rescinding the traditional confidentiality of juvenile records, and expanding the number of state laws mandating (or permitting, solely at the prosecutor's discretion) automatic transfer of juveniles to adult court for certain offenses.

Despite the fact of political and public support for harsh juvenile sanctions that are not proven to reduce recidivism, there is a growing body of research, largely unused by policy makers, on programs that actually work to prevent juvenile crime and are additionally cost-effective. The Center for the Study and Prevention of Violence at the University of Colorado (*Blueprints*, 2000) has analyzed hundreds of violence prevention programs and identified a number that meet a rigorous scientific standard of effectiveness. The criteria for selection include demonstrated deterrent effects, replication at multiple sites with successful case outcomes, and evidence of sustained positive impact after youths leave the program. These have been labeled Blueprints Model Programs. Included among the *Blueprints* programs are (a) prenatal and infancy home visitation programs, discussed in the chapter by MacFarlane, Doueck, and Levine and a decade ago urged by the U.S. Advisory Board on Child Abuse and Neglect as a national policy priority (*Creating Caring Communities*, 1991); (b) an elementary school–based program for promoting emotional and social competencies while reducing behavior problems and aggression; (c) bullying prevention programs; (d) a life skills training program for middle/high school students to prevent or reduce the use of alcohol, tobacco, and marijuana; (e) the Big Brothers, Big Sisters program; (f) a multidimensional "treatment foster care" program for troubled adolescents; and (g) the Multisystemic Therapy and Functional Family Therapy intensive multidisciplinary family and community-based treatment programs.

The Blueprints programs and the *Comprehensive Strategy for Serious, Violent, and Chronic Juvenile Offenders* (1993) materials published by the Office of Juvenile Justice and Delinquency Prevention, U.S. Department of Justice, should be carefully studied by political leaders who are sincere in their desire to address effectively juvenile crime and violence. The *Comprehensive Strategy* and a follow-up guide (Howell, 1995) for implementing it describe model prevention approaches, application of graduated sanction principles, and use of risk assessment and offender classification scales. Two other essential resources for policy makers intent on achieving positive reform of the juvenile justice system's services for at-risk youth include the organization Fight Crime: Invest in Kids, made up of hundreds of police chiefs, sheriffs, prosecutors, crime survivors, and leaders of police organizations, and Building Blocks for Youth, a collaboration among national groups (headed by the Youth Law Center) seeking to develop a fair and effective youth justice system.

Late in 1999, a special committee of the U.S. House of Representatives issued a report (*Bipartisan Working Group on Youth Violence*, 1999) concluding that prevention and early intervention programs are essential to reducing youth violence. This report also addressed two topics that have been the focus of some of my work at the ABA Center on Children and the Law. The first is the nexus between child abuse and neglect and later juvenile crime and violence. The report notes that children who experience or witness violence are 50% more likely to be arrested as juveniles and 40% more likely to be arrested as adults. The report says that we need to make sure that child protective services staff have sufficient resources to identify

and treat abused and neglected children and that we must act before children are hurt by expanding the programs proven to reduce
abuse and neglect. For the most part, elected officials have done neither. The report, however, further acknowledges that making criminal justice funds available to prevent child abuse recognizes that
preventing child abuse prevents crime and that community-based
programs supporting families can be implemented to prevent child
abuse for far fewer dollars than it costs now to treat and manage the
far-reaching consequences of child abuse and neglect. Why aren't
we listening?

The fact that so many abused and neglected children later
find themselves in the juvenile justice system raises another child
maltreatment–juvenile offender policy link that has been insufficiently addressed. Congress created, 20 years ago, a system of
child-focused legal protections for children entering the foster care
system. A few years ago, that system was refined though the
Adoption and Safe Families Act (ASFA, 1997). The federal government spends billions of dollars annually to share costs with
the states for foster care, and legal protections within ASFA are
required for state eligibility for this (Title IV-E) money. It is not
widely known among youth advocates that state and local placement and service costs for delinquent or status offender children
can be financially assisted by participation in this IV-E funding program (Hemrich, 1999) but that, as a condition, certain protections
for youth must be provided. These protections include a specially
tailored case plan for the youth, judicial findings that continuation
in the youth's home would be contrary to his or her welfare, court
and placement agency findings that reasonable efforts were made to
help the family avoid unnecessary placement of the youth, and judicial reviews and hearings to ensure that a permanent plan for the
youth is implemented. Much of this is *not* characteristic of current
juvenile justice and youth services practice, but it *is* representative of
good, individualized, "least-restrictive alternative" case planning
for kids, and it could help avoid many unnecessary incarcerations of
juveniles. This *IV-E eligibility for delinquents* issue should be further
explored by juvenile justice policy reformers.

The second topic within the recent congressional report that I
want to address is a topic the House Bipartisan Working Group

referred to as *parental responsibility*. The report stated that negative parenting is the biggest factor indicative of children having a propensity toward violence. They highlighted that the prevalence of parental disengagement with their kids, among all American families, is in the 25–30% range (!) and called parental engagement the single most important factor in a child's healthy development. The report went on to say that law enforcement efforts that enlist the active involvement of parents or guardians are among the most successful and cost-effective strategies for early intervention and prevention, and it spotlighted a Brooklyn truancy program that requires active participation by parents.

The topic of parental involvement with the juvenile justice system has been inadequately studied, and for some juvenile justice professionals it is controversial. Juvenile delinquency intervention literature has contained little information on strategies for working with a youth's parents, either before serious offenses are committed (i.e., in status offense situations such as truancy, incorrigibility, or curfew violations) or in pre- and postjuvenile offender placement situations. Juvenile court literature also has little information on judge–parent interactions. The media have occasionally looked at the issue of parents as potentially responsible (civilly or criminally) for their child's criminal misbehavior rather than exploring how courts and agencies could more positively involve parents in decision-making and parenting skills enhancement. Parental involvement was the topic of an ABA Center on Children and the Law/Consortium on Children, Families, and the Law invitational conclave (*Parental Interventions to Prevent Child Violence*, 1999), and it is the focus of our Center's recent national research study, *Parental Involvement Practices of Juvenile Courts* (Davies & Davidson, 2001).

More organizations, courts, and researchers should focus on this subject. As Small and Limber mention in their chapter, one of the core principles of the Convention on the Rights of the Child is that policies and services for children should respect parents and support the family. Any juvenile justice system that ignores the possibilities of, or does nothing to promote, more positive involvement by mothers and fathers in the lives of youth in that system is violating this important premise.

HELPING CHILDREN IN THE COURTS BE BETTER HEARD
AND REPRESENTED

Many of the chapters in this book center on the barriers to children
having their voices effectively heard, whether as alleged victims of
or witnesses to crime, in the civil and criminal justice systems. If
children or youth fail to understand the role and potential impact
of the justice system, they and whatever "system advocates" they
are fortunate to have will be at a great disadvantage.

There is a fundamental problem with how children experience
America's justice system. Schmidt and Reppucci reveal problems
with children's understanding of the law. Small and Limber highlight the Convention on the Rights of the Child's core principle
(often unmet in this country) of viewing children as important actors in matters affecting them. Haralambie and Nysse-Carris com-
plain of the lack of role clarity of many court-appointed lawyers
for children. Woolard cites evidence of deficits in preteens' comprehension of law-related waivers of rights. Depner describes how the
application of social science research in California helped develop
counseling and treatment programs for children undergoing family transition, parenting education programs for divorcing families,
specialized family drug courts, programs for perpetrators and victims of domestic violence, and supervised visitation resources – but
that has been inadequately implemented nationwide.

Through our Center's work with the California-based Judith
Wallerstein Center for the Family in Transition, research was conducted on another important family-relevant topic not addressed
by Depner: assessing the risk of child custody violations. This study
resulted in recommendations for courts (Johnston & Girdner, 1998;
Johnston, Girdner, & Sagatun-Edwards, 1999) to impose special cus-
tody/visitation-related protections and restrictions where there are
prior custodial violations, or evidence of plans to abduct or overt
threats to take a child; great potential obstacles to a child's return
due to retention in an uncooperative jurisdiction or country; or possible substantial harm to a child if abducted (e.g., the abductor has a
severe mental or personality disorder, a history of abuse/violence,
or little or no prior relationship with the child). I worry that
this important study will not result in universal judicial reform

because of the disconnect between research and policy/practice changes.

In short, we have poorly applied the findings of the dedicated research scholars who have explored how children and their families experience the legal system to the *implementation* of practical reforms in that system. This situation must change.

In many ways, America's systems of appointment for legal representation of children in the courts are the most advanced in the world (Grasso, Davidson, Finley, & Rollin, 1998). Yet, those of us who have represented children know too well how difficult and undervalued such advocacy can be. Many highly competent lawyers for children are forced out of the field by compensation rates too low for a long-term professional commitment to this area, caseloads for children's attorneys in public agencies that are so high as to unwittingly invite malpractice and burn-out, and a lack of respect from their colleagues in the bar who practice in other fields. Many children are pressured to waive their right to counsel; and worse, in some types of serious cases, they are afforded no legal representation at all (especially in high-conflict, contested custody and visitation disputes, as well as in immigration/political asylum cases).

Little government or foundation funding has been available for thorough evaluations of various systems of child representation. In some states, legislation has permitted courts to dispense entirely with appointed counsel for children in child abuse/neglect cases, substituting only a lay advocate: a court-appointed special advocate (CASA). Although I strongly support the use of CASAs on behalf of maltreated children before the courts, this is not a viable substitute for, but should be a supplement to, every child having court-appointed legal counsel. States that do not require counsel for children in abuse/neglect cases are unlikely to change this policy unless there is more funding for studies of the impact on children of having, or not having, true legal representation.

In our work at the ABA Center on Children and the Law, we have noted that a good deal of attention is being given to upgrading legal representation of children through state "court improvement committees" receiving federal support (Hemrich, Hardin, Rauber, & Lancour, 1999). This includes the development of new guidelines and standards for such advocacy. However, social scientists have

not yet been adequately engaged in efforts to study child representation systems, and there have been few sources of adequate
support for creation of model child representation programs or the
ongoing support of such programs.

I fear the basic intent of Congress in enacting the Adoption and
Safe Families Act (ASFA), to speed permanency for maltreated children removed from their homes, may be frustrated by inadequate
advocacy for children within the courts. Therefore, evaluations of
the implementation of ASFA must include studies of how representation of children has helped, or hindered, that legislation's goals
of child safety, permanence, and well-being.

Several authors of this book (McAuliff and Kovera; Schaaf,
Alexander, Goodman, Ghetti, Edelstein, and Castelli; Lyon) address
another key issue affecting children's experiences in the courts: how
their testimony is utilized within judicial proceedings. Twenty years
ago, the ABA Center on Children and the Law began studying and
reporting on legislative, court, and prosecutor office reforms related
to child sexual abuse victims. We were among the first national organizations to highlight child-related evidentiary innovations such as
special hearsay exceptions and technical innovations such as the use
of closed-circuit television, as well as to inform the legal field about
innovative community-based, multidisciplinary approaches to the
handling of child sexual abuse cases (e.g., special prosecution units,
offender treatment-related diversion programs, and children's advocacy centers). We also recognized the importance of good interviewing of children, especially the impact of child-related forensic
linguistics, so that communications could be clearer, more likely to
be understood by both adult interviewers and children, and produce more accurate information. Our book on this topic has been
the Center's all-time best-seller (Walker, 1999).

The research cited in earlier chapters is simultaneously reassur-
ing and distressing. Although technical innovations that substitute for traditional child witness testimony are used very sparingly
throughout the country, it is encouraging to know that studies have
generally supported the propriety and effectiveness of their use, and
that children's sexual abuse memories generally have been found to
be accurate. However, testimony via closed-circuit television may,
for some jurors, produce dissonance from how they *expect* children

to behave in court, and those in the justice system should be aware of this.

More disturbingly, there has been an inadequate effort to ensure that research findings on the following topics, explored earlier in this book, inform and guide the work of prosecutors, attorneys, and judges: jurors' expectancies concerning child witnesses; reluctance of children to disclose abuse; the reliability of child eyewitness testimony concerning abuse; the reliability of children's memories of past abuse; and the ability to implant false suggestions of abuse. The lack of properly informed legal/judicial professionals, combined with growing use of aggressive defense strategies focused on allegedly tainted child revelations (including the use of misleading, inaccurate, or irrelevant research findings), pose serious threats to the courts in doing justice for children. In his chapter, Lyon makes a good argument for *not permitting* most expert testimony on child witness suggestibility because of (a) its scientific *unreliability* and (b) its lack of focus on the *facts* of the case at hand.

Because research suggests that some children *can* be led into making false statements about abuse, although with great difficulty, there is an urgent need for upgrading and possibly standardizing the interviewing techniques of those in law enforcement, social services, and mental health programs who may be the first professionals to question children about their abuse (and whose interviews may become the focus of defense-requested taint hearings). Although little can be done to remedy the contaminating effect of some parents' questioning of children about possible abuse, especially where some parental perceptions or misperceptions of their child's abuse may be so strong that they lead to improperly suggestive questioning, the government can do much to improve the skills of professionals whose work involves interviewing suspected child sexual abuse victims.

There is considerable interest in the child sexual abuse response field to the concept of *forensic interviewing*. Although we've learned that research does not support the assumption that improper questioning renders children incapable of later remembering and telling the truth in court, authors such as Schaaf et al. inform us that there is still an urgent need for dissemination of empirically validated interviewing techniques that work best for various ages, and other categories, of children. Support for such research and dissemination, as well as for much greater expansion of the acclaimed Children's Advocacy Center model, is critical. Research is also needed on a growing practice not discussed earlier in this book: the audiotaping or videotaping of child victim statements and the later effects/utilization of these recordings. State laws or policies have begun to promote or require the recording of "official" child interviews, in part to meet challenges of improperly suggestive questioning and to provide the best possible evidence of what the interviewer asked and the child said.

MAKING EFFECTIVE TREATMENT AND SERVICES AVAILABLE
TO MORE CHILDREN AND FAMILIES IN NEED

Several authors of this book suggest that our country is not doing enough to provide the assistance troubled families and children require. Small and Limber conclude that services are fragmented and their provision does not meet the "highest priority" standard enunciated as a core principle of the Convention on the Rights of the Child. Berman, Silverman, and Kurtines note the lack of adequate school-based programs for younger children exposed to violence in the school environment. Fried and Reppucci inform us that most youth violence preventive interventions are unevaluated or poorly evaluated, with the exception of a few programs like Multisystemic Therapy. MacFarlane et al. reveal that there is a lack of empirical research on the effectiveness of school-based child sexual abuse prevention programs. Haugaard and Avery observe that family reunification services in child maltreatment cases are not only often inadequate but also tend to end prematurely due to imposed time limits, which leads to enhanced risks to children returned home from foster care. Depner describes services provided to California families involved in high-conflict custody disputes that are often unavailable to parents and children throughout the country. And Wilcox, Colman, and Wyatt acknowledge the lack of sufficient child-care funding to aid properly parents in the Temporary Assistance to Needy Families (TANF) program in seeking and holding employment.

The failure of the president, federal and state legislators, governors, mayors, county executives, and others to acknowledge that services to children have been grossly underfunded in so many areas has contributed to the benign neglect of the child protection, child welfare, child care, family court, juvenile justice, and so many other systems of intervention. As the federal leadership of 30–40 years ago (which created such holistic child and family programs as Head Start) has been replaced by the concept of *devolution* to the states for flexible program implementation, it has been more difficult for child advocates to develop sustained congressional or presidential interest in anything but individual worthwhile topics of reform (e.g., speeding adoptions and finding missing children).

For example, when the U.S. Advisory Board a decade ago (*Child Abuse and Neglect*, 1990) urged the development and implementation of a model planning process aimed at generating plans for the coordinated, comprehensive, community-based prevention, identification, and treatment of child abuse and neglect, its call fell on deaf ears. Although the federal Child Abuse Prevention and Treatment Act (CAPTA) has been reauthorized and amended many times since its original 1974 enactment, Congress has never taken the time to refine an underlying federal policy that could better support nationwide child protection improvement. Rather, it has simply revisited CAPTA approximately every 4 years when its authorization was about to expire.

Thus the routine political process, affected by the issues/crises of the moment and the loudest voices of dissent, have led to most changes in CAPTA (what I call "tinkering around the edges" rather than any logical planning/review process). The same is true for the handling of most child abuse/neglect issues at the state level. No wonder our services to children and families are primarily delivered through narrow, categorically funded programs rather than by holistic approaches.

If we are ever to achieve nationally the child-centered, family-focused, neighborhood-based, integrated child protection system that the Advisory Board called for, it will require sustained, well-funded efforts that bring together political, business, and religious leaders for a prolonged look at how federal laws addressing child protection, and their state law counterparts, might be changed to promote real community partnerships for the protection of children. The same is true for other systems discussed in this book: juvenile justice, the courts, and "welfare reform."

Part of our more thoughtful, holistic work must be attention to the fact that strengthening our poorest communities *must* be a central part of any reform, including increasing housing and job opportunities and decreasing the availability of guns. Moreover, extreme poverty and pervasive family, community, and media violence are at the very core of most of the child-related social problems that have been described in this book, and they are America's shame. We must eradicate these scourges if we are ever going to be able to substantially reduce child abuse, juvenile crime, and other serious youth problems.

We are living at a time when few political leaders do *not* publicly voice the sentiment that children's issues are important. That was not always the case. Yet, troubled youth are still scapegoated and demonized, "get tough" speeches by fear-mongering politicians often get better public reception than announcements of new funding proposals for family services, and despite research on what works, few leaders appear ready to fight for considerable expansion, let alone universal availability, of such programs. I hope this book will *not* be read principally by academics or practitioners already convinced of the need for changes articulated herein. We *must* get social scientists, practitioners, policy wonks, key private sector movers and shakers, foundation heads, and political leaders together. Reading of this book, by all of them, would be a good start.

References

Adoption and Safe Families Act, Public Law 105–89, November 19, 1997.
Bipartisan working group on youth violence: Final report. (1999). Washington, DC: U.S. House of Representatives.
Blueprints Model Programs. (2000). Boulder, CO: University of Colorado Center for the Study and Prevention of Violence. Available at: www.colorado.edu/csp/blueprints.
Child abuse and neglect: critical first steps in response to a national emergency. (1990). Washington, DC: U.S. Department of Health and Human Services, U.S. Advisory Board on Child Abuse and Neglect.

Cohen, C. P., & Davidson, H. A. (1990). *Children's rights in America: U.N. convention on the rights of the child compared with United States law.* Washington, DC: ABA Center on Children and the Law.

Comprehensive strategy for serious, violent, and chronic juvenile offenders. (1993). Washington, DC: U.S. Department of Justice, Office of Juvenile Justice and Delinquency Prevention.

Creating caring communities: Blueprint for an effective federal policy on child abuse and neglect. (1991). Washington, DC: U.S. Department of Health and Human Services, U.S. Advisory Board on Child Abuse and Neglect.

Davies, H., & Davidson, H. (2001). *Parental involvement practices of juvenile courts.* Washington, DC: ABA Center on Children and the Law.

Grasso, K. L., Davidson, H. A., Finley, B., & Rollin, M. A. (1998). *A judge's guide to improving legal representation of children.* Washington, DC: ABA Center on Children and the Law.

Guide for implementing the comprehensive strategy for serious, violent, and chronic juvenile offenders. (1995). Washington, DC: U.S. Department of Justice, Office of Juvenile Justice and Delinquency Prevention.

Hemrich, V. E. (1999). Applying ASFA to delinquency and status offender cases. *ABA Child Law Practice* 18(9), 129–148.

Hemrich, V. E., Hardin, M., Rauber, D. B., & Lancour, R. (1999). *Representing clients: Vol. 1. State court assessments 1995–1998: Dependency proceedings.* Washington, DC: ABA Center on Children and the Law.

Howell, J. C. (Ed.). (1995). *Guide for implementing the comprehensive strategy for serious, violent, and chronic juvenile offenders.* Washington, DC: U.S. Department of Justice, Office of Juvenile Justice and Delinquency Prevention.

Johnston, J. R., & Girdner, L. K. (1998). Early identification of parents at risk for custody violations and prevention of child abduction. *Family and Conciliation Courts Review, 36*(3), 392–409.

Johnston, J. R., Girdner, L. K., & Sagatun-Edwards, I. (1999). Developing profiles of risk for parental abduction of children from a comparison of families victimized by abduction with families litigating custody. *Behavioral Sciences and the Law 17*, 305–322.

Parental interventions to prevent child violence. (1999). Washington, DC: ABA Center on Children and the Law.

Walker, A. G. (1999). *Handbook on questioning children* (2nd ed.). Washington, DC: ABA Center on Children and the Law.

Resources

ABA Center on Children and the Law, American Bar Association, 740 15th Street, NW, Washington, DC 20005. Available at: http://www.abanet.org/child.

Building Blocks for Youth, Youth Law Center, 1325 G. Street, NW, Washington, DC 20005. [Online] Available at: http://www.buildingblocksforyouth.org/.

Consortium on Children, Families, and the Law, Institute on Family and Neighborhood Life, Clemson University, 158 Poole Agricultural Center, Clemson, SC 29634. Available at: http://virtual.clemson.edu/groups/ifnl/consortium.htm.

Fight Crime: Invest in Kids, 1334 G Street, NW, Suite B, Washington, DC 20005. [Online] Available at: http://www.fightcrime.org/.

Author Index

Case Index

Subject Index

DATE DUE

OhioLINK			
DEC 03 REC'D			
APR 2 6 2005			
APR 1 2 REC'D			
APR 1 8 2007			
FEB 2 0 REC'D			
APR 1 4 REC'D			
DISCARDED			
LIBRARY			
GAYLORD			PRINTED IN U.S.A.

KF 3735 .C48 2002

Children, social science,
and the law